Epidemiology of Aging: An Ecological Approach

William A. Satariano, PhD, MPH

Professor of Epidemiology and Community Health
School of Public Health
University of California, Berkeley

JONES AND BARTLETT PUBLISHERS
Sudbury, Massachusetts
BOSTON   TORONTO   LONDON   SINGAPORE

World Headquarters

Jones and Bartlett Publishers
40 Tall Pine Drive
Sudbury, MA 01776
978-443-5000
info@jbpub.com
www.jbpub.com

Jones and Bartlett Publishers
Canada
6339 Ormindale Way
Mississauga, ON L5V 1J2
CANADA

Jones and Bartlett Publishers
International
Barb House, Barb Mews
London W6 7PA
UK

Jones and Bartlett's books and products are available through most bookstores and online book-sellers. To contact Jones and Bartlett Publishers directly, call 800-832-0034, fax 978-443-8000, or visit our website www.jbpub.com.

Substantial discounts on bulk quantities of Jones and Bartlett's publications are available to corporations, professional associations, and other qualified organizations. For details and specific discount information, contact the special sales department at Jones and Bartlett via the above contact information or send an email to specialsales@jbpub.com.

Production Credits
Publisher: Michael Brown
Production Director: Amy Rose
Associate Production Editor: Tracey Chapman
Editorial Assistant: Kylah Goodfellow McNeill
Associate Marketing Manager: Marissa Hederson
Manufacturing and Inventory Coordinator: Amy Bacus
Composition: Auburn Associates, Inc.
Cover Design: Timothy Dziewit
Printing and Binding: Malloy, Inc.
Cover Printing: Malloy, Inc.

Library of Congress Cataloging-in-Publication Data
Satariano, William.
  Epidemiology of aging / William Satariano.
     p. ; cm.
  Includes bibliographical references and index.
  ISBN 0-7637-2655-9 (pbk.)
  1. Aging. 2. Older people—Diseases—Epidemiology.
  [DNLM: 1. Chronic Disease—epidemiology—Aged. 2. Aging. 3. Health Policy. 4. Health Services for the Aged. 5. Mortality—Aged. 6. Population Dynamics. WT 500 S253e 2005]
  I. Title.
  QP86.S27 2005
  614.4'2'0846—dc22

                                                                                    2004029250

Printed in the United States of America
09 08 07 06 05   10 9 8 7 6 5 4 3 2 1

Table of Contents

Introduction

It is often stated that the human population is aging. While this remains in most cases a rather abstract notion, from time to time we have personal experiences that make that statement much more real and immediate. For me, that recognition came in 1989 when I returned to California to begin a faculty appointment at the University of California, Berkeley. One morning, my father and I were driving through our old neighborhood and we passed my former elementary school. I commented about how well the school had been maintained over the years. My father replied that, yes, it was in good shape, but that it was no longer an elementary school; it was now a senior center. He went on to say that he was currently taking a class there, and, as I later learned, in the same room where my sixth grade class met in 1957. That for me was a very personal example of how the population had aged and how some of one town's resources had shifted from children to seniors.

My purpose in writing this book is to provide an overview of research in the epidemiology of aging. Although this was a new experience, I knew that I did not want to prepare a book that would consist simply of a series of somewhat disparate chapters. Instead, I wanted to illustrate, to the extent that I could, that the leading topics in this field, such as physical functioning, depression, and survival, were, in fact, interrelated. I felt that such an approach would illustrate both what was being done—and what needed to be done—to learn more about the causes and consequences of an aging population. I decided that an ecological model, which is now receiving so much attention in epidemiology and public health, was well suited to undertake this task. Although I knew at the beginning this would be difficult, I did not fully appreciate *how* difficult. I realized that the direction and content of the book would evolve, but I did not fully appreciate the extent of that evolution. I realized that I would learn a lot about the epidemiology of aging by writing this book, but I did not realize how much I would learn or how little I really knew at the outset about this topic. This has been a very humbling, but also very satisfying and rewarding, experience. At best, I hope this book identifies some of the larger questions and summarizes some of the important current research. Obviously, new research is being published every day. As is true of other textbooks, over time these chapters will need to be revised and updated. I do hope, however, that researchers and students will find the *framework* (i.e., the ecological model) that I used to present and discuss this material useful for a longer period of time. I hope that readers will find the framework presented here to be valuable for interpreting and locating new research within the broader context that is the epidemiology of aging.

Acknowledgments

I have been very fortunate in my life to learn from a number of wonderful teachers and mentors. These people include Witold Krassowski at Santa Clara University, California, Walter Hirsch and Robert Eichhorn at Purdue University, and lastly, Leonard Syme at the University of California, Berkeley, who remains one of my close friends and faculty colleagues. I want to acknowledge those mentors and to indicate how much they have contributed to my intellectual and personal development.

I also want to acknowledge a number of my friends and colleagues who have significantly contributed to the preparation of this book. These people include Ira Tager, Thomas Boyce, Meredith Minkler, Ray Catalano, Marcia Ory, Kokos Markides, Jay Magaziner, and Thomas Prohaska. My Dutch colleagues and friends also have contributed significantly. These people include Francois Schellevis, Trudi van den Bos, Dorly Deeg, and Brenda Prennix. From February to June 1999, I had the good fortune to spend a sabbatical, under the auspices of a Fulbright Senior Scholarship, at the National Center for Public Health and the Environment in Bilthoven, the Netherlands. During my stay, I benefited tremendously from my Dutch colleagues' advice and counsel as we discussed my tentative steps to prepare an outline for this book.

Michael B. Brown, my editor at Jones and Bartlett, has been an important source of support and guidance during the long process of writing this book.

Finally, I want to thank my wife, Enid, and my children, Erin and Adam. They have been remarkably patient and supportive throughout the preparation and writing of this book. One of the joys of aging for me will be spending future years with them.

CHAPTER 1

The Aging of Human Populations: The Significance of an Epidemiologic Perspective

INTRODUCTION

Today, older people constitute a larger segment of the population than at any other time in history. For example, in the United States in 1900, only 4% of the population was aged 65 and older. One hundred years later, people in that age group represent nearly 13% of the population, and by 2030, when the last wave of people born between 1946 and 1964 (the baby boom generation) reaches the age of 65, they are expected to constitute just over 20% of the country's population. This historic, demographic transformation has had, and will continue to have, dramatic and far-reaching social, political, and economic consequences for all segments of the society. This transformation can be demonstrated graphically by reviewing the age structure of the nation from 1905 to 2030. Figure 1–1 displays the number of males and females in each age group, from the youngest ages at the base upward to the oldest groups, for the years 1905, 1975, 2010, and 2030. In addition to a general increase in the size of the population, these figures indicate that there has been over the four periods a more even distribution in the number of people across the age groups

1

Population by Age and Sex: 1905

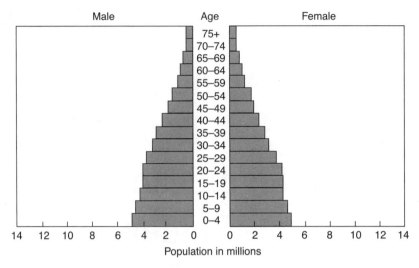

Source: From *Estimates of the Population of the United States, by Single Years of Age, Color, and Sex: 1900 to 1950,* Current Population Reports, Series P-25, No. 311, U.S. Bureau of the Census, 1965, Washington, DC: U.S. Government Printing Office.

Population by Age and Sex: 1975

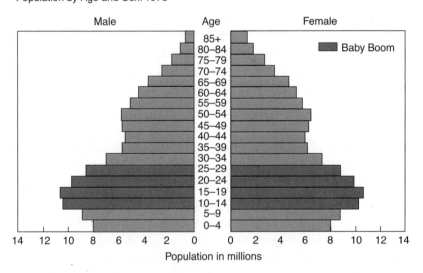

Source: From *Preliminary Estimates of the Population of the United States, by Age, Sex, and Race: 1970 to 1981,* Current Population Reports, Series P-25, No. 917, U.S. Bureau of the Census, 1982, Washington, DC: U.S. Government Printing Office.

FIGURE 1–1 Estimates of the Population of the United States, by Age and Gender, 1905, 1975, 2010, 2030, U.S. Bureau of Census.

Projected Population by Age and Sex: 2010

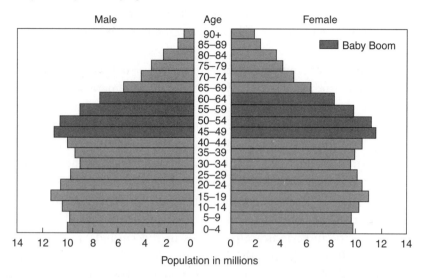

Source: From *Population Projections of the United States, by Age, Sex, Race, and Hispanic Origin: 1993 to 2050,* Current Population Reports, P25-1104, Jennifer C. Day, U.S. Bureau of the Census, 1993, Washington, DC: U.S. Government Printing Office.

Projected Population by Age and Sex: 2030

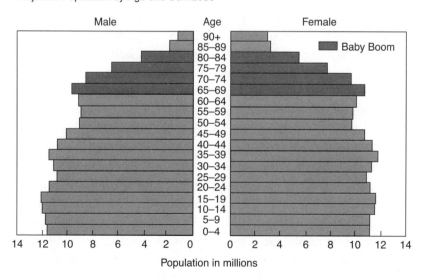

Source: From *Population Projections of the United States, by Age, Sex, Race, and Hispanic Origin: 1993 to 2050,* Current Population Reports, P25-1104, Jennifer C. Day, U.S. Bureau of the Census, 1993, Washington, DC: U.S. Government Printing Office.

for both males and females. It is clear that what was once labeled a "population pyramid" (in fact, still the generic name for this type of demographic display) will, in the future, more closely resemble a "population dome."

The aging of human populations represents one of the most significant public policy issues facing society. Not only has the increase in the sheer number of the older population focused the public's attention, but the current and future levels of that population's health and vitality are also of widespread concern. The fundamental question is whether an increase in the proportion of older people will result in an increase in the prevalence of chronic disease and disability. That simple question is the basis of public debate about anticipated increases in health care costs, federal spending for entitlement programs, and in particular, the future viability of the Social Security and Medicare programs in the United States (Rice & Fineman, 2004). Although the Medicare population (in other words, people 65 and older) represents approximately 13% of the population, they accounted for 31% of national health care spending in 1999 (Rice & Fineman, 2004). The enrollment in the Medicare program will increase significantly after 2010. It is anticipated that the enrollment will grow by 2.4% a year between 2010 and 2030. This is in contrast to a projected, average annual growth rate of 1.4% between the late 1990s and 2007. During the same period, the number of workers in the United States, that is, those people whose payroll deductions sustain the program, will decline. The ratio of workers to Medicare beneficiaries, coupled with an anticipated decrease in the absolute number of workers, has stimulated intense debate about policy options for the Medicare programs, including slowing the growth of provider payments, increasing beneficiary cost-sharing requirements, placing the cost of monthly premiums on a graduated scale to better reflect differences in household income, advancing the age of eligibility, increasing Medicare revenues, and introducing guidelines that will "privatize" elements of the programs. Further compounding the issue is a growing increase in calls for expanding Medicare coverage to include increased pharmaceutical benefits and long-term care beyond current coverage for rehabilitative care following hospitalization. In February 2004, the chairman of the U.S. Federal Reserve questioned in public testimony to the Congress whether current Medicare benefits could be maintained for future generations of older retirees in light of current and projected federal deficits. Following the reelection of President Bush in

November 2004, both Social Security and Medicare became the focus of extensive political debate. Not surprisingly, the specter of generational conflict has been raised as public debate addresses the question of what proportion of society's resources should be allocated to support its growing senior population. This debate has led to fundamental questions about the need for what James Madison, in a letter to Thomas Jefferson in 1790, called a "web of obligatory connections between past and present generations," something Madison saw as being "essential for continuation of civilized society" (Ellis, 1998, p. 132). Of course, the aging of the population is not confined to the United States, nor is public discussion and debate about the implications of that aging population for increases in the prevalence of chronic disease, disability, and their associated social and economic costs.

In this chapter, we will examine aging as a global phenomenon; consider the Epidemiologic Transition Theory as one framework for understanding regional differences in aging populations; describe the development of the epidemiology of aging as a viable field of study and practice; and finally, outline the core epidemiological questions that serve to frame the study of aging, health, and functioning in populations. The main purpose is to highlight the special significance and contribution of the epidemiology of aging for addressing these important issues and, it is hoped, make the case for the importance of a text in this field.

HUMAN AGING AS A GLOBAL PROCESS

The aging of the population is a global issue. Table 1–1 displays the current and future projections for the size of the senior population by region of the world between the years 2000 and 2050 (National Research Council, 2001). Two points are clear. First, there is considerable variation among regions. In 2000, the percentage of the population aged 65 and older ranged from 14% in Europe to 2.9% in sub-Saharan Africa. Second, in 2050, although Europe is expected to continue to lead the world in the percentage of older people in its population (nearly 30%), seniors in a number of other regions, most notably, Asia, Latin America and the Caribbean, and the Near (or Middle) East and North Africa, are expected to constitute a much higher percentage of the total populations of those areas than they do today, in some cases, approximating the percentages that are expected for North America and Oceania.

Table 1-1 Percent Elderly, by Age and Region: 2000 to 2050

Region	Year	65 Years and Over	75 Years and Over	80 Years and Over
Europe	2000	14.0	5.6	2.8
	2015	16.3	7.7	4.3
	2030	23.1	10.8	6.3
	2050	28.6	15.7	10.2
North America	2000	12.6	6.0	3.3
	2015	14.8	6.3	3.8
	2030	20.3	9.4	5.4
	2050	20.7	11.6	8.0
Oceania	2000	10.2	4.5	2.4
	2015	12.7	5.4	3.2
	2030	16.3	7.5	4.4
	2050	20.0	10.6	6.6
Asia	2000	5.9	1.9	0.8
	2015	7.7	2.7	1.3
	2030	11.9	4.5	2.2
	2050	18.0	8.5	4.9
Latin America/Caribbean	2000	5.5	1.9	0.9
	2015	7.4	2.8	1.5
	2030	11.6	4.5	2.4
	2050	18.1	8.4	4.9
Near East/North Africa	2000	4.3	1.4	0.6
	2015	5.2	1.8	0.9
	2030	8.1	2.8	1.3
	2050	13.3	5.4	2.9
Sub-Saharan Africa	2000	2.9	0.8	0.3
	2015	3.1	1.0	0.4
	2030	3.7	1.3	0.6
	2050	5.3	1.8	0.9

Source: From *Preparing for an Aging World: The Case for Cross-National Research*, by the National Research Council, 2001, Washington, DC: National Academy Press.

Although regional comparisons of this kind are very useful, it should be kept in mind that there are variations in the percentage of older people *within* each region. For example, in 2000, the percentage of people aged 65 and older in Europe ranged from a high of 18.1% in Italy to 12.3% in Poland. Even more dramatically, in Asia, the percentage of seniors ranged from 17.1% in Japan to 3.3% in Bangladesh.

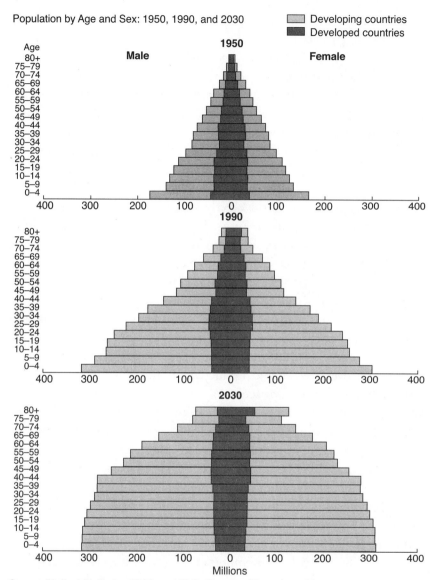

Source: United Nations, 1999 and U.S. Census Bureau, 2000a.

FIGURE 1–2 Population by Age and Sex: 1950, 1990, and 2030

It is clear that there is a difference in the percentage of people aged 65 and older between the so-called developed and developing worlds. Between 1950 and 2030, we can see again the transformation from a population pyramid to a population dome (Figure 1–2). In this case, the greater absolute size of the population in the developing world contributes significantly to the shape of that dome. Without the population from the developing world, the global age structure would more closely resemble an elongated tower, with very little difference in the size and distribution of the population across age groups for both males and females.

The elderly support ratio also provides a useful summary of the age distribution of the population. This ratio represents the number of people aged 65 and over per 100 aged 20 to 64. In the United States, the ratio is anticipated to increase from 21 in 2000 to 37 in 2030. While this increase is noteworthy, it is even more dramatic in other developing nations. For example, the ratio in Italy is expected to increase from 29 to 49 between 2000 and 2030, and in Japan, from 27 to 52 over the same time period. Although less pronounced, the elderly support ratio is also expected to increase among developing nations. For example, in Asia the ratio is expected to increase from 12 to 26 in China between 2000 and 2030, in India from 9 to 15, and in Thailand from 11 to 27. In Latin America and the Caribbean, the ratio will range from 13 to 28 in Chile and from 8 to 11 in Guatemala (Kinsella & Velkoff, 2001).

In addition to summarizing the age distribution of the population, the elderly support ratio is also useful for estimating the proportion of the population (those aged 20 to 64 years) theoretically available to contribute to the overall economic productivity of the country in general and to the economic support for seniors aged 65 and older in particular. (In the United States, this support comes in the form of such transfer programs as Social Security and Medicare.) The significance of the ratio will vary with each country's economic transfer programs and the perceived need demonstrated by the country's elderly, as reflected by their level of health and functioning. With recent attempts to reduce trade and immigration barriers among countries, there are also incentives for developed countries to reduce their elderly support ratio by encouraging migration of younger workers from other countries, most notably developing countries. No doubt, this will be an important area of future research and policy, especially regarding the effect of this migration on the elderly support ratio of the migratory workers' home countries.

Global patterns of aging, migration, and travel also will have implications for the development and transmission of infectious and chronic health conditions. For example, the recent epidemic of sudden acute respiratory syndrome in China and Canada in 2002 and 2003 focused attention on exposure and transmission patterns associated with travel among countries. Although younger people are most likely to contact the condition, reduced age-related resistance to infection and the presence of other, comorbid health conditions make the condition especially lethal for elderly people (Leung, Hedley, Ho, Chau, Wong, Thach et al., 2004; Liang, Zhu, Guo, Liu, He, Zhou et al., 2004; Xu, Laird, Dockery, Shouten, Rijchen, & Weiss, 1995).

In general, global patterns of aging have important implications for current and future incidence and prevalence of health conditions and disability. The specific patterns of disease and disability, of course, will depend on a variety of factors that include specific environmental and behavioral risk factors as well as the resources devoted to preventive and health care services. This will be addressed in more detail in subsequent sections. At this point, however, it is important to consider the reasons why there are regional variations in older populations and the effect the health status of these populations has had on those patterns.

EPIDEMIOLOGIC TRANSITIONS AND CHANGES IN LIFE EXPECTANCY

What accounts for differences in age distribution of the population around the world? The Epidemiologic Transition Theory, as first published by Omran in 1971, was originally presented as an attempt to both describe and explain these global patterns. In this section, we will review the original formulation of this theory as well as its critiques and proposed modifications.

The reasons for the improvements in life expectancy represent an important area of investigation. The basic proposition of the Epidemiologic Transition Theory (Omran, 1971) is that the increases in life expectancy have been caused in part by a substitution in late-onset degenerative causes of death, such as heart disease and cancer, replacing deaths caused by early-onset infectious and parasitic diseases. This epidemiologic transition was due to a variety of factors that were associated with socioeconomic factors and, more specifically, forces of modernization. These factors include improvements in public hygiene, sanitation, and housing; improvements in nutrition, food production, and processing; and later, immunization and other medical innovations. Improved access to formal education by females also has been identified as an important factor (Aviles, 2001). Because infants and children of both genders and adolescent and young adult women were at greatest risk of early death from infectious and parasitic conditions, reduction in the incidence of these conditions results in an improvement in life expectancy. Initial improvements in life expectancy, therefore, were due to early reduction of infant and maternal mortality. People typically survived their early years to develop degenerative, chronic conditions later in life.

The epidemiologic transition, as originally proposed, took place in three stages:

- The age of pestilence and famine
- The age of receding pandemics and
- The age of degenerative and man-made diseases

High fertility and high mortality characterized the age of pestilence and famine. Although the mortality rates were high, there were also periodic fluctuations in those rates due to epidemics that regularly affected the population. Influenza, pneumonia, diarrhea, smallpox, and tuberculosis, as well as trauma and infections associated with childbirth, were conditions that most commonly affected the population during this period. During the age of receding pandemics, basic improvements in living standards, public sanitation, housing, and nutrition reduced the incidence of the pandemics of infectious and parasitic disease, especially among infants and young women. The development and dissemination of medical and public health measures, such as new immunization and community screening programs, sustained this transition. Following a reduction in mortality rates, a reduction in birth rates occurred. Finally, as the risk of early death from infectious and parasitic diseases declined, more people survived to their later years. Life expectancy improved. During this third period, the age of degenerative and man-made diseases, the major causes of disease are the late-onset conditions of heart disease, cancer, and stroke. Relatively low and stable birth and death rates characterize this period. Overall, the transition from the first to the third stage has resulted in a progressive aging of the population. Regions of the world are currently in different stages of development. Some regions of the world are presently in the third stage of development; others are not. As noted previously, the age distribution of the world population is quite variable. Indeed, Omran (1971) proposed that the nature and timing of the transition depend on the time period, country, the stage of modernization, and, it may be hypothesized, the degree of contact a country has with regions in different stages of transition. This is important. While each region may proceed through a similar demographic and epidemiologic transition, each region is characterized by a different pattern, pace, determinants, and consequences.

Three models were identified (Omran, 1971). The Classic or Western Model is characterized by a gradual, progressive transition from high mortality and high fertility to low mortality and low fertility. This transition, as experienced by Western Europe and the United States, was stimulated in large part by socioeconomic factors. Specific factors included the sanitary revolution of the late 1800s, coupled with the development and dissemination of medical and public health innovations during the early period of the 1900s. In the second and third decades of the 1900s, chronic and degenerative disease replaced infectious diseases as the primary causes of death. In contrast, the Accelerated Epidemiologic Transition Model occurred in countries such as Japan. Although the factors that stimulated the transition were similar to the factors that affected the transition in the Classic Model, Omran contends that the process occurred more quickly. The epidemiologic transition that occurred at this time and region of the world was affected by interaction with regions—the United States and Western Europe—that had made that same transition decades before. Finally, the Contemporary (or Delayed) Epidemiologic Transition Model characterizes the ongoing transition that is taking place today in many of the developing nations. Mortality rates in a number of these nations began to decline at the end of the 1800s, but accelerated after World War II. Many of these nations are still characterized by high fertility rates. Although socioeconomic factors contributed significantly to this transition, as was the case with the first two models, public health and medical interventions played, and continue to play, a more significant role.

There is evidence to support the premise that the aging of the populations in the developing countries is occurring more rapidly than it did in developed countries. One measure used by the U.S. Census Bureau is the time it takes for the percentage of people aged 65 and older in a country's population to increase from 7% to 14% of its total population. For example, in the developed world, it took over 115 years (1865–1980) for the senior population in France to increase from 7% to 14%, compared to only 26 years (1970–1996) in Japan. In contrast, among developing countries, it is estimated that the time will range from 30 years for Chile (2000–2030) to only 15 years in Tunisia (2020–2035) (National Research Council, 2001).

The Epidemiologic Transition Theory provides a parsimonious framework for considering the interrelationship of life expectancy, morbidity, and mortality within a global-historical context. In addition, the model underscores the significance of socioeconomic and environmental factors in this transition. That is not to say, of course, that aspects of the theory have not been questioned or that the theory itself has not been modified over time. Indeed, Omran (1971) concluded his original paper by acknowledging that there are inherent difficulties in attempting to formulate such a comprehensive theory, especially when it attempts to incorporate such a vast array of social, economic, demographic, and epidemiologic factors. He called on other researchers to assist in expanding or refining the theory.

Three types of modifications or critiques have been proposed. First, there have been proposals to extend the number of stages from three to four and, in some cases five, to better account for recent events. Second, there are critiques that question some of the theory's fundamental assumptions. Finally, there have been proposals to include additional variables, for example, regional differences in natural resources and climatic patterns.

NEW STAGES

Fifteen years after the publication of Omran's paper, Olshansky and Ault (1986) proposed that the final stage of the theory (the age of man-made diseases) no longer accurately characterized many of the developed nations. Instead, they proposed that many of these countries could be better specified by a fourth stage—the age of delayed degenerative diseases.

At the time the original paper was published in 1971, Olshansky and Ault argued that Omran and others did not fully appreciate the long-term significance of the decline in coronary heart disease that began in 1967 and 1968. The general consensus at the time was that life expectancy, approximately 70 years at that time, had reached its biologic limit and it was very unlikely that there would be any meaningful improvement in life expectancy beyond that point. This proved not to be the case. While the death rates declined initially among middle-aged people, later declines occurred among older age groups. The development of new drugs and antibiotics and improved methods of diagnosing and treating degenerative diseases and their complications served to postpone deaths from these diseases by slowing the rate of chronic disease progression and by reducing case-fatality rates. In addition to advances in medical technology, there were lifestyle changes, such as reductions in smoking and improved exercise and dietary behavior. Improved access to health services in the United States also was provided to the elderly through the introduction of the Medicare program in the 1960s. In contrast to improvements in life expectancy that were driven by reductions in infant and maternal mortality at the turn of the century, current and future gains in life expectancy are reducing mortality among older age groups. Just as the initial epidemiologic transitions resulted in infectious and parasitic diseases being replaced by chronic diseases, the most recent transition has resulted in the age at death changing from the young old to the old old.

Olshansky and Ault (1986) argued that this period of increased age at onset of degenerative conditions is important for two reasons: (1) the size, age, and gender distribution of the older population, and (2) the health and vitality of the older population. Indeed, the relationship between increased age at onset and associated levels of health and vitality has been the topic of some debate, especially in the United States.

EPIDEMIOLOGIC TRANSITIONS AND THE COMPRESSION OF MORBIDITY

It is fair to say that this debate was first joined in 1980 with the publication of a paper in *The New England Journal of Medicine* by James Fries on "the compression of morbidity." According to Fries, his paper challenged the "common anticipation" that there would be in the future "an ever older, ever more feeble, and ever more expensive-to-care-for populace" (Fries, 1980). Instead, Fries predicted a future in which morbidity and disability would be "compressed" into the final years or even months of life. This "compression of morbidity" hypothesis, which was dismissed by some commentators at the time as "dangerous optimism" (Schneider & Brody, 1983), is based on the following propositions:

- There is a fixed life span. Fries argued that although there has been an improvement in life expectancy, all species have, at some point, a fixed life span, in other words, the maximum expected number of years of life. Based on his projections, most humans can expect to live to approximately 85 years.
- There is a common course for most chronic conditions. The onset of disease is followed by a period or morbidity or disability, which, in turn, is followed by death.
- The onset of chronic disease is occurring later in life. This is the result of the improvements in preventive health behavior (such as

exercise and nutritional improvements) and medical innovations. (Less attention is given to socioeconomic factors.)

- With a fixed life span, a delay in the onset of disease should be followed by a "compression" of morbidity. This process, in turn, would result in a "rectangularization" of the survival curve (Figure 1–3). People will survive for a longer period of life before developing chronic disease. Moreover, the late onset of chronic diseases would be followed by a relatively short period of disability, which, in turn, would be followed by, to use Fries's term, a more "natural death."

Fries also proposed a new research agenda. This research would first assess the variability of one or more markers of aging, such as oxygen uptake or cognitive function. This would be followed by examinations of the associations between differences in those markers and differences in health behavior. This would determine whether differential aging in these outcomes is associated with differences in health behavior. Finally, prospective intervention studies would be designed to determine whether there is a causal relationship between particular types of health

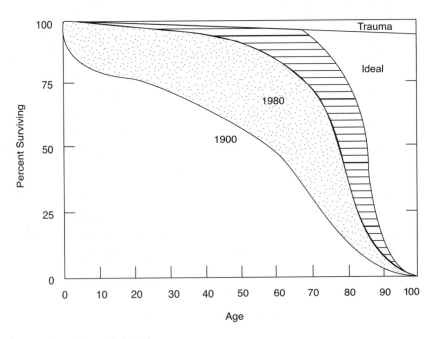

Source: From Fries, J.F. (1980).

FIGURE 1–3 Rectangularization of the Survival Curve

behavior, such as exercise and dietary practices, and differences in the markers of aging.

Not surprisingly, the compression of morbidity hypothesis proved to be quite controversial. Concerns were expressed about whether the hypothesis was based on sound research, whether it was testable, and finally, whether it unwittingly served to justify reduced support for gerontological research and reduced support for programs assisting disabled older populations (Schneider & Brody, 1983). First, it was somewhat unclear whether Fries was using the term "life span" to mean a fixed end point or something that was more akin to "life expectancy" when he proposed that the human life span was age 85 years. Second, it was questioned whether there was a generic relationship between disease, disability, and death, that is, disease leads to disability, which, in turn, leads to death. Some commentators argued instead that it was impossible to think in terms of a generic, linear process, given that the severity, timing, and course of functional limitations and disability were so variable across conditions (Rice, Haan, Selby, & Satariano, 1991). In fact, some very common conditions, such as osteoarthritis and cataracts, often lead to disabilities, but are not necessarily lethal. It was argued that older people were increasingly avoiding or surviving chronic conditions, only to develop nonlethal, disabling conditions (Gruenberg, 1977). Living longer is often associated with living more years with functional limitations and disability. It also was argued that Fries's formulation of diseases, disability, and death seemed to ignore the presence of multiple, concurrent health conditions, so common in older populations (Rice et al., 1991). The compression of morbidity hypothesis also seemed to ignore, some charged, that the severity of disability may vary over the disease course, increasing in the years just prior to death, especially for those aged 85 and older (Guralnik, 1991). Instead of being compressed, the years of disability may be extended by initiating an early predisability period. The feasibility of testing the hypothesis also was questioned, as the age of the onset of a chronic condition, such as heart disease and cancer, is difficult to establish (Kaplan, 1991). Finally, there was concern about the political implications of the hypothesis. Schneider and Brody (1983) concluded a critical assessment of the compression of morbidity hypothesis with the hope that political leaders and policy makers would not be "seduced" by Fries's statements and assume that resources should not be committed to meet the needs of an aging population. Unfortunately, much of the debate during those early years focused on the political and ideological implications of the hypothesis, resulting in what Fries later characterized as producing "more heat than light" (Fries, 2003).

In 1990, the National Institute on Aging convened a conference in Pacific Grove, California, to establish a research agenda for the compression of morbidity hypothesis, an agenda that would be designed to provide some light on this critical issue (Haan, Rice, Satariano, & Selby, 1991). The conference concluded with a number of recommendations (Rice et al., 1991). First, it was concluded that predictions about the effects of aging on health would require a comparison of the incidence and survival time in different time periods. Longitudinal studies of well-characterized cohorts were needed, therefore, to determine the onset and duration of disease, to compare how different cohorts of people age, and to assess differences in disease patterns. This included the recommendation that each cohort should be characterized by age, gender, race, ethnicity, and socioeconomic status, so that the diversity of the population should be presented. Second, based on the position that the aging process does not necessarily involve an immutable progression toward deterioration, disability, and death, it was proposed that health transitions associated with single and multiple health conditions should be studied in more detail. Third, biologic, behavioral, medical, social, economic, and environmental risk factors for disease and disability should be identified, especially in terms of how chronological age affects the strength and direction of those risk factors. Fourth, it was recommended that better measures of comorbidity (or multiple occurrence of health conditions) and quality of life should be developed and tested. Fifth, more attention should be given to strategies to promoting health and preventing disease, including research on assistive devices and low-cost aids to improve mobility, sight, and hearing for older persons. Sixth, research was recommended to examine long-term care services, medical care, alternatives to institutionalization, housing, financial support, retirement patterns, and barriers to service and care. Seventh, methodological research and data needs were identified. It was argued that refined statistical models, as well as new measures of "active life expectancy," were required to characterize the relationship between age changes and the onset of single and comorbid conditions, disability, and mortality. Active life expectancy is an estimate of the remaining years of life that are spent in independence and mobility. (See Chapter 4 for a more complete description.) Finally, a strong recommendation was made that national and local longitudinal surveys were needed to develop more refined forecasts of life expectancy, health, and vitality.

DEVELOPMENT OF A LONGITUDINAL RESEARCH BASE

Progress has been made. Since 1995, a series of papers has been published, based on a number of different longitudinal data sets. Most important, these studies have provided an opportunity to examine levels of health and functioning among different cohorts or generations of older people. While there have been eight surveys to address the trends in functioning and disability among older populations, only the National Long-Term Survey and the National Health Interview Survey were judged in a recent review (Freedman & Martin, 1998) to be of sufficient quality (rated "good") to address a number of the key issues. This means that each of the two surveys met most of the following criteria:

- Independent repeated cross-sectional assessments
- A national sample that included institutionalized residents
- A time frame of eight years or more
- Five or more annual assessments
- Identical interview methods
- Detailed self-reported outcomes
- Low loss to follow-up, less than 5%
- Fewer than 10% proxy respondents
- Low missing data of less than 5%
- A sample size that is large enough to detect 1–2% change per year.

Three examinations by Manton and colleagues were based on data from the National Long-Term Survey. This survey, judged in the evaluation to be "one of the best designed surveys for analyzing national disability trends," consisted of a series of cross-sectional surveys of representative samples of older people aged 65 and older, including people who were institutionalized, that were administered through the 1980s and 1990s. Each survey was based on consistent field methods with relatively high follow-up rates. Based on data from 1982, 1984, and 1989, a consistent decline was reported in the prevalence of 16 medical conditions. In subsequent examinations, Manton and colleagues reported a consistent decline in the prevalence of chronic disability, as measured by activities of daily living (ADL) and instrumental activities of daily living (IADL), first between 1989 and 1994 (Manton, Corder, & Stallard, 1997) and later in a subsequent analysis from 1992 to 1999 (Manton & Gu, 2001). Manton argued that while there was an increase in the prevalence of chronic conditions, the severity of those conditions, as measured by limitations and disabilities, was less.

In a series of papers based on the data in the National Health Interview Survey, there was a consistent decline in reports of "any disability" from 1982 to 1993 and in a later paper from 1982 to 1996. Although declines were noted for IADL, there was no consistent decline in ADL. The National Health Interview Survey consisted of annual assessments of samples of national residents aged 70 and older.

Although judged as only of "fair" quality, consistent declines in "any disability," IADL disability, and in selected physical functional and sensory limitations were reported for studies based on the Supplements on Aging and the Survey of Income and Program Participation. As will be addressed in more detail in Chapter 4, Freedman and Martin (1998) report that generic measures of functioning, such as reported difficulty seeing words in a newspaper, lifting and carrying 10 pounds, climbing a flight of stairs, and walking a quarter of a mile, may represent assessments of function that are less dependent on social and technological resources, as would be the case with ADL and IADL measures.

Although there seems to be consistent evidence of a decline in general measures of disability among the best national surveys, there is no clear explanation for why this is the case. Without consistent findings regarding differences by age, gender, race, and education, it is difficult to develop explanatory hypotheses. As Freedman and colleagues (2002, p. 3145) report, "Future work would do well to focus on rigorously examining trends in important disparities. A thorough understanding of trends in disparities is critical not only for identifying groups that might benefit from various health-related interventions but also for projecting the future course of population-level health trends." Possible explanations that have been offered for the decline include the role of medical care and, in particular, technological devices for detecting disease at an early stage, for determining best treatment strategies, and devices to improve the prospects of rehabilitation. Other reasons include an increase in the prevalence of healthful behaviors and higher years of education among later cohorts of older people, although, as noted, research to date shows no consistent pattern between the prevalence of education and declines in the prevalence of disability.

In a recent paper, Fries (2003) claims that recent reports based on data from the National Long-Term Survey and the National Health Interview

Survey support the original compression of morbidity hypothesis. He also notes, however, that more definitive assessments can be obtained only by tracking age-specific disability and age-specific mortality, although he makes no mention about the importance of tracking age of onset of conditions. If age-specific disability declines more quickly than age-specific mortality, then there is evidence of a compression of morbidity, especially if this is shown serially across successive cohorts of older people. Other evidence, he indicates, could be obtained by examining whether disability could be postponed by specific interventions (such as exercise, weight control, total joint replacement, influenza vaccination, or smoking cessation) by more than projected increases in the length of life from these interventions.

Two additional sources of information are necessary to provide a more definitive test of the compression of morbidity hypothesis. First, it is necessary to determine whether there is a difference in the prevalence of generic functional limitations and measures of disability. As Freedman and Martin (1998) indicate, the generic measures, such as report of level of difficulty in the performance of such generic tasks as lifting items less than 10 pounds, provide a "cleaner" measure of morbidity that is less influenced by social expectations, as is the case of ADL and IADL. Second, it is necessary to develop more sophisticated assessments that include measures of the severity of functional limitations and disability. As noted at the Pacific Grove Conference, the severity of limitations and disability is not uniform and the severity of such limitations and disability, in fact, may be more pronounced in the later years. Clearly, more sophisticated surveys need to be introduced to capture this more detailed information, information that is necessary to test the compression of morbidity hypothesis and, more generally, to assess the nature of the proposed stage of epidemiologic transition, "age of delayed degenerative disease," as suggested by Olshansky and Ault (1986).

In a recent review of the research on trends in health among the elderly, Crimmins (2004) concludes with two observations: First, health as measured in most ways has improved during the past 20 years. Second, although the prevalence of most conditions has increased, any particular condition may be less disabling. Again, while the reasons for this improvement are not completely clear, there are some tentative explanations. It may be that there has been an improvement in diagnosis, treatment, and rehabilitation for older people with specific conditions. If recent cohorts of elderly are in better health and adhere to better health practices, they are less likely to be diagnosed with severe disease and less likely to experience functional limitations.

CRITIQUE OF BASIC ASSUMPTIONS

Progressive and sustained improvements in life expectancy and the resultant aging of the population are fundamental propositions of the Epidemiologic Transition Theory. It is assumed that all societies and regions of the world will experience improvements in life expectancy, admittedly in their own time and in their own way. Thus, improvements in life expectancy are presented as a positive force of nature. However, recent events in Russia and other states in the former Soviet Union indicate that life expectancy can be quite fragile and gains can be lost in a relatively short period of time (Notzon, Komarov, Ermakov, Sempos, Marks, & Sempos, 1998; Shkolnikov, McKee, & Leon, 2001). Specifically, between 1990 and 1994, life expectancy for Russian men and women declined dramatically from 63.8 and 74.4 years to 57.7 and 71.2 years respectively, while in the United States, life expectancy increased for both men and women from 71.8 to 78.8 years to 72.4 and 79.0 years respectively. Closer inspection revealed that more than 75% of the decline in Russian life expectancy was due to increased mortality rates for ages 25 to 64 years. Leading causes of death included cardiovascular diseases, injuries, pneumonia, influenza, chronic liver diseases, and cirrhosis and other alcohol-related causes. Researchers conclude that the dramatic decline in life expectancy was due to a variety of factors, including economic and social instability, high rates of tobacco and alcohol consumption, poor nutrition, depression, and deterioration of the health care system (Leon, Chenet, Shkolnikov, Zakharov, Shapiro, Rakhmanova, et al., 1997). Interestingly, some of the most dramatic declines occurred in the wealthiest regions. Recent data indicate that life expectancy is beginning to rebound, attributed by some to reduction in the social and economic trauma occurring following the collapse of the Soviet Union. It is interesting to consider whether the events in Russia suggest that epidemiologic transition is not always progressive, moving from stages 1 to 3 (and perhaps 4). Moreover, it is unknown whether events could be so dramatic to reverse the transition, moving from stages 3 to 1.

There are also criticisms of the presumption that the Epidemiologic Transition Model is uniform within countries (Gaylin & Kates, 1997; Heuveline, Guillot, & Guatkin, 2002; Mackenbach, 1994). For example, the United States is included with other developed nations in the third or fourth stages of transition. This presumption neglects, some charge, the heterogeneity that exists within both developed and developing countries. It may be, for example, that the epidemiologic profile of some residents of developed countries may be more akin to stage 2 than stages 3 and 4. This is reflected, in turn, in the health disparities that exist in countries such as the United States and other developed countries, disparities that are often associated with differences in race, ethnicity, and socioeconomic status. Rather than one epidemiologic transition, there may be multiple transitions occurring within single countries, reflected as well in the heterogeneity of multiple health conditions. Developed and developing countries are characterized by a variety of conditions, including both chronic and infectious diseases.

Robine and Michel (2004) argue that a general theory of population aging must take these multiple patterns into account. In a commentary that accompanied the Robine–Michel paper, Guralnik (2004, p. 606) summarizes their position as follows:

> There may be a circling back, where, first, sicker people survive into old age and disability rises, then the number of years lived with disability decreases as new cohorts of healthier people enter old age, but, finally, the number of years lived with disability rises again when the average age of death goes so high that many people spend their last years at advanced old age burdened by multiple chronic diseases and frailty. And as if all of this were not complex enough, Robine and Michel proposed that it is happening at different times in different countries and perhaps even at different times in the same country within different population subgroups. Particularly provocative and worthy of serious consideration is their proposal that all these changes, both expansion and compression of morbidity, are part of a single unifying process, a "general theory on population aging," and are simply different stages of a single transition.

ADDITIONAL DETERMINANTS

One of the significant features of Omran's Epidemiologic Transition Theory is the role of socioeconomic context and the so-called historic forces of modernization. Improvements in life expectancy, the aging of the population, and changes in the causes of death are due to these factors. Recent work, although not presented in the context of the Epidemiologic Transition Theory, suggests that other factors may have affected this transition. For example, Jared Diamond's recent book, *Guns, Germs, and Steel* (1999, p. 16), is based on a question that is very similar to the basic questions that led to the Epidemiologic Transition Theory: "Why did human development proceed at such different rates on different continents?" Diamond contends that differences in human development and demography, such as the aging of populations, may have been affected by differences in land topography and natural resources. Specifically, differences in topography may have affected both the opportunities for the production and accumulation of food through the availability and domestication of wild plant and animal species as well as the likelihood for contact among populations and resultant opportunities for the diffusion of technology and social, political, and economic organization. According to Diamond, Eurasia had a greater variety of wild plant and animal species available for domestication. Moreover, sustained contact with domesticated animal species led to the establishment of immunities to particular types of infectious and bacterial diseases. In addition, contact and diffusion of innovations among populations were more likely in Eurasia, because of its east–west major axis and the relative absence of such geographic barriers as major north–south mountain ranges. In contrast, interhemispheric diffusion made no contribution to Native America's complex societies, isolated from Eurasia at low latitudes by broad oceans, and at high latitudes by geographic barriers and a climate suitable only for hunting and gathering. Together these factors helped to support the development of a larger, more diverse, and more organized population in Eurasia. Work similar to Diamond's can serve as a model to broaden the scope of the Epidemiologic Transition Theory.

THE EPIDEMIOLOGIC TRANSITION THEORY: SOME SUGGESTED MODIFICATIONS

The Epidemiologic Transition Theory has contributed to our understanding of the global patterns of aging and longevity among developed and developing nations. The strengths of this theory can be summarized as follows: First, the theory casts the study of aging, health, and longevity into a broad historical and global context. The causes and consequences of aging and longevity are not restricted to one country, in one period of history. Second, the theory emphasizes the effects of social, economic, and political forces on changes in patterns of longevity and the age profile of nations. Together, these characteristics set the stage for the development of global and regional strategies to understand and enhance the health and functioning of older populations.

Thirty years ago, Omran (1971) acknowledged that this theory must be refined over time. In that spirit, we propose the following modifications, taking into account recent commentaries and research in this area.

- Following from Diamond and others, it is reasonable to consider a broader array of factors that affect the epidemiologic transition. While Diamond considers the role of topography, land use, and the diffusion of innovation to explain the past and current state of development in nations, it is reasonable to also consider the significance of such factors for future development, especially as we continue to think of aging, health, and longevity within an interconnected, global context.
- Along those lines, one of the most significant issues to address in more detail is the relationships among nations, in particular, the relationships among developed and developing nations to explain patterns and timing of aging and longevity. As noted previously, the traditional Epidemiologic Transition Theory indicates that the time required for nations to advance from one stage to another depends on the historical context and the relationship that one nation has with nations at a more "advanced" stage. Omran points to the diffusion of technology and other markers of modernization as contributing significantly to the improvement of longevity in developing nations. This, of course, is the fundamental issue of contemporary globalization. Following the observation made by at least one commentator (Aviles, 2001), relationships among nations can be multifaceted and may not always contribute positively to the improvement of longevity among residents of developing countries. From the perspective of this theory, future researchers should be cognizant of this possibility and consider a variety of outcomes associated with contact among nations.
- The nature and timing of transitions from one stage to another also can be variable, as evidenced by reductions in life expectancy among segments of the Russian population, a point underscored by Robine and Michel in their discussion of a new theory of population aging. There may be times in which improvements in life expectancy are

delayed or even reversed by social, political, and economic events. The Epidemiologic Transition Theory should be modified to allow for these occurrences. It is reasonable to speculate, for example, that the current epidemic of obesity among children and adolescents in the United States may have a negative effect on future life expectancy when that generation reaches its middle years.

- Perhaps the most significant concern is that little attention has been given to the heterogeneity of life changes within countries and regions. As noted previously, the theory should be expanded to consider and assess the number and type of transitions within countries that will assist in accounting for differences in aging, longevity, and, in general, health disparities.

- It is reasonable to expand the number of stages from three to four, allowing for what Olshanksy and Ault (1986) refer to as the age of delayed degenerative diseases (Rogers & Hackenberg, 1987). Some commentators also have proposed a fifth stage that reflects the reemergence of infectious diseases in developed nations (the age of emergent and re-emergent infections) (Smallman-Raynor & Phillips, 1999). Although this, in fact, represents a fifth stage, it also may reflect recognition that chronic and infectious diseases can occur concurrently. Moreover, the presence of concurrent infectious and chronic diseases may characterize the heterogeneity of the nations or, as noted previously, the fact that there may be concurrent epidemiologic transitions within nations.

Despite these suggested modifications, it is important to realize that, at the very least, the Epidemiologic Transition Theory has served as a typology for the description of global aging and longevity by geographic area and historical period. At best, the theory holds the promise for also explaining patterns of aging, health, functioning, and longevity. To do so, the theory must be expanded conceptually to account for the heterogeneity that exists among and within nations. As we will see, it is precisely in this area that the epidemiology of aging may make its most significant contribution.

TOWARD AN EPIDEMIOLOGY OF AGING

Chronological age historically has been a key variable in epidemiological studies of disease and disability. Indeed, age is so closely aligned with the incidence of disease and disability that it has been necessary to adjust or "hold constant" the effects of age, so that the significance of other variables could be noted. It is ironic, therefore, that while chronological age has figured so prominently in the study of epidemiology, the epidemiology of aging, as a separate field, is of relatively recent origin.

It is useful to consider in what ways the field of epidemiology compares to other fields that focus on aging, such as demography, gerontology, and geriatrics. Recently, the *Annals of the New York Academy of Science* devoted a special issue in 2001 to articles that compared the two fields of epidemiology and demography and addressed the likelihood of a collaboration or synthesis of methods between the two fields to provide a more comprehensive view of aging, health, and function in populations (Weinstein, Hermalin, & Stoto, 2001). Robert Wallace (2001), one of the contributors to that special issue, reports that both demography and epidemiology are applied disciplines that address the issue of population health as well as issues of social and economic well-being. In addition, however, Wallace notes that demography, being more closely connected to the social sciences, typically does not include biologic factors in descriptive and analytic reports, as is done in epidemiologic studies. Moreover, demography is more likely to examine global patterns of aging and longevity than is the case in epidemiology. Epidemiology, on the other hand, is more likely to examine the causes and consequences of disease with specific populations. In addition, epidemiology, as noted by Wallace (2001, p. 64), is "more willing to engage in randomized population experiments and quasi-experiments in order to scientifically validate its hypotheses and suppositions, as well as to test potentially health-enhancing interventions." Gerontology is a multidisciplinary field that focuses on the biology, psychology, and sociology of aging. Unlike epidemiology, gerontology is not restricted to the study of the causes and consequences of aging, health, and functioning. Moreover, gerontology addresses subjects at both the individual, familial, and community levels. Finally, geriatrics is a branch of medicine that focuses on age-related factors associated with the causes and consequences of disease, limitations, and disability, typically at the individual or patient levels. In addition, geriatrics focuses on the development of age-related protocols that enhance the diagnosis, treatment, and rehabilitation of the older patient.

In 1972, the National Institutes of Health (NIH) convened the first conference on the epidemiology of aging in Washington, DC. The epidemiology of aging was presented (in many ways, introduced) at this conference as a field that should address the underlying physiological factors that characterized aging, in fact, factors that served as markers of aging. The markers were considered to be distinct from individual chronic conditions, but perhaps represented the physiological foundation that affected relative host susceptibility to all health conditions and disabilities. As Adrian Ostfeld, chairperson of the NIH conference, indicated in his opening remarks (Ostfeld & Gibson, 1975, p. 1):

> The epidemiologic method has been traditionally used in the study of specific diseases, first the communicable and later the chronic disorders. Some of us think that the time has come to apply these fruitful methods to a phenomenon broader and more complex than any illness, the condition of aging itself.

Ostfeld went on to describe the challenges faced by researchers in this new field (Ostfeld & Gibson, 1975, p. 1):

> But the challenge of applying epidemiologic methods to the study of aging is a far more difficult one than applying them to a disease. A clear, valid, and reliable definition of aging remains to be formulated. The units of aging capable of study range from intracellular enzyme activity to overall mortality rates, with subcellular particles, cells, hormones, immune processes, tissues, organs, and neural and endocrine biofeedback mechanism[s] in between. This conference represents a small beginning in considering how we may use epidemiologic methods in partnership with other disciplines in attempting to improve our understanding of aging at all levels of living organisms.

Fourteen questions were raised at the 1972 NIH conference:

1. Is there a valid and reliable definition of aging independent of the common chronic diseases?
2. What does the remarkably high prevalence of carbohydrate intolerance in the elderly mean in terms of morbidity and mortality? What is the mechanism and should it be treated?
3. What are the precursors of Alzheimer's disease and chronic brain syndrome in the elderly?
4. In elderly cohorts, how do endocrine and immune functions decline over time, and how is the decline correlated with morbidity and mortality?

5. What is the value of intervention studies on blood pressure in older populations in reducing the incidence of stroke and senile dementia?
6. Why is life span so extraordinarily short after the onset of senile dementia?
7. What living arrangements for the elderly will produce the lowest morbidity and mortality and the highest indices of life satisfaction?
8. What aspects of socioeconomic status make it so important a determinant of longevity?
9. What can we learn from studying the effects of retirement, relocation, bereavement, and economic loss in cohorts of elderly persons?
10. Why are mortality rates lower in the Midwestern United States than in the Southeast and Northeast?
11. What are the differential effects on aging of sex?
12. Do dietary habits adversely or favorably affect morbidity and mortality in populations?
13. Can Comfort's measures provide a useful index of aging? (Alex Comfort was the author of a popular book at the time on sexuality and aging. Although aging and sexuality remains an important area of study, today, the Comfort book receives less attention.)
14. Can studies of aging be grafted on to existing cohorts, for instance, the Framingham, Albany, Evans County, and Tecumseh studies?

In 1977, a second conference was convened, in part, to take stock of the progress that may have been made in the intervening five years (Haynes & Feinleib, 1980). The consensus was that some progress had been made, but more governmental support was required to support the methods and sources of longitudinal data that were necessary to develop this field.

In 1974, the National Institute on Aging was established, as part of the Research on Aging Act, as one of the institutes of NIH. One of the branches of this new institute was dedicated to epidemiology, demography, and biometry. One of the primary objectives of this branch was to describe and explain patterns of aging, health, and functioning in human populations. This, of course, helped to provide additional focus to the emerging field of the epidemiology of aging. The epidemiology, demography, and biometry branch stimulated the development of new national population surveys on aging, such as the National Health and Nutrition Examination Survey I. This survey, together with other collaborative studies, provided a picture of the aging population. In addition, a series of analytical studies were undertaken nationally and in collaboration with other countries to better understand the causes and consequences of aging populations. A consideration of economic factors figured prominently in these investigations. Finally, the branch and institute gave special attention to the development of new methods, especially related to the meaning of impaired functional status.

Since the second NIH conference, two edited volumes in the epidemiology of aging have been published—one by Jacob Brody and George Maddox in 1988 and the second by Robert Wallace and Robert Woolson in 1992. The Brody–Maddox volume includes the proceedings of a series of symposia on epidemiology and aging at the International Association of Gerontology in 1985. The volume consists of four parts: Epidemiology and the Challenge of Aging; Epidemiology and Aging in International Perspective; The Epidemiology of Psychiatric Disorders in the Elderly; and Uses of Epidemiological and Social Survey Research in Program Planning and Evaluation and in Policy Analysis. In contrast, the Wallace–Woolson volume consists of individually invited pieces on a variety of topics, organized in four parts: Interdisciplinary Contributions to the Epidemiologic Study of the Elderly; Issues in Surveying Older Persons; Important Measurement Themes in the Elderly; and Analytic Issues in the Epidemiologic Study of the Elderly. In addition to highlighting recent research in the epidemiology of aging, these volumes helped to advance the field by identifying the important topics and describing the methodological approaches needed to address those topics.

There also has been an increase in the number of studies worldwide in the epidemiology of aging, most notably, longitudinal studies that provide an opportunity to examine health, functioning, and longevity in aging populations. Many of these studies will be described in the subsequent chapters. The studies can be summarized as follows:

Clinic/Laboratory-Based Populations for Epidemiologic Studies of the Elderly

These are early studies based on selected samples of relatively homogeneous populations that include detailed assessments of physiological markers of aging as well as behavioral and social factors. The exemplar for studies in this area is the Baltimore Longitudinal Study of Aging (BLSA).

The BLSA was established in 1958 and consisted of male subjects aged 20 and older. Male subjects consisted primarily of employees at the Department of Agriculture, the George Washington University, or the University of Maryland. Subjects were invited to the laboratory in Baltimore, Maryland, for two and a half days to be assessed in terms of over 100 tests. The test interval has varied across age groups and over time. The BLSA provided some of the most detailed assessments of the physiologic markers of aging populations.

Adapted Populations for Epidemiologic Studies of the Elderly

These are population-based studies that developed into epidemiologic studies of aging as the original cohorts of those studies aged. Exemplars for this type of study include the Framingham Heart Study, the Honolulu Heart Study, and the Alameda County Study. This was the type of study called for by Ostfeld and others at the first NIH meeting on the epidemiology of aging: aging studies that reflected an efficient and effective use of current resources. The advantage of this type of study is that information has been collected for extended periods of time, often following the cohort from the middle to senior years. Unlike the BLSA, these studies are more representative of the larger population of older residents.

Established Populations for Epidemiologic Studies of the Elderly

The more recent epidemiologic studies have been based on longitudinal studies that were designed specifically for the purpose of research on aging. Reflecting the global significance of aging, there have been a variety of emergent studies of this kind throughout the world. The National Institute on Aging initiated a collaborative study in 1984 that serves as an exemplar for many studies of this kind. The study, the Established Populations for Epidemiologic Studies of the Elderly (EPESE), was the first collaborative, community-based study devoted specifically to the study of the epidemiology of aging, health, and functioning. It was based on three population-based samples: East Boston, MA; New Haven, CN; and selected counties in Iowa. Later, the collaboration was expanded to include selected counties in North Carolina. The study is important for a variety of reasons. First, although not representative of the nation, the collaboration was perhaps the largest and most representative study in the United States. The samples from New Haven and North Carolina included valuable information about African-Americans. Second, the study protocol consisted of a home interview that included the respondents' reports of health and functioning as well as direct assessments of physical performance. Respondents were asked to perform specific tasks that were designed to assess upper- and lower-body function, walking speed, balance, and fine dexterity. The inclusion of these items was a major innovation to population-based studies and supported an observation made by Robert Wallace that many of the research methods used in community studies were first developed in laboratory and clinical settings. Third, the EPESE protocol arguably has become the standard protocol for epidemiologic studies of this kind, providing the bases for comparisons of aging populations throughout the world. For example, the protocol or key components of the protocol have been used as part of longitudinal studies in Amsterdam, Berlin, and Beijing. In the United States, there are notable examples, such as the Hispanic EPESE, which includes a comprehensive examination of Mexican-American seniors in Texas, Arizona, New Mexico, and California. Other community studies that have included core elements of the protocol have been conducted in Marin County and the City of Sonoma in California. The study in Sonoma (the Study of Physical Performance and Age-Related Changes in Sonomans) also includes a laboratory component, with assessments of pulmonary function, cardiovascular fitness, and vision.

Special Populations of Epidemiologic Studies of the Elderly

There are also longitudinal studies that focus on important subgroups of older populations. For example, the MacArthur Study on Successful Aging is designed to examine those older subjects who perform at the highest levels and are most able to preserve their health and functioning. Subjects for this study were recruited from the EPESE cohort aged 70 and older who scored in the top 20% of selected performance measures. On the other hand, the Women's Health and Aging Study consisted of female residents of Baltimore aged 65 and older who scored in the lowest one-third on a number of selected items. Other studies included the NIA ABC study and also the Centenarian study, which consisted of respondents aged 100 and older.

Special Populations of Epidemiologic Studies of Elderly with Selected Chronic Conditions

These longitudinal studies consist of older people diagnosed with specific chronic conditions. Their purpose is to examine the causes and consequences of older people diagnosed with those specific conditions. Representative collaborative studies include the Cardiovascular Health Study, the NCI/NIA Comorbidity and Cancer Study, and the Osteoporatic Fracture Study. In some cases, studies of this kind have included control groups of older people of the same age without the diagnosed condition. The Health and Functioning in Older Women with Breast Cancer study included a sample of female residents in the Detroit metropolitan area aged 40 to 84 years newly diagnosed with invasive breast cancer. In addition, female residents of the Detroit metropolitan area of the same age without a past or current diagnosis of invasive breast cancer were recruited through telephone random-digit dialing. The cases were interviewed at 3 and 12 months after diagnosis to assess, in part, patterns of functional limitations and disability. The controls were interviewed twice over the same period. This represented an attempt to identify the number and types of functional limitations and disability that may be likely to occur among women with breast cancer from those limitations and to identify any disability that may be found among women of the same age without the disease.

SUMMARY

Although this list does not represent by any means the number and diversity of studies in the epidemiology of aging, it does identify five common categories of studies in this area. In addition to characterizing the etiology and course of chronic disease in older populations, epidemiologic studies of this kind also have focused on geriatric syndromes, such as frailty, falls and injury, incontinence, vision and hearing difficulties, dizziness, postural instability, and delirium. Geriatric syndromes are conditions caused by a variety of different pathological processes. Finally, studies in the epidemiology of aging have focused on functioning and disability, identified by the Institute of Medicine in 1991 as the first priority in studies of older populations.

Finally, nearly 30 years after the first NIH conference on the epidemiology of aging, Linda P. Fried, a leading geriatrician and epidemiologist of aging, published a review article for *Epidemiologic Reviews* in 2000 that evaluated the accomplishments in the field and included a new research agenda for this century. Using the study of falls and injuries as an exemplar, Fried (2000) reports that six findings related to this area have generic implications for the epidemiology of aging in general:

- The level of risk for a fall or injury increases steadily with each risk factor.

- Nearly 50% of falls are due to an interplay of host susceptibility and environmental risks, an important connection that is the basis of an ecological approach, a point to which we will return in Chapter 2.
- The effectiveness of interventions in this area depends in part on the underlying functional status of the aging population.
- Both primary and secondary prevention are effective in reducing the incidence of falls.
- The goal of an intervention should be based on the type of fall. For example, in the general population, the objective may be to reduce the likelihood of a fall, whereas in a more frail population, the objective may be to reduce the number of falls.
- The risk factors for falls may be associated with the likelihood of other geriatric syndromes associated with frailty.

These six points, then, represent the tenets of the epidemiology of aging. These tenets also underscore a point that was made by Adrian Ostfeld 30 years earlier at the first NIH conference on the epidemiology of aging: This field will require a new set of sophisticated methods and research designs. As Fried (2000, p. 102) goes on to write:

> This [the need for new methodological strategies] is due to the heterogeneity of health and functional status among the aged; the prevalence of subclinical disease or disability, which alters risk for future outcomes; and the fact that risk associated with a characteristic may change because of survivorship characteristics, such that an increased proportion of persons still living with a risk characteristic at age 80, for example, may be resistant to the risk factor. In addition, the study of trajectories in health status over time has to account for improvement as well as decline—in physical function, for example. In order to develop the most effective scientific bases for prevention and health promotion for an aging population in the 21st century, we must take these issues into account.

THE EPIDEMIOLOGY OF AGING: THE CORE QUESTIONS

Epidemiology, both as a perspective and as a set of analytic methods, is especially well suited to examine patterns of health and functioning in an aging population. Epidemiology is based on the premise that health outcomes are not distributed randomly in the population. Rather, the incidence and prevalence of health outcomes, as well as the duration and quality of life, follow specific patterns. The purpose of epidemiology is to describe and explain those patterns in the population. This information, in turn, will establish the foundation for future public health interventions. The important questions are how best to prevent and postpone disease and disability and to maintain the health, independence, and mobility of an aging population:

1. What is the overall distribution of the health outcome in the population, such as number and types of subclinical conditions, diseases, levels of functioning, limitations, disability, and survival? How does the health outcome vary among age groups? How does it change as people age? To what extent does the health outcome vary within age groups?
2. To what extent do differences among and within age groups vary by gender, race, ethnicity, socioeconomic status, and geographic region? One example is the difference among groups in the age of the onset of a particular condition.
3. To what extent do differences among and within age groups vary by other factors associated with health, functioning, behavior, social factors, and the physical environment? Although these factors are important in their own right, they also serve to explain the associations between health outcomes and age, gender, race, ethnicity, socioeconomic status, and geographic region.
4. To what extent are differences among and within age groups associated with age differences in:
   a. The prevalence of the same risk factors
   b. The salience or strength of the same risk factors
   c. The frequency and timing of exposure over the life course to the same risk factors
   d. Exposure to a different set of risk factors?
   How does the timing of these factors across the life course, coupled with developmental physiological factors, affect the subsequent risk of disease, disability, and death in the middle and senior years?
5. What are the biologic, behavioral, social, and environmental factors associated with maintenance of health and functioning among older people, or so-called healthy aging? Special attention should be given to those older people who maintain health and functioning, in spite of a risk-factor profile that should elevate their risk for disease, disability, and death.

Finally, epidemiology provides an opportunity to distinguish between "sick individuals" and "sick populations" (Rose, 1985). The study of "sick individuals" is designed to understand the reasons why some people are at risk for health problems, while other people are not. In contrast, the study of "sick populations" focuses on an understanding of differences in the incidence of disease and other disorders among populations. At first glance, the difference between sick individuals and sick populations may seem trivial, a largely semantic distinction. It is not. The study of sick individuals depends on the overall distribution of risk factors in a specific population. For example, the risk of disease associated with a particular factor, such as a high-fat diet, would appear to be modest or even non-existent in a population in which most of the people consume a high-fat diet. In that population, the risk of disease among sick individuals would be found to be associated with one or more other factors, whose prevalence is sufficiently variable in the population. This group of high-risk individuals would be relatively small. The true significance of a high-fat diet would become apparent only by comparing the incidence of the disease in a country with high-dietary fat consumption to a country with low-dietary fat consumption. In addition to contributing to our understanding of the etiology of disease, this distinction has important implications for prevention. Although people at high risk should receive attention, a more substantial impact may be achieved by changing the entire population distribution to reduce exposure to particular factors. For example, more may be achieved by reducing the fat consumption by a small amount for a large number of people than may be achieved by reducing the risk of a small number of high-risk individuals. With regard to the epidemiology of aging, this underscores the significance of global studies that include comparative studies among nations. In the next chapter, we will focus on the utility of an ecological model for examining the intersection of biologic, behavioral, and environmental factors over the life course to organize and conduct studies in the epidemiology of aging.

CONCLUSION

The aging of population is a global issue. It is not just the sheer number of older people in the population, but the implications of that aging population for patterns of health, functioning, and longevity, as well as the number and types of resources that will be needed to address the needs of this aging population. The Epidemiologic Transition Theory was presented as one common framework for describing and explaining the patterns of health and functioning in the population. Moreover, the epidemiologic perspective is presented as being ideally suited to understanding the causes and consequences of an aging population. In the next chapter, we will argue that an ecological model should serve as a multidisciplinary foundation for future research and practice in the epidemiology of aging.

REFERENCES

Aviles, L. A. (2001). Epidemiology as discourse: The politics of development institutions in the epidemiological profile of El Salvador. *Journal of Epidemiology & Community Health, 55*(3), 164–171.

Brody, J. A., & Maddox, G. L. (Eds.). (1988). *Epidemiology and aging: An international perspective.* New York: Springer.

Crimmins, E. M. (2004). Trends in the health of the elderly. *Annual Review of Public Health, 25,* 79–98.

Diamond, J. (1999). *Guns, germs, and steel: The fates of human societies.* New York: W. W. Norton.

Ellis, J. J. (1998). *American sphinx: The character of Thomas Jefferson.* New York: Vintage Books.

Freedman, V. A., & Martin, L. G. (1998). Understanding trends in functional limitations among older Americans. *American Journal of Public Health, 88*(1), 1457–1462.

Freedman, V. A., Martin, L. G., & Schoeni, R. F. (2002). Recent trends in disability and functioning among older adults in the United States: A systematic review. *Journal of the American Medical Association, 288*(24), 3137–3146.

Fried, L. P. (2000). Epidemiology of aging. *Epidemiologic Reviews, 22*(1), 95–106.

Fries, J. F. (1980). Aging, natural death, and the compression of morbidity. *The New England Journal of Medicine, 303*(3), 130–135.

Fries, J. F. (2003). Measuring and monitoring success in compressing morbidity. *Annals of Internal Medicine, 139*(5, Pt. 2), 455–459.

Gaylin, D. S., & Kates, J. (1997). Refocusing the lens: Epidemiologic transition theory, mortality differentials, and the AIDS pandemic. *Social Science and Medicine, 44*(5), 609–621.

Gruenberg, E. M. (1977). The failure of success. *Milbank Memorial Fund Quarterly, 55*(1), 3–24.

Guralnik, J. M. (1991). Prospects for the compression of morbidity: The challenge posed by increasing disability in the years prior to death. *Journal of Aging & Health, 3*(2), 138–154.

Guralnik, J. M. (2004). Robine and Michel's "Looking forward to a general theory on population aging": Population aging across time and cultures: Can we move from theory to evidence? *Journals of Gerontology: Medical Sciences, 59*(6), M606–M608.

Haan, M. N., Rice, D. P., Satariano, W. A., & Selby, J. V. (Eds.). (1991). Living longer and doing worse? Present and future trends in the health of the elderly [Special issue]. *Journal of Aging & Health, 3*(2), 133–307.

Haynes, S. G., & Feinleib, M. (1980). *Second Conference on the Epidemiology of Aging.* (NIH Publication No. 80-969). Bethesda, MD: National Institutes of Health.

Heuveline, P., Guillot, M., & Guatkin, D. R. (2002). The uneven tides of the health transition. *Social Science and Medicine, 55*(2), 313–322.

Kinsella, K., & Velkoff, V. A. (2001). *U.S. Census Bureau, Series P95/01-1, An Aging World: 2001.* Washington, DC: U.S. Government Printing Office.

Kaplan, G. A. (1991). Epidemiologic observations on the compression of morbidity: Evidence from the Alameda County Study. *Journal of Aging & Health, 3*(2), 155–171.

Leon, D. A., Chenet, L., Shkolnikov, V. M., Zakharov, S., Shapiro, J., Rakhmanova, G., et al. (1997). Huge variation in Russian mortality rates 1984–94: Artifact, alcohol, or what? *The Lancet, 350*(9075), 383–388.

Leung, G. M., Hedley, A. J., Ho, L. M., Chau, P., Wong, I. O., Thach, T. Q., et al. (2004). The epidemiology of severe acute respiratory syndrome in the 2003 Hong Kong epidemic: An analysis of all 1755 patients. *Annals of Internal Medicine, 141*(9), 662–673.

Liang, W., Zhu, Z., Guo, J., Liu, Z., He, X., Zhou, W., et al. Beijing Joint SARS Expert Group. (2004). Severe acute respiratory syndrome, Beijing, 2003. *Emerging Infectious Diseases, 10*(1) [serial online], cited December 20, 2004.

Mackenbach, J. P. (1994). The epidemiologic transition theory. *Journal of Epidemiology and Community Health, 48*(4), 329–331.

Manton, K. G., & Gu, X. (2001). Changes in the prevalence of chronic disability in the United States black and nonblack population above age 65 from 1982 to 1999. *Proceedings of the National Academy of Sciences, 98*(11), 6354–6359.

Manton, K. G., Corder, L., & Stallard, E. (1997). Chronic disability trends in elderly United States populations: 1982–1994. *Proceedings of the National Academy of Sciences, 94*(6), 2593–2598.

National Research Council. (2001). *Preparing for an aging world: The case for cross-national research.* Washington, DC: National Academy Press.

Notzon, F. C., Komarov, Y. M., Ermakov, S. P., Sempos, C. T., Marks, J. S., & Sempos, E. V. (1998). Causes of declining life expectancy in Russia. *Journal of the American Medical Association, 279*(10), 793–800.

Olshansky, S. J., & Ault, A. B. (1986). The fourth stage of the epidemiologic transition: The age of delayed degenerative diseases. *Milbank Quarterly, 64*(3), 355–391.

Omran, A. R. (1971). The epidemiologic transition: A theory of population change. *The Milbank Memorial Fund Quarterly, 49*(4), 509–538.

Ostfeld, A., & Gibson, D. C. (Eds.). (1975). *Epidemiology of aging.* Summary Report and Selected Paper from a Research Conference on Epidemiology of

Aging, June 11–13, 1972, Elkridge, Maryland. Bethesda, MD: National Institutes of Health.

Rice, D. P., & Fineman, N. (2004). Economic implications of increased longevity in the United States. *Annual Review of Public Health, 25,* 457–473.

Rice, D. P., Haan, M. N., Selby, J. V., & Satariano, W. A. (1991). Epilogue: Research agenda on the compression of morbidity. *Journal of Aging & Health, 3*(2), 301–304.

Robine, J. M., & Michel, J. P. (2004). Looking forward to a general theory on population aging. *Journals of Gerontology: Medical Sciences, 59*(6), M590–M597.

Rogers, R. G., & Hackenberg, R. (1987). Extending epidemiologic transition theory: A new stage. *Social Biology, 34*(3–4), 234–243.

Rose, G. (1985). Sick individuals and sick populations. *International Journal of Epidemiology, 14*(1), 32–38.

Schneider, E. L., & Brody, J. A. (1983). Aging, natural death, and the compression of morbidity: Another view. *The New England Journal of Medicine, 309*(14), 854–856.

Shkolnikov, V., McKee, M., & Leon, D. A. (2001). Changes in life expectancy in Russia in the mid-1990s. *The Lancet, 357,* 917–921.

Smallman-Raynor, M., & Phillips, D. (1999). Late states of epidemiologic transition: Health status in the developed world. *Health and Place, 5*(3), 209–222.

Wallace, R. B. (2001). Bridging epidemiology and demography: Theories and themes. *Annals of the New York Academy of Sciences, 954* (December), 63–75.

Wallace, R. B., & Woolson, R. F. (Eds.). (1992). *The epidemiologic study of the elderly.* New York: Oxford University Press.

Weinstein, M., Hermalin, A. I., & Stoto, M. A. (Eds.). (2001). Population health and aging: Strengthening the dialogue between epidemiology and demography. *Annals of the New York Academy of Sciences, 954.*

Xu, X., Laird, N., Dockery, D. W., Schouten, J. P., Rijcken, B., & Weiss, S. T. (1995). Age, period, and cohort effects on pulmonary function in a 24-year longitudinal study. *American Journal of Epidemiology, 141*(6), 554–566.

CHAPTER 2

Aging, Health, and the Environment: An Ecological Model

INTRODUCTION

Research in the epidemiology of aging addresses a variety of topics that are related to health, functioning, and longevity. Leading areas of research include the study of the effects of age and aging on survival and mortality; physical functioning and activities of everyday life; cognitive functioning; depression and other psychosocial disorders; falls and injuries; and, of course, disease and comorbidities. In each case, the central question is to what extent and for what reasons are some people and, indeed, some populations, able to do well as they age, while others are not. Moreover, there is a strong interest in learning how these age-associated patterns of health, functioning, and longevity are affected by differences in geography or place, gender, race, ethnicity, and socioeconomic status.

Epidemiologic research in aging has drawn from a wide range of scientific disciplines, including the biologic, behavioral, social, and environmental health sciences. In this chapter, an *ecological model* is proposed as a comprehensive framework to summarize the diversity of that research and to provide a sense of the "big picture." Aging represents a complex blending of physiological, behavioral, social, and environmental changes that occur at both the level of the individual and at the level of the wider community. An ecological model, we believe, is ideally suited to describe and explain that complex blend.

The ecological model has a long history in the biologic, behavioral, social, and health sciences (Bronfenbrenner, 1979; Green & Kreuter, 2004; McLeroy, Bibeau, Steckler, & Glanz, 1988; Sallis & Owen, 1997). Depending on the time and discipline, the model has taken different forms. Some forms of the model highlight the connections among biologic, behavioral, and social factors, while other forms emphasize the significance of the social and physical environments—the "context." Elements of the model are reminiscent of the components of "agent," "host," and "environment" that make up the traditional epidemiologic perspective. It is important to note that the word "ecological" also has been used in epidemiology to characterize a largely descriptive approach to population health that is based on associations between, on the one hand, a summary measure of the population such as per capital consumption of high-fat foods, and, on the other hand, the incidence or mortality rate of some health outcome, such as colorectal cancer (Morgenstern, 1998). This approach often has been used for international comparisons and, more importantly, as a way of generating hypotheses that are then tested directly in case-control or prospective studies of individual consumption patterns and disease outcomes among people in that population. In some cases, such "aggregate" or group-level associations found in the population have been used incorrectly as evidence that specific individuals in those populations who consume high-fat diets are themselves at elevated risk for colorectal cancer. This, of course, is an example of the "ecologic fallacy"— falsely generalizing from associations found at the level of the population to associations found at the level of the individual. It is fair to say that the prospect of committing this fallacy has discouraged and even intimidated some researchers from conducting systematic investigations of population health—a point to which we will return in later chapters.

THE ECOLOGICAL MODEL—AN OVERVIEW

Today, there is a renewed interest in the utility of an ecological approach in public health and epidemiology. Recent position statements by leading scientific bodies, including the National Institutes of Health, the National Academy of Sciences, and the Institute of Medicine, are based on the ecological model as a framework to characterize and to encourage multidisciplinary work in the health sciences. The Ottawa Charter on Health Promotion also uses the ecological model as a foundation for its recommendations (www.euro.who.int/AboutWHO/Policy/20010827_2). Although there are different versions of the ecological model, the version included in *Healthy People 2010*, a government document that outlines the U.S. public health agenda for the first part of this century, includes the key elements of the ecological model, as shown in Figure 2–1 (U.S. Department of Health and Human Services, 2000a).

An ecological model is based on the assumption that patterns of health and well-being are affected by a dynamic interplay among biologic, behavioral, and environmental factors, an interplay that unfolds throughout the life course of individuals, families, and communities (Smedley & Syme, 2000). This model also assumes that age, gender, race, ethnicity, and socioeconomic differences shape the context in which individuals function, and therefore directly and indirectly influence health risks and resources. In addition, the ecological model serves to identify multiple points of possible intervention in public health, from the microbiologic to the environmental levels, to postpone the risks of disease, disability, and death; and enhance the chances for health, mobility, and longevity. The metaphor of the "Chinese box" (boxes within boxes) has been used by some researchers to capture the multilevel, integrated quality of the ecological model (Susser & Susser, 1996, p. 676): "The outer box may be thought of as representing the overall physical environment which, in turn, contains societies and populations (the epidemiologic terrain), single individuals, and individual physiological systems, tissues, and cells, and finally (in biology) molecules." Whether referred to as "eco-epidemiology," "social

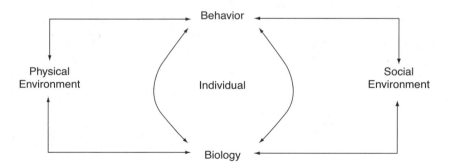

Source: From U.S. Department of Health and Human Services.

FIGURE 2–1 Ecological Model. Determinants of Health (Detail).

ecological," or "ecosocial," in each case, the value of viewing epidemiology and public health in a broader historical, social, economic, political, and environmental context is underscored (Krieger, 2001; Stokols, 1992; Susser & Susser, 1996).

An ecological model has been used to describe and explain the effects of multilevel factors on both the causes (or etiology) of health conditions as well as on the consequences (or course) of those conditions. Later, we will examine the age-associated causes of major health conditions, such as cardiovascular disease, cancer, diabetes, Alzheimer's disease, and osteoarthritis. We will also examine the extent to which the course of those conditions contributes to patterns of health, functioning, and longevity. The likelihood of disability among people and populations has received special attention and has been explained as a multilevel process—"the disablement process." The process, as described originally by Verbrugge and Jette (1994) and adapted by Guralnik and Ferrucci (2003), is initiated by a pathology with an associated level of physiological or cognitive impairment that may lead, in turn, to functional limitations and, ultimately, to a disability (Figure 2–2). The transition from pathology to disability, especially from functional limitations to disability, depends on the intersections of the individual's capacity and behaviors, as well as the relative resources and demands of the social and physical environments. Functional limitations are defined as restrictions or difficulty in the performance of generic tasks that typically involve upper- and lower-body strength, balance, fine dexterity, and walking speed. Disability, on the

Pathology⟶	Impairment⟶	Functional Limitation⟶	Disability
Disease, injury, congenital developmental condition	Dysfunction and structural abnormalities in specific body systems (musculoskeletal, cardiovascular, etc.)	Restrictions in basic physical and mental actions (ambulate, reach, grasp, climb stairs, speak, see standard print)	Difficulty doing activities of daily life (personal care, household management, job, hobbies)

Example			
Denervated muscle in arm due to trauma	Atrophy of muscle	Cannot pull with arm	Change of job; can no longer swim recreationally

Source: Reprinted from Verbrugge and Jette (1994) as adapted by Guralnik and Ferrucci (2003), with permission from the American Journal of Preventive Medicine.

FIGURE 2–2 The Disablement Model

other hand, refers to the inability to perform specific social roles in everyday life because of health or physical problems.

The Verbrugge–Jette Disablement Model (1994) has served as an important frame of reference for research in the epidemiology of aging and disability. In fact, a recent Cooper Conference in Dallas, Texas, used the model as the basis and foundation for a symposium on the significance of physical activity as a strategy to prevent physical disablement in older adults (Rejeski, Brawley, & Haskell, 2003). While the model continues to play a critical role in facilitating research in this area, suggestions for revision have been made. For example, Anita Stewart (2003) has recommended that the model be expanded to include physiologic aging and disuse, in addition to the current focus on disease pathology, as primary engines of disablement. This is based on the observation, to be discussed in more detail in Chapter 4, that functional limitations and disabilities are not only found among older people with frank disease pathology. She also recommends that assessments of functioning be expanded and not defined negatively, as is the case with "impairments" and "limitations." Recommendations of this kind are leading to a more comprehensive assessment of aging, health, and functioning.

In addition to the study of the causes and consequences of disease, the ecological model has been used to study the process of aging itself. By far the clearest connection between epidemiology and gerontology is found in the work of M. Powell Lawton and his colleagues in what has come to be defined as the "general ecological model of aging" (Lawton & Nahemow, 1973; Lawton, 1986; Nahemow, 2000). However, unlike the model in epidemiology, which is focused on a variety of health and functional outcomes, the work of Lawton and colleagues focuses exclusively on behavior and well-being. The primary thesis is that human behavior and function result from the competencies of the individual, the demands or "press" of the environment, and the interaction or adaptation of the person to the environment. Moreover, the relationship between individual competency and the environment is viewed as a dynamic process; both the press of environments and levels of individual competencies change as part of the process of aging. This interaction is summarized in terms of the "Press-Competence Model" (see Figure 2–3).

Competence lies on a continuum from low to high along the vertical axis, while environmental press goes from weak to strong, along the horizontal axis. The line moving from low to high on both axes represents

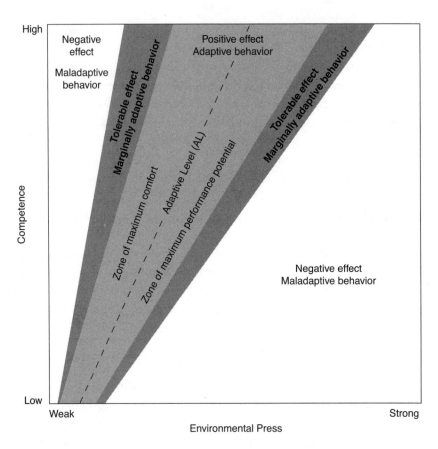

Source: Lawton, M. P. & Nahemow, L. (1973).

FIGURE 2–3 Lawton and Nahemow's Press-Competence Model

adaptation, the theoretical point at which the level of environmental press matches the level of individual competence. With aging, there is a general, although highly variable, reduction in individual competence. If environmental press remains constant, individual behavior and function are adversely affected. To the right of the line is the "zone of maximum performance," which is characterized by high press, challenges, and stimulation. This zone encourages active behavior by eliciting motivating responses. To the right of this zone is a marginal zone, where individuals continue to function, but with some difficulty. Falls, stress, and other indicators of maladaptive behavior start to occur here. To the right of the marginal zone is the zone of negative effect and maladaptive behavior, where the individual can no longer maintain an acceptable degree of functioning. This is the point at which the demands of the environment exceed the individual's ability to meet those demands. According to Verbrugge and Jette (1994), this is the point of disablement. On the other hand, to the left of the adaptation line is the zone of maximal comfort, an area characterized by weak environmental press and a general relaxation from environmental demands. To the left of that zone is another marginal zone, in which the absence of environmental stimulation begins to lead to boredom. Finally, the final zone is the zone of negative affect and maladaptive behavior. In this case, the environment is so unchallenging that it contributes to functional passivity, disuse, and limitation. This, in turn, perhaps may lead to a sense of "helplessness" (Seligman, 1975).

Lawton also distinguished between environmental docility and environmental proactivity. Environmental docility refers to those situations in which personal competence declines and behavior is increasingly affected by characteristics of the environment. In contrast, environmental proactivity describes situations in which an increase in personal competence enhances a person's ability to make use of environmental resources and achieve a more positive outcome.

Proposals have been made to enhance the utility of Lawton's person-environment fit model for research in epidemiology and public health (Glass & Balfour, 2003). While acknowledging the strengths of this model, Glass and Balfour report that the person-environment fit model rarely has been used to assess physical health. They note that "environmental press" has proven to be difficult to operationalize in epidemiologic research, especially regarding the identification of hypothesized pathways between neighborhood characteristics and health outcomes. Second, they indicate that little attention has been given to how person-environment fit is affected over time. Third, and perhaps most significantly, Glass and Balfour argue that the model underestimates the inverse of environmental press, that is, features that are conducive to functioning and that may lead to the "buoying" of behavioral competence. This is an important observation. It underscores the point that successful adaptation is not simply due to the absence of barriers, similar to the preamble to the constitution of the World Health Organization, that health is not merely the absence of disease or infirmity, but rather complete physical, mental and social well-being. In this case, environmental buoying is associated with environmental flexibility, as well as prostheses, resource availability, enrichment, and social support. Environmental buoying and press are placed in a broader context that affects person-environment fit and, in turn, affects the likelihood of personal competence, level of adaptive or maladaptive responses, and ultimately health and functional outcomes.

One of the dilemmas of the person-environment model, as noted by Benyamin Schwartz (2003, p. 14) in a recent review of Powell's work, is the nature of the interrelationship between the individual and the environment:

> The interactional approach to the relationships between older persons' behavior and the environment introduced the subject–object problem into the philosophical foundation of environment aging studies. This dualistic concept of the individual allowed two simultaneous but mutually exclusive interpretations under which the theories of environmental gerontology would be developed. At the same time it created a fundamental problem: On the one hand, the older individual is perceived as one of the "elderly," whose actions and behavior are determined by the external forces of the environment; on the other hand, the individual is seen as a freely thinking, freely acting subject whose actions and behavior are determined by his or her own personal inner drives and desires. The problems that emerge from this duality revolve around two issues: Is the individual's behavior determined by conditions in his or her environment, or in his or her own internal wiring? And how can the environment and the person interactively shape each other?

The relationship between the individual and the larger social and physical environments, which is one of the central questions in sociology and social philosophy, is a key component of the ecological model. Increasingly, commentators see the distinction between the individual and the larger environment as a false dichotomy. Anthony Giddens, a leading British sociologist (1984, p. 139), for one, opposes this conceptual distinction between the individual and social–physical environment, or what he refers to as "micro-sociological" and "macro-sociological" study, noting that "The two are not infrequently set off against one another, with the implication that we have to choose between them, regarding one in some way more fundamental than the other." Rather than a dualism, in Giddens' view, the individual and the broader social and physical structure are, by definition, interrelated. It is not possible to understand one without a consideration of the other. Put differently, the interaction is both constraining and enhancing. For example, interaction among individuals takes place in a particular setting or place at a particular point in time. The interaction, of course, is prescribed or constrained by societal and cultural patterns of behavior—the context. While the interaction itself may serve to reinforce those societal and cultural prescriptions, it may be modified to adapt to new societal and environmental challenges. Of course, the opportunities to enhance or modify those patterns are affected as well by social and economic resources, such as summarized by positions of class, status, and power. In general, those with greater resources, such as those of higher socioeconomic status, have a greater range of choices and are in the best position to adapt to changing circumstances to affect change. In contrast, those of lower socioeconomic status have a more restricted range of choices and less opportunity to adapt or alter the course of events. It is important to emphasize, however, that even among the people with fewer options, choices are still available and choices are still made. Carol Ryff and colleagues (1999, p. 17) have addressed this issue with specific reference to aging and the significance of life events:

> The experiential substance of people's lives becomes a profitable context for joint focus on how life opportunities and life difficulties are distributed across the social order, and what their consequences are for individual functioning.

THE ECOLOGICAL MODEL—KEY COMPONENTS

In this section, we will address the central components of the ecological model that will serve as the framework for a consideration of the topics to follow. If the biologic, behavioral, social, and environmental nodes of this model enable us to see the scope of work in the epidemiology of aging, the connections among those nodes suggest the causal pathways that either have been or should be examined. In this way, the model serves as both a typology of what has been done and as an agenda for what should be done in this field. This will be challenging. As Ana Diez Roux (1998, p. 220) has written, "Perhaps the most challenging aspect of multilevel analysis is it requires a theory of causation that integrates micro- and macro-level variables and explains these relationships and interactions across levels." Accordingly, we will begin by considering some key themes that set the stage for a theory of causation across these multilevel levels of biologic, behavioral, social, and environmental factors.

Theories of Aging as Explanations of "Weathering"

There are a number of major theories of aging (Carey, 2003). Each theory can be arrayed hierarchically from the molecular level, to the cellular, to the systematic, and, finally, to the evolutionary level. In general, a theory can be defined as a set of logically connected propositions designed to both describe and explain some phenomenon. A theory serves to identify a set of important variables, to specify the relationship between those variables, and, most importantly, to provide an explanation or reason for the relationship among those variables.

Although the molecular, cellular, and systematic theories of aging address the aging process at different levels of biologic organization, a common theme is the proposition that the likelihood of an error or malfunction in processes increases with time. The site and etiology of the error differ depending on the scope or level of the theory. These errors or malfunctions, in turn, render the organism more susceptible to the onset of disease, disability, and death. The timing and extent of those age-related errors or malfunctions, followed later by an elevation in the risk of ill health and overall "weathering," seem to be due to the interplay of genetic and environmental factors throughout the life course.

Molecular theories of aging focus on the extent to which cellular function and integrity change over time. Along these lines, the gene regulation theory is based on the proposition that genetic expression is diminished and structurally altered following reproductive maturity, resulting in a loss of genetic integrity. Other theories posit that accumulation of random molecular damage inhibits regular genetic expression. Important from our perspective, in some cases, these theories include the proposition that the accumulation of environmental damage is associated with age-associated errors and malfunctions.

One of the most well known *cellular* theories of aging is the free-radical theory or free-radical accumulation theory, which is based on a mechanistic link between aging and metabolism. Free or unstable oxygen molecules are a byproduct of metabolism. These unstable molecules, in turn, are a source of cellular damage in a number of different cell components, such as lipids, protein, carbohydrates, and nucleic acids. Of particular significance, especially for our purposes, is that the free-radical theory of aging is proposed as a generalized mechanism for aging, or as Carey (2003, p. 91) writes, "a 'public' mechanism of aging—common mechanisms among diverse organisms that are conserved over the course of evolution." A related cellular theory is based on the proposition of finite cell life. It is hypothesized that there is a finite period of population doublings, known generically as The Hayflick Limit, after Leon Hayflick, the scientist who first proposed "replicative senescence." Current research is focusing on telomeres. Telomeres are located on the ends of chromosomes and are necessary for proper chromosomal function and replication. Following from this theory of aging, research indicates that there is a progressive loss in the length of the telomeres and, as a result, a progressive loss in the ability to transmit the full genetic complement across generations (Aviv, Levy, & Mangel, 2003). In addition, recent research indicates a connection between this cellular process and difficulties of everyday life (Epel, Blackburn, Lin, Dhabhar, Adler, Morrow, et al., 2004). As summarized by Carey (2003, p. 92): "The simplest theory for accounting for the Hayflick Limit is one in which permanent cell-cycle arrest is due to a checkpoint mechanism that interprets a critically short telomere length as damaged DNA and causes cells to exit the cell cycle." Later, Carey writes (2003, p. 92): "Although telomere length has historically been used as a means to predict the future life of cells, a new model frames the connection between telomere shortening and cellular senescence by introducing the concept of a stochastic and increasing probability of switching to the uncapped/noncycling state."

System theories of aging are based on aging and the regulation and coordination of organ systems. One well-known theory is the immunological theory of aging, which is based on the competencies of mechanisms that operate before and after infection (innate and adaptive immunity), and is supported by evidence that indicates that immunological function declines with age.

Unlike these theories, the *evolutionary* theories of aging address the issue of the aging of the human species. Rather than focusing primarily on the weathering and ultimate destruction of the system, this theory examines to what extent aging confers an evolutionary advantage to the human species. Moreover, unlike other theories, evolutionary theories of aging provide a comprehensive underpinning for an ecological model of aging. For that reason, we will discuss the evolutionary theory of aging in more detail.

Evolutionary Theories of Aging

Why do humans age, or to put it differently, what is the evolutionary advantage of an aging population for the human species? Moreover, why do humans live so long after their reproductive capacity is gone—what some have referred to as the "menopause paradox"? Some have argued that there is an "aging gene," which manifests itself in one of two ways. First, it is claimed that aging is a genetically programmed means to limit population size and avoid overcrowding. Second, aging is an adaptive process to facilitate the turnover of generations, thus aiding in the adaptation of the species to a changing environment. In contrast, others, such as Thomas Kirkwood (1999), argue that these explanations run counter to one of the basic principles of evolution: Species are programmed to survive, not to die.

Kirkwood (1999) and others have proposed a Disposable Soma Theory. This theory assumes that aging is probably caused by the gradual and progressive accumulation of damage in the cells and tissues that comes from the need to react and adjust to a changing and demanding environment. Over time, the capacity to react to this changing environment becomes more difficult. With age, physiological systems need more resources and time to adjust to environmental demands. As Kirkwood writes (1999, p. 145):

> Natural selection did not design us to age, but it did design us to cope with all kinds of vicissitudes, such as illness, cold, and hunger. Many of the challenges that occur as a result of aging doubtless mimic other challenges that occur in younger individuals as a result of the sheer unpredictability of life. In time, the cumulative effects of aging test even the cleverest of homeostatic mechanism to the limit. That is why, as we age, we find that our adaptive response to physiologic stress declines.

With aging, the maintenance of the human body (soma) becomes more difficult. More metabolic resources are diverted from reproduction to somatic maintenance. As humans evolved and became more sophisticated, they were better able to control and manage environmental risks, especially within the context of social groups. As Kirkwood (1999, p. 68) writes, "Our ancestral species found that living in social groups made good sense because there was safety in numbers, especially if those around you were your kin, who would have a genetic interest in your survival."

The aging of the population helps to maintain the human species in other ways. While aging requires that increased resources be directed away from reproduction to somatic maintenance, that is not to say that older people fail to help maintain the species. Quite the contrary, for as a social species humans require extended time for nurturance and socialization. In terms of maintenance of the species, it is more appropriate for aging humans to spend time assisting in the nurturance of their children and grandchildren than it is for them, such as would be the case with aging women, to actually give birth to more children. In fact, some have argued that menopause makes evolutionary sense in that it protects aging women from the rigors of childbirth and makes them available to assist in the nurturance of developing children and grandchildren. Ronald Lee (2003) recently expanded on this idea by arguing that the need for "intergenerational transfers" not only explains the aging of people beyond their reproductive years but also explains relative survival across the life course and the reasons why juvenile mortality declines with age. More important, this evolutionary theory of aging explains why humans age and adjust to a changing environment within a social context. For our purposes, it suggests an *evolutionary explanation* for why age-associated patterns of health, functioning, and longevity in human populations result from multilevel connections across biologic, behavioral, social, and environmental factors over the life course.

Homeostasis, Allostasis, and Allostatic Load

Human aging can be described in terms of the maintenance of physiological balance (homeostasis) through an ongoing process of adaptation (allostasis) to changing, stressful environmental demands (Brunner, 2000). Allostasis was first introduced by Sterling and Eyer (1988, pp. 631–651) to explain why human survival requires that "an organism must vary parameters of its internal milieu and match them appropriately to environmental demands." The autonomic nervous system, the hypothalamic-pituitary-adrenal (HPA) axis, and the cardiovascular, metabolic, and immune systems protect the body by responding to internal and external stress. This is sometimes explained in terms of the "fight or flight" mechanism. When acute or chronic environmental threat persists, allostatic mechanisms become impaired, and a weathering process is initiated that is described as "allostatic load (AL)." This, of course, is particularly important to consider in the context of aging. Not only do older people experience an accumulation of environmental challenges and, in some cases, insults, but they also experience declines in the capacity to meet those challenges. AL represents the cumulative biologic burden exacted on the body through attempts to adapt to life's demands (McEwen & Seeman, 1999; Seeman, Singer, Rowe, Horwitz, & McEwen, 1997; Seeman, McEwen, Rowe, & Singer, 2001).

Dysregulation in one or more of the biologic systems involved in allostatis is reflected in characterizations of the multiple pathways to pathophysiology and a diversity of chronic conditions. As Taylor and colleagues (1997) have noted, this process helps to explain how "an unhealthy environment gets under the skin."

Different analytical strategies have been used to calculate AL scores for individuals. An initial operationalization of the notion of AL used assessments of 10 biologic parameters reflecting functioning of the HPA axis, sympathetic nervous system, cardiovascular system, and metabolic processes. Dysregulation was defined in terms of scores in the upper quartiles. Overall severity of AL was based on the number of systems in which resting scores were recorded in the extreme quartiles. Higher scores on a summary numerical measure of AL were shown to predict four major health outcomes: incident cardiovascular disease, decline in physical functioning, decline in cognitive functioning, and mortality. Although the summary measure of AL was a significant predictor of outcomes, none of the individual components exhibited strong predictive capacity. This finding suggests that risk for the above outcomes is related to the overall impact of dysregulation across multiple regulatory systems. Later formulations, based on canonical weights, were based on the full range of scores and did not assume that the indicators of dysregulation were uniform across the different physiologic systems. The purpose of this analysis was to determine which linear combination of biomarkers was maximally correlated with which linear combination of functional change scores. The weights in the best linear combinations for predicting decline in physical and cognitive functioning served as the basis for a more comprehensive scoring scheme for AL. It was determined that four primary mediators—epinephrine, norepinephrine, cortisol, and DHEA-S represented the most parsimonious set of prognostic indicators of AL. Finally, the most sophisticated strategy to date for the measurement of AL is based on a technique referred to as recursive partitioning (Zhang, Yu, & Singer, 2003). Based on a set of candidate independent variables and study outcomes, this technique systematically identifies the most parsimonious set of physiologic items as well as the best cut points for determination of severity. This strategy affords an opportunity to identify specific combinations and cut points of physiologic systems.

Despite the promise of research in this area, it is important to realize that this is a relatively new area of study and that criticisms have been raised. First, there are concerns that the measurements are based on resting levels and may not accurately reflect the actual allostastic process, a process that may be better reflected in a setting based on an environmental challenge. Second, there is concern that only a small number of indicators of dysregulation have been available for examination. Finally, the indicators used have been those that have been available in existing population studies, such as the MacArthur Study on Successful Aging (Seeman et al., 1997, 2001). As a result, it has not been possible to examine a full complement of possible biologic systems. It is recommended that future studies include immune measures that reflect general levels of proinflammatory activity in an individual.

One of the interesting questions is why some aging people have better allostatic capacity than others. There is evidence that genetic, familial factors may play a role. For example, there is a growing body of research stating genetic factors may be associated with extreme longevity (Perls, Kunkel, & Puca, 2002). It is reported that the life spans of human monozygotic twin pairs are statistically more similar to each other than life spans of dizygotic twins; the magnitude of this difference indicating that approximately one quarter to one third of what determines life span is genetic (Finch & Tanzi, 1997). Behavioral and social factors are important as well. Those who engage in healthful behaviors and those who maintain social bonds with others are less likely to exhibit dysregulation.

There is evidence that experiences in the early years affect allostatic competence in adulthood. For example, life history profiles were constructed using data from the Wisconsin Longitudinal Study (Singer & Ryff, 1999). Individual lives were represented by information from five domains:

1. Family background and early life experiences
2. Occupational experiences from first job through employment status at ages 59–60
3. Adult family life
4. Mental health, psychological outlooks, and beliefs in adulthood
5. Physical health in adulthood

Persons who had predominantly negative experiences in three of the first four domains were defined to have essentially negative profiles. Persons who had very positive childhood experiences but who had negative experiences on at least two of the other domains were defined to have poor adult profiles subsequent to positive childhood profiles. The results indicate that there is a long-term protective effect from a positive childhood, even in the face of considerable adversity in adulthood. These results underscore the importance of the life course, another key component of the ecological model.

Research to date has been based on the availability of data in existing study populations. Recently, there has been a call for researchers to step back and consider the types of physiological data that should be used to provide a more definitive test of the AL hypothesis.

Life Course

It follows logically that the interplay of biologic, behavioral, social, and environmental factors must occur over time. The important task is to determine how development at the individual level is affected by broad demographic factors, such as age, period, and cohort effects. Although this may seem at first glance to be a rather abstract notion, it is really the basis of most historical novels, novels in which the lives of individuals are played out against a historical background of social, political, and economic forces.

There are two bodies of research that underscore the importance of the life course in epidemiologic studies (Kuh & Ben-Shlomo, 2004). The first body of research, based on the work of David Barker and his colleagues (Barker, Eriksson, Forsen, & Osmond, 2002), assumes that events surrounding critical periods of early development, most notably during gestation, affect the subsequent risk of chronic diseases. The second body of research assumes that the accumulation of exposures and "insults" over the life course affect later risk for disease. Although these two approaches are often presented as distinct, there is no apparent reason why the risk of disease in adulthood and the senior years cannot be due to both accumulated risk and exposures occurring at critical points of development. In fact, Neal Halfon and Miles Hochstein (2002, p. 433) argue that one of the key components of a life course perspective is recognition that "different health trajectories are the product of cumulative risk and protective factors and other influences that are programmed into biobehavioral regulatory systems during critical and sensitive periods."

Age differences in health outcomes may be the result of a variety of factors. A cross-sectional examination reflects, in many ways, a simple snapshot of differences in health outcomes among people in different age groups. Because older people are survivors, the magnitude of the age difference may be less than would be found for an examination of a cohort of people across the life course. Accordingly, a longitudinal examination that compares a cohort of people as they age would provide a more precise estimate of age-related differences. It is important to emphasize that such age-related differences could not necessarily be attributed to factors associated with aging. The differences may reflect characteristics of specific cohorts of people, that is, generations of people "moving through time." T. Kue Young (1998, p. 180) provides a succinct description of derivation and significance of "cohort" in epidemiologic research:

> It comes from the Latin cohors, meaning "warriors." A Roman legion consisted of 10 cohorts, each with 300–600 soldiers. In epidemiology, cohort is initially used to refer to a birth cohort, a group of individuals born at the same time (usually the same year) whose health experience can be followed as the group ages.

Young (1998, p. 180) goes on to write that, "Cohort effect, also called generation effect, refers to the unique set of environmental conditions to which a particular generation or birth may have been exposed during some time in its life span." This means that some of the age differences may be due to specific characteristics and events that affected a particular generation of older people at some point in their lives. Age differences also may be due to period effects, that is, extrinsic factors, such as environmental factors that were present in a particular calendar year, which affected people across the life course. Together, these factors are summarized as age, period, and cohort effects.

The circumstances of exposures and behaviors over the life course point to the importance of broad demographic factors occurring at the population level that affect the subsequent patterns of disease within populations. As noted previously, age, period, and cohort effects are three well-known demographic variables. Age, in this case, refers to the age distribution or composition of a population. A period effect, often represented by one or more calendar years, refers to an event, such as the Dutch famine—a time during the Nazi occupation of Holland in 1944 in which access to food was severely limited, in which the health of the population regardless of age was affected (Roseboom, van der Meulen, Ravelli, Osmond, Barker, & Bleker, 2001). A cohort effect refers to events that affect a generation of people as they age. Although these factors are presented as three independent variables, there is considerable discussion about whether the effects are truly independent. This, in turn, has important implications for describing and explaining the association between aging and health. Despite these concerns, which will be addressed in more detail in later chapters, it is important to note that there are demographic factors that operate at the level of the population that affect health at both the level of the population and at the level of the individual.

Age-period-cohort analysis is a technique, then, that is used to describe the relative effects of each of the three factors. The traditional method is to present health data, for example, age-specific mortality rates for different cohorts of people, in other words, people with different birth years, who died in different years. Figure 2–4 is an example of an age-period-cohort analysis of age-specific mortality rates for people who died from a particular condition.

While the descriptive tabular analysis of age, period, and cohort effects is useful, it is not designed to provide precise estimates of the independent effects of each factor. Analytic strategies have been developed to examine the independent and joint effects of each of the three factors through multivariate statistical analysis. There remains considerable controversy, however, about the appropriateness of this strategy, as it is argued that the three factors are not independent and, in fact, are confounded by definition. With information on two of the factors, the value of the third factor can be derived. This issue, referred to in the literature as "the identifiability problem," will be discussed in more detail in Chapter 10 (Xu, Laird, Dokery, Schouten, Rijcken, & Weiss, 1995). Although there are significant concerns about the best analytic strategy to use to examine age, period, and cohort effects, it is important to emphasize again how useful these three factors are for obtaining a more complete qualitative description of aging, health, and function than would be the case if we relied on chronological age alone.

Elaine M. Brody provides another example of the utility of this approach in her book, *Mental and Physical Health Practices of Older People* (Brody, 1985). Instead of presenting data for an entire cohort of people, she presents data for a single individual—a 75-year-old woman. She highlights key biographical events in the woman's life, compared to events that were occurring at the same time in society. It provides a very effective way to compare the biographies of individuals against the backdrop of history, noting in particular, the key political and social events of the period.

In addition to age, period, and cohort effects presented at either the level of the population or, as is the case with Brody's example, a life-course approach must include an appreciation of how older people interpret

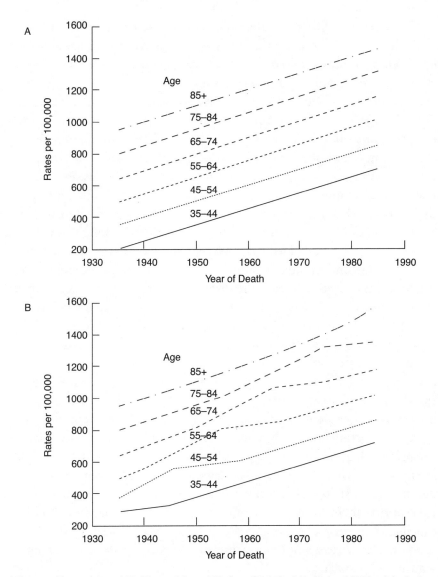

Source: Figure 4.1, p. 106, Figure 4.2, p. 107, from Statistical Analysis of Epidemiological Data, Second Edition, by Steve Selvin, Copyright 1991, 1996, by Oxford University Press, Inc. Used by permission of Oxford University Press, Inc.

FIGURE 2–4 Age-Specific Curves for Hypothetical Data Showing Mortality Rates per 100,000 Population by Year of Death (A) Without a Cohort Effect Present and (B) With a Cohort Effect Present.

change and how it affects their self-concept, as well as their expectations for the future. Work in this area is part of a broader research agenda in the "Developmental Sciences" (Halfon & Hochstein, 2002; Settersten, 1999).

The issue of the life course and time figure prominently in the standard research designs used in epidemiology—the case-control design and the longitudinal or prospective design. Each design addresses time in a different way. With regard to the case-control study, cases are people with the health outcome of interest, for example, breast cancer, heart disease, or diabetes. The controls are people who are similar to the cases with the exception of their disease status. The task is to obtain information about the cases and controls, typically retrospective information, such as past behaviors and exposures, that preceded the onset of the disease, which may provide an opportunity to establish how the cases are different from the controls. This information, in turn, ideally provides insight into the etiology or causes of the disease. In the case of the longitudinal or prospective design, the objective is to identify a group of people without the health outcome of interest and then follow them over time and record which of these people develop the disease. Recent research suggests that the time interval that is typically used in most studies in epidemiology—including studies in the epidemiology of aging—must be extended.

In summary, the topics of theories of aging, most notably the evolutionary theory of aging; homeostasis, allostasis, and AL; and the life course represent three underlying themes that serve as a foundation for a specific consideration of the ecological model. Together, these themes underscore three points: First, a consideration of the epidemiology of aging, health, functioning, and longevity should be based on a multilevel perspective that includes biologic, behavioral, social, and environmental levels. Second, those levels are interrelated. For example, health outcomes depend on physiological factors, such as allostatic capacity, to respond to environmental challenges. That capacity depends on a variety of factors that include genetics, behavioral patterns, and level of social contacts and support. Third, these multilevel factors unfold over the life course of individuals and populations.

EPIDEMIOLOGY OF AGING—AN ECOLOGICAL MODEL

The ecological model presented in this section builds on the previous themes and other models used in the fields of epidemiology, gerontology, sociology, environmental psychology, developmental science, environmental design, and urban planning (Catalano, 1979, 1989; Macintyre & Ellaway, 2000; McLeroy et al., 1988; Smedley & Syme, 2000; Stokols, 1992). Our purpose here is to use the ecological model both as a typology for what is being done and as an agenda for what should be done in the field of the epidemiology of aging. Rather than thinking of the major topics in this field, such as survival, physical functioning, and disease and comorbidities, as distinct areas of research, this model serves to underscore that the areas are, in fact, interrelated. Indeed, it is only by thinking of the field in this way that we can appreciate recent work to identify the causal pathways in aging, health, functioning, and longevity. The model, then, serves as a blueprint of what is to follow in the book. Subsequent chapters will address each of the key topic areas in this field as outcomes. These include survival and mortality; physical functioning and activities of everyday life; cognitive functioning; depression; falls and injuries; and disease and comorbidities. For example, research on physical functioning and activities of everyday life will be addressed in Chapter 4. This will include examinations of both the independent and joint effects of biologic, behavioral, social, and environmental factors on patterns of physical functioning in aging populations. In Chapter 3, research on aging and survival will be addressed. Research on physical functioning also will be included, but only as it relates to patterns of survival, and so on. It is hoped that this approach will underscore the connections among the key topic areas. Moreover, it will point to areas of needed research, a topic that will be described in more detail in Chapter 12.

In the subsequent sections of the present chapter, we will describe the components of the ecological model by starting, as researchers in public health often do, by addressing the demographic and socioeconomic patterns of aging, health, and longevity in the population. This often establishes the framework for subsequent examinations. In other words, after describing the demographic and socioeconomic patterns of health and longevity, the next task is to attempt to explain the reasons for these patterns. This will include a consideration of characteristics of the physical environment, in terms of both toxic environmental exposures and characteristics of the built environment; the social environment, including living arrangements and social networks; and health behaviors, such as tobacco consumption, diet and nutrition, and alcohol consumption; and levels of physical activity. Although we will not devote separate chapters to these topics, each will figure in the discussion of survival;

physical and cognitive functioning; depression; falls, injuries, and automobile crashes; disease and comorbidities; and general health, frailty, and successful aging.

This ecological model (Figure 2–5) is only intended to illustrate the range of variables and underscore the point that the variables are interrelated. The model is divided into three sections (circles). The top circle includes demographic (age, gender, race, and ethnicity), socioeconomic, environmental (physical and built), social (social capital, living arrangements, social networks, and social support), psychosocial (self-efficacy, social control, and sense of coherence), and physiological factors. The second circle includes standard health and functional outcomes. It is important to note that with the exception of the demographic factors, the variables are interrelated (in other words, each variable affects and, in turn, is affected by each other variable). Indeed, the outcomes that are displayed in the second circle also may affect over time the variables listed in the first circle. The third circle represents vital status (alive or dead). It is important to realize that the model is not intended to present specific, hypothesized causal relationships (or causal links across independent, intermediary, and dependent variables.) Rather, the model represents a simple heuristic device to guide our consideration of research in the epidemiology of aging.

The following sections present a more detailed description of the variables included in the first two, interrelated circles of the ecological model.

Age

Age, as noted previously, is one of the key variables in epidemiology. Chronological age is associated with the incidence and prevalence of most conditions, as well as the risk of death. Because age is considered to be a marker for a variety of biologic, behavioral, social, and environmental factors, much of epidemiologic research is designed to understand what it is about age that affects patterns of health and well-being. These age-associated patterns, in turn, may be due to the aging process itself, coupled with exposures resulting from the shared experiences of a specific cohort or generation of people over time as well as exposures associated with living in a particular historical period. Although birth date and age are often readily available for purposes of research, the manner in which age is summarized may affect the nature of a study. For example, if age is summa-

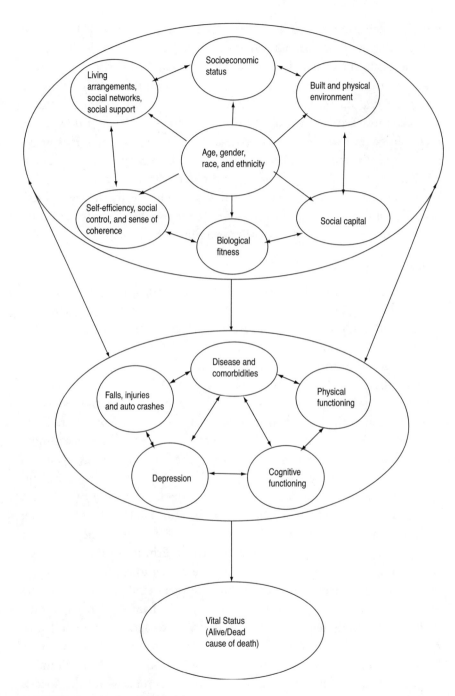

FIGURE 2–5 Ecological Model

rized as a continuous variable, the estimate of risk may be based on a unit change of age, often summarized as one year. So, for example, if the risk for colon cancer associated with age is 1.15, it can be interpreted to mean that the risk of that cancer increases by 1.15 (approximately 15%) for every one-year increase in age. Although this is a useful summary, it does not take into account the extent to which the absolute magnitude of risk may change over specific periods of age. This may be captured by categorizing age into "meaningful categories," for example, ages 45–54, 55–64, 65–74, 75–84, and 85 years of age and older. If the age group of 45–54 years is used as a referent, each risk estimate would specify the level of risk for each subsequent age group. This strategy assists in determining whether the magnitude of risk varies as a function of age.

Gender

Gender is also an important variable in epidemiologic studies. Patterns of health, functioning, and longevity have been shown to be associated with gender. Although women tend to have a greater life expectancy than men, women tend to report more functional limitations and disability than men. In addition to biologic factors, such as levels of estrogen or testosterone, there are behavioral, social, and environmental factors that account for gender differences in health outcomes. For example, research indicates that with the exception of sedentary behavior, women are more likely than men to engage in healthful behavior. Specifically, men are more likely than women to engage in risky behavior, such as exposure to tobacco, poor dietary practices, excessive alcohol consumption, and aggressive behaviors that elevate risk for violence and injury (Berrigan, Dodd, Troiano, Krebs-Smith, & Barbash, 2003). One recent national study indicated that men were 2.6 times more likely than women to report nonadherence to recommendations to five healthful behaviors. In contrast, women were 1.6 times more likely than men to report adherence to every one of the five recommendations (Berrigan et al., 2003). Men also are more likely than women to be employed in hazardous occupations. Although it is only relatively recently that women have been included in clinical research trials, there is a growing body of research on women's health. Although historically included in studies as the "generic" human subject, there is relatively little research that has focused on the special health needs of men (International Longevity Center, 2004). This includes cultural prescriptions regarding the socialization of sex roles and how those prescriptions change over the life course as well as how they have changed in different historical periods. Of course, as we consider the issue of global patterns of aging, health, and functioning, the similarities and differences in cultural prescriptions for sex-role socialization in different parts of world must be taken into account.

Race and Ethnicity

As noted in Chapter 1, the aging population is not only becoming larger, it is becoming more diverse. In the United States, for example, the proportion of African-, Hispanic-, and Asian-Americans aged 65 and older is becoming larger, relative to non-Hispanic whites. In 2000, 83.5% of the U.S. population aged 65 and older was non-Hispanic white, compared to 8.1% African-American, 5.6% Hispanic white, 2.4% Asian or Pacific Islander, and 0.4% American Indian or Alaska native. In 2050, however, non-Hispanic whites will represent only 64.2% of those aged 65 and older. African-Americans will increase to 12.2%, Hispanic whites to 16.4%, Asian or Pacific Islander to 6.5%, and American Indian or Alaska native to 0.6% (Federal Interagency Forum on Aging Related Statistics, 2005).

As will be described in subsequent chapters, compared to non-Hispanic whites, African-American seniors are at elevated risk for a broad array of health conditions, functional limitations, and disabilities. Although Hispanic whites are typically in better health than African-American seniors, they too are at elevated risk for serious chronic health conditions, such as diabetes. Although Asian-American seniors represent a heterogeneous group, including Chinese-, Korean-, and Vietnamese-Americans, their health status is often comparable to that of non-Hispanic whites. Patterns of health, functioning, and longevity tend to vary by gender and, most notably, age. In general, racial and ethnic differences, especially between African-Americans and non-Hispanic whites, are most pronounced in the middle years. Less difference, especially among women, is found among seniors. Nevertheless, because health disparities are associated with differences in race and ethnicity, it is important to understand the implications of the increase in race and ethnic diversity in the growing senior populations for future incidence of health problems, limitations, and disabilities. As evidence of the importance of this topic, the National Academy of Sciences has recently published a comprehensive report titled *Understanding Racial and Ethnic Differences in Late Life: A Research Agenda* (Bulatao & Anderson, 2004).

The scientific consensus is that race is a social category of individuals who share certain phenotypic characteristics. Race is no longer thought of as a category characterized by homogeneous biologic inheritance. Ethnicity, on the other hand, refers to a social group that shares a distinctive social and cultural tradition. Interestingly, the U.S. Bureau of the Census and U.S. governmental health statistics restrict the use of ethnicity to people of Hispanic ancestry. In the 2000 U.S. census, if a person answered in the affirmative to the question, "Do you consider yourself Hispanic/Latino?" he or she then had the option of selecting one of eight categories of Hispanic from Puerto Rican to Other Hispanic/Latino.

Respondents also were asked to designate one or more racial/ethnic classifications from a list of 16 categories. Unlike the ethnic/Hispanic classifications, race is classified in terms of white, African-American, Indian (American), and Asian/Pacific Islander. As will be discussed in more detail in later chapters, racial and ethnic classification remains a controversial issue. In 2003, an initiative was placed on the California state ballot calling for the termination of the collection of all race and ethnic data for state activities. Although the initiative was defeated, it prompted considerable debate and raised concern among public health researchers about the loss of these important demographic data. The important question is what is it about race and ethnicity that is associated with health outcomes? The answer to this question includes factors associated with genetic and familial patterns, socioeconomic status, environmental exposures, social and behavioral status, and, in many cases, experiences of racism and discrimination (Ren, Amick, & Williams, 1999; Williams, Neighbors, & Jackson, 2003). In addition, relative accessibility and quality of health care as well as use of native home remedies may play a role. How does age as well as the timing of experiences over the life course affect the association between race and ethnicity and health outcomes? To what extent do race and ethnicity affect life chances in terms of both the challenges that are faced and the resources that are available to meet those challenges?

There are a number of factors that complicate this investigation. For example, some racial and ethnic groups, such as Hispanic and Asian groups, have higher proportions of immigrants than other groups, such as African-Americans. This means that those who were able to migrate may be healthier than those who remained in the home country. Moreover, in some racial and ethnic groups, those who become ill are likely to return to their home country to receive care, the so-called "Salmon Effect" (Bulatao

& Anderson, 2004). These selection factors may result, therefore, in an inaccurate estimate of racial and ethnic differences in health outcomes.

Socioeconomic Status

Socioeconomic status, often assessed in terms of independent and aggregate levels of family income, education, and occupational status, as well as community-level indicators, is associated with health, functioning, and longevity over the life course (Lynch & Kaplan, 2000; Seeman & Crimmins, 2001). In general, those of lower socioeconomic status are at elevated risk and have a higher incidence of acute and chronic health conditions, functional limitations and disabilities, and premature death. There is evidence of a socioeconomic health gradient, that is, at each level of socioeconomic status, there is a higher level of overall health (Adler, Boyce, Chesney, Cohen, Follerman, Kahn, et al., 1994). There is evidence that racial and ethnic differences in health and well-being are due at least in part to differences in socioeconomic status.

Age and aging affect the consideration of socioeconomic status and health in several ways. First, while socioeconomic status may affect levels of health and functioning across the life course and across generations, the magnitude of that effect may vary with age (House, Lepkowski, Kinney, Mero, Kessler, & Herzog, 1990). As with race and ethnicity, socioeconomic status, family income, education, and occupational status may have different implications in older populations. The strength of the association between family income and health may differ across different age groups. Among seniors, income may not reflect resources as well as measures of overall wealth. Because most seniors may no longer be employed in the jobs they had for most of their lives, occupational status may not be as indicative a measure of socioeconomic status as it is for younger groups. Although educational attainment is not affected with time, the meaning, significance, and past rewards associated with a specific number of years of formal education may be different across different generations. Second, the measurement of older people's current socioeconomic status may be less closely associated with current health status than is socioeconomic status at earlier points in the life course (Beefe-Dimmer, Lynch, Turrell, Lustgarten, Rahunathan, & Kaplan, 2004; Seeman & Crimmins, 2001). Finally, there is discussion about the significance of the "drift hypothesis," or the extent to which one's current health and level of functioning affect subsequent socioeconomic status (Harkey, Miles, & Rushing, 1976). In other words, serious health problems and functional limitations may have an adverse effect on a person's socioeconomic status and cause the person to drift downward in the social hierarchy. To the extent that older people are at greater risk for health problems and disabilities, they may be at greater risk for loss of economic resources. This all depends, of course, on the extent to which an older person can rely on an economic and social safety net.

Increasingly, socioeconomic status is being assessed at both individual and community levels (Daly, Duncan, Kaplan, & Lynch, 1998; Macintyre, Maciver, & Sooman, 1993; Robert, 1999). In addition to individual levels of income, years of education, and occupational position, summary measures of socioeconomic status at the community level are associated with individual and community health outcomes. The summary measures include median income, percentage of adults with 12 or more years of education, and inequality in income distribution (Robert, 1999). Haan, Kaplan, and Camacho (1987) have investigated the reasons for the association between socioeconomic status and poor health by studying mortality for nine years in a random sample of residents aged 35 years and more in Oakland, California. They found that residents of a federally designated poverty area experienced higher age-, race-, and sex-adjusted mortality, compared to residents of nonpoverty areas. Most important, the relationship between quality of health and places of residence persisted, even after adjusting for characteristics of the individual residents. These factors included baseline health status, race, income, employment status, access to medical care, health insurance coverage, tobacco use, and alcohol consumption. These findings suggest that characteristics of the physical environment should be investigated.

There is evidence of a health gradient associated with levels of socioeconomic status (Adler et al., 1994). In other words, it is not simply that those in poverty are in poorer health than those with higher levels of socioeconomic status. Instead, at each level of socioeconomic status, there is a corresponding increase in health. Of course, the magnitude of this difference may vary by the specific health outcome. There is little information about the extent to which the association between socioeconomic status and health outcomes varies by chronological age.

There is also research that indicates that the absolute level of inequality, that is, the extent of the socioeconomic difference in the population, has an effect that is independent of the association between socioeconomic status and health. Those communities with less extensive income differential have an overall lower mortality rate than communities with more extensive income differential (Lobmayer & Wilkinson, 2002). There is some controversy about the mechanisms by which income differentials affect specific health outcomes. Some researchers contend that the material disadvantages associated with lower socioeconomic status, such as less access to nutritious food, offer the primary explanation for the association (Lynch, Smith, Hillemeir, Shaw, Rahunathan, & Kaplan, 2001; Lynch, Smith, Kaplan, & House, 2000). Others contend that adverse psychosocial factors, such as greater anxiety and less social cohesion, associated with poorer socioeconomic status, are the primary explanations for ill health (Kawachi & Kennedy, 1997; Subramanian, Lochner, & Kawachi, 2003; Lobmayer & Wilkinson, 2002). Some commentators question the nature of this argument, noting instead that these explanations are not mutually exclusive. In other words, it is possible that both material and psychosocial pathways may account for the association between socioeconomic status and the magnitude of income inequity and health outcomes. To our knowledge, it is unknown to what extent the independent and joint effects of those factors on health vary by chronological age. It is also unknown whether the independent and joint effects of those factors vary over the life course and whether the relative strength and sequencing of those factors affect patterns of health later in life.

As noted previously, most measures of socioeconomic status, whether assessed at the individual or community levels, are based on objective indicators, such as family income, years of education, occupational status, as well as measures of wealth, including real estate and stock. There is also evidence that subjective indicators of social status are associated with measures of ill health (Singh-Manoux, Adler, & Marmot, 2003). One such measure includes a "ten-rung self-anchoring scale," displayed in the form of a ladder. Subjects are presented with a figure of the ladder and given the following instructions:

> Think of this ladder as representing where people stand in society. At the top of the ladder are the people who are best off—those who have the most money, most education, and the best jobs. At the bottom are the people who are worst off—who have the least money, least education, and the worst jobs or no job. The higher up you are on this ladder, the closer you are to people at the very top and the lower you are, the closer you are to the bottom. Where would you put yourself on the ladder? Please place a large "X" on the rung where you think you stand.

There is evidence that this measure provides an overall summary of various socioeconomic indicators. However, when such measures are held constant, the subjective measure is independently associated with health outcomes (Singh-Manoux et al., 2003). Importantly from our perspective, it is also argued that this subjective measure "reflects both changes in socioeconomic circumstances over the life course and cumulative social position better than current employment grade" (Singh-Manoux et al., 2003, p. 1332).

The Physical Environment

The physical environment refers to both the level of exposure to environmental pollutants and toxins as well as characteristics of the built environment, including housing, transportation, and land use. As noted previously, allostasis refers to a process by which physiological systems adjust and adapt to challenges resulting from stressors in the environment. It is well known that exposure to environmental pollutants and toxins is associated with a variety of acute and chronic health conditions. Much of the work in this area has focused on children, because of their physiological vulnerability, and on workers, because of the level of environmental exposures and workplace hazards (Committee on Chemical Toxicity and Aging, 1987). Although less attention has focused on the elderly, this is changing for a number of reasons. First, as noted previously, there is a growing recognition that current health status, for example, in the elderly is due to events and exposures occurring over the life course. Because the elderly by definition have lived a long time, there is a greater likelihood of elevated risk associated with accumulated exposures and environmental insults. Second, as with children, the elderly are physiologically vulnerable. This vulnerability is due to past and current health conditions as well as reductions in immunologic capacity associated with aging.

In 1985, the National Academy of Sciences prepared a report on the effects of environmental exposures on the aging processes, at the request of the Environmental Protection Agency and the National Institute of Environmental Health Sciences (Committee on Chemical Toxicity and Aging, National Research Council, 1987). The preparation of this report was based on the proposition that the principles of toxicology should be integrated with the principles of gerontology. As stated in the preface of that report (1987, p. vii): "The formation of the committee constituted one of the country's first organized efforts to bring together experts in the field of gerontology and toxicology to consider the interface between the two scientific disciplines." Although the report provides an excellent review of the principles of environmental health sciences, toxicology, and gerontology, it concludes that research in this area is scant (Committee on Chemical Toxicity and Aging, National Research Council, 1987, p. 163). Research recommendations in this area include the following: First, it is argued that the identification of biomarkers of aging is necessary to examine the effects of environmental agents on aging processes. A biomarker of aging is defined as "a biologic event or measurement of a biologic sample that is considered to be an estimate or prediction of one or more of the aging processes" (Committee on Chemical Toxicity and Aging, 1987, p. 39). Second, special effort should be made to take advantage of information that may be available on toxic exposures in particular populations. It is recommended that "persons exposed to specific chemical substances in an industrial setting or as a result of an 'experiment in nature' should be followed throughout life, so that the effects of such exposure that have long latent periods can be identified and investigated" (Committee on Chemical Toxicity and Aging, 1987, p. 167). Third, the development of animal models to investigate aging and environmental exposures is proposed. Finally, it is recommended that research be conducted on the effects of advancing age on pharmacokinetics (absorption, distribution, metabolism, and elimination), bioaccumulation, and other drug and chemical interactions and the influence of dietary factors, smoking, and other environmental factors.

In 2002, the National Academy of Sciences, the National Academy of Engineering, the Institute of Medicine, and the National Research Council, in cooperation with the Environmental Protection Agency and the National Institute on Aging, convened a second conference to examine environmental exposures in older populations in Washington, DC. The purpose of the conference was to initiate a yearlong effort to develop a national agenda on the environment and aging. A number of themes were identified, including the following:

1. There are significant age differences in pharmacokinetics, absorption, metabolism, and excretion that are likely to influence the retention of toxic environmental chemicals as well as the potential for these chemicals to cause adverse effects.

2. Because lung and liver functions tend to decline with age, there may be increased susceptibility to chemical and physical and environmental agents.

3. Older adults may be more susceptible to some chemicals than to others, especially those chemicals that are more likely than others to accumulate in the bone, lipids, and tissues. For example, although exposure to lead is less common today than in the past, older people, because of past exposures, may have greater concentrations of lead in their bones, leading to adverse health and functional effects.

There is also a growing interest in characteristics of the built environment, including housing, transportation, and overall patterns of land use (Carp, 1987; Lindheim & Syme, 1983). In fact, the Institute of Medicine convened a conference in collaboration with the National Institute of Environmental Health Sciences to propose a "new vision of environmental health for the 21st century". The final report, *Rebuilding the Unity of Health and the Environment* (Hanna & Coussens, 2001) included a chapter devoted to "Human Health and the Built Environment." Historically, most of the work in this area has focused on falls and injuries. There is evidence that certain elements of housing design, such as placement of stairs and lighting, are associated with the risk of falls, one of the leading causes of accidental death in older populations. Today, there is a growing appreciation that overall functioning is associated with both individual level of capacity as well as the level of environmental resources. Put differently, functional limitations and disabilities result when environmental demands exceed the capacities and resources of the individual or the population. A number of recent studies have indicated that one of the key mechanisms for fostering health and functioning is physical activity. More specifically, those who reside in neighborhoods that are characterized by greater housing density, with street and sidewalk grid pattern, and in proximity to goods and services are more likely to walk than people who reside in areas that are less dense, without grid patterns, and in less proximity to goods and services. More recently, research indicates that level of physical activity and functioning is associated with characteristics of the built environment (Moudon & Lee, 2003). As noted previously, Lawton (1986) argued that with age, physical capacity generally declines, and characteristics of the built environment and environmental design become more strongly associated with physical activity and functioning.

A number of different measures have been used to assess characteristics of the built environment (Macintyre, Ellaway, & Cummins, 2002). First, there are environmental audits. These audit measures provide an opportunity to systematically enumerate characteristics of the built environment at the street level. Items include width of street, presence and conditions of sidewalks, traffic flow, and presence of walking hazards and litter. Although professional researchers typically conduct the audits, residents also have used environmental audits of communities. Second, the built environment also can be surveyed by using available environmental sources of data. The geographic information system consists of a "layering" of information on a geographic map. For example, it is possible to identify the number and type of housing, location of goods and services, street patterns, locations of parks and walking trails, and traffic flow. Third, self-reports also have been used. In addition to reporting on the characteristics of the environment, respondents also may provide evaluations of the environment. For example, respondents may be asked to evaluate the quality of the sidewalk or the extent to which they feel safe while walking in a particular area. The issue of safety prompts us to consider another important variable that we have included in the ecological model—"social capital."

Social Capital

Social capital is defined as "those features of social structures—such as levels of interpersonal trust and norms of reciprocity and mutual aid—which act as resources for individuals and facilitate collective action" (Kawachi & Berkman, 2000, p. 175). It is important to emphasize at this point that social capital is a characteristic of neighborhoods and communities and not individuals, a point to which we will return (Subramanian et al., 2003). In fact, communities with higher levels of social capital may provide greater "opportunity structures," such as attractive and safe places to walk, to shop, and visit friends. Following from previous research in the social sciences (Coleman, 1988; Gouldner, 1960; Putnam, 2000), social capital has typically been measured in a variety of ways, such as number of voters, number of voluntary associations, or reports of customs or "norms of reciprocity" in neighborhoods. It is presently unknown, however, to what extent social capital affects health through the development and maintenance of self-efficacy and to what extent social capital operates directly on healthful behaviors, such as physical activity and proper diet and nutrition.

Living Arrangements, Social Networks, and Social Support

The social environment refers to living arrangements, marital status, and social networks. A number of studies have indicated that those with stronger social ties experience greater health, functioning, and longevity than those who are socially isolated (Seeman, 1996). This is important for a consideration of health and functioning in older populations. First, the association between social networks and health has been reported across the life course, including among older populations. Second, older people are at risk for losing important social contacts as they age. There is less contact with children and friends, and relatives may be lost to death or institutionalization. The loss of a spouse has been associated with subsequent health problems and an elevated risk of death in the surviving spouse, especially among widowers. Third, providing care for an ill or disabled spouse can cause health problems for the caregiver, especially if the ill spouse suffers from dementia.

There is evidence that social networks are associated with positive health for a number of reasons. First, contact with friends and relatives may provide opportunities of tangible, informational, or emotional support. Second, contact with friends and relatives may be associated with healthful behaviors, such as proper nutrition and physical activity. There is evidence that those older males living with a spouse eat more regularly and eat more nutritious foods than older males who live alone. In addition, married women and males with five or more friends and relatives are more likely to engage in regular physical activity than women who are not married and males with less than five friends and relatives.

Health Behaviors

It is well known that health behaviors, such as tobacco exposure, dietary practices, alcohol consumption, and physical activity, are associated with health, functioning, and longevity across the life course (Emmons, 2000; McGinnis & Foege, 1993). The likelihood for engaging in particular types of behavior, for example, the extent to which the older person is physically active, is associated with characteristics of the physical and social environments. This information, in turn, contributes to a better understanding of the racial, ethnic, and socioeconomic patterns of health, functioning, and longevity in aging populations.

Although research is often based on examinations of the health effects of single health behavior, recent research has examined specific patterns of behavior (Berrigan et al., 2003). Based on standard recommendations for such specific health behaviors as tobacco exposure, alcohol consumption, physical activity, and diet and nutrition, Berrigan and colleagues examined patterns of behavior by age, gender, race, and ethnicity. Overall, adherence to tobacco and alcohol recommendations represented the most common combination of behaviors in the national sample. In contrast, the recommendations for physical activity and diet and nutrition were least likely to be followed. Overall, adherence in all five behaviors increased with age as well as higher levels of education and family income. As noted previously, women are more likely than men to adhere to positive health behaviors, with the exception of physical activity. African-Americans were least likely to observe proper health behaviors.

Tobacco Exposure

Exposure to tobacco is associated with a variety of health conditions (Giovino, Hennifingfield, Tomar, Escobedo, & Slade, 1995; Giovino, 2002). Major exposures to tobacco smoke include direct exposure, in the form of cigarette smoking, and indirect exposure, in the form of passive exposure associated with environmental sources. As we will see, exposure to tobacco is associated with a variety of health conditions, functional limitations, disabilities, and premature death. Although the frequency of exposure, especially direct exposure, declines with age, it is necessary to review the history of tobacco exposure over the life course. It also has been reported that tobacco exposure varies by cohort and period effects. For example, among the current cohort of older people in the United States and Western Europe, older males have had a greater exposure to tobacco than older women. Between the 1920s and the release of the U.S. Surgeon General's Report on tobacco in 1964, there was an increase in the prevalence of smoking among young adult women. Although smoking resulted in an increase of premature death, female smokers who survived to senior years are at greater risk for a variety of health conditions, functional limitations, and disabilities. Measurement of tobacco exposure is typically based on self-report, including reports of direct and indirect exposures over the life course. People are typically asked about the type, amount, and frequency of tobacco exposure during their lives. This is sometimes supplemented with tests to assess contemporary levels of nicotine in the blood. Measures of indirect exposure typically are based on questions following a household census. After asking about the number and relationships of others in the household, subjects are asked to indicate which of these people are regular smokers in the home. Measures of environmental smoke also include questions that ask the number of times in a regular day when the subject is in a situation in which he or she can smell or see cigarette smoke.

Alcohol Consumption

Alcohol consumption refers to the type, frequency, and occasion of drinking alcohol. Unlike tobacco exposure and more akin to diet and nutrition, alcohol consumption is a type of health behavior that is not necessarily associated with problems of health, well-being, and longevity. Moderate consumption of alcohol, shown in some cases to be associated with some positive health outcomes, tends to decline with age. This decline, in turn, may be associated with problems of ill health. On the other hand, moderate consumption of alcohol, in some cases, may be associated with health conditions. For example, alcohol could lead to health problems and injuries, if it is taken in conjunction with one or more types of medications. If the older person is also operating an automobile, the combination of moderate amounts of alcohol and medications could lead to driving difficulties and elevate the risk of a crash (U.S. Department of Health and Human Services, 2000b).

The measurement of alcohol is often based on self-report. The Alameda County Survey (Berkman & Breslow, 1986) developed a series of questions on alcohol that represent a core set of items that have been adapted for use in other population surveys. For each type of alcohol (beer, wine, and spirits), respondents are asked whether they have consumed alcohol in the past year and, if so, how often they consumed alcohol and how much (number of glasses or drinks) was drunk at each sitting. In addition to providing an opportunity to examine consumption of each type of alcohol, it is possible to calculate an overall summary measure of alcohol.

Physical Activity

Level of physical activity is associated with a variety of health outcomes, functional limitations, disability, and longevity (U.S. Department of Health and Human Services, 1996). Physical activity is typically classified as either leisure-time physical activity (LTPA) or as utilitarian or everyday activities. Research indicates that men are more physically active than women, and that the overall prevalence of both LTPA and utilitarian walking declines with age. Reasons for the decline seem to vary by gender.

Our own work in this area suggests a gender-age difference (Satariano, Haight, & Tager, 2000). In a study of older people in Sonoma, California, the absence of an exercise companion was identified as one of the major reasons for avoiding or limiting LTPA. Among men of the same age, the leading reason was disinterest. With increasing age, the reasons were more likely to be health-related and a fear of falling for both men and women.

The measurement of physical activity is based on both self-reports and direct assessments of activity. Direct measures of physical activity are based on the use of pedometers and accelerometers. Global position devices can now also be incorporated in the survey studies of physical activity.

Diet and Nutrition

Past and current diet and nutritional patterns are associated with health, functioning, and longevity in older populations. Although obesity is an important public health problem in many countries, most notably in the developed countries, undernutrition and malnutrition are also problems among older people as well. This may be due to a variety of factors, including health problems, depression, poor physical and cognitive functioning, impairment in the senses of smell and taste, as well as poor oral health. In addition, there is research that suggests that social and environmental factors also are associated with dietary and nutritional patterns in older persons (Davis, Murphy, Neuhaus, 1988; Davis, Murphy, Neuhaus, Gee, & Quiroga, 2000). Older people who limited physical access to markets that sell a variety of nutritious foods at reasonable prices are more likely to have poor nutritional status (Morland, Wing, Diez Roux, & Poole, 2002). Older people who live alone, especially older men, are less likely to consume nutritional meals on a regular basis (Davis et al., 1988). It is also reasonable to hypothesize that older migrants may be less likely to have an adequate diet, if their traditional foods are not readily available. With a reduction in energy needs, there is a concomitant decrease in nutritional intake. Wakimoto and Block (2001, p. 79) report that "Mean energy intake declines by 1000 to 1200 kcal in men and by 600 to 800 kcal in women between those aged in their 20s and those in their 80s." There appears to be significant declines in median protein, zinc, calcium, vitamin E, and other nutrients, especially in men. There also appears, however, to be an increase in the consumption of some other nutrients, especially among women. These include vitamin A, vitamin C, and potassium. This is consistent with consumption patterns that indicate that older women in particular consume higher levels of fruits and vegetables than younger women. It is important to realize that there are very few data available to judge the nutritional needs of older people as they age, especially for some nutrients such as proteins. In addition, although older adults are more likely than younger adults to take supplements, there is little information about nutritional needs in this area as well.

There are different methods for the assessment of diet and nutritional status. These include 24-recall and multiple-day diet diaries. There are also methods available, such as the Block questionnaire, that have been automated to provide nutritional assessment of specific foods.

Sense of Control, Coherence, and Self-Efficacy

Psychosocial factors have been identified as central explanatory variables in social epidemiology. For example, Leonard Syme (1989) argues that a sense of control or control of destiny serves to explain the association between a variety of social factors, such as socioeconomic status and social networks, and different health outcomes. This position is also associated with the work of Martin Seligman on a "sense of helplessness." Seligman writes (1975, p. 106):

> The life histories of those individuals who are particularly resistant to depression or resilient to depression may have been filled with mastery. These people may have had extensive experience controlling and manipulating the sources of reinforcement in their lives and may therefore perceive the future optimistically. These people who are particularly susceptible to depression may have had lives relatively devoid of mastery.

Seligman speculates that learned helplessness may be associated with a variety of health outcomes.

Aaron Antonovsky (1979) introduced a related term, "sense of coherence." Like Syme and Seligman, Antonovsky argued that the concept represented a parsimonious psychosocial variable that helped to explain the associations between a variety of demographic, socioeconomic, and social and behavioral factors on the one hand and a host of health outcomes on the other. In contrast, he defined a sense of coherence as a generalized sense of understanding events in everyday life as well as a sense of optimism that future events would unfold as well as one could expect. When he was once asked to distinguish between a sense of control and a sense of coherence, he explained that a person with a sense of coherence understands the rules of the game without necessarily being able to control those rules (Antonovsky, personal communication, Spring, 1979).

Albert Bandura helped to introduce the concept of self-efficacy, and, as the subtitle of his book in this area indicates, viewed the concept as a vehicle for the exercise of control (Bandura, 1997). The concept of self-efficacy is one of the most commonly used concepts in public health and epidemiology. As we will see, there is a substantial body of research that indicates that people who demonstrate a sense of self-efficacy, defined here to mean a sense of confidence and competence, are more likely than others to reflect positive health outcomes. Bandura (1997, p. 3) defines self-efficacy as "beliefs in one's capabilities to organize and execute the courses of action required to produce given attainments." Unlike a sense of control and a sense of coherence, self-efficacy does not refer to a generalized sense of competence. Instead, it is perceived as being specific to particular tasks, such as physical activity. This conceptual distinction is reflected in how the concepts are measured.

Measurement of a sense of control and a sense of coherence reflects generalized concepts. For example, Antonovsky designed a linking sentence to capture the key components and the possible relationships between those components. In contrast, measures of self-efficacy are specific to particular types of outcomes. For example, there are measures of self-efficacy regarding physical activity and other types of behavior. To my knowledge, neither measure of social control, competence, or self-efficacy has been designed for older populations.

Health, Functioning and Longevity

The remaining components of the ecological model include measures of health, functioning, and longevity. With the exception of longevity and vital status, each of the measures of health and functioning serve both as outcomes and predictors. In the subsequent chapters, specific health outcomes, beginning with mortality and cause of death, will be examined.

CONCLUSION

The ecological model assumes that patterns of health and well-being in human populations are associated with a dynamic interplay of biologic, behavioral, social, and physical environmental factors, an interaction that unfolds over the life course of individuals, families, and communities. In the subsequent chapters, this model will serve as a blueprint for reviewing and evaluating the concepts, methods, and research in the epidemiology of aging.

REFERENCES

Adler, N. E., Boyce, T., Chesney, M. A., Cohen, S., Folkman, S., Kahn, R. L., et al. (1994). Socioeconomic status and health: The challenge of the gradient. *American Psychologist, 49*(1), 15–24.

Antonovsky, A. (1979). *Health, stress, and coping.* San Francisco: Jossey-Bass Company.

Aviv, A., Levy, D., & Mangel, M. (2003). Growth, telomere dynamics and successful and unsuccessful human aging. *Mechanisms of Aging and Development, 124,* 829–837.

Bandura, A. (1997). *Self-efficacy: The exercise of control.* New York: W. H. Freeman and Company.

Barker, D. J., Eriksson, J. G., Forsen, T., & Osmond, C. (2002). Fetal origins of adult disease: Strength of effects and biological basis. *International Journal of Epidemiology, 31*(6), 1235–1239.

Beefe-Dimmer, J., Lynch, J. W., Turrell, G., Lustgarten, S., Rahunathan, T., & Kaplan, G. A. (2004). Childhood and adult socioeconomic conditions and 31-year mortality risk in women. *American Journal of Epidemiology, 159*(5), 481–490.

Berkman, L. F., & Breslow, L. (1986). *Health and ways of living: The Alameda County Study.* New York: Oxford University Press.

Berrigan, D., Dodd, K., Troiano, R. P., Krebs-Smith, S. M., & Barbash, R. B. (2003). Patterns of health behavior in U.S. adults. *Preventive Medicine, 36*(5), 615–623.

Brody, E. M. (1985). *Mental and physical health practices of older people.* New York: Springer.

Bronfenbrenner, U. (1979). *The ecology of human development: Experiments by nature and design.* Cambridge, MA: Harvard University Press.

Brunner, E. J. (2000). Toward a new social biology. In L. F. Berkman & I. Kawachi (Eds.), *Social epidemiology* (pp. 306–331). New York: Oxford University Press.

Bulatao, R. A., & Anderson, N. B. (2004). *Understanding racial and ethnic differences in health in late life: A research agenda.* Washington, DC: National Academies Press.

Carey, J. R. (2003). Theories of life span and aging. In P. S. Timiras (Ed.). *Physiological basis of aging and geriatrics* (pp. 85–89). New York: CRC Press.

Carp, F. (1987). Environment and aging. In D. Stokols & I. Altman (Eds.), *Handbook of environmental psychology* (pp. 329–360). New York: John Wiley & Sons.

Catalano, R. (1979). *Health, behavior, and the community: An ecological perspective.* New York: Pergamon Press.

Catalano, R. (1989). Ecological factors in illness and disease. In H. Freeman & S. Levine (Eds.), *Handbook of medical sociology* (pp. 87–101). Englewood Cliffs, NJ: Prentice Hall.

Coleman, J. S. (1988). Social capital in the creation of human capital. *American Journal of Sociology, 94*(Suppl.), S95–S120.

Committee on Chemical Toxicity and Aging, National Research Council (1987). *Aging in today's environment.* Washington, DC: National Academies Press.

Daly, M. C., Duncan, G. J., Kaplan, G. A., & Lynch, J. W. (1998). Macro-to-micro links in relation between income inequality and mortality. *Milbank Quarterly, 76*(3), 315–339.

Davis, M. A., Murphy S. P., Neuhaus, J. M., Gee, L., & Quiroga, S. S. (2000). Living arrangements affect dietary quality for U.S. adults aged 50 years and older: NHANES III 1988–1994. *Journal of Nutrition, 130*(9), 2256–2264.

Davis, M. A., Murphy, S. P., & Neuhaus, J. M. (1988). Living arrangements and eating behaviors of older adults in the United States. *Journal of Gerontology, 43*(3), S96–S98.

Diez Roux, A. V. (1998). Bringing context back into epidemiology: Variables and fallacies in multi-level analysis. *American Journal of Public Health, 88*(22), 216–222.

Emmons, K. M. (2000). Health behaviors in a social context. In L. F. Berkman & I. Kawachi (Eds.), *Social epidemiology* (pp. 242–266). New York: Oxford University Press.

Epel, E. S., Blackburn, E. H., Lin, J., Dhabhor, F. S., Adler, N. E., Morrow, J. D., et al. (2004). Accelerated telomere shortening in response to life stress. *Proceedings of the National Academy of Sciences, 101*(49), 17312–17315.

Federal Interagency Forum on Aging Related Statistics. (2005). *Older Americans 2004: Key Indicators of Well-Being.* www.agingstats.gov/chartbook2004/Tables-population.html (Accessed, February 5, 2005).

Finch, C. E., & Tanzi, R. E. (1997). Genetics of aging. *Science, 278*(5337), 407–411.

Giddens, A. (1984). *The constitution of society.* Berkeley, CA: University of California Press.

Giovino, G. A., Hennifingfield, J. E., Tomar, S. L., Escobedo, L. G., & Slade, J. (1995). Epidemiology of tobacco use and dependence. *Epidemiologic Reviews, 57,* 411–422.

Giovino, G. A. (2002). Epidemiology of tobacco use in the United States. *Oncogene, 21,* 7326–7340.

Glass, T., & Balfour, J. (2003). Neighborhoods, aging, and functional limitations. In I. Kawachi & L. F. Berkman, *Neighborhoods and health* (pp. 303–334). New York: Oxford University Press.

Gouldner, A. W. (1960). The norm of reciprocity: A preliminary statement. *American Sociological Review, 25*(April), 161–178.

Green, L. W., & Kreuter, M. W. (2004). *Health program planning: An educational and ecological approach.* New York: McGraw-Hill.

Guralnik, J. M., & Ferrucci, L. (2003). Assessing the building blocks of function: Utilizing measures of functional limitation. *American Journal of Preventive Medicine, 25*(3ii), 112–121.

Haan, M., Kaplan G. A., & Camacho, T. (1987). Poverty and health: Prospective evidence from the Alameda County Study. *American Journal of Epidemiology, 125*(6), 989–998.

Halfon, N., & Hochstein, M. (2002). Life course health development: An integrated framework for developing health, policy, and research. *The Milbank Quarterly, 80*(3), 433–479.

Hanna, K., & Coussens, C. (2001). *Rebuilding the unity of health and the environment: A new vision of environmental health for the 21st century.* Washington, DC: National Academies Press.

Harkey, J., Miles, D. L., & Rushing, W. A. (1976). The relation between social class and functional status: A new look at the drift hypothesis. *Journal of Health and Social Behavior, 17*(3), 194–204.

House, J. S., Lepkowski, J. M., Kinney, A. M., Mero, R. P., Kessler, R. C., & Herzog, A. R. (1990). Age, socioeconomic status, and health. *The Milbank Quarterly, 68*(3), 383–411.

International Longevity Center. (2004). *Promoting men's health: Addressing barriers to healthy lifestyle and preventive health care.* New York: International Longevity Institute.

Kawachi, I., & Berkman, L. (2000). Social cohesion, social capital, and health. In L. F. Berkman & I. Kawachi (Eds.), *Social epidemiology* (pp. 174–190). New York: Oxford University Press.

Kawachi, I., & Kennedy, B. P. (1997). Health and social cohesion: Why care about income inequality? *British Medical Journal, 314*(7086), 1037–1040.

Kirkwood, T. (1999). *Time of our lives: The science of human aging.* New York: Oxford University Press.

Krieger, N. (2001). Theories for social epidemiology in the 21st century: An ecosocial perspective. *International Journal of Epidemiology, 30*(4), 668–677.

Kuh, D., & Ben-Shlomo, Y. (Eds.). (2004). *A life course approach to chronic disease epidemiology* (2nd ed.). New York: Oxford University Press.

Lawton, M. P., & Nahemow, L. (1973). Ecology and the aging process. In C. Eisdorfer & M. P. Lawton (Eds.), *The psychology of adult development and aging* (pp. 619–674). Washington, DC: American Psychological Association.

Lawton, M. P. (1986). *Environment and aging.* Albany, NY: Center for the Study of Aging.

Lee, R. D. (2003). Rethinking the evolutionary theory of aging: Transfers, not births, shape senescence in social species. *Proceedings of the National Academy of Sciences, 100*(16), 9637–9642.

Lindheim, R., & Syme, S. L. (1983). Environments, people, and health. *Annual Review of Public Health, 4,* 335–359.

Lobmayer, P., & Wilkinson, R. G. (2002). Inequality, residential segregation by income and mortality in U.S. cities. *Journal of Epidemiology & Community Health, 56*(3), 165–166.

Lynch, J., & Kaplan, G. (2000). Socioeconomic position. In L. F. Berkman & I. Kawachi (Eds.), *Social epidemiology* (pp. 13–35). New York: Oxford University Press.

Lynch, J., Smith G. D., Hillemeir, M., Shaw, M., Rahunathan, T., & Kaplan, G. (2001). Income inequality, the psychosocial environment, and health: Comparisons of wealthy nations. *Lancet, 358*(9277), 194–200.

Lynch, J. W., Smith, G. D., Kaplan, G. A., & House, J. S. (2000). Income inequality and mortality: Importance to health of individual income, psychosocial environment, or material conditions. *British Medical Journal, 320*(7243), 1200–1204.

Macintyre, S., & Ellaway, A. (2000). Ecological approaches: Rediscovering the role of the physical and social environment. In L. F. Berkman & I. Kawachi (Eds.), *Social epidemiology* (pp. 332–348). New York: Oxford University Press.

Macintyre, S., Ellaway, A., & Cummins, S. (2002). Place effects on health: How can we conceptualize, operationalize and measure them? *Social Science & Medicine, 55,* 125–139.

Macintyre, S., Maciver, S., & Sooman, A. (1993). Area, class and health: Should we be focusing on places or people? *Journal of Social Policy, 22*(2), 213–234.

McEwen, B. S., & Seeman, T. E. (1999). Protective and damaging effects of mediators of stress: Elaborating and testing the concepts of allostasis and allostatic load. *Annals of the New York Academy of Science, 896,* 30–47.

McGinnis, J. M., & Foege, W. H. (1993). Actual causes of death in the United States. *Journal of the American Medical Association, 270,* 2207–2212.

McLeroy, K. R., Bibeau, D., Steckler, A., & Glanz, K. (1988). An ecological perspective on health promotion programs. *Health Education Quarterly, 15*(4), 351–377.

Morgenstern, H. (1998). Ecologic studies. In K. J. Rothman & S. Greenland (Eds.), *Modern epidemiology* (pp. 459–480). New York: Lippincott.

Morland, K., Wing, S., Diez Roux, A., & Poole C. (2002). Neighborhood characteristics associated with the location of food stores and food serve places. *American Journal of Preventive Medicine, 22*(1), 23–29.

Moudon, A., & Lee, C. (2003). Walking and bicycling: An evaluation of environmental audit instruments. *American Journal of Health Promotion, 18*(1), 21–37.

Nahemow, L. (2000). The ecological theory of aging: Powell Lawton's legacy. In R. Rubinstein, M. Moss, & M. Kleban (Eds.), *The many dimensions of aging* (pp. 22–40). New York: Springer.

Perls, T., Kunkel, L. M., & Puca, A. A. (2002). The genetics of exceptional human longevity. *Journal of the American Geriatrics Society, 50*(2), 359–368.

Putnam, R. D. (2000). *Bowling alone: The collapse and revival of American community.* New York: Simon & Schuster Publishers.

Rejeski, W. J., Brawley, L. R., & Haskell, W. L. (2003). The prevention challenge: An overview of this supplement. *American Journal of Preventive Medicine, 25*(3Sii), 107–109.

Ren, X. S., Amick, B. C., & Williams, D. R. (1999). Racial/ethnic disparities in health: The interplay between discrimination and socioeconomic status. *Ethnic Disparity, 9*(2), 151–165.

Robert, S. A. (1999). Socioeconomic position and health: The independent contribution of community socioeconomic context. *Annual Review of Sociology, 25,* 489–516.

Roseboom, T. J., van der Meulen, J. H., Ravelli, A. C., Osmond, C., Barker, D. J., & Bleker, O. P. (2001). Effects of prenatal exposure to the Dutch famine on adult disease in later life: An overview. *Molecular Cell Endocrinology, 185*(1–2), 93–98.

Ryff, C. D., Marshall, V. W., & Clarke P. J. (1999). Linking the self and society in social gerontology: Crossing new territory via old questions. In C. D. Ryff & V. W. Marshall (Eds.), *The self and society in the aging processes* (pp. 3–41). New York: Springer Publishing Co.

Sallis, J. F., & Owen, N. (1997). Ecological models. In K. Glanz, F. M. Lewis, & B. K. Rimer (Eds.), *Health behavior and health education: Theory, research, and practice* (pp. 403–424). San Francisco: Jossey-Bass.

Satariano, W. A., Haight, T. J., & Tager, I. B. (2000). Reasons given by older people for limitation or avoidance of leisure time physical activity. *Journal of the American Geriatrics Society, 48*(5), 505–512.

Schwarz, B. (2003). M. Powell Lawton's three dilemmas in the field of environment and aging. In R. J. Scheidt & P. G. Windley (Eds.), *Physical environments and aging: Critical contributions of M. Powell Lawton to theory and practice* (pp. 5–22). New York: Haworth Press.

Seeman, T. E. (1996). Social ties and health: The benefits of social integration. *Annals of Epidemiology, 6*(5), 442–451.

Seeman, T. E., & Crimmins, E. (2001). Social environment effects on health and aging: Integrating epidemiologic and demographic approaches and perspectives. *Annals of the New York Academy of Sciences, 954,* 88–117.

Seeman, T. E., McEwen, B. S., Rowe, J. W., & Singer, B. H. (2001). Allostatic load as a marker of cumulative biological risk: MacArthur Studies of Successful Aging. *Proceedings of the National Academy of Science, 98,* 470–475.

Seeman, T. E., Singer, B. H., Rowe, J. W., Horwitz, R. I., & McEwen, B. S. (1997). The price of adaptation–allostatic load and its health consequences: Macarthur Studies of Successful Aging. *Archives of Internal Medicine, 157,* 2259–2268.

Seligman, M. E. P. (1975). *Helplessness: On depression, development, and death.* San Francisco: W. H. Freeman.

Selvin, S. (1996). *Statistical analysis of epidemiologic data.* New York: Oxford University Press.

Settersten, R. A. (1999). *Lives in time and place: The problems and promises of developmental science.* Amityville, NY: Baywood.

Singer, B., & Ryff, C. D. (1999). Hierarchies of life histories and associated health risks. *Annals of the New York Academy of Science, 896,* 96–115.

Singh-Manoux, A., Adler, N. E., & Marmot, M. C. (2003). Subjective social status: Its determinants and its association with measures of ill health in the Whitehall II Study. *Social Science & Medicine, 56*(6), 1321–1333.

Smedley, B. D., & Syme, S. L. (Eds.). (2000). *Promoting health: Intervention strategies from social and behavioral research.* Washington, DC: National Academies Press.

Sterling, P., & Eyer, J. (1988). Allostasis: A new paradigm to explain arousal pathology. In S. Fisher & J. Reason (Eds.), *Handbook of life stress, cognition and health* (pp. 629–649). New York: John Wiley & Sons.

Stewart, A. L. (2003). Conceptual challenges in linking physical activity and disability research. *American Journal of Preventive Medicine, 25*(3Sii), 137–140.

Stokols, D. (1992). Establishing and maintaining healthy environments: Toward a social ecology of health promotion. *American Psychologist, 47*(1), 6–22.

Subramanian, S. V., Lochner, K. A., & Kawachi, I. (2003). Neighborhood differences in social capital: A compositional artifact or a contextual construct? *Health & Place, 9*(1), 33–44.

Susser, M., & Susser, E. (1996). Choosing a future for epidemiology II. From black box to Chinese boxes and eco-epidemiology. *American Journal of Public Health, 86*(5), 674–677.

Syme, S. L. (1989). Control and health: A personal perspective. In A. Steptoe & A. Appels (Eds.), *Stress, personal control & health* (pp. 3–18). New York: John Wiley & Sons.

Taylor, S. E., Repetti, R. L., & Seeman, T. E. (1997). Health psychology: What is an unhealthy environment and how does it get under the skin? *Annual Review of Psychology, 48,* 411–447.

U.S. Department of Health and Human Services (1996). Physical Activity and Health: A Report of the Surgeon General. Washington, DC: Author.

U.S. Department of Health and Human Services (2000a). *Healthy people 2010: Understanding and improving health.* Washington, DC: Author.

U.S. Department of Health and Human Services (2000b). *Tenth special report to the U.S. Congress on alcohol and health: Highlights from current research. Drinking over the life span: Issues of biology, behavior, and risk.* Washington, DC: Author.

Verbrugge, L., & Jette, A. M. (1994). The disablement process. *Social Science & Medicine, 38*(1), 1–14.

Wakimoto, P., & Block, G. (2001). Dietary intake, dietary patterns, and changes with age: An epidemiological perspective [Special issue 2]. *Journal of Gerontology: Medical Sciences, 56,* 65–80.

Williams, D. R., Neighbors, N. W., & Jackson, J. S. (2003). Racial/ethnic discrimination and health: Findings from community studies. *American Journal of Public Health, 93*(2), 200–208.

Xu, X., Laird, N., Dokery, D. W., Schouten, J. P., Rijcken, B., & Weiss, S. T. (1995). Age, period, and cohort effects on pulmonary function in a 24-year longitudinal study. *American Journal of Epidemiology, 141*(6), 554–566.

Young, T. K. (1998). *Population health: Concepts and methods.* New York: Oxford University Press.

Zhang, H., Yu, C. Y., & Singer, B. (2003). Cell and tumor classification using gene expression data: Construction of forests. *Proceedings of the National Academy of Sciences, 100*(7), 4168–4172.

CHAPTER 3

Survival, Mortality, and Cause of Death

INTRODUCTION

One of the most profound demographic changes has been the significant improvement in life expectancy. As noted in Chapter 1, this improvement has been achieved among people in every age group. In the early 1900s, the most dramatic improvement was achieved by infants and by women in their childbearing years. Today, the improvement has been realized by older people, especially among those who have reached the age of 65.

Despite the overall aging of the society, there is considerable variation in the extent of life expectancy within populations, and, as we shall see, among people who have already reached the age of 65. Some people, indeed, some populations, survive longer than others. Life expectancy is greater for women than men, and greater for non-Hispanic whites and Asian-Americans than for African-Americans and Hispanic whites. The level of difference in life expectancy among gender, race, and ethnic groups also has been found to vary across different geographic areas. Recognition of these demographic and geographic patterns in life expectancy has stimulated considerable research in epidemiology to understand the biologic, behavioral, social, and environmental reasons for these broad patterns within and among populations. Research in these areas is based on the premise that explanations for these population patterns will contribute significantly to our understanding of human aging and longevity. It is further assumed that this research will lead to public health strategies to improve the life chances of those at risk for premature death.

In this chapter, we will review the epidemiology of aging, survival, and mortality. Research in this area is extensive and varied, including the independent and joint effects of biologic, behavioral, social, and environmental factors. The ecological model presented in Chapter 2 underscores the point that in the epidemiology of aging, as in life, all paths lead to the question of survival and, ultimately, mortality.

VITAL STATUS AND CAUSE OF DEATH

Studies of survival and mortality depend on the quality of information on vital status, defined to mean whether the person is alive or dead. It would appear at first glance that this information is not only reasonably accurate, but also readily available. Although it is true that data on vital status are perhaps the most widely available population health indicator, ensuring the quality of this information represents an important public health challenge.

Cause-specific mortality statistics serve as the basic source of data for many epidemiologic studies on aging. A mortality rate is the number of deaths in a given time period divided by the number of person-years lived in that time period by those at risk for death. For cause-specific rates, the deaths are restricted to those in which a particular condition or disease is listed as the *underlying* cause of death on the death certificate.

The death certificate is a legal document that is used as proof for insurance, to obtain a burial permit, and to determine cause of death in court. The death certificate consists of two parts (see Figure 3–1). Part 1 consists of a listing of the causal conditions leading to death: the *immediate* cause of death is entered first; following by one or more *intermediate* conditions; and, finally, the *underlying* cause of death. The underlying cause of death is that disease or condition that initiated the chain of events that led to death. The premise is that without that disease or condition, the particular death could not have occurred. Part 2 includes the addition of other significant conditions that contributed, but were not directly related, to the death. For example, septicemia, a systemic infection, may be listed as the immediate cause of death, followed by pneumonia as an intermediate condition, with lung cancer listed as the underlying cause of death. Diabetes may be listed as a contributory cause. This particular decedent case would be included in the numerator as part of a calculation of a lung cancer mortality rate. Figure 3–1 displays a sample of a death certificate from the State of Michigan.

TYPE/PRINT IN PERMANENT BLACK INK

LF _____
CF _____

STATE OF MICHIGAN
DEPARTMENT OF COMMUNITY HEALTH
CERTIFICATE OF DEATH

STATE FILE NUMBER

DECEDENT

| 1. DECEDENT'S NAME (First, Middle, Last) | 2. DATE OF BIRTH (Month, Day, Year) | 3. SEX | 4. DATE OF DEATH (Month, Day, Year) |

5. NAME AT BIRTH OR OTHER NAME USED FOR PERSONAL BUSINESS (include AKA if any) | 6a. AGE - Last Birthday (| 6b. UNDER 1 YEAR MONTHS DAYS | 6C. UNDER 1 DAY HOURS MINUTES

7a. LOCATION OF DEATH (Give place officially pronounced dead HOSPITAL OR OTHER INSTITUTION - Name (if not in either give name and number and zip code) | 7b. CITY, VILLAGE, OR TOWNSHIP OF DEATH | 7c. COUNTY OF DEATH

8a. CURRENT RESIDENCE - STATE | 8b. COUNTY | 8c. LOCALITY (check which best describes the location) ☐ City or Village ☐ Township ☐ Place | 8d. STREET AND NUMBER Include Apt. No. (If applicable)

9a. ZIP CODE | 9b. BIRTHPLACE (City and State) | 10. SOCIAL SECURITY NUMBER | 11. DECEDENT'S EDUCATION - What is the highest grade or level of school completed at the time of death?

12. RACE - American Indian, White, Black, (If Asian, give i.e., Chinese, Filipino, | 13a. ANCESTRY - Mexican, Cuban, Asian, African, French, Dutch, etc. (all that apply) If American Indian race, enter tribe | 13b. HISPANIC ORIGIN (Yes or No) | 14. WAS DECEDENT EVER IN THE U.S. ARMED FORCES? (Yes or No)

15. USUAL OCCUPATION Give list of during most of working life. Do | 16. KIND OF BUSINESS OR INDUSTRY | 17. MARITAL STATUS - Married, Never Married, Widowed, Divorced (Specific) | 18. NAME OF SURVIVING SPOUSE wife give name before

PARENTS

19. FATHER'S NAME (First, Middle, Last) | 20. MOTHER'S NAME BEFORE FIRST MARRIAGE (First, Middle, Last)

INFORMANT

21a. INFORMANT'S NAME (Type/Print) | 21b. RELATIONSHIP TO DECEDENT | 21c. MAILING ADDRESS (City or Village, State, Zip Code)

DISPOSITION

22. METHOD OF DISPOSITION Burial, Cremation, Donation, Removal, Storage (Specify) | 23a. PLACE OF DISPOSITION Name of cemetery, Crematory or other | 23b. LOCATION - City or Village, State

24. SIGNATURE OF MORTUARY SCIENCE LICENSEE | 25. LICENSE NUMBER (of licensee) | 26. NAME AND ADDRESS OF FUNERAL FACILITY

SAMPLE COPY

CERTIFICATION

27a. CERTIFIER (Check only one) ☐ Certifying Physician - To the best of any knowledge, ☐ MedicaL Examiner - Signature and Title _____ | 28a. ACTUAL OR PRESUMED TIME OF DEATH | 28b. PRONOUNCED DEAD ON (Mo., Day, Yr.) | 28c. TIME PRONOUNCED DEAD

29. MEDICAL EXAMINER CONTACTED? (Yes or No) | 30. PLACE OF DEATH (Home, Nursing Home, Hospital, Ambulance) (Specify) | 31. IN HOSPITAL Emergency Room, DOA (Specify)

27b. DATE SIGNED | 27c. NUMBER | 32. MEDICAL EXAMINER'S CASE NUMBER (if applicable) | 33. NAME OF ATTENDING PHYSICIAN IF OTHER THAN CERTIFIER (Type or Print)

34. NAME AND ADDRESS OF ATTENDING PHYSICIAN (Type or Print)

35a. REGISTRAR'S SIGNATURE | 35b. DATE FILED (Month, Day, Year)

CAUSE OF DEATH

36. PART I. Enter the chain of events, diseases, injuries, or complications - that directly caused the death. DO NOT write such as cardiac arrest, respiratory irreg., or vestibular fibrillation without knowing the . Enter only one reason on a line.

Approximate Interval Between Onset and Death

a. _____
DUE TO (OR AS A CONSEQUENCE OF)

IMMEDIATE CAUSE (Final disease or condition resulting in death)
b. _____
DUE TO (OR AS A CONSEQUENCE OF)

c. _____
DUE TO (OR AS A CONSEQUENCE OF)

UNDERLYING CAUSE (disease or injury that initiated the result-ing in death) LAST
d. _____

NAME OF DECEDENT For use by physician or institution

continues

Source: State of Michigan, Department of Community Health.

FIGURE 3–1 Sample Death Certificate, State of Michigan

FIGURE 3–1 continued

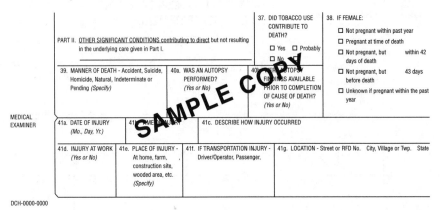

DCH-0000-0000

The death certificate also contains demographic information about the decedent, such as age, race, gender, residence, occupation, and the location of the death. Information is also maintained on the certifier of the death, in most cases the physician of record, and on the burial or other method of handling the remains of the deceased.

The classification of the cause of death is based on 17 general categories of diseases that are grouped by system (such as diseases of the circulatory system and diseases of the respiratory system), or by type of disease (such as infectious and parasitic diseases, and neoplasms). Although the certifier of death, a physician, determines the underlying and intermediate causes of death, a medical coder or nosologist processing the certificate may change data within certain guidelines established by the World Health Organization. Local health departments in the United States submit data to their state health departments, which, in turn, transmit the data to the National Center for Health Statistics (NCHS) in Washington, DC. Once the data reach NCHS, further reclassification may occur. Automated Classification of Medical Entities is a computerized algorithm that programmatically reviews and evaluates the data and assigns causes of death based on established criteria. The results of this programmatic review are used, in turn, to generate national statistics on cause-specific mortality rates by age, gender, race, and geographic area.

In 2001, the leading causes of death in the United States for those aged 65 and over include diseases of the heart (1,632 deaths per 100,000 people), malignant neoplasms (cancer) (1,100 per 100,000), cerebrovascular diseases (stroke) (404 per 100,000), chronic lower respiratory diseases

(301 per 100,000), influenza and pneumonia (155 per 100,000), and diabetes mellitus (151 per 100,000) (Federal Interagency Forum on Aging-Related Statistics, 2005).

The validity of data on cause of death has been a subject of concern both for studies of the general population and for studies of older populations in particular. With regard to older populations, there is concern that it may be difficult to identify a definitive cause of death, as older people are very likely to have multiple, concurrent health conditions (comorbidity). As Sherwin Nuland writes (1993, p. 78) in his book, *How We Die: Reflections on Life's Final Chapter:*

> Every group of lethal diseases of the elderly consists predominantly of the usual suspects. Of hundreds of known diseases and their predisposing characteristics, some 85% of our aging population will succumb to the complications of one of only seven major entities: atherosclerosis, hypertension, adult-onset diabetes, obesity, mentally depressing states such as Alzheimer's and other dementias, cancer, and decreased resistance to infection. Many of those elderly who die will have several of them; and not only that, the personnel of any large hospital's intensive care unit can confirm the everyday observation that terminally ill people are not infrequently victims of all seven. The seven make up the posse that hunts down and kills the elderly among us. For the vast majority of those of us who live beyond middle age, they are the horsemen of death.

In keeping with Nuland's observations, results from the National Health Interview Survey indicate that the percentage of people aged 60 years and greater that reported having two or more of the nine most common conditions increased steadily with age (Guralnik, La Croix, Everett, & Kovar, 1989). Specifically, the percentage of women who reported two or more conditions increased from 45% among those aged 60 to 69 years, to 61% for those aged 70 to 79 years, and to 70% for those aged 80 years and over. Among men, the percentages were 35%, 47%, and 53% respectively. Compared to cancer patients without comorbid conditions, those with comorbid conditions are more likely to die with an underlying cause of death other than the index cancer (Satariano & Ragland, 1994). In a national study of mortality patterns, Manton and colleagues (1991) reported that cancer is often found on death certificates as contributing to the risk of noncancer causes of death. The occurrence of cancer as a nonunderlying cause of death increased with age and was highest for treatable and slowly growing tumor types. Breast cancer patients from the Detroit metropolitan area who had three or more of seven selected comorbid conditions had a 20-fold higher rate of mortality from causes other than breast cancer and a 4-fold higher rate of all-cause mortality when compared with patients who had no comorbid conditions (Satariano & Ragland, 1994). In a recent study of the cause of death among men diagnosed with prostatic cancer in Kaiser hospitals in the San Francisco Bay Area, increasing age and comorbidity, in particular, cardiovascular comorbidity, were independently associated with death due to a cause other than prostate cancer (Satariano, Ragland, & Van Den Eeden, 1998).

In view of the potential difficulties associated with the study of mortality statistics for the elderly, it has been recommended that research focus on multiple causes of death, based on data that include all of the causes of death listed on the death certificate, not just the underlying cause. The NCHS now generates public use data tapes, which include two different coding schemes for all the cause-of-death information on the death certificate as well as the single underlying cause. Mortality statistics based on multiple causes of death have a number of advantages, including opportunities to study disease combinations associated with high mortality, to understand more about the contribution of less lethal diseases to death, and to monitor increases and declines in causes of death in a more accurate way. With increasing age of the decedent, a greater number of associated conditions are listed on the death certificate. It is also reported that diabetes is more likely to be included as an associated or contributing cause of death than it is to be listed as an underlying cause of death. In addition, examinations of multiple causes of death over time by age and gender suggest that as the incidence of coronary heart disease (CHD) declines, different forms of cancer are likely to become the leading underlying causes of death, especially among the elderly (Manton et al., 1991). Despite the importance of data regarding multiple causes of death, there are limitations. In particular, it is impossible to establish from the death certificate either the timing or sequence of multiple health conditions, or the relative severity of those conditions. To complement studies of comorbidity from death certificates, other studies are being conducted based on data from medical records and personal interviews. This work will be discussed later in Chapter 8.

STUDIES OF SURVIVAL

There are generally two types of survival studies. First, there are studies of survival based on general population surveys. The objective is to describe and explain patterns of survival in a specific population. Baseline assessments of subjects are conducted and then followed for particular periods of time, coupled with regular assessments of vital status. In addition to vital studies, these studies also may entail periodic assessments of other, hypothesized predictor variables. With this type of study, there is an opportunity to determine whether patterns of survival are associated with not only the independent and joint effects of independent variables, but also the association of survival with *changes* in those independent variables. This type of study is ideally suited for the investigation of aging and longevity. Examples of such longitudinal studies include the National Institute on Aging (NIA) Established Populations for Epidemiologic Studies of the Elderly (EPESE) (Cornoni-Huntley, Brock, Ostfeld, Taylor, & Wallace, 1986) and the NIA-funded Study of Physical Performance and Age-Related Changes in Sonomans (Satariano, Smith, Swanson, & Tager, 1998). Second, there are longitudinal studies based on older people recently diagnosed with a particular health condition. In this case, identification and recruitment are not based solely on the residence of subjects in a particular geographic area, but rather a particular diagnosis among people of a particular age and geographic area. It is also possible, as with the previous types of study, to monitor the levels and changes in hypothesized independent variables. Examples of this type of study include the NIA/NCI Cancer in the Elderly Study, a population-based study of older cancer patients recruited from selected areas in the United States (Yancik, Havlik, Wesley, Ries, Long, Rossi, et al., 1996), and the Cardiovascular Health Study, a study of heart disease in older populations (Fried, Borhani, Enright, Furberg, Gardin, Kronmal, et al., 1991).

The quality of the results from longitudinal studies of this kind depends on the extent to which members of the study cohort are actively followed. Losing members of the study cohort over time, termed "loss to follow-up," may result in biased results. Although in most cases a decedent subject can be located through the U.S. National Death Index, it is more difficult to obtain information about a subject who is not known to be dead. Moreover, if the loss of contact is not random, but rather associated with one or more of the hypothesized independent variables, the study results may be biased. Even in situations in which contact is maintained with cohort members, bias may be introduced because of the differential survival rate. Without taking into account the timing of the death of the decedents and the characteristics of those decedents, an incorrect estimation of the association between independent variables, such as physical activity and survival, may result. With this brief introduction to the measurement of vital status and survival, we now turn to a consideration of some of the basic epidemiologic patterns in this area.

DEMOGRAPHIC PATTERNS

Age

There is a strong association between chronological age and the risk of death. However, the relationship between age and the risk of death varies by other demographic and socioeconomic factors. Moreover, the strength of the association between chronological age and the risk of death varies by the cause of death. This is most evident in the area of cancer. Among men, the strongest association between age and cancer is found for prostatic cancer, less so for cancer of the colon and rectum. As we will see, the most important question has to do with the reasons for this association with age.

In addition to age, the variables of gender, race, ethnicity, and socioeconomic status (SES) are strongly associated with the length of survival and risk of death in most human populations. What is of interest is the manner in which chronological age seems to moderate the association between the other demographic factors, SES, and vital status. In general, among adults, the extent of the difference by gender, race, ethnicity, and SES is greatest among people in their middle years (approximately, age 40 to 60). With increasing age, the extent of the difference becomes less pronounced. It is also interesting to determine the reasons for these differences and whether those reasons vary over the life course. Put differently, are the reasons for gender or racial differences in mortality among people in their middle years the same reasons for those differences among people in their senior years? These questions are among the most central to an understanding of the epidemiology of aging and longevity.

Gender

It is well known that women live longer than men (Hazzard, 1986; 1989). Today, a woman has an excellent chance of surviving well into her 80s, and women who survive to age 85 can expect to live another 6 years on average. At each point in the life course, females have a greater life expectancy than men. As William Hazzard (1986, p. 458–459) has written:

It would appear that the only clear point of advantage occurring to the male over the female of the human species is at the point of fertilization: various estimates have placed the male:female sex ratio at conception to be as high as 170:100. In the first trimester of pregnancy, the point at which the earliest secure estimates of sex ratios can be ascertained, the sex ratio has already diminished to almost 130:100, with a decline throughout fetal life to a sex ratio at birth of 106:100. Before adulthood the greater mortality of male infants and children than girls of comparable age is largely attributable to infections and accidents. Parity in numbers between the sexes is accomplished at the time of adolescence, the gap thereafter to favor female over male survival throughout the remainder of the human life span.

The extent of gender difference varies globally. Based on the Epidemiologic Transition Theory described in Chapter 1, Newman and Brach (2001) report that gender differences in longevity are related to the stage of economic and social development. As noted earlier, the relatively high maternal mortality rate limits life expectancy among women in developing countries. With improvements in maternal and infant mortality, often used as a health indicator of economic development, life expectancy improves significantly, especially for women. Newman and Brach (2001, p. 343) hypothesized that in the latest stage of development, "Life expectancy for women is so high that it may be near its maximum." Moreover, subsequent improvements are found for elderly men, even though the percentage of older women still far exceeds the percentage of older men (Newman & Brach, 2001, p. 343):

> Thus, in developed countries such as the United States, Canada, and the countries of Western Europe the gender gap in longevity is now decreasing between men and women. However, the larger number of women surviving at every age has resulted in a much larger number of older women than of men. In the United States, there are about 20 million [women] over age 65 years compared with 14 million men. The ratio of women to men at age 65 is about 120 women for every 100 men, and by age 85, it is 250 women to 100 men. Because of these trends, the majority of older patients in the health care system are women. Of those over age 65 years, about 60% are women, and more than 70% of those over 85 years are women.

Males are more likely to develop and to die from the leading chronic health conditions, including CHD, stroke, cancer (most notably, lung, colorectal, and, of course, prostate cancers), diabetes, as well as motor vehicle accidents and occupation-related injuries. It is generally hypothesized that gender differences in longevity are due to a variety of factors, or as Newman and Brach (2001, p. 343) describe them, "a complex interaction of environmental, behavioral, and biologic factors." No doubt, the nature of that complex interaction will vary geographically as well as over time. One leading hypothesis is that the gender difference in sex hormone levels gives rise to the gender differential in lipoprotein metabolism. Among men, testosterone raises low-density lipoproteins and lowers high-density lipoproteins. Among females, estrogen has the opposite effect. Over time, this leads to a gender differential in arteriosclerosis, which, in turn, leads to a gender difference in longevity, given that CHD is the leading cause of death. Support for this hypothesis is based on the fact that gender differences in longevity vary by age. It is reported that the male–female coronary risk ratio is greater than 1.0 at all ages, though it narrows progressively with age; and the median female cholesterol ratios are greater than 1.0 at all ages beyond puberty but also narrow progressively with age, most notably after menopause. Despite this change, males remain at higher risk than females for CHD.

Differences in socialization and health behaviors are offered as contributing to gender differences in longevity. Most recently, Berrigan and colleagues (2003) reported on the patterns of health behavior among U.S. adults. They noted that with the exception of physical activity, men are more likely than women to engage in behaviors that elevate the risk of major chronic health conditions. These behaviors include tobacco exposure, excessive alcohol consumption, poor dietary and nutritional practices, and other "risky behaviors." In the Berrigan (2003) study, men were reported to be 2.6 times more likely than women to report they did not adhere to any of the five national recommendations on physical activity, tobacco use, alcohol consumption, fruit and vegetable consumption, and dietary fat intake. In contrast, women were approximately 60% more likely than men to report that they adhered to all five healthful behaviors (Berrigan et al., 2003).

As noted in the previous chapter, the International Longevity Institute (2004) recently convened a conference to examine men's health issues. In addition to noting differences in health behaviors, conference participants identified other factors that may account for differences in health and longevity between men and women. For example, men are reported to be more likely than women to underestimate the risk associated with particular behaviors, such as reckless driving and exposure to the sun. Compared to women, men also are reported to be less knowledgeable about basic health information and less likely to obtain preventive health services or seek care following the onset of particular symptoms. While these are important points, it is still unclear to what extent these gender differences vary by geographic area as well as by race, ethnicity, SES, and, of course, age.

Even though differences in health behaviors and access to health services may help to explain gender differences in longevity, it is important to report the findings of one community study as a caution against assuming that we completely understand the reasons for these differences. Based on a random sample of 6928 adult residents of Alameda County, California, researchers examined gender differences in mortality over the following nine years (Seeman, Kaplan, Knudsen, Cohen, & Guralnik, 1987). The unadjusted relative mortality risk for men compared to women was 1.5, that is, the mortality risk was 50% greater for men than for women. An attempt was made to explain the gender difference by a systematic adjustment for 16 demographic and behavioral risk factors. These factors included age, race, SES, occupation, physical health status, use of health services, smoking, alcohol consumption, physical activity, weight, sleeping patterns, marital status, social contacts, church and group membership, and life satisfaction. Adjustment for some of the factors, such as smoking and alcohol consumption, reduced the gender difference, suggesting that the excess risk of death found for men may be due, at least in part, to the fact that males are more likely than females to have a history of smoking and alcohol consumption. Interestingly, adjustment for other factors, such as physical activity, physical health status, and marital status, actually increased the gender difference. This means that women were more likely than men to be physically sedentary, report poorer health status, and less likely to be married—all factors associated with an elevated risk of death. Therefore, when those factors were held constant between men and women, the elevated risk of death for men increased. Overall, adjustment for 16 factors slightly increased the relative risk of death from 1.5 to 1.7. It was concluded that in general these demographic, social, and behavioral factors do not completely explain the gender difference in longevity. Moreover, it was recommended that a more fruitful course would be to examine the possible interaction of biologic and behavioral risk factors.

Race and Ethnicity

Racial and ethnic minorities have poorer survival than non-Hispanic whites, across the life course. Most research has focused on differences between non-Hispanic whites, African-Americans, and Hispanic whites. Considerably less attention has been directed to the different Asian-American groups, one of the fastest growing populations in the United States. In general, African-American males have poorer life expectancy than Asian-American, Hispanic white, or non-Hispanic white males. Although the racial and ethnic differences in longevity are also evident for females, it is much less pronounced. Not only are racial and ethnic minorities at elevated risk for acute and chronic conditions, but also they tend to be diagnosed at a more advanced stage and have less access to care and rehabilitation services. These factors contribute significantly to an elevated risk of death. It is interesting to note, however, that the extent of that racial difference is considerably reduced among those aged 75 years and older (Hummer, Benjamins, & Rogers, 2004) (see Figure 3–2).

Double-Jeopardy Hypothesis

Research has focused on the extent to which race and ethnic patterns of health, disease, and longevity vary by age. The double-jeopardy hypothesis, an early characterization of the interplay of race, age, and health, states that the association between chronological age and a decline in health outcomes occurs more precipitously for minorities than others (Dowd & Bengston, 1978). Put differently, the hypothesis suggests that aging has greater negative consequences for members of minority groups who must face the burdens and difficulties associated with growing old, as well as the burdens and difficulties associated with their minority status. Racial and ethnic memberships serve to modify, therefore, the association between age and health outcomes. Although there is some evidence to support the double-jeopardy hypothesis, primarily studies based on self-reports of general health between African-American and non-Hispanic white populations, there have been very few direct tests of the hypothesis. Moreover, the tests that have been conducted have been based on cross-sectional data. Although cross-sectional data provide a snapshot of racial differences in health by age and by gender, a true test of the hypothesis requires a longitudinal investigation. Such data are necessary to determine whether and to what extent there are differences in health status based on a variety of indicators between members of a minority group and members of the majority,

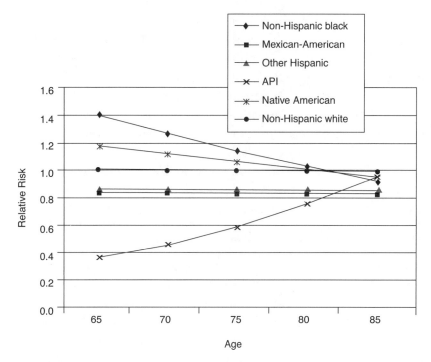

Source: Hummer, R. A., Benjamins, M. R., & Rogers, R. G. (2004).

FIGURE 3–2 Predicted Racial/Ethnic Mortality Disparities by Age, United States, 1989–1997

in most cases, non-Hispanic whites, as they age. Although the results of the test seem to depend on the type of health outcome, most research to date, from both cross-sectional and a limited number of longitudinal studies, seems to support the converse of double jeopardy—a decline in health differences with age (Ferraro & Farmer, 1996). While there may be health differences across the life course, those differences, in fact, are most pronounced at earlier points in life, in particular, during the middle years.

Selective survival, associated with racial and ethnic differences in life expectancy, seems to account for the decline in health differences in the later years. The selective survival hypothesis argues that higher early mortality in disadvantaged populations leads to greater survival of biological robust members of minority populations at advanced ages. The middle years, therefore, may represent a watershed. The accumulation of insults associated with minority status, coupled with reduced physiological resistance, may make the middle years critical for determining who subsequently survives and who does not. Moreover, the health status of minorities who survive their middle years may be somewhat more akin to the health status of their non-Hispanic white age peers. In fact, there is considerable evidence to indicate that there is a black–white mortality crossover in the later years, meaning the age-specific mortality rate for whites aged 75 and older and 85 and older may exceed that found for the age-specific mortality rate for African-Americans of the same age. In the end, the double-jeopardy hypothesis may be conceptually flawed. It ignores the presence of subgroups within the racial and ethnic groups. Second, it ignores latency, i.e., early-life susceptibilities and exposures may only become manifest later in life. The double-jeopardy hypothesis is based on the assumption that negative health outcomes that occur in the later years are due primarily to factors that occur at that time.

Black–White Mortality Crossover

US national vital statistics show that black mortality rates at advanced ages converge with and then drop below white mortality rates (see Figure 3–2). Although some argue that the crossover is due, at least in part, to methodological difficulties, for example, an undercount of the middle-aged minority population, there is general consensus that the black/white mortality crossover is real and due, in a greater extent, to the premature death of subpopulations of blacks, primarily black males.

The most compelling evidence for the mortality crossover comes from epidemiologic research. Evidence from the Charleston Heart Study and Evans County Study indicate that part of the black–white differential in the early and middle years seems to be attributed to specific groups in the black population with multiple risk-factor exposures, especially high rates of alcohol consumption, cigarette smoking, and violence (Keil, Sutherland, Knapp, Lackland, Gazes, & Tyroler, 1993; Keil, Sutherland, Hames, Lackland, Gazes, Knapp, et al., 1995). These factors, together with differences in sexual and reproductive behavior, nutritional and dietary differences, hypertension and obesity elevate the risk of infant mortality, heart disease, accidents, and homicide. In terms of premature or excess deaths, the greatest impact is found for chronic conditions between the ages of 45 and 70. Two recent epidemiologic studies confirm the black/white mortality crossover (Corti, Guralnik, Ferrucci, Izmirlian, Leveille, Pahor, et al., 1999; Ny-Mak, Dohrenwend, Abraido-Lanza, & Turner, 1999). Mortality hazard ratios between African-Americans and non-Hispanic whites during nine years of follow-up were estimated from the National Longitudinal Mortality Study (Ny-Mak et al., 1999). Black persons younger than 65 years were at higher risk than others for all-cause and cardiovascular mortality. The excess mortality was greatest for African-Americans aged 25 to 44. Similar results were reported for a study of African-Americans and non-Hispanic white residents of North Carolina as part of the NIA EPESE. A total of 4136 men and women living in North Carolina were interviewed in 1986 and followed until 1994 to examine differences in subsequent mortality. Black persons had higher mortality rates than whites at young old age (65–80 years) but had significantly lower mortality rates after age 80. Black persons age 80 or older had a significantly lower risk of all-cause mortality and of CHD mortality (hazard ratio of blacks vs. whites = 0.75 and 0.44 respectively). It is important to note that these race and age patterns were not found for other causes of death. The authors conclude that the results were due either to differences in the selective survival of the healthiest oldest African-Americans or to other biomedical factors affecting longevity after age 80. The authors also conclude that as the crossover was observed only for deaths due to CHD, it was unlikely that the results could be explained by the overreporting of age by older African-Americans (Corti et al., 1999).

Despite these results, there are reports of similar race and age patterns for deaths due to stroke as well as ischemic heart disease. Recent trends in ischemic heart disease and stroke mortality were compared in California among six major gender-racial or gender-ethnic groups (Karter, Gazzaniga, Cohen, Casper, Davis, & Kaplan, 1998). Rates of age-specific and age-adjusted mortality were calculated for persons aged 35 and older during the years 1985 to 1991. Between 1985 and 1991, mortality rates for ischemic heart disease and stroke were generally highest for African-Americans, intermediate for non-Hispanic whites, and lowest for Hispanics. In keeping with the crossover effect, African-Americans had excess ischemic heart disease mortality relative to non-Hispanic whites until later in life, whereas stroke mortality in non-Hispanic whites was higher at older ages. In general, similar results were reported from a national study of stroke mortality. Data were obtained from among participants age 45 and older in the National Longitudinal Mortality Study. The hazard ratios for African-American men and women (relative to non-Hispanic whites) were nearly identical, at > 4.0 at age 45, but marginally significant < 1.0 by age 85. For both Hispanic men and women, the hazard ratios (relative to non-Hispanic whites) were approximately 1.0 at age 45 but were marginally significant < 1.0 at older ages. The ethnic differences in stroke death rates reveal differences in age distributions of fatal strokes between these groups. Approximately 6% of fatal strokes for non-Hispanic whites occurred before age 60, whereas > 15% occurred in both Hispanic whites and blacks. In conclusion, the results indicate that for Hispanics, stroke risk is similar to that for non-Hispanic whites at younger ages but is marginally lower at older ages, the excess stroke mortality in blacks mainly occurs at younger ages (between 45 and 55 years), and the relationship between stroke risk for blacks and Hispanics relative to whites is similar by gender. Most important, proportionally more strokes occur at older ages in non-Hispanic whites than in either African-Americans or Hispanic whites.

There is also evidence of race by age interactions in population-based studies of prostate and female breast cancers (Austin & Convery, 1993; Simon & Severson, 1997). A retrospective analysis was made of men diagnosed with prostate cancer, based on data from the National Cancer Institute's SEER program. A total of 12,907 men diagnosed from 1973 to 1987 were included in the study. The results indicated that African-American men had poorer survival than white men for all stages of prostate cancer when the cancer was diagnosed at younger ages. However, these differences in survival were not demonstrated for men diagnosed with prostate cancer after age 70 (Austin & Convery, 1993). In a study of racial differences in breast cancer survival in metropolitan Detroit, 10,502 invasive breast cancer cases were included (Simon & Severson, 1997). African-American women were more likely than white women to have more advanced disease, a higher tumor grade, and a tumor that was estrogen-receptor negative. After controlling for age, tumor size, stage, histological grade, census-derived SES, and the presence of a residency training program at the treatment hospital, the relative risk of dying for African-Americans compared with whites was 1.68 for women less than 50 years of age, and 1.33 for women older than 50 years of age. In a separate study of breast cancer patients in Wisconsin and in the nation at large, the results indicate that the black:white gap in mortality for those among women of all ages, but especially for those under the age of 55 (Russell, Langlois, Johnson, Trentham-Dietz, & Remington, 1999).

Racial differences in mortality are affected by age at death (Berkman, Singer, & Manton, 1989). African-Americans, especially African-American men, are at elevated risk of premature death from CHD, stroke, and prostate cancer. African-American women, in turn, have poorer survival than white women following early-onset breast cancer. In contrast, there is little if any racial difference in survival following late-onset disease or when death occurs later in life, either after ages 65 or 75, depending on the disease in question. In fact, there is evidence of a black/white crossover in late-age mortality from deaths due primarily to CHD.

As part of the recent report on racial and ethnic differences in health in later life published by the National Academy of Sciences, Robert A. Hummer and colleagues (2004, p. 55) nicely summarize the research in this area:

> Although researchers for many years have documented such a mortality crossover using a number of different data sets and have concluded that it appears to be real, others have been more skeptical because of the data quality concerns. The most recent, carefully produced evidence by a research team from the latter group continues to find a racial mortality crossover occurring at ages 90 to 94 for females and 95+ for males (Hill, Preston, & Rosenwaike, 2000). Although the crossover is identified at an older age than a number of other researchers have found, the weight of the evidence, using a number of nationally based U.S. data sources, is strong that a black-white crossover exists.

SOCIOECONOMIC STATUS

SES has been found to be associated with a variety of health outcomes, including survival and mortality, in older populations. SES has been assessed in terms of both the characteristics of the individual as well as characteristics of the place of residence, across the life course. Just as we found for gender, race, and ethnicity, the strength of the association between SES and mortality is affected by age, such that the most pronounced difference is noted for people in their middle years and much less difference is found among the elderly (House, Kessler, & Herzog, 1990; Kaplan, Seeman, Cohen, Knudsen, & Guralnik, 1987; Sorlie, Baclund, & Keller, 1995). Based on the data from the NIA EPESE study, Bassuk and colleagues (2002) examined whether specific indicators of SES, including education, family income, and occupational history, were differentially associated with all-cause mortality among populations of people aged 65 and older. In addition, this analysis addressed whether the strength of the association varied by age and gender as well as place by focusing on the following locales and regions: East Boston, Massachusetts; New Haven,

Connecticut; east-central Iowa; and the Piedmont region of North Carolina. The results confirm the association between SES and all-cause mortality, with overall family income being the strongest predictor among men and women and across the geographic areas. In addition, adjustment for social and behavioral factors reduced but did not extinguish the association. Although these findings suggest that social and behavioral factors are on the causal pathway between SES and mortality, there are clearly other factors as well. The strength of the association also varied by place. Specifically, the relationship between SES and mortality was more pronounced among elders in New Haven and North Carolina than among elders in East Boston and Iowa. Bassuk and colleagues (2002, p. 530) explained this difference in terms of the "relative deprivation hypothesis":

> A low income may be more deleterious in communities where the majority of the population is wealthy than in poorer communities, either because of invidious social comparison processes or because of economic barriers to purchasing goods and services at prices geared toward more affluent residents.

Bassuk and colleagues (2002) conclude that future research should address the extent to which community factors serve to affect the association between socioeconomic factors and mortality. In addition, it would be valuable in the future to obtain more information about the significance of socioeconomic factors across the life course.

In a separate study, lower levels of educational attainment were shown to be associated with higher rates of mortality, based on data from the National Longitudinal Mortality Survey (Elo & Preston, 1996). The authors argue that educational attainment is an ideal indicator of SES. First, it can be obtained for most individuals and it is readily quantifiable. Second, unlike occupational status and family income, it is less likely to be affected by adult health status. Although moderated among those aged 65 and older, there is evidence that educational attainment is associated with subsequent longevity. The researchers also conclude that the findings suggest that levels of health and functioning should improve in future cohorts of seniors (Elo & Preston, 1996, p. 56):

> The responsiveness of mortality to years of schooling at ages 65 and above give support to the view that older age mortality will continue to decline in the United States in the coming decades as better-educated cohorts replace those currently aged 65+.

This is an interesting hypothesis that would seem to depend on the extent to which the causal mechanism between educational attainment and longevity for the current cohort of seniors will remain constant for future generations of seniors. This will be discussed in greater detail in Chapter 12.

The effect of SES over the life course is a critical issue and will require detailed investigation. There is some interesting preliminary work in this area. For example, the risk of death associated with SES at different points in the life course and by place was assessed in a study in Great Britain (Breeze, Sloggett, & Fletcher, 1999). The study was based on the Longitudinal Study, a 1% sample of the populations of England and Wales. These data include a linkage of successive censuses since 1971 with routinely collected vital registration data from the National Health Service Central Register. The purpose of the study was to examine the association between socioeconomic and demographic factors and mortality over a 21-year period. The specific objective was to assess whether circumstances occurring in the first 10 years of life affected subsequent mortality and institutionalization. The results indicated that SES (assessed here in terms of access to a car and type of housing) during middle age predicted subsequent mortality 20 years later. This was found for both men and women.

There is also evidence that elevated mortality is associated with geographic indicators of SES. Although census tract data in the United States are often used as proxy measures for the individual's SES, other studies suggest that census data may capture more global, ecological effects on mortality. For example, Mary Haan and colleagues (1987) reported that residents of a federally designated poverty area experienced higher age-, race-, and sex-adjusted mortality rates than residents of nonpoverty areas over a 9-year follow-up period (Relative Risk = 1.71), independently of a variety of individual characteristics, including race, income, and employment status. There is also evidence from a separate study of 276 metropolitan areas in the United States that a measure of income segregation, i.e., the extent to which people with different levels of income live in separate census tracts, was associated with mortality (Lobmayer & Wilkinson, 2002). Although neither study focused on age differences in mortality or the elderly in particular, the results suggest that both *compositional* factors (characteristics of the people) and *contextual* factors (characteristics of the place) may contribute to longevity. For example, based on data from the National Longitudinal Study, it is reported that residents of rural areas aged 55 and older have lower mortality rates than those in urban areas, following adjustment for age, gender, race/ethnicity, education, income, and marital status (Smith, Anderson, Bradham, & Longino, 1995). The extent of the rural-urban difference was increasingly reduced with increasing age. These overall results were confirmed in a separate study that indicated that older residents of rural areas of the United States have lower rates of mortality than those who reside in urban areas, even though those in urban areas have greater socioeconomic resources and greater access to health services (Hayward, Pienta, & McLaughlin, 1997). It is hypothesized that the lower rate of mortality may be associated with an apparently more equitable distribution of life chances across different socioeconomic positions. In the Alameda County study, Haan and colleagues (1987) concluded that properties of the sociophysical environment might contribute to the relationship between low socioeconomic status and excess mortality, independently of individual behaviors.

PHYSICAL ENVIRONMENT

Environmental factors include both chemical and toxic exposures as well as characteristics of the built environment. There is evidence that environmental exposures such as air pollution and lead exposures elevate the risk of illness and death across the life course (Committee on Chemical Toxicity and Aging, 1987). As noted earlier, there is a recent initiative to examine effects of environmental exposure on health and longevity of older people. Segments of the older population may be at elevated risk because of combinations of exposures over the life course, coupled with reduced immunological resistance later in life.

There is also evidence that characteristics of the built environment, e.g., land use patterns, are associated with mortality. In a longitudinal study of senior residents of Tokyo born in 1903, 1908, 1913, and 1918, it was determined that environmental area characteristics in the place of residence were associated with survival (Takano, Nakamura, & Watanabe, 2002). Specifically, it was determined that those who live in areas with walkable streets and spaces had better survival than those who did not, after adjustment of the residents' age, sex, marital status, and SES. While this is one of the few studies to examine a hypothesized association between the built environment and mortality, it is very suggestive for future projects in this area. In the future, it will be necessary to determine whether length of residence in the area or area characteristics at other points in the life course affect the strength of this association. As noted earlier, in studies of this kind, it is important to understand whether the elevated risk of death is due to compositional or contextual factors. This too will be examined in more detail in Chapter 12.

There are also a number of studies that have examined the association between residential characteristics and the risk of accidental death in older populations. In addition to research on the environmental correlates of falls and injuries, which we will examine later in the chapter, there are a number of recent studies that have examined fire- and heat-related deaths in older populations. Although deaths associated with fatal fires may seem rather capricious, some people are at greater risk than others (Marshall, Runyan, Bangdiwala, Linzer, Sacks, & Butts, 1998). In a study of fire-related deaths in North Carolina, Marshall and colleagues (1998) determined that people at greatest risk for death include those under the age of 5 years and those over age 64, those suffering with a physical or cognitive disability, and those who were impaired by alcohol or other drugs. There are also studies of older people at risk for heat-related deaths. Kilbourne and colleagues (1982) reported that those most likely to die of heatstroke in St. Louis, Missouri, were those who were elderly, ill, poor, and socially isolated. These results were confirmed in a subsequent study of St. Louis health-related mortality (Smoyer, 1998), in which it was also determined that health-related deaths were more likely to occur in the "warmer, less stable, and most socioeconomically disadvantaged areas" of the city (Smoyer, 1998, p. 1821). Finally, Eric Klinenberg's (2002) chronicle of the 1995 Chicago heat wave, *Heat Wave: A Social Autopsy of Disaster in Chicago*, provides further confirmation of the results reported first in St. Louis. In the Chicago study, Klinenberg called attention to the general fear and isolation that characterized many of the city's seniors, in particular, those seniors who lived in the poorest parts of the city. These are the areas, like those in St. Louis, with the fewest resources and highest rates of crime (Sampson, Raudenbush, & Earls, 1997). Although Chicago had made "cooling stations" available throughout the city, many seniors were apprehensive about leaving their apartments and houses to travel to those stations. Moreover, the seniors who lived alone and who were most isolated were either least likely to be aware of the service or lacked the resources, in most cases, a friend or relative, to accompany them to a station. This illustrates that places can either enhance opportunities for social connection or not. As Klinenberg (2002, p. 103) writes,

> Old people in all parts of Chicago complain about the difficulties of navigating across broken sidewalks, rickety stairways, and forbidding open spaces left dark by burned-out street lamps. The fear of falling is a real concern of senior citizens, who know all too well that a stumble from which they once would have recovered could cripple or kill them when their bodies become frail. In North Lawndale, where the city government has done little to repair streets, sidewalks, alleys, and empty lots in the area and poverty prevented many residents from making major repairs on their homes, porches, and stairways, the condition of the physical environment contributes to the local seniors' sense of precariousness and increases the risks of leaving home. The social costs of fear in and of the streets made a brutal appearance during the heat wave, when the barriers North Lawndale residents established to keep themselves safe became the sources of their demise.

SOCIAL CAPITAL

In keeping with these observations, it is often reported that place provides a context for social interaction. Along these lines, researchers have addressed the topic of social capital. As noted in Chapter 2, social capital refers to the quality of social relationships and community life. Following from research and commentary in sociology and political science (Coleman, 1988; Putnam, 2000), social capital has been defined in terms of social and community relationships characterized by trust and reciprocity (Kawachi, Kennedy, Lochner, & Prothrow-Stith, 1997; Lochner, Pamuk, Makuc, Kennedy, & Kawachi, 2001; Lochner, Kawachi, Brennan, & Buka, 2003). It is important to emphasize again that social capital is a term used to characterize populations and communities rather than individuals. Research indicates that communities (both at the level of the state and the neighborhood) characterized by high social capital have lower rates of mortality than communities with lower levels of social capital, following adjustment for individual and population characteristics (Kawachi et al., 1997; Lochner et al., 2003). To my knowledge, the relationship between social capital and mortality has not been examined by age or length of residence in the area.

LIVING ARRANGEMENTS, SOCIAL NETWORKS, AND SOCIAL SUPPORT

One of the most persistent findings in social epidemiology is the association between social contacts and health outcomes (Berkman and Kawachi, 2000). In general, those people with regular contacts with friends and relatives and those who reported regular sources of social support have the best health outcomes. In fact, one of the earliest studies in this area demonstrated that residents of Alameda County, California, with the most developed social network index (a composite measure of personal and group relationships) in 1965 had the lowest age-adjusted mortality rate in 1974, following adjustment for baseline health status and health behaviors (Berkman & Syme, 1979). In a subsequent examination of the Alameda County cohort, this relationship was also found for seniors (Seeman et al., 1987). In addition to confirming the association between a general social network index and subsequent 17-year mortality among residents aged 70 years and older, research indicated that the strength of the association varied among specific measures of social networks and mortality by age. Specifically, the relationship between marital status and mortality was strongest for those less than 60 years of age at baseline. In contrast, the relationship between ties with close friends and relatives and mortality was most pronounced for those over the age of 60. In a subsequent study of social ties and mortality based on data from three geographic areas of the NIA EPESE, the strength of the association was affected by the geographic area and by gender (Seeman, Berkman, Kohout, LaCroix, Glynn, & Blazer, 1993). The age-adjusted analysis revealed that those with the least developed social network were at elevated risk of death between 1982 and 1987 for both men and women (relative hazard ranged from 1.97 to 3.06 across the three areas). After adjustment for measures of health, functioning, and health practices, social ties was associated with subsequent mortality only in New Haven, Connecticut, and among men in Iowa. No significant association was demonstrated for men and women in East Boston. The results suggest that the relationship between social ties and mortality may operate through other factors, in particular situations, and for certain groups of people. The variation in results across the different geographic areas also underscores yet again that compositional and contextual characteristics of place may help to account for differences in health outcomes.

In a separate study based on data from the New Haven component of the NIA EPESE, social and productive activities, even those that do not involve physical activity, was associated with survival over a 13-year period (Glass, Mendes de Leon, Marottoli, & Berkman, 1999). Those elderly who engaged in those activities had better survival than those who did not, following adjustment for a variety of factors including age, gender, race/ethnicity, marital status, income, body mass index, smoking, functional disability, and history of cancer, diabetes, stroke, and myocardial infarction.

Particular types of social relationships seem to be especially important. For example, there is a growing body of evidence that older people who engage in religious activities and belong to religious organizations have lower rates of mortality and higher survival rates than those who do not (Helm, Hays, Flint, Koenig, & Blazer, 2000; Omran & Reed, 1998). It has been hypothesized that religious affiliation is important for at least two reasons. First, as with membership in other organizations, it provides fellowship with others and potential sources of social support. Second, participation in this organization may provide meaning and "a sense of coherence," to use Aaron Antonovsky's (1979, p. 123) term, to cope with the issues of everyday life as well as more profound existential issues.

Marital status has been shown to be associated with health outcomes (Mendes de Leon, Kasl, & Jacobs, 1993). In general, those who are married are in better health than those who are not, especially among those who are divorced and separated. The health of those who are never married seems to depend on gender as well as their contacts with friends and relatives. As we shall see, those who have lost a spouse are at elevated risk of death, but this is associated with the timing and circumstances of the loss and gender of the surviving spouse.

Results from the National Longitudinal Mortality Study indicate that divorced and separated men had a higher mortality rate, especially for deaths due to suicide, than those who were married (Kposowa, 2000). Being single or widowed had no significant effect on suicide risk. As is true of other findings, the relationship between marital status and the risk of death was reduced among older people (Johnson, Backlund, Sorlie, & Loveless, 2000).

The loss of a spouse to death is also associated with a subsequent risk of death among the surviving spouse. A critical review of this literature was conducted by Osterweis, Solomon, and Green (1984). It was determined that there was a relationship between a loss of a spouse and a subsequent risk of death, especially among middle-aged men. In addition, the risk of death was most pronounced with the first year following the loss of the spouse. Subsequent studies have continued to identify this relationship. For example, in a study of 12,522 spouse pairs belonging to a prepaid health care plan in northern California, it was determined that there was an elevated risk of death among the surviving spouse, most notably within the first seven months, but continuing for as long as two years (Schaefer, Quesenberry, & Wi, 1995). Among surviving women, the risk was 1.9 between 7–12 months following the death of the spouse. Among surviving men, the risk was associated with the level of preexisting health conditions. The risk for men with no preexisting health conditions was 2.12, and for those with preexisting conditions, it was only 1.5. It is unknown whether the timing and circumstances of the spouse's death affected the subsequent risk of death. This is an intriguing issue, as there is research indicating that stressful caregiving can have a negative effect on the health of the caregiving spouse. Another important issue is homicide and elder abuse (Schiamberg & Gans, 2000). Some commentators have speculated that stressful caregiving may be one of the factors that contribute to abuse, and in some cases, elder homicide.

HEALTH BEHAVIORS

It is well known that specific types of behavior are associated with subsequent risk of death. In general, this is evident across the life course, but it is less pronounced among those aged 65 and older.

Tobacco Exposure

A history of cigarette smoking is associated with the risk of death from all of the leading causes of death, including CHD, stroke, chronic obstructive lung disease, and a number of different forms of cancer, such as cancers of the lung and bronchus, head and neck, stomach, and esophagus, as well as infections (Arcavi & Benowitz, 2004; Burns, 2000; Rivara, Ebel, Garrison, Christakis, Wiehe, & Levy, 2004). The quantity of tobacco consumed and length of time one has smoked are associated with the subsequent risk of death. As Burns (2000, p. 357) writes, "Disease consequences of smoking occur disproportionately among the elderly because of long duration of cumulative injury or change that underlies the bulk of tobacco-caused disease." There is also evidence that older smokers are more likely than younger smokers to develop lung cancer, a cancer with a relatively long latency. On the other hand, younger smokers are at elevated risk for the development of cardiovascular disease.

Alcohol Consumption

Heavy and sustained consumption of alcohol is associated with an elevated risk of death (Camacho, Kaplan, & Cohen, 1987). Unlike tobacco exposure, there is evidence that moderate consumption of alcohol may be associated with reduced risk of CHD. Heavy consumption, however, is associated with an elevated risk of death associated with conditions such as cancer of the head and neck, liver cancer, cirrhosis, suicide, and deaths due to accidents and injuries. An elevated risk of death is also associated with alcohol consumption, even moderate consumption, in combination with multiple medications and comorbidities (Reid, Boutros, O'Connor, Carariu, & Concato, 2002).

Physical Activity

There is considerable research indicating that older people who engage in physical activity have a reduced risk of death. In contrast, those who are sedentary are at elevated risk for many of the leading causes of death, including CHD, stroke, and specific forms of cancer, most notably colorectal cancer (Rakowski & Mor, 1992; Rosengren & Wilhelmsen, 1997). A reduction of risk is noted for people who engage in a variety of forms of physical activity, both weight-bearing exercise as well as aerobic forms of activity. The reasons for this reduction of risk include increased lung capacity, increased lean muscle mass, and increase in anti-oxidant activity.

Diet and Nutrition

Research also indicates that diet and nutrition are associated with a reduction in the risk of premature mortality (Meyyazhagan & Palmer, 2002; Pirlich & Lochs, 2001). Although there is considerable debate about the types of foods that should be consumed, there is general consensus that moderate consumption of food is healthful. In terms of specific foods, there is general agreement that a low-fat diet coupled with consumption of fruits and vegetables is associated with reduced risk of premature death. Ironically, the twin problems facing older populations that are associated with diet and nutrition are obesity on the one hand and undernutrition on the other. Obesity is associated with increased intake of food, coupled with sedentary activity. Undernutrition is associated with inadequate consumption of nutritious foods, a condition that many researchers consider to be the primary source of nutrition-related mortality in older populations. This may be associated with poor oral health, reduction in sense of smell and olfaction, as well as comorbid conditions of cognitive dysfunction and depression.

SENSE OF CONTROL, COHERENCE, AND SELF-EFFICACY

There is evidence that particular types of psychosocial factors, such as self-efficacy and a sense of control, are associated with vital status. Those people who lack control and a sense of confidence do not do as well as those who have those characteristics. One of the earliest studies to examine this issue, and in many ways still the most profound and the most compelling, was an intervention study to investigate the health effects of providing seniors with responsibility (Langer & Rodin, 1976). Seniors in a nursing home were randomly assigned to two groups. Members of one group were given a potted plant and told that they were responsible for its care and well-being. Members of the second group also were given a plant but told that members of the staff would be responsible for its care. After 18 months, there was a mortality difference between the two groups. Those who were told that members of the staff would care for their plants had a higher mortality rate than those who were told that they were responsible. While some commentators have since criticized the study's small sample size and other elements of its design and interpretation, the results were quite startling and stimulated other researchers to examine the issue of control in more detail. As indicated in Chapter 2, Leonard Syme (1998) and Aaron Antonovsky (1979) contributed significantly to this area of research. Both Syme and Antonovsky argue that this concept (either a sense of control or a sense of coherence) help to explain the connection between many of the social and behavioral factors and health outcomes, not the least of which is survival and mortality. Also, as noted previously, Albert Bandura (1997) introduced the concept of self-efficacy, which describes a person's level of confidence in being able to complete a particular task. In keeping with Syme's and Antonovsky's observations, Bandura argued that the successful completion of a task depends in large part in one's confidence that it can be done. As we will see in subsequent chapters, in particular, Chapter 11, self-efficacy is a core concept in public health and epidemiology and the basis of a new generation of public health interventions for populations in general as well as interventions that are focused on the elderly. A sense of control, a sense of coherence, and self-efficacy all seem to be pointing to an underlying factor that includes a sense of competence, confidence, well-being, and optimism about the future (Penninx, van Tilbrug, Kriesgsman, Deeg, Boeke, & van Eijk, 1997). This underlying factor was captured well and seems to be summarized best by Edith Wharton (1923, p. vii) in her autobiographical work, *A Backward Glance:*

> In spite of illness, in spite of the arch-enemy sorrow, one can remain alive long past the usual date of disintegration if one is unafraid of change, insatiable in intellectual curiosity, interested in big things, and happy in small ways.

DISEASE AND COMORBIDITIES

As we saw earlier, disease and comorbidities are central to a consideration of survival and mortality. Indeed, the causes of death, as reflected on the death certificate and mortality statistics, are not defined in terms of social and behavioral factors, even though they figure in the causal pathways, but rather in terms of disease categories. As shown in later chapters, some conditions have a higher case-fatality rate than others. Leading conditions include CHD, stroke, chronic obstructive lung disease, diabetes, and, of course, the various forms of cancer, most notably, cancers of the lung and bronchus, colon and rectum, female breast, and prostate. The number and types of conditions a person may have is also strongly associated with survival and mortality (Feinstein, 1970). As noted earlier, a set of concurrent health conditions or comorbidity is especially common in older populations. In addition to specific categorical disease conditions, there is also evidence that very simple, general measures of health have prognostic significance (Idler, 1992; Idler & Benyamini, 1997). Respondents are usually asked to provide an overall assessment of their health: "How would you classify your overall health—excellent, good, fair, or poor?" or "Compared to other (men or women) your age, would you say that your health is better than most, same as most, or worst than most?" A recent prospective study based on data from the NHANES I epidemiologic follow-up study, which used a representative sample of US adults aged 25–74, indicated that self-reported health predicted subsequent mortality for men, but less so for women (Idler, Russell, & Davis, 2000). The researchers (2000, p. 874) conclude that "Self-rated health contributes unique information to epidemiologic studies that is not captured by standard clinical assessments or self-reported histories." It may be that self-rated, overall assessments of health may be based not only on the number and types of conditions a person may have, but also that person's assessment of the impact of those conditions in his or her everyday life. This leads to a consideration of other factors that have been shown to have an independent effect on survival and mortality, and also may help to explain the mechanisms of the association between health status and the risk of death.

FALLS AND INJURIES

Falls and automobile crashes represent the two leading causes of accidental death among people aged 65 and older. Although concepts and measurement of falls, injury, and automobile crashes will be addressed in more detail in Chapter 8, it is important to realize that fatalities are due to important factors. First, there is the force of the trauma itself, i.e., the circumstances of the fall or the crash. Second, there is the vulnerability of the person, i.e., the extent to which a person can withstand the trauma. Of course, falls and automobile crashes can result directly in loss of life. In addition, falls and crashes can render older people functionally limited or disabled, which in turn can initiate a chain of events that will lead to death. Finally, a fall or injury can lead to fear of a subsequent fall or injury. This fear can lead to sedentary behavior, which, in turn, can elevate the risk for a subsequent fall, injury, serious injury, or, over time, death. Laurence Rubenstein and colleagues (2003, p. 3) summarize the research on fall-related mortality as follows:

> Accidents are the fifth leading cause of death in older adults (after cardiovascular, cancer, stroke, and pulmonary causes), and falls constitute two thirds of these accidental deaths. About three fourths of deaths due to falls in the United States occur in the 13% of the population aged 65 and older (Hogue, 1982; Rubenstein & Josephson, 2002). Fall-related mortality increases dramatically with advancing age, especially in populations over age 70 years, and nursing home residents 85 years and older account for one out of five fatal falls (Baker & Harvey, 1985). The estimated 1% of fallers who sustain a hip fracture have a 20% to 30% mortality rate within one year of the fracture (Magaziner, Simonsick, Kashner, Hebel, & Kenzora, 1990).

PHYSICAL FUNCTIONING

Physical functioning refers to the relative ease in the performance of tasks that are necessary for adaptation to everyday life. The tasks may range from generic tasks, such as lifting and balance, to more complicated, everyday tasks, such as driving a car and engaging in voluntary or occupational tasks. In addition to being an important outcome associated with quality of life, research indicates that level of physical functioning is associated with subsequent survival and mortality. For example, a battery of self-reported assessments of function and direct measures of physical performance were administered to subjects (Reuben, Siu, Kimpau, 1992). At follow-up (average 22 months), each of the four measures was shown to be independently associated with either death or nursing home placement. In a subsequent study by the same research group, a set of functional measures predicted subsequent survival over a 4-year period, following adjustment for a variety of demographic, health, and social measures (Reuben et al., 1992). There is also evidence that direct measures of performance and computation are associated with survival (Williams, Gaylord, & Gerritty, 1994). The timed manual performance requires the participant to unlock, open, and close latches on a series of small doors. Those who required less time to perform the task, a task requiring the integration of a variety of tasks including cognition, vision, and manual dexterity, had lower mortality than those who required more time.

COGNITIVE FUNCTIONING

Cognitive function refers to a variety of different mental tasks that include short- and long-term memory, computation, orientation, and executive processing. Research indicates that cognitive functioning, like physical functioning, is independently associated with survival and mortality in older populations. For example, the longitudinal studies conducted by Reuben and colleagues (1992, 2004) that were noted previously, included the Folstein Mini-Mental State Examination, a standard summary test of general cognitive functioning, as one of the tests independently associated with mortality. Research based on the Longitudinal Aging Study, Amsterdam, a study of 2380 residents of Amsterdam aged 55–85 years, indicated that five areas of cognitive functioning (general cognitive functioning, information processing speed, fluid intelligence, learning, and proportion retained) were associated with subsequent mortality, after adjustment of age, gender, education, and depressive symptoms (Smits, Deeg, Kriegsman, & Schmand, 1999). Even after adjustment for self-rated health, medication use, physical perform-ance, functional limitations, lung function, specific chronic diseases, information-processing speed, fluid intelligence, learning and proportion retained were still independent predictors of mortality.

DEPRESSION

Depressive symptoms and cognitive functioning often are both present and, in fact, interact among older people (Black & Markides, 1999; Ostier, Markides, Black, & Goodwin, 2000). There is evidence as well that people with depressive symptoms are at elevated risk of death. In fact, depression is considered to be one of the leading comorbid conditions for older people diagnosed with other conditions. Put differently, no matter what combination of diagnosed health conditions an older person may have, the addition of depressive symptoms makes it worse. It is fair to ask what is it about depression that elevates the risk of death. Should we think of depression as a separate condition or should it be thought of as part of the sequelae of one or more other conditions? As is true of both physical and cognitive functioning, does depression affect the immune system directly or does it operate through other pathways, adversely affecting proper health behaviors or relationships with others? Blazer and col-leagues (2001) addressed this question in a recent study. In this study, a cohort of elderly subjects was followed for three years. The results indi-cated that as a variety of social, behavioral, health, and functional vari-ables were systematically introduced into the model, the risk of death associated with depression declined from nearly a two-fold elevation in risk (1.98) to less than a 25% increase (1.21). The researchers conclude (2001, p. 505) that "Unlike other known risk factors for mortality in the elderly population, depression appears to be associated with mortality through a number of independent mechanisms, perhaps through com-plex feedback loops of known risk factors."

PHYSIOLOGICAL FACTORS

Following Blazer's and his colleagues' observation about the prognostic significance of depression, the ecological model suggests that multiple pathways, integrating biologic, behavioral, social, and environmental factors are associated with patterns of longevity in older populations. Given the range of possible paths, it is fair to say that different biological factors may come into play. These factors may range from affecting the cardiovascular and/or immune systems, to affecting not only the risk of the death, but the specific cause of death. A variety of studies have been conducted to examine biological factors, including body mass index, lean and fat body mass, muscle mass, and changes in weight. Clearly, the specific health outcome and the specific cause of death will determine the specific causal hypotheses. Following John Cassel's (1976) recommendation, it is useful to consider the combination of factors that affect overall host susceptibility. According to Leonard Syme and Claudine Torfs (1987), there are two important questions: Why do some people become ill, while others do not? And, of those who become ill, why do some people develop one health condition, while others develop another? With regard to the first question, it may be possible to identify a set of factors that may be common across a variety of situations and conditions. Why are some people and some populations more likely than others to become ill? As we explained in the previous chapter, it is that question that makes the concept of allostasis and allostatic load so important. To recall that discussion, allostasis is defined as a summary measure of a range of regulatory systems pertinent to disease risks (Seeman, Singer, Roue, & McEwen, 2001). Allostatic load, a summary measure of impaired physiological response or adaptation to cumulative stress, is measured by the dysregulation of those systems. In a prospective study of 1189 men and women aged 70–79, enrolled in the MacArthur Successful Aging Study, those with higher measures of allostatic load were at an elevated risk of death (Odds ratio = 1.23) following adjustment for age, gender, ethnicity, education, income, and baseline health conditions.

CONCLUSION

We began this chapter with the observation that in the epidemiology of aging, as in life, all roads lead to survival and mortality. We have attempted to illustrate, as noted previously, that there are a variety of biologic, behavioral, social, and environmental factors associated with vital status and survival. It should be clear at this point that we do not consider these factors to be independent and disparate. We have proposed the ecological model as a template to describe and explain multiple pathways. In the subsequent chapters, we will, in effect, move back from vital status along the multiple paths to better characterize the backdrop that is the epidemiology of aging, functioning, and longevity.

REFERENCES

Antonovsky, A. (1979). *Health, stress, and coping.* San Francisco: Jossey-Bass.

Arcavi, L., & Benowitz, N. (2004). Cigarette smoking and infection. *Archives of Internal Medicine, 164*(20), 2206–2016.

Austin, J. P., & Convery, K. (1993). Age-race interaction in prostatic adenocracinoma treated with external beam irradiation. *American Journal of Clinical Oncology, 16*(2), 140–145.

Baker, S. P., & Harvey, A. H. (1985). Fall injuries in the elderly. *Clinics in Geriatric Medicine, 1*(3), 501–512.

Bandura, A. (1997). *Self-efficacy: The exercise of control.* New York: W.H. Freeman.

Bassuk, S. S., Berkman, L. F., & Amick, B. C., III. (2002). Socioeconomic status and mortality among the elderly: Findings from four U.S. communities. *American Journal of Epidemiology, 155*(6), 520–533.

Berkman, L., Singer, B., & Manton, K. (1989). Black/white differences in health status and mortality among the elderly. *Demography, 26*(4), 661–678.

Berkman, L. F., & Syme, S. L. (1979). Social networks, host resistance, and mortality: A nine-year follow-up study of Alameda County residents. *American Journal of Epidemiology, 109*(2), 186–204.

Berkman, L., & Kawachi, I. (2000). *Social epidemiology.* New York: Oxford University Press.

Berrigan, D., Dodd, K., Troiano, R. P., Krebs-Smith, S. M., & Barbash, R. B. (2003). Patterns of health behavior in U.S. adults. *Preventive Medicine, 36*(5), 615–623.

Black, S. A., & Markides, K. S. (1999). Depressive symptoms and mortality in older Mexican Americans. *Annals of Epidemiology, 9*(1), 45–52.

Blazer, D. G., Hybels, C. F., & Pieper, C. F. (2001). The association of depression and mortality in elderly persons: A case for multiple, independent pathways. *Journals of Gerontology: Medical Sciences, 56*(8), M505–M509.

Breeze, E., Sloggett, A., & Fletcher, A. (1999). Socioeconomic and demographic predictors of mortality and institutional residence among middle aged and older people: Results from the Longitudinal Study. *Journal of Epidemiology and Community Health, 53*(12), 765–774.

Burns, D. M. (2000). Cigarette smoking among the elderly: Disease consequences and the benefits of cessation. *American Journal of Health Promotion, 14*(6), 357–361.

Camacho, T. E., Kaplan, G. A., & Cohen, R. D. (1987). Alcohol consumption and mortality in Alameda County. *Journal of Chronic Diseases, 40*(3), 229–236.

Cassel, J. (1976). The contribution of the social environment to host resistance. *American Journal of Epidemiology, 104*(2), 107–123.

Coleman, J. (1988). Social capital in the creation of human capital. *American Journal of Sociology, 94*(Suppl.), S95–S120.

Committee on Chemical Toxicity and Aging, National Research Council (1987). *Aging in today's environment.* Washington, DC: National Academies Press.

Cornoni-Huntley, J., Brock, D. B., Ostfeld, A. M., Taylor, J. O., & Wallace, R. B. (Eds.). (1986). *Established populations for epidemiologic studies of the elderly.* Washington, DC: National Institutes of Health (NIH Publication No. 86-2443).

Corti, M. C., Guralnik, J. M., Ferrucci, L., Izmirlian, G., Leveille, S. G., Pahor, M., et al. (1999). Evidence for a black-white crossover in all-cause and coronary heart disease mortality in an older population: The North Carolina EPESE. *American Journal of Public Health, 89*(3), 308–314.

Dowd J., & Bengston, V. (1978). Aging in minority populations: An examination of the double jeopardy hypothesis. *Journal of Gerontology, 33*(3), 427–436.

Elo, I. T., & Preston, S. H. (1996). Educational differentials in mortality: United States, 1979-1985. *Social Science & Medicine, 42*(1), 47–57.

Federal Interagency Forum on Aging Related Statistics. (2005). *Older Americans 2004: Key indicators of well-being.* www.agingstats.gov/chartbook2004/ healthstatus.html (Accessed February 5, 2005).

Feinstein, A. R. (1970). The pre-therapeutic classification of co-morbidity in chronic disease. *Journal of Chronic Diseases, 23,* 455–469.

Ferraro, K. F., & Farmer, M. M. (1996). Double jeopardy, aging as leveler, or persistent health inequality? A longitudinal analysis of white and black Americans. *Journals of Geronotology: Social Sciences, 51*(6), S319–S328.

Fried, L. P., Borhani, N. O., Enright, P., Furberg, C. D., Gardin, J. M., Kronmal, R. A., et al. (1991). The Cardiovascular Health Study: Design and rationale. *Annals of Epidemiology, 1*(3), 263–276.

Glass, T. A., Mendes de Leon, C., Marottoli, R. A., & Berkman, L. F. (1999). Population-based study of social and productive activities as predictors of survival among elderly Americans. *British Medical Journal, 319,* 478–483.

Guralnik, J. M., LaCroix, A. Z., Everett, D. F., & Kovar, M. G. (1989). *Aging in the eighties: The prevalence of comorbidity and its association with disability.* Hyattsville, MD: National Center for Health Statistics, Advanced Data from Vital and Health Statistics, No. 170.

Haan, M., Kaplan, G. A., & Camacho, T. (1987). Poverty and health: Prospective evidence from the Alameda County Study. *American Journal of Epidemiology, 125*(6), 989–998.

Hayward, M. D., Pienta, A. M., & McLaughlin, D. K. (1997). Inequality in men's morality: The socioeconomic status gradient and geographic context. *Journal of Health and Social Behavior, 38*(4), 313–330.

Hazzard, W. R. (1986). Biological basis of the sex differential in longevity. *Journal of the American Geriatrics Society, 34*(6), 455–471.

Hazzard, W. R. (1989). Why do women live longer than men? Biologic differences that influence longevity. *Postgraduate Medicine, 85*(5), 271–278.

Helm, H. M., Hays, J. C., Flint, E. P., Koenig, H. G., & Blazer, D. G. (2000). Does private religious activity prolong survival? A six-year follow-up study of 3,851 older adults. *Journals of Gerontology: Medical Sciences, 55*(7), M400–M405.

Hill, M. E., Preston, S. H., & Rosenwaike, I. (2000). Age reporting among white Americans aged 85+: Results of a record linkage study. *Demography, 37*(2), 175–186.

Hogue, C. (1982). Injury in late life: Part I. Epidemiology. *Journal of the American Geriatrics Society, 30*(3), 183–190.

House, J. S., Kessler, R. C., & Herzog, A. R. (1990). Age, socioeconomic status, and health. *Milbank Quarterly, 68*(3), 383–411.

Hummer, R. A., Benjamins, M. R., & Rogers, R. G. (2004). Racial and ethnic disparities in health and mortality among the U.S. elderly population. In N. B. Anderson, R. A. Bulatao, & B. Cohen (Eds.), *Critical perspectives on racial and ethnic differences in health in late life* (pp. 53–94). Washington, DC: National Academies Press.

Idler, E. L. (1992). Self-assessed health and mortality: A review of studies. In S. Maes, H. Leventhal, & M. Johnston (Eds.), *International Review of Health Psychology, 1*, 33–56.

Idler, E. L., & Benyamini, Y. (1997). Self-rated health and mortality: A review of twenty-seven community studies. *Journal of Health and Social Behavior, 38*(1), 21–37.

Idler, E. L., Russell, L. B., & Davis, D. (2000). Survival, functional limitations, and self-rated health in the NHANES I Epidemiologic Follow-up Study, 1992. First National Health and Nutrition Examination Survey. *American Journal of Epidemiology, 152*(9), 874–883.

International Longevity Institute. (2004). *Promoting men's health: Addressing barriers to healthy lifestyle and preventive health care.* New York: International Longevity Institute.

Johnson, N. J., Backlund, E., Sorlie, P. D., & Loveless, C. A. (2000). Marital status and mortality: The National Longitudinal Mortality Study. *Annals of Epidemiology, 10*(4), 224–238.

Kaplan, G. A., Seeman, T. E., Cohen, R. D., Knudsen, L. P., & Guralnik, J. (1987). Mortality among the elderly in the Alameda County Study: Behavioral and demographic risk factors. *American Journal of Public Health, 77*(3), 307–312.

Karter, A. J., Gazzaniga, J. M., Cohen, R. D., Casper, M. L., Davis, B. D., & Kaplan, G. A. (1998). Ischemic heart disease and stroke mortality in African-American, Hispanic, and non-Hispanic white men and women, 1985 to 1991. *Western Journal of Medicine, 169*(3), 139–145.

Kawachi, I., Kennedy, B. P., Lochner, K., & Prothrow-Stith, D. (1997). Social capital, income inequality, and mortality. *American Journal of Public Health, 87*(9), 1491–1498.

Keil, J. E., Sutherland, S. E., Hames, C. G., Lackland, D. T., Gazes, P. C., Knapp, R. G., et al. (1995). *Archives of Internal Medicine, 155*(14), 1521–1527.

Keil, J. E., Sutherland, S. E., Knapp, R. G., Lackland, D. T., Gazes, P. C., & Tyroler, H. A. (1993). Mortality rates and risk factors for coronary disease in black as compared with white men and women. *The New England Journal of Medicine, 329*(2), 73–78.

Kilbourne, E. M., Choi, K., Jones, T. S., & Thacker, S. B. (1982). Risk factors for heatstroke: A case-control study. *Journal of the American Medical Association, 247*(24), 3332–3336.

Klinenberg, E. (2002). *Heat wave: A social autopsy of disaster in Chicago.* Chicago, IL: University of Chicago Press.

Kposowa, A. J. (2000). Marital status and suicide in the National Longitudinal Mortality Study. *Journal of Epidemiology and Community Health, 54*(4), 254–261.

Langer, E. J., & Rodin, J. (1976). The effects of choice and enhanced personal responsibility for the aged. *Journal of Personality and Social Psychology, 34,* 191–198.

Lobmayer, P., & Wilkinson, R. G. (2002). Inequality, residential segregation by income, and mortality in U.S. cities. *Journal of Epidemiology & Community Health, 56*(3), 165–166.

Lochner, I. K., Pamuk, E., Makuc, D., Kennedy, B. P., & Kawachi, I. (2001). State-level income inequality and individual mortality risk: A prospective multilevel study. *American Journal of Public Health, 91*(3), 385–391.

Lochner, K. A., Kawachi, I., Brennan, R. T., & Buka, S. L. (2003). Social capital and neighborhood mortality rates in Chicago. *Social Science & Medicine, 56*(8), 1797–1805.

Magaziner, J., Simonsick, E. M., Kashner, T. M., Hebel, J. R., & Kenzora, J. E. (1990). Predictors of functional recovery one year following hospital discharge for hip fracture: A prospective study. *Journal of Gerontology, 45*(3), M101–M107.

Manton, K. G., Wrigley, J. M., Cohen, H. J., & Woodbury, M. A. (1991). Cancer mortality, aging, and patterns of comorbidity in the United States: 1968 to 1986. *Journal of Gerontology, 46*(4), S225–S234.

Marshall, S. W., Runyan, C. W., Bangdiwala, S. I., Linzer, M. A., Sacks, J. J., & Butts, J. D. (1998). Fatal residential fires: Who dies and who survives? *Journal of the American Medical Association, 279*(20), 1633–1637.

Mendes de Leon, C. F., Kasl, S. V., & Jacobs, S. (1993). Widowhood and mortality risk in a community sample of the elderly: A prospective study. *Journal of Clinical Epidemiology, 46*(6), 519–527.

Meyyazhagan, S., & Palmer, R. M. (2002). Nutritional requirements with aging: Prevention of disease. *Clinics in Geriatric Medicine, 18*(3), 557–576.

Newman, A. B., & Brach, J. S. (2001). Gender gap in longevity and disability in older persons. *Epidemiologic Reviews, 23*(2), 343–350.

Ny-Mak, D. S., Dohrenwend, B. P., Abraido-Lanza, A. F., & Turner, J. B. (1999). A further analysis of race differences in the National Longitudinal Mortality Study. *American Journal of Public Health, 89*(11), 1748–1751.

Nuland, S. B. (1993). *How we die: Reflections on life's final chapter.* New York: Vintage Books.

Omran, D., & Reed, D. (1998). Religion and mortality among the community-dwelling elderly. *American Journal of Public Health, 88*(10), 1469–1475.

Osterweis, M., Soloman, F., & Green, M. (Eds.). (1984). *Bereavement: Reactions, consequences, and care.* Washington, DC: National Academies Press.

Ostier, G. V., Markides, K. S., Black, S. A., & Goodwin, J. S. (2000). Emotional well-being predicts subsequent functional independence and survival. *Journal of the American Geriatrics Society, 48*(5), 473–478.

Penninx, B. W., van Tilbrug, T., Kriesgsman, D. M., Deeg, D. J., Boeke, A. J., & van Eijk, J. T. (1997). Effects of social support and personal coping resources on mortality in older age: The Longitudinal Aging Study, Amsterdam. *American Journal of Epidemiology, 146*(6), 510–519.

Pirlich, M., & Lochs, H. (2001). Nutrition in the elderly. *Best Practice & Research Clinical Gastroenterology, 15*(6), 869–884.

Preston, S. H., & Elo, I. T. (1995). Are educational differential in adult mortality increasing in the United States? *Journal of Aging and Health, 7*(4), 476–496.

Putnam, R. D. (2000). *Bowling alone: The collapse and revival of American community.* New York: Simon & Schuster Publishers.

Rakowski, W., & Mor, V. (1992). The association of physical activity with mortality among adults in the Longitudinal Study of Aging Study (1984–1988). *Journals of Gerontology: Medical Sciences, 47,* M122–M129.

Reid, M. E., Boutros, N. N., O'Connor, P. G., Carariu, A., & Concato, J. (2002). The health-related effects of alcohol use in older persons: A systematic review. *Substance Abuse, 23*(3), 149–164.

Reuben, D. B., Seeman, T. E., Keeler, E., Hayes, R. P., Bowman, L., Sewall, A., et al. (2004). Refining the categorization of physical functional status: The added value of combining self-reported and performance measures. *Journals of Gerontology: Medical Sciences, 59*(10), 1056–1061.

Reuben, D. B., Siu, A. L., & Kimpau, S. (1992). The predictive validity of self-report and performance-based measures of function and health. *Journal of Gerontology, 47*(4), M106–M110.

Rivara, F. P., Ebel, B. E., Garrison, M. M., Christakis, D. A., Wiehe, S. E., & Levy, D. T. (2004). Prevention of smoking-related deaths in the United States. *American Journal of Preventive Medicine, 27*(2), 118–125.

Rosengren, A., & Wilhelmsen, L. (1997). Physical activity protects against coronary death and deaths from all causes in middle-aged men: Evidence from a 20-year follow-up of the primary prevention study in Goteberg. *Annals of Epidemiology, 7*(1), 69–75.

Rubenstein, L. Z., Castle, S. C., Diener, D. D., Hooker, S. P., Jones, C. J., & Vasquez L. (2003). *Best practice interventions for fall prevention.* Prepared for "A California Blueprint for Fall Prevention Conference," Invitational Conference, Sacramento, California, February 5–6, 2003.

Rubenstein, L. Z., & Josephson, K. R. (2002). The epidemiology of falls and syncope. *Clinics in Geriatric Medicine, 18*(2), 141–158.

Russell, A., Langlois, T., Johnson, G., Trentham-Dietz, A., & Remington, P. (1999). Increasing gap in breast cancer mortality between black and white women. *Western Journal of Medicine, 98*(4), 47–49.

Sampson, R. J., Raudenbush, S. W., & Earls, F. (1997). Neighborhoods and violent crime: A multilevel study of collective efficacy. *Science, 277*(5328), 918–924.

Satariano, W. A., Ragland, K. E., & Van Den Eeden, S. K. (1998). Cause of death in men diagnosed with prostate carcinoma. *Cancer, 83*(6), 1180–1188.

Satariano, W. A., & Ragland, D. R. (1994). The effect of comorbidity on 3-year survival of women with primary breast cancer. *Annals of Internal Medicine, 120,* 104–110.

Satariano, W. A., Smith, J., Swanson, A., & Tager, I. B. (1998). A census-based design for the recruitment of a community sample of older adults: Efficacy and costs. *Annals of Epidemiology, 8*(4), 278–282.

Schaefer, C., Quesenberry, C. P., Jr., & Wi, S. (1995). Mortality following conjugal bereavement and the effects of a shared environment. *American Journal of Epidemiology, 141*(12), 1142–1152.

Schiamberg, L. B., & Gans, D. (2000). Elder abuse by adult children: An applied ecological framework for understanding contextual risk factors and the intergenerational characteristics of quality of life. *International Journal of Aging and Human Development, 50*(4), 329–359.

Seeman, T. E., Kaplan G. A., Knudsen, L., Cohen, R., & Guralnik, J. (1987). Social network ties and mortality among the elderly in the Alameda County study. *American Journal of Epidemiology, 126*(4), 714–723.

Seeman, T. E., Berkman, L. F., Kohout, F., LaCroix, A., Glynn, R., & Blazer, D. (1993). Intercommunity variations in the association between social ties and mortality in the elderly: A comparative analysis of three communities. *Annals of Epidemiology, 3*(4), 448–450.

Seeman, T. E., Singer, B., Rowe, J. W., & McEwen, B. S. (2001). Exploring a new concept of cumulative biological risk—allostatic load and its health consequences: MacArthur studies of successful aging. *Proceedings of the National Academy of Sciences of the United States of America, 98*(8), 4770–4775.

Simon, M. S., & Severson, R. K. (1997). Racial differences in breast cancer survival: The interaction of socioeconomic status and tumor biology. *American Journal Obstetrics & Gynecology, 176*(6), S233–S239.

Smith, M. H., Anderson, R. T., Bradham, D. D., & Longino, C. F., Jr. (1995). Rural and urban differences in mortality among Americans 55 years and older: Analysis of the National Longitudinal Mortality Study. *Journal of Rural Health, 11*(4), 274–285.

Smits, C. H., Deeg, D. J., Kriegsman, D. M., & Schmand, B. (1999). Cognitive functioning and health as determinants of mortality in an older population. *American Journal of Epidemiology, 150*(9), 978–986.

Smoyer, K. E. (1998). A comparative analysis of heat waves and associated mortality in St. Louis, Missouri—1980 and 1995. *International Journal of Biometerology, 42*(1), 44–50.

Sorlie, P. D., Baclund, E., & Keller, J. B. (1995). U.S. mortality by economic, demographic, and social characteristics: The National Longitudinal Mortality Study. *American Journal of Public Health, 85*(7), 903–905.

Syme, S. L. (1998). Social and economic disparities in health: Thoughts about intervention. *The Milbank Quarterly, 76*(3), 493–505.

Syme, S. L., & Torfs, C. (1987). Epidemiologic research in hypertension: A critical appraisal. *Journal of Human Stress, 4*(1), 43–48.

Takano, T., Nakamura, K., & Watanabe, M. (2002). Urban residential environments and senior citizens' longevity in megacity areas: The importance of walkable green spaces. *Journal of Epidemiology and Community Health, 56*(12), 913–918.

Wharton, E. (1923). *A backward glance.* New York: Scribners Publishing.

Williams, M. E., Gaylord, S. A., & Gerritty, M. S. (1994). The time manual performance test as a predictor of hospitalization and death in a community-based elderly population. *Journal of the American Geriatric Society, 42*(1), 21–27.

Yancik, R., Havlik, R. J., Wesley, M. N., Ries, L., Long, S., Rossi, W. K., et al. (1996). Cancer and comorbidity in older patients: A descriptive profile. *Annals of Epidemiology, 6*(5), 399–412.

CHAPTER 4

Physical Functioning and Activities of Everyday Life

The study of aging and longevity not only deals with length of life, but also with what that life entails—its quality. The critical debate about the impact of an aging population on health care and long-term care costs will be advanced by obtaining an accurate assessment of the connections between life expectancy, age at the onset of chronic conditions, and the timing and duration of functional limitations and disability associated with those conditions. Functioning refers to the ease with which people are able to complete basic tasks of everyday life. These tasks range from basic generic activities associated with independence, such as walking and eating, to more complicated activities associated with employment, running errands, and driving an automobile. The level and ease of functioning depend on the interplay between the capacity of the individual and population on the one hand and the demands and resources of the social and physical environments on the other. As such, the study of functioning is really an exemplar for a demonstration of the intersections among biologic, behavioral, and environmental factors.

ACTIVE LIFE EXPECTANCY

Active life expectancy, a key concept in the epidemiology of aging, is used to summarize the remaining years that people can expect to spend free of disability (Katz, Branch, Branson, Pasidero, Breck, & Greer, 1983). Put differently, if the measure of life expectancy defines the number of years

125

individuals can expect to live, given that they have survived to a particular age, then the measure of active life expectancy defines the number of years that individuals can expect to live in independence, free of functional disability. In many ways, this is a hybrid measure. It combines well-validated measures of functional health with common demographic and public health statistics. It supports Robert Wallace's observation that the history of the epidemiology of aging can be thought of as a process that began in clinical settings and then moved to the field (Wallace, 1992). For our purposes, a discussion of active life expectancy provides an excellent transition from our discussion in the previous chapter of survival, mortality, and cause of death to a discussion here of physical functioning and activities of everyday life.

Age

Katz and his colleagues first introduced the concept of active life expectancy in a 1983 paper based on longitudinal data from the Massachusetts Health Care Panel Study, which was designed to assess the feasibility of forecasting functional health for the elderly. Active life expectancy was described in that paper as representing the convergence of improvement in the techniques used to create life tables and the availability of well-validated and well-accepted measures of functional health, most notably, activities of daily living (ADL) (Katz et al., 1983). ADL, to be discussed later in more detail, measures the extent to which individuals can complete basic tasks that are necessary for independent living, such as feeding oneself and dressing oneself without assistance (Katz, 1963). It is arguably one of the earliest, most common, and most well-accepted measures of functional health. Following the recommendations of Katz and colleagues, subsequent studies have expanded the concept of active life expectancy to include other generic measures of physical functioning as well as measures of higher-level functioning (Branch, Guralnik, Foley, Kohout, Wetle, Ostfeld, et al., 1991), such as instrumental activities of daily living (IADL) (Lawton & Brody, 1969). These studies also assessed how well the initial results from the Massachusetts study could be generalized to a wider population by studying active life expectancy in different, more heterogeneous samples. Finally, subsequent studies employed more sophisticated models to assess active life expectancy (Crimmins, Hayward, & Saito, 1996). The initial Katz paper was based on a single-decrement model, designed to assess the expected proportion of people who are independent in ADL tasks at baseline (time 1) who will remain independent, become dependent in one or more ADL tasks, become institutionalized, or die by a subsequent time (time 2), in this case, 15 months. The single-decrement model is thus based on the expectation of either functional maintenance or decline. On the other hand, multivariate, *multistate models* were introduced to assess expected active life expectancy among a more heterogeneous population of independent and dependent people (Land, Guralnik, & Blazer, 1994). This later model is also based on the common observation that aging does not necessarily imply a uniform and constant decline in function; there are different patterns of active life expectancy. While some people maintain their level and others decline, there are still others whose level of functioning varies over time, varying periods of decline, recuperation, and maintenance. As such, the multistate model takes into account differences in the frequency, degree, and timing of recuperation and decline. Together, these studies have contributed to an expanding literature on active life expectancy, the results of which are summarized below. Indeed, the promotion and maintenance of an "active life" are now considered as key national health objectives for an aging population, and are highlighted prominently in both *Healthy People 2000* and *Healthy People 2010* (US Department of Health & Human Services, 2000). Efforts to expand measures of the global burden of disease to include estimates of lost years of active life are part of this more general research agenda to broaden traditional public health statistics to better reflect the characteristics of everyday life.

Gender

It is reported that, "One of the real paradoxes of the aging process is the longer life but worse health of women" (Hazzard, 1986). This observation has been confirmed, with some qualifications, in various studies on active life expectancy. Specifically, although women have greater life and active life expectancies than men, women can expect to live a smaller percentage of their remaining years in independence than men (see Table 4–1). As reported by Katz and colleagues (1983), the percentage of independent years declines from 54% to 36% for women between the ages of 65–69 to 85 and older. For men, the percentage of independent years declines from 71% to 51%. Later studies that used broader measures of function and the multistate model confirmed the initial findings for gender (Crimmins et al., 1996). Similar to what was presented in a single-decrement model, compared to men of the same ages, women have approximately equal percentages of remaining years of dependence. When coupled with the

Table 4-1 Age and Gender Differences of Total and Active Life Expectancy

Age	Male Life Expectancy		Female Life Expectancy	
	Total	Active	Total	Active
65–69	13.2	9.3	19.5	10.6
70–74	11.9	8.2	15.9	8.0
75–79	9.6	6.5	13.2	7.1
80–84	7.4	4.8	9.8	4.8
85+	6.5	3.3	7.7	2.8

Source: Adapted from Katz et al., 1983.

long-recognized phenomenon of greater life expectancy for women as described in the previous chapter, these comparable percentages imply that women can expect a greater number of years in dependence than men of the same age. Overall, compared to the single-decrement model, the multistate model resulted in an increase in the expected number of active years for older men and women: from 9.3 years for men and 10.6 years for women to 11.3 to 13.0 years for men and 15.5 to 17.1 years for women. Although gender differences are relatively consistent, some qualifications are offered. For example, gender differences in living arrangements and institutionalization also may affect the results, recalling that institutionalization has been used as one indicator, together with functional decline and death, to assess "inactive life." Specifically, because of the gender differences in mortality, older women are more likely than older men to be widowed and later institutionalized because they have no caregiving spouse. Thus, higher male mortality could be the cause, in part, for what appears to be a greater functional decline among women. This and other explanations for gender differences in active life expectancy will be examined in more detail.

Race and Ethnicity

There is evidence that African-American elders have poorer active life expectancy than non-Hispanic white elders. Most notably, a recent study examined total and active life expectancy in a sample of 2219 blacks and

1838 whites who were 65 years of age or older in the Piedmont region of North Carolina—one of the sites for the Established Populations for Epidemiologic Studies of the Elderly (EPESE), described in Chapter 2 (Guralnik, La Croix, Abbott, Berkman, Satterfield, Evans, et al., 1993). In this disability or "inactivity" was defined as the inability to perform independently one or more basic ADL functional tasks such as walking, bathing, dressing, eating, and using the toilet. For subgroups defined by gender, race, and education, statistical models were used to estimate for persons at each age the probability of transition from not being disabled or being disabled at baseline to not being disabled, being disabled, or having died one year later. Multistate, increment–decrement life tables were used to generate estimates of total, active, and disabled life expectancy (with total life expectancy equal to active life expectancy plus disabled life expectancy). The results indicate an interesting race–education pattern for both men and women. Specifically, black men aged 65 and over had a lower total life expectancy (11.4 years) and active life expectancy (10 years) than white men (total life expectancy of 12.6 years and an active life expectancy of 11.2 years) (Guralnik, Land, Blazer, Fillenbaum, & Branch, 1993). In contrast, there was much less of a difference in either total or active life expectancy between black and white women. Interestingly, there was evidence of a cross-over at age 75 years and older. Black men and women aged 75 and older had higher values for total life expectancy and active life expectancy than whites, and the racial differences were larger after stratification for education. Overall, education had a stronger relation to total and active life expectancy than did race. At the age of 65, those with 12 or more years of education had an active life expectancy that was 2.4 to 3.9 years longer than the levels for those with less education. This educational difference was evidence for each race–gender group. Consistent with other studies, educational level may serve as a powerful social protective mechanism that delays the onset of health problems at older ages. The significance of education for health and functioning will remain one of the interesting and transcendent questions in this book.

Socioeconomic Status

Research in active life expectancy has shown consistently that those of lower socioeconomic status have poorer total and active life expectancy than those of higher socioeconomic status. In the initial 1983 paper, the results indicate that in each age group, active life expectancy was greater for the "nonpoor" than for the poor (Katz et al., 1983). The difference in favor of the nonpoor ranged from 2.4 additional years for those aged 65–69, to less than one additional year for those aged 75 or older. In this study, the nonpoor was defined as residents who did not receive old age assistance or supplementary security income and did not have medical expenses covered by Medicaid or other public-assistance programs. In contrast, "poor" was defined as including residents who received income from old age assistance or supplemental security income, or had medical expenses covered by Medicaid or other public-assistance programs. Subsequent studies also have identified the significance of socioeconomic status as measured by education in both black and white populations.

The measurement of active life expectancy serves, then, as an introduction to the discussion of physical functioning and activities of everyday life. We will now examine in more detail the standard functional measures. In addition to a consideration of the theory of health and functioning, we will address the specificity, timing, and level of functional assessment. This will require a consideration of at least two themes of research. First, we will examine the different types of functional assessments. Second, we will consider the process of disablement and, in particular, the natural history of functional limitations and disability. As part of this discussion, we will examine the epidemiology of disablement, including the biologic, behavioral, social, and environmental "causes" of functional limitations and disability.

MEASURES OF PHYSICAL FUNCTIONING AND ACTIVITIES OF EVERYDAY LIFE

As noted previously, functioning is defined as the relative ease in the performance of tasks that are necessary for independence and mobility in everyday life. Functioning ranges from individual, generic tasks, such as ease in lifting, to more complicated tasks associated with the performance of social roles. Unlike other public health statistics, such as the incidence of disease or mortality, the measurement of functioning is not limited to dichotomous classification. Instead, measures of functioning are more likely to be based on an ordinal, interval, or continuous scale, typically expressed as the level of difficulty in completing a particular task. Moreover, the level of functioning is generally variable and can decline or improve at different points in the life course. This has implications for the timing of assessment as well as the establishment of criteria for judging functional change. Although physicians and other health personnel make functional assessments of their patients, most functional assessments used in epidemiologic studies are based on the person's report of his or her own capacities and actions.

Measures of functioning represent an appreciation of the necessity, indeed, the reality of "being in the world." These measures are based on the premise, so clearly stated by the World Health Organization in 1946, that health is not simply the absence of disease. Rather, health represents the complete state of physical, psychological, and social well-being. Along these lines, functioning represents the intersection between the capacities of the individual and the population on the one hand and the resources and demands of the social and physical environments on the other hand. Functioning provides, therefore, a more comprehensive and complete picture of health and well-being. It is one of the few concepts shared by researchers and practitioners in the health sciences, clinical medicine, epidemiology, and health services. It also represents, as we shall discuss later, a concept that serves to link the health sciences with other disciplines, such as environmental design, architecture, and human factors research.

It is fair to say that there is a direct link between many functional measures in use today and two early measures that were developed to monitor the severity of the impact of specific acute health events and the timing and extent of recuperation following the onset of that acute event. These two measures are the Karnofsky Scale (Table 4–2) and the ADL Scale (Table 4–3).

The Karnofsky Scale

In 1948 the first issue of the journal *Cancer* included a report of the effect of a common chemotherapeutic agent on the course of lung cancer (Karnofsky, Abelmann, Craver, & Burchenal, 1948). In this article, the senior author, Karnofsky, introduced an index that would later bear his name. The Karnofsky index provided a ranking of overall health and functioning on a scale from 0 (death) to 100 (complete health and functioning) and was based on a clinician's assessment. Despite the large numbers of functional measures that are currently available (McDowell & Newell, 1996), the Karnofsky index continues to be used in clinical practice and is often used to assess overall functioning in clinical trials in oncology. Moreover, it is often used as a standard for the assessment of validity in the

---

Table 4-2 Karnofsky Scale

100	Able to work. Normal; no complaints; no evidence of disease.
90	Able to work. Able to carry on normal activity; minor symptoms.
80	Able to work. Normal activity with effort; some symptoms.
70	Independent; not able to work. Cares for self; unable to carry on normal activity.
60	Disabled; dependent. Requires occasional assistance; cares for most needs.
50	Moderately disabled; dependent. Requires considerable assistance and frequent care.
40	Severely disabled; dependent. Requires special care and assistance.
30	Severely disabled. Hospitalized, death not imminent.
20	Very sick. Active supportive treatment needed.
10	Moribund. Fatal processes are rapidly progressing.

Source: Karnofsky, D. A. et al. CA: Cancer Journal for Clinicians 1948; 634–656. Copyright Lippincott, Williams and Wilkins. Used with permission.

development of other scales. Although not specifically developed for use in studies of functioning in older populations, the Karnofsky index is one of the earliest measures to assess overall health and functioning.

Activities of Daily Living

As noted previously, ADL is one of the most common and widely accepted measures of functioning in gerontological studies (Katz et al., 1963). The ADL index assesses the extent to which the subject requires personal or technical assistance in basic tasks that are necessary for independence. Although there is some difference between versions of ADL, the tasks typically include bathing, dressing, toileting, transferring from a bed to a chair, continence, and feeding.

The items were originally derived from a theory of human development. Katz and colleagues demonstrated in a 1963 paper that the sequence of six basic activities of daily living from an acute health event (in this case, a stroke) was similar to that experienced by children as they develop. Measures of ADL are a standard component of comprehensive geriatric assessments in clinical and long-term care settings. As noted in Chapter 3, ADL has prognostic significance. In the general population, only a small percentage of people aged 65 and older cannot complete one or more ADL tasks. It is only at the age of 75 and older that the percentage of people with dependencies exceeds 5%. Moreover, in addition to increasing age, women and blacks are more likely to have difficulty with

Table 4–3 Activities of Daily Living

Activities Points (1 or 0)	Independence (1 POINT) No supervision, direction, or personal assistance.	Dependence (0 POINTS) With supervision, direc- tion, personal assistance, or total care.
Bathing Points: _____	(1 Point) Bathes self com- pletely or needs help in bathing only a single part of the body such as the back, genital area, or dis- abled extremity.	(0 Points) Needs help with bathing more than one part of the body and get- ting in or out of the tub or shower. Requires total bathing.
Dressing Points: _____	(1 Point) Gets clothes from closet and drawers and puts on clothes and outer garments complete with fasteners. May have help tying shoes.	(0 Points) Needs help with dressing self or needs to be completely dressed.
Toileting Points: _____	(1 Point) Goes to toilet, gets on and off, arranges clothes, cleans genital area without help.	(0 Points) Needs help transferring to the toilet and cleaning self, or uses bedpan or commode.
Transferring Points: _____	(1 Point) Moves in and out of bed or chair unassisted. Mechanical transferring aids are acceptable.	(0 Points) Needs help in moving from bed to chair or requires complete transfer.
Continence Points: _____	(1 Point) Exercises com- plete self-control over uri- nation and defecation.	(0 Points) Is partially or totally incontinent of bowel and bladder.
Feeding Points: _____	(1 Point) Gets food from plate into mouth without help. Preparation of food may be done by another person.	(0 Points) Needs partial or total help with feeding or requires parenteral feeding.

Source: Katz et al., 1963.

ADL tasks. Results from the baseline EPESE study indicate that assistance is most often needed for walking or bathing and least often needed for grooming or eating. This pattern is similar to the hierarchy of activities first observed in the development of the original Index of Activities of Daily Living, in which patients recovering from disability usually regained independence in feeding and continence first, then recovery in transferring and toileting, and finally, recovery of dressing and bathing (Cornoni-Huntley, Brock, Taylor, & Wallace, 1986).

Instrumental Activities of Daily Living

Although ADL represent a critical set of tasks that are necessary for independent living, there are other types and levels of functioning that assess adaptation to the environment—so-called higher levels of functioning. It is obvious that there is tremendous variability in functioning among the large numbers of people who are independent in ADL tasks. Powell Lawton and Elaine Brody (1969) contributed significantly to the assessment of the level of functioning among those people by introducing the measure of IADL. While ADL was designed to assess independence in areas of self-maintenance, IADL assesses ease in adaptation to the environment. As shown in Table 4–4, the Lawton-Brody IADL scale often includes all or a subset of the following nine items:

- Housekeeping
- Home maintenance
- Telephone use
- Shopping
- Food preparation
- Laundering
- Use of transportation
- Use of medicine
- Financial management

Levels of IADL functioning depend on whether the person performs the task, and, if so, the level of difficulty the person reports in the completion of that task. It is important to realize that, as complex tasks, IADL include a number of different capacities, such as physical and cognitive abilities, as well as access to personal and social resources. Since some of the tasks are sex linked, there is also concern that some people may report not performing the tasks because they are not expected to perform the task, not because they are unable. Some researchers have attempted to avoid this problem by asking subjects who report not performing the task whether they *could* perform it if they were required to do so (Satariano, Ragheb, Branch, & Swanson, 1990). It is not surprising that one early paper characterized IADL limitations as a "social disability" (Branch & Jette, 1981). As a social function, Branch and Jette made a distinction between a met need for assistance in performing a particular task and an unmet need for assistance to do so. They reasoned that a need for assistance implies a situation in which the individual is not self-sufficient in

Table 4–4 Instrumental Activities of Daily Living

Patient's Name: _____   Date: _____

I = Independent   A = Assistance Required   D = Dependent

Obtained from Patient	Obtained from Informant	Activity	Guidelines for Assessment
I	I		I = Able to look up numbers, dial, receive and make calls without help
A	A	Using telephone	A = Unable to use telephone
D	D		D = Able to answer phone or dial operator in an emergency but needs special phone or help in getting number, dialing
I	I		I = Able to drive own car or travel alone on buses, taxis
A	A	Traveling	A = Able to travel but needs someone to travel with
D	D		D = Unable to travel
I	I		I = Able to take care of all food/clothes
A	A	Shopping	A = Able to shop but needs someone to shop with
D	D		D = Unable to shop
I	I		I = Able to plan and cook full meals
A	A	Preparing meals	A = Able to prepare light foods but unable to cook full meals alone
D	D		D = Unable to do any housework
I	I		I = Able to do heavy housework, e.g., scrub floors
A	A	Housework	A = Able to do light housework but needs help with heavy tasks
D	D		D = Unable to do any housework
I	I		I = Able to prepare/take medications in the right dose at the right time
A	A	Taking medicine	A = Able to take medications, but needs reminding or someone to prepare them
D	D		D = Unable to take medications
I	I		I = Able to manage buying needs, e.g., write checks, pay bills
A	A	Managing money	A = Able to manage daily buying needs but needs help managing checkbook, paying bills
D	D		D = Unable to handle money

Source: Lawton, M. P., Brody, E. M. Assessment of older people: self-maintaining and instrumental activities of daily living. *Gerontologist* 1969, 9:179–180. Copyright The Gerontological Society of America. Reproduced by permission of the publisher.

performing an activity. If the person is not self-sufficient, then he or she is faced with locating the necessary support or assistance, or failing that, remaining with an unmet need. For those who find the support, whether it comes formally or informally, the unmet need no longer exists. On the other hand, if support cannot be located, then the unmet need remains. As Branch and Jette (1981, p. 203) write, "This is the person whose quality of life or independence is in immediate jeopardy, one who is socially disabled, one who might be frail or vulnerable." This important distinction between "met" and "unmet" needs also illustrates how the study of functioning may serve to link research in epidemiology with research and practice in health services and public health interventions.

Not surprisingly, the prevalence of limitation or difficulty in the performance of IADL tasks is considerably greater than that reported for ADL tasks. For example, research from the Framingham Disability Study indicates that 19% of the women aged 55 to 64 had a potential or actual problem with transportation, compared with only 1% of women of the same age who were unable to bathe independently (Branch & Jette, 1981; Jette & Branch, 1981).

ADL/IADL Scale

In an effort to develop a more comprehensive functional assessment tool, Spector and colleagues (1987) combined ADL and IADL scales into a single instrument. This work followed from earlier reports that there was a hierarchical relationship between the items in the two scales. The Guttman scale that was developed included the following categories: independent in IADL and ADL, dependent in IADL only, and dependent in IADL and ADL (see Table 4–5). The ordering of the categories is based on the assumption, which was confirmed in the analysis conducted by Spector and his colleagues, that because ADL represents a more basic generic form of functioning, those with ADL limitations also would be

---

Table 4–5 The IADL–ADL Hierarchy

· Independent in IADL and ADL
· Dependent in only IADL
· Dependent in IADL and ADL

Source: Adapted from Spector, W. D., Katz, S., Murphy, J. B., Fulton, J. P. (1987). The hierarchical relationship between activities of daily living and instrumental activities of daily living. *Journal of Chronic Diseases, 40*(6), pp. 481–489.

limited in IADL functioning, but not vice versa. In addition to meeting the criteria for an ordered Guttman scale, the measure also was shown to predict subsequent functional decline, hospitalization, and death.

Physical Functioning

A third set of measures was developed to capture generic tasks associated with daily functioning. In many ways, these are the underlying tasks that make ADL and IADL possible. There are two common sets of questions. First, Rosow and Breslau (1966) proposed two questions that assess cognition, balance, and lower-body strength. Respondents are asked to report (1) whether they are able to walk up and down stairs without help, and (2) whether they are able to walk half a mile (the equivalent of a city block) without help. As is true of most measures of function, the percentages of people who report an inability to complete those tasks increases with age and is greater for women than men. Second, another common set of functional questions asks subjects to report their level of difficulty in completing a set of 10 tasks, with the levels of difficulty labeled as "No difficulty," "A little difficulty," "Some difficulty," and "A lot of difficulty" (Nagi, 1976). These tasks, initially identified by Nagi, are associated with upper- and lower-body strength, balance, and fine dexterity (see Table 4–6). In some cases, the Nagi and Rosow and Breslau items have been combined into a single instrument (Satariano et al., 1990). In this case, the two Rosow and Breslau (1966) questions were rephrased to match the Nagi format for the level of reported difficulty.

THE DISABLEMENT PROCESS

The disablement process described in Chapter 2 characterizes (a) the phased transition from pathology to impairment to functional limitation to disability; and (b) the multilevel factors (from the biologic to the behavioral to the social to the environmental) that affect the extent and timing of that transition from pathology to disability. As defined originally by Verbrugge and Jette (1994), pathology refers to biochemical and physiologic abnormalities that are detected and medically labeled as disease, injury, or congenital or developmental conditions. Impairments are dysfunctions and significant structural abnormalities in specific body systems. Functional limitations are restrictions in performing fundamental physical and mental actions used in daily life by one's age–sex group. Finally, disability, a social concept, refers to the difficulty people experi-

Table 4–6 Standard Physical Functioning Items

A subject is asked to report the level of difficulty he or she has experienced in performing each of the following tasks during the past month (a lot, some, a little, or none). If the subject reports that he or she has performed the task, the reason is requested (not able to perform, never perform the task, or do not perform the task on doctor's orders).

1. Pushing objects such as a living room chair
2. Stooping, crouching, or kneeling
3. Getting up from stooping, crouching, or kneeling position
4. Lifting or carrying items under 10 pounds, such as a bag of potatoes
5. Lifting or carrying items over 10 pounds, such as a bag of groceries
6. Reaching or extending your right arm above your shoulder
7. Reaching or extending your left arm above your shoulder
8. Writing or handling small objects
9. Standing in place for 15 minutes or longer
10. Standing for long periods, about 1 hour
11. Standing up after sitting in a chair
12. Getting up or down a flight of stairs
13. Walking two to three neighborhood blocks

Items 01, 02, 04, 05, 09, 10 are obtained from Rosow and Breslau (1969).
Items 12, 13 are obtained from Nagi (1976).
Items 06, 07 were adapted from Nagi (1976).
Items 03, 08, 11 were developed from Tager et al. (1998).

ence as they engage in activities in any domain of life (the domains typical for one's age–sex group) due to a health or physical problem. Put differently, disability reflects the inability to meet the expectations of a particular social role because of reduced physiological capacity associated with a health or physical problem.

The process from pathology to disability is not fixed, and depends on a variety of factors associated with physiologic competence and reserves, the severity of medical conditions, individual resiliency, social connections, and characteristics of the natural and built environments. Just as epidemiology is designed to identify and explain the patterns of health outcomes, the disablement process identifies the range of factors that describe and explain the patterns of disability.

The disablement process was introduced in Chapter 2 as an example of an ecological approach to describe and explain the epidemiology of disability. The model is reintroduced here to highlight the strengths and limitations of research in this area. As the disablement model increasingly became a common frame of reference, it prompted a consideration of some fundamental conceptual and measurement issues associated with aging, health, and functioning. These issues include the measurement of functional limitation and disability and the assessment and measurement of the pathway from disease to disability.

MEASUREMENT OF FUNCTIONAL LIMITATIONS AND DISABILITY

Although there is general agreement that the study of physical functioning is important and has served to expand our understanding of aging, health, and longevity, there are concerns that the measurement of functioning is not sufficiently precise or physiologically meaningful. Physical performance measures were originally introduced to improve that precision (Guralnik, Branch, Cummings, & Curb, 1989). Specifically, these measures were designed to capture a person's ability to complete specific tasks under test circumstances. Unlike the ADL, IADL, and physical functional measures that were described previously, the physical performance measures do not include the subject's assessment of his or her level of dependency or difficulty. Instead, subjects are asked to perform specific tasks in a test situation. Level of performance is typically assessed in terms of whether the tasks are completed and, more important, how long it took to complete the tasks. Most tests are time dependent. Although an ordinal level of measurement is often used for the self-reported measures, continuous levels of measurement are often used for the performance measure (e.g., seconds to complete the task, and pounds of pressure of grip strength reported by a hand dynamometer). Although physical performance measures were initially developed for clinical or laboratory-based studies, many have been adapted for administration in a home setting, making them well suited for incorporation in field-based epidemiology studies (see Table 4–7). This is yet another example of Wallace's observation that the epidemiology of aging developed in clinical settings and laboratories and later was applied to samples of seniors in communities.

The strengths and limitations of physical performance measures have been reported (Guralnik et al., 1989). The strengths of these measures include greater face validity for the tasks being evaluated; better reproducibility; greater sensitivity to change; influenced less by poor cognitive functioning (i.e., the need to consider the question and respond verbally); and finally, these measures are influenced less by culture, language, and education. This has been highlighted as a strategy to facilitate the development of international and cross-cultural studies in the epidemiology of

Table 4–7 Examples of Physical Performance Measures

Name	Description
Water jug test	A measure of upper-extremity strength. From a seated position, subjec\t is asked to lift a 1-gallon plastic jug filled with water in sequence from lap to mid-chest level, to eye level, and then overhead.
Chair stand	A measure of lower-body strength. From a seated position with arms folded across chest, the subject is asked to stand and then sit in sequence until told to stop. The interviewer records the time required to complete 5 maneuvers.
Standing test	A measure of leg strength and balance. From a standing position with the feet placed at a comfortable distance, the subject is asked first to assume a semitandem position with the toes of one foot placed midway along the side of the other foot. If this position is achieved for 10 seconds, the subject is then asked to place the toes of one foot at the heel of the other foot. Finally, if that position is achieved for 10 seconds, the subject is then asked to stand on one leg with the other leg elevated and bent at the knee. Again, the interviewer records whether the subject can assume this position for 10 seconds.
360-degree turn	A measure of leg strength and balance. From a standing position with the feet placed at a comfortable distance, the subject is asked to step to either the left or right and make a complete rotation. The interviewer records the number of steps the subject takes to make the rotation.
Reaching down test	A measure of lower-body strength and balance. The subject is asked to assume a standing position with the feet placed at a comfortable distance. The interviewer places a pencil on the floor in front of the subject. From the standing position, the subject is asked to stoop, retrieve the pencil, and then return to a standing position, without holding on to any other object, such as a chair or table. The interviewer records the time needed to perform the maneuver.
Walking test	The interviewer extends a 10-foot length of rope on the floor. The subject is asked to begin at one end of the rope, and then at a normal pace, walk the length of rope, turn, and return. The subject is asked to continue this maneuver until told to stop. After 60 seconds, the interviewer records the number of lengths that have been walked during the period. Later, these data are summarized as number of feet traveled per second.

Source: Adapted from Tager et al., 2001.

aging. Potential difficulties include concern that the use of performance measures may be more time consuming; require adequate space and special equipment; require special training; require modification of standard home surveys; and increase the likelihood that subjects and/or interviewers may be injured. There is also concern that simple ·performance tests may not reflect execution of complex tasks or capture how people adapt to challenges in everyday life. With regard to adaptation, performance tests may not capture the "compensatory strategies" that people may use to adapt to their environments in the face of functional limitations. These compensatory strategies, which some consider to be a marker of "successful" or "healthy" aging, may take the form of modifications of behavior and alterations in the physical environment, such as installation of grab bars in the bathroom. There is also concern that there has been a proliferation in the number and variety of performance tests without due consideration given to conceptual overlap and more important, without a clear understanding of what, in fact, is being measured.

Physical performance measures were initially recommended by a number of commentators as representing a more precise and objective way of assessing physical functioning than could be obtained by self-reports (Guralnik et al., 1989). Today, there is a growing consensus that measures of physical performance may capture something different than is captured by the subject's reports. Specifically, whereas reports of difficulty in functioning, such as lifting 10 pounds, may assess functional limitations, measures of physical performance, such as grip strength, may assess functional capacity under test circumstances. Moreover, performance measures may assess a state that is logically prior to reports of the relative ease in functioning of generic tasks and social roles in everyday life. One study indicated that baseline performance measures predicted subsequent levels of limitations and disability among seniors who reported no limitations or disabilities at baseline. Specifically, lower scores on a baseline performance were associated with a statistically significant, graduated increase in the frequency of disability in ADL and reported mobility-related disability at follow-up among older people who were not disabled at baseline. After adjustment for age, sex, and the presence of chronic disease, those with the lowest scores on the performance tests were 4.2 to 4.9 times as likely to have disability at four years as those with the highest performance scores (Fried, Bandeen-Roche, Chaves, & Johnson, 2000). The authors conclude that measures of physical performance may identify older persons with a "preclinical stage of disability" who may benefit from interventions to prevent the development of frank disability. In general, these and other results suggest that performance measures may help elucidate the disablement process. Most performance measures are thought to assess possible impairments.

The disablement model also has assisted in the refinement of the self-reported measures. Although the model specifies a conceptual distinction between functional limitations and disabilities, the measurement of the concepts was ambiguous and often overlapped. For example, in some cases, the Nagi items (such as reports of difficulty in the performance of tasks, e.g., lifting items over 10 lbs) were considered to be a functional limitation and, in other cases, a disability. As of late, there have been calls for standard strategies of distinguishing and measuring the two components. Since the Nagi items typically assess generic characteristics of upper- and lower-body strength, balance, and fine dexterity, they are used to assess functional limitations. On the other hand, since ADL, IADL, and the Rosow-Breslau items (climbing stairs and walking a city block) more closely assess living in the world and fulfilling a social role, they are used to assess disability. Other areas noted by Jette (2003) that can be used to measure the extent and type of disability include paid and unpaid role activities (e.g., occupation, parenting, grandparenting); social activities (e.g., attending church and other group activities, socializing with friends and relatives); and leisure activities (e.g., sports and physical recreation, reading, and distant travel).

Despite the utility of the functional measures that have been used to assess possible functional limitations and disabilities, there is concern that the current measures are not sufficiently comprehensive and do not fully capture the range of social activities in everyday life. Recent evidence indicates that this is especially problematic for measures of social roles, thus limiting the ability to assess potential disabilities. Based on a review of 31 studies of physical activities and function in older populations, Keysor and Jette (2001) concluded that late-life exercise interventions improved strength, aerobic capacity, flexibility, walking, and standing balance. In contrast, of the few studies that focused on physical, social, emotional, or overall disability, few improvements were noted. Possible reasons for this finding include variations in sample size, differences in the type and length of the exercise intervention, inadequate sample size and power, and, most notably, shortcomings with the measures of disability used by the investigators. In addition to including a broader range of role functions, it also is recommended that new measures must take into account a person's interaction with the environment. It is necessary to recall that social and physical environmental resources and demands help to distinguish between functional limitations on the one hand and disabilities on the other. Two people may have the same level of functional limitations, e.g., reduced lower-body strength. One person, living in a one-story home, may be able to meet all of his or her everyday responsibilities, e.g., cooking, cleaning, and dressing, and is not disabled. However, another person with the same level of functional limitation, but living in a two-story home, may not be able to complete all of his or her daily activities, because to do so would require walking upstairs, a task that is no longer possible. Accordingly, Keysor and Jette (2001, p. 418) write:

> Perhaps in addressing disability we need to target directly the person-environment interaction. Therefore, more research is needed to examine the mediating and moderating role of beliefs, emotions, coping strategies, and physical and social environments so that we can develop and evaluate interventions to enhance behaviors and reduce late-life disability.

There have been recent attempts to expand both the number and diversity of items to capture a more comprehensive set of measures that can be used to assess possible functional limitations and disabilities. Jette and colleagues (2002) developed the Late-life Function and Disability Instrument to provide an expanded set of items around three functional dimensions: (1) basic lower-extremity function, (2) advanced lower-extremity function, and (3) upper-extremity function (see Table 4–8).

Later, Jette (2003) used these functional items to expand the set of items to capture higher levels of role function so that potential disabilities could be assessed more precisely. Jette and colleagues (2002, p. 123) identified 16 items that reflected everyday activities, including personal maintenance, travel in one's environment, exchange of information, social activities, home life, paid or volunteer work, and involvement in economic activities and in community and civic activities. Factor analysis indicated that the 16 items included four distinct factors: social roles, personal role, instrumental role, and management role.

Self-reports also have been used to better understand "preclinical disability." As noted previously, physical performance items have been used to illustrate that it may be possible to identify a subset of people who report no difficulty in function (either in generic tasks or in completing higher-level role functions), but have difficulty in the performance of a

Table 4–8 Late-Life Function and Disability Instrument: Functional Component by Area of Function

Basic Lower-Extremity Function	Advanced Lower-Extremity Function	Upper-Extremity Function
Walk around one floor of home.	Hike a few miles, including hills.	Remove wrapping with hands only.
Pick up a kitchen chair.	Carry something while climbing stairs.	Unscrew lid without assistive device.
Get into and out of a car.	Walk a brisk mile.	Pour from a large pitcher.
Reach overhead while standing.	Go up and down one flight, no rails.	Hold full pitcher in one hand.
Wash dishes while standing.	Walk one mile with rests.	Put on and take off pants.
Step up and down from a curb.	Walk on a slippery surface.	Reach back.
Put on and take off coat.	Go up and down three flights indoors.	Use common utensils.
Open heavy outside door.	Walk several blocks.	
Get on and off bus.	Run one-half mile.	
Make bed.	Get up from floor.	
Bend over from standing position.		
Go up and down a flight of stairs.		
Move on and off a step stool.		
Stand up from a low, soft couch.		

Source: Reprinted from Guralnik, J. M., and Ferrucci, L. (2003). Assessing the building blocks of function: Utilizing measures of functional limitation. *American Journal of Preventive Medicine, 25, 35ii*, 112–121, Copyright (2003) with permission from the American Journal of Preventive Medicine.

test-based task, such as having reduced hand grip strength. Fried and colleagues (1996) also developed a set of questions that help to identify people who may be at risk for subsequent limitations or disabilities. Even though people may report that they can complete a task without difficulty, those who also report that they now complete the task in a different way, including doing it more slowly, are more likely than those who do not report a change in how the task is performed to be subsequently limited or disabled. In a separate study, Avlund and colleagues (2003) determined that seniors aged 75 and 80 years who reported fatigue in completing daily tasks were more likely than those of the same age who did not report fatigue to demonstrate a greater level of subsequent functional decline.

The disablement model is also important because it emphasizes that the process of disablement is the result of a series of transitions and changes from pathology to impairment to limitation, and, finally, to disability. As noted previously, the extent and timing of those transitions depend on a variety of factors. In addition to biologic, behavioral, and environmental factors, the extent and timing of transition also depend on errors in reporting and measurement. Quantitative estimates of the reliability (reproducibility) of measures of function are necessary for the assessment of functional changes over time. Large random errors in tests of function, on average, will lead either to underestimation of the magnitude of change or to the complete obscuring of the occurrence of changes in function with age and disability or lead to the obscuring of improvements with targeted interventions. The reliability both of self-reported physical function and direct measures of physical performance has been examined in several epidemiological studies. In two of the studies, a 2- to 3-week interval between test and retest was used. Pearson correlations ranged from .58 to .73 for a modified ADL index, a Rosow-Breslau index, and a Nagi index (Smith, Branch, Scheer, Wetle, & Evans, 1990). For direct measures of physical performance (balance, chair stand, time for a fast walk, writing a signature), Pearson correlations between .61 and .91 have been reported (Seeman, Charpentiar, & Berkman, 1994). However, the use of a 2- to 3-week interval limits the interpretation of these results, as "real" acute changes in the status of these elderly subjects could have occurred, and this possibility is not specifically addressed in these studies.

More recent evaluation studies have used shorter time intervals and more appropriate measures to assess test–retest reliability. In the Sonoma, California, Study of Physical Performance and Age-Related Changes in Sonomans (SPPARCS) project, a sample of 199 elderly subjects was assessed twice over a 48-hour period (Tager, Swanson, & Satariano, 1998). Items included measures of physical performance and self-reported physical function. There was a high level of agreement for the self-reported functional items. While these seem to be reliable measures, the positive results seem to be due in part to the fact that most subjects reported no difficulty for the particular tasks. Although there was reasonable agreement for the performance measures, there is clear evidence of a practice effect, i.e., there was an improvement in performance over the 48-hour period. The importance of practice effects has not been given sufficient attention in studies published to date. Although direct measures hold the promise of providing more detailed and complete assessments of functioning and performance, the data from the Sonoma study indicate that the measures may be less reliable than previously thought. As a result, the sample sizes that may be needed by such studies to detect change over time may have been underestimated, given the apparent underestimation of the imprecision of these measures. It was recommended that future research should evaluate the utility and feasibility of completing multiple replicates of tests at the same visit to provide more stable estimates of performance, as was done in the Sonoma study for grip strength and reaching down. To assess the reliability of measures in the Women's Health and Aging Study, Mendes de Leon and colleagues (2002) recruited a sample of women from the main study to be interviewed and assessed daily over a 2-week period. This "nested study" provided an ideal opportunity to assess reliability over an extended period and, more important, provided an opportunity to more precisely assess the possibility of a test effect. In fact, more for measures of performance, it was demonstrated that, like the SPPARCS assessment of reliability, there was evidence of an improvement or practice effect between the first and second assessments. However, the third assessment showed a return to the general level of the first assessment and subsequent consistency after that. It is fair to conclude, therefore, that the standard measures—both self-report and direct assessment—satisfy the general requirements of reliability.

There is a growing body of research that indicates that the timing and nature of transitions from impairments, functional limitations, and disability are quite variable. For example, there is evidence of a particular sequence of decline in basic ADL (Jagger, Arthur, Spiers, & Clarke, 2001). Based on data from the UK, the order of activity restriction was bathing, mobility, toileting, dressing, transfers from bed and chair, and feeding. There is also evidence of a particular sequence of decline among discrete measures of physical performance. For example, Onder and colleagues (2002), using data from the Women's Health and Aging Study, report that in moderately to severely disabled women aged 65 or older, lower-extremity measures show more change over three years than upper-extremity measures. There is also evidence that the transitions from impairments to disability are not unidirectional. There may be instances in which older people are limited, but then recuperate, only to become limited and disabled later.

In addition to conceptual distinctions between functional limitations and disabilities, attention also has been directed to the development of more meaningful summary measures of severity. Although there are standard items for self-reported functional assessment, reported levels of difficulty have been measured and summarized in a variety of ways, and there is no generally agreed upon standard summary protocol. This makes comparisons across studies difficult. In the SPPARCS study, a comparison was made among different strategies for summarizing and scoring key Nagi and Rosow-Breslau self-reported items (Tager, Haight, Hollenberg, & Satariano, 2003). The comparison was based on how well each scoring scheme predicted mortality among the 1246 female participants aged 55 and older in the study. Thus, all-cause and cardiovascular mortality were used as the gold standards for assessment of the different scoring methods. In light of the argument that measures of function provide an opportunity to move beyond simple mortality and duration of life to learn more about quality of life, it may seem curious then to use mortality as a standard to assess the severity of function. However, mortality is important; it is associated with prior levels of function, and there are very few other standards available.

In the Tager study, three summary measures were developed. Each measure was based on a different scoring configuration of energy equivalence and level of difficult. Because the functional items were derived from Nagi and Rosow and Breslau, the summary measures were identified as NRB 1, NRB 2, and NRB 3. NRB 1 is based on the most detailed information and NRB 3 on the least. NRB 1 included information on the average energy equivalent associated with a task and multilevel scoring of self-reported difficulty. Following research on physical activity, a metabolic equivalent table (MET) value was used for each of the five NRB tasks. The total MET value for the sum of the five items was 25 METs. A separate value for level of difficulty was assigned (Table 4–9). These values ranged from 0.0 for a lot/unable to 1.0 for no difficulty. For NRB 2, differences in levels of energy equivalents were not included. The difficulty score for each item was calculated as it was for NRB 1, and the final NRB 2 score was based on the sum of the total difficulty scores. The final score was rescaled to range from 0 to 1. NRB 3 was the simplest summary measure of physical functioning. As with NRB 2, the item/energy values were held constant. Unlike NRB 1 and NRB 2, the difficulty items were dichotomized: 1 = no/little, and 0 = all other levels of difficulty/nonperformance. The final score ranged from 0 to 5 and was rescaled to a 0 to 1 scale to facilitate comparison with the other two scores.

The results indicate that both NRB 1 and 2 were associated with all-cause and cardiovascular mortality assessed over a 6.5 year period. No consistent association was shown for NRB 3. Since there was no signifi-

Table 4–9 Details of Formulation of NRB Scores

Question Item	MET Value Assigned	Ainsworth Codes	Fraction of 25 MET
Walking stairs	8.0	17130 *(up)*	0.32
Walking city blocks	2.5	17070 *(down)*	0.10
Lifting > 10 lb	6.0	17170	0.20
Lifting < 10 lb	3.5	17027	0.14
Pushing heavy object	6.0	17020	0.24
		05120	
Total	25		1.00

The final score was calculated as follows: $\sum_1^s w_i f_i$

Source: Reprinted from Tager, I. B., Haight, T. J., Hollenberg, M., & Satariano, W. A. (2003). Physical functioning and mortality in older women: Assessment of energy costs and level of difficulty. *Journal of Clinical Epidemiology 56*(8), 807–813, Copyright (2003), with permission from Elsevier.

cant difference between NRB 1 and 2, it was concluded that the additional information about energy expenditure did not improve prediction beyond that obtained for interval scale for level of difficulty. However, the researchers qualify that conclusion by noting that "Pooling of the actual data from a large number of population-based studies would provide for a more precise determination of whether weighting by energy equivalents provides additional information for the classification of self-reported physical functioning" (Tager et al., 2003, p. 812).

To summarize, the disablement model has contributed significantly to a better understanding of the process of disablement from pathology to disability. This has resulted in a better understanding of the physiologic basis and measurement of the key variables. In the next section, we will address the epidemiology of physical functioning and the extent to which patterns of aging, functioning, and disability are caused by the interplay of biologic, behavioral, social, and environmental factors over the life course.

DEMOGRAPHIC PATTERNS

Age

There is agreement that chronological age is strongly associated with functional status (Berkman, Seeman, Albert, Blazer, Kahn, Mohs, et al., 1993; Fried & Guralnik, 1997). Although there is a general decline in overall functional status with increasing age, there is considerable variation in the level of function and the timing of decline among older people of the same age (Beckett, Brock, Lemke, et al., 1996). Some older people fare better than others. Not surprisingly, the level of age-related decline varies by the type of function. For example, activities such as pushing heavy objects (coordination of upper- and lower-body strength) are more likely to be difficult than activities that involve extending one's arms above shoulder level (Cornoni-Huntley et al., 1986). Among white male residents of New Haven, Connecticut aged 85 and older, 17.2% reported that they were unable to move large objects or did so with a lot of difficulty, compared to only 8% who reported the same level of difficulty in extending arms above shoulder level.

Gender

Women are more likely than men to report lower levels of functional status, a finding in keeping with reports of poorer overall health (Fried & Guralnik, 1997). Interestingly, with the exception of measures of upper-body strength, such as measures of grip strength, there is less difference between older men and women in the performance of other types of tasks (Simonsick, Kasper, Guralnik, Bandeen-Roche, Ferrucci, Hirst, et al., 2001). Based on data from the EPESE project, there is evidence that within age group, women are more likely to have difficulty with upper-body tasks (Cornoni-Huntley et al., 1986). For example, 24% of white female residents of New Haven, Connecticut, reported that they were unable to move heavy objects or did so with a lot of difficulty, compared to 12.1% who reported the same level of difficulty with extending arms above shoulder level.

Race and Ethnicity

Most of the racial and ethnic differences in functioning reported for the United States are based on differences between African-American and non-Hispanic white populations (Hummer, Benjamins, & Rogers, 2004). For each functional outcome, African-American elders are more likely than non-Hispanic white elders to report dependency in ADL, dependency or difficulty with IADL, and greater difficulty with generic physical functional tasks (Hummer et al., 2004; Mendes de Leon, Fillenbaum, Williams, Brock, Beckett, & Berkman, 1995).

Less comprehensive comparisons are available for other racial and ethnic groups. There are recent data, however, that suggest that among men, African-American elders, together with Native Americans, are more likely to demonstrate greater limitations in daily activities than non-Hispanic whites, Hispanic whites, and Asian and Pacific Islanders (Hummer et al., 2004). Among females, the same general racial/ethnic pattern is apparent, although the overall prevalence of activity limitations is greater for women ages 80 to 84 (Hummer et al., 2004). These findings are important for several reasons. First, the results demonstrate that racial and ethnic differences in activity limitation vary by age and gender. Second, there are limited national data on the diversity of racial and ethnic groups in the United States. The categories of "Hispanic white" and "Asian Pacific Islander" are very diverse. It is not possible from most national studies to examine the variation in aging, health, and functioning that exists among Hispanic and Asian Pacific Islander groups. As noted previously, there is the Hispanic EPESE study that includes Mexican-American seniors. The results from that study are quite interesting. Summarizing results from Markides, Rudkin, Angel, & Espino (1997), Hummer and colleagues (2004, p. 74) report the following:

> Interestingly, Mexican Americans are characterized by their most favorable level of activity limitations compared to non-Hispanic whites ages 20 to 24, when their mortality rates are highest compared to non-Hispanic whites. At ages 60 to 64 and 70 to 74, reports of activity limitations are modestly higher among Mexican-American compared to non-Hispanic whites.

With the exception of Japanese-American elders in the Honolulu Aging Study, there is very little information about Asian-American elders, especially Chinese-American seniors, the largest group of US residents of Asian descent. With this in mind, there is no significant difference in the level of functioning between non-Hispanic whites and that reported for Japanese-Americans in the Honolulu Aging Study.

Levels of functional status among elderly groups also differ by geographic region. Regional differences in levels of functional dependency and difficulty are evident in reports of national data in the United States. In general, elders in the Southeast are more likely than elders in other regions of the country to report greater functional dependency and difficulty; in general, these results parallel regional differences in mortality in the United States. It is not clear, of course, to what extent these regional differences are due to the demographic and social characteristics of the seniors who reside in those areas and to what extent they are due to other aspects of the social and physical environments (for example, constructed or built environments) of those areas. This represents one of the important topics in the epidemiology of aging and will be discussed in more detail later in the chapter.

SOCIOECONOMIC STATUS

At this point, it will be useful to step back from a consideration of age-related patterns of health and functioning and examine the broader socioeconomic and behavioral context. This is in keeping with the disablement model and its basic premise that the extent and severity of the effects of health and physiological factors on impairments, limitations, and disabilities are affected by the broader socioeconomic, behavioral, and environmental context (Verbrugge & Jette, 1994). It is also in keeping, as noted previously, with the basic approach in public health to report the broad demographic and social patterns in the population. The next task is to attempt to explain the reasons for those patterns. That, in turn, leads to a consideration of other variables that may figure in the pathways from pathology to disability.

There is evidence that socioeconomic status is associated with functional limitations and disability (Seeman et al., 1994). Those of lower socioeconomic status are more likely than others to be associated with increased limitations and a greater risk of disability. There are a variety of hypothesized reasons for this pattern. Older people of lower socioeconomic status may be more likely than others to develop specific chronic conditions, to be diagnosed with more severe cases of those conditions, and to receive less adequate care, which may lead, in turn, to a more difficult course. Socioeconomic status, in turn, may be associated with other factors that affect level of functioning and disability. These factors include living arrangements, social networks, and social support; health behaviors; psychosocial factors, such as self-efficacy; and characteristics of the physical and built environments.

PHYSICAL ENVIRONMENT

The resources and demands of the physical and built environments also may affect the level of functional limitations and, in particular, the level of disability. There is evidence that characteristics of the physical environment and, more specifically, characteristics of neighborhoods, defined in a variety of ways, are associated with different health behaviors. For example, research from the Alameda County Study indicated that residence in an impoverished area was associated with a significant decline in levels of physical activity, after adjustment for other factors, including individual income, education, smoking status, body mass index, and alcohol consumption (Yen & Kaplan, 1999). In a separate study of neighborhood environments in Alameda County, residents aged 55 and over who reported specific problems in their neighborhoods (e.g., traffic, noise, crime, trash and litter, poor street lighting, and transportation difficulties) were more likely than others to report loss of lower-extremity function (Balfour & Kaplan, 2002). There is also evidence from environmental audits that indicate that people who reside in areas that are characterized as single use, low-density housing are less likely to walk and engage in other outdoor activities (Frank, Engle, & Schmid, 2003). In addition to restricting the health and functional benefits from physical activity, a problematic environment may restrict access to goods and services and reduce contacts with friends and relatives.

SOCIAL CAPITAL

Measures of social capital (norms of reciprocity and civic trust) and behaviors (participation) were shown to be associated with self-reported overall health, depression, and functional limitations in a comparative study between the United States and Germany (Pollack & von dem Knesebeck, 2004). To my knowledge, there are no other studies that have examined the association between social capital and physical functioning in older populations. It is reasonable to hypothesize that such a relationship exists. For example, there are reports of associations between feelings of safety in a neighborhood (an indicator of social capital) and the likelihood that a person will walk in that area. Walking, in turn, has been associated with the maintenance of physical functioning.

LIVING ARRANGEMENTS, SOCIAL NETWORKS, AND SOCIAL SUPPORT

Living arrangements, or the number and types of people that share a common residence, have been shown to be associated with levels of functioning and disability. There is evidence, for example, that those who are separated and divorced are more likely to experience functional limitations and disabilities. In a study of seniors in Baltimore, Maryland, the association between living arrangement and change in IADL depended on the level of physical impairment (Sarwari, Fredman, Langenberg, & Magaziner, 1998). Among women without severe impairment, IADL deterioration was significantly less for those living alone compared with those living with spouses or nonspouse others. For women with severe impairment, however, those living alone had a greater decline in IADL, especially when compared with those living with nonspouse others. There is also evidence that married couples who live alone or with children have the highest levels of functioning (Waite & Hughes, 1999). In contrast, single adults who live with others (not a spouse) are more likely to have functional difficulties. Often this type of living arrangement, e.g., living with an adult child, represents a middle step in the transition from living independently, either with a spouse or alone, to residence in a long-term care facility. Indeed, the health consequences of relocation among the aged are associated with the type of housing environment and whether the older person voluntarily makes the move (Ferraro, 1983). Looking beyond the household, older people with a stronger web of social relations with others and a greater number of connections to outside organizations are more likely than more isolated seniors to have better health and overall functioning (Mendes de Leon, Glass, & Berkman, 2003). Older people with a stronger social network may have greater access to social support and are more likely to have people to call on to complete everyday tasks, especially older people with some type of functional need. For example, Moritz, Kasl, and Berkman (1995) found that social isolation and lack of participation in social activities were associated with incident limitations in ADL. It also may be that living arrangements and social networks are associated with more positive health behavior (e.g., reduced cigarette smoking, proper nutrition, and physical activity).

HEALTH BEHAVIORS

Health behaviors are associated with functioning status and disability. In this section, we review the research on the association between tobacco, alcohol, physical activity, and diet and nutrition.

Tobacco

There is evidence that current or former smoking is a risk factor for functional decline (Branch, Katz, Kniepmann, Papsidero, et al., 1984; Ferrucci, Izmirlian, Leveille, Phillips, Corti, Brock, et al., 1999; House, Lepkowski, Kinney, Mero, Kessler, & Herzig, 1994). Most recently, results from the Medicare Health Outcome Survey indicate that smokers report worse physical and mental functional status than those who have never smoked (Arday, Milton, Husten, Haffer, Wheeless, Hones, et al., 2003). In addition, long-term quitters have better functional status than those who still smoke. There is also evidence from the Marin County Health and Aging Study that current smokers aged 55 and older had significantly more difficulty maintaining their balance (i.e., a full-tandem stand with the toes of one foot placed at the heel of the second foot) than nonsmokers, after adjustment for other demographic, social, behavioral, health, and functional measures (Satariano, DeLorenze, Reed, & Schneider, 1996).

Alcohol Consumption

Stuck and colleagues (1999), as part of an extensive review of the risks for functional limitations and disability, reviewed a number of articles on the association between alcohol consumption and level of functioning. Although Stuck and colleagues expressed concern about the lack of precision in the measurement of alcohol, the results seem to be consistent with the relationship between alcohol consumption and the risk of death. In comparison to moderate consumers of alcohol, heavy drinkers were more likely to experience a decline in functional status. Older people who consumed small to moderate amounts of alcohol were more likely to maintain their functional status, compared to abstainers.

Physical Activity

Physical activity has been consistently shown to be associated with higher levels of physical functioning (Cress, Buchner, Questad, Esselman, de Lateur, Schwartz, 1999; LaCroix, Guralnik, Berkman, Wallace, & Satterfield, 1993; Mor, Murphy, Materson-Allen, Willey, Razmpour, Jackson, et al., 1989; Seeman, 1995; Stewart, Hays, Wells, Rogers, Spritzer, & Greenfield, 1994). Interestingly, most studies indicate that engagement in any form of activity, such as leisure walking, is associated with the maintenance of physical functioning. According to Stuck and colleagues (1999), there is little evidence indicating a strong dose response between level of physical activity and level of physical functioning.

Diet and Nutrition

Nutritional factors are also associated with functional health (Amarantos, Martinez, & Dwyer, 2001; Pirlich & Lochs, 2001). Despite the significance of obesity and health, the most significant problem is undernutrition, for example, poor diet and eating too little. This may be due to a variety of factors, such as less access to nutritious foods as well as reductions of sensory functioning (e.g., reductions in sense of taste and smell), which may reduce appetite.

SENSE OF CONTROL, COHERENCE, AND SELF-EFFICACY

Psychosocial factors, such as self-efficacy, are associated with levels of functioning (Mendes de Leon, Seeman, Baker, Richardson, & Tinetti, 1996). As noted previously in Chapter 2, self-efficacy refers to the extent of confidence a person has in the completion of a particular task. There is evidence that those with higher levels of self-efficacy are more likely than others to have higher levels of physical functioning. Self-efficacy is not simply a reflection of physical abilities. Seeman and colleagues (1999) report that self-efficacy beliefs have significant impacts on perceptions of functional disability, independent of actual underlying physical abilities. She and her colleagues conclude that perceptions of confidence in the completion of particular tasks may affect lifestyles and quality of life at older ages.

DISEASE AND COMORBIDITIES

Acute and chronic disease and conditions are strongly associated with patterns of functional limitations and disability (Fried & Guralnik, 1997). There are two types of studies in this area. First, there are studies that examine the association between diagnosis and treatment of a particular health condition and levels of functional limitations and disability (Boult, de Regt, Andries, Van Agt, Bijl, de Boer, et al., 1994; Guccione, Felson, Anderson, Anthony, Zhang, Wilson, et al., 1994; Sprangers, Kane, Louis,

Boult, McCaffrey, et al., 2000). Second, there is research that investigates the history of past diagnosis, including both specific index conditions and levels of comorbidity (i.e., number and types of past diagnoses) and subsequent levels of functioning and disability.

Verbrugge and colleagues (1989) examined the relationship between single and multiple chronic conditions on the prevalence of disability (really, limitations and disabilities), based on data from the National Health Interview Survey. ADL, IADL, and self-reported functional imitations were used as measures of the outcome. The research can be summarized as follows (Verbrugge et al., 1989, pp. 476–477):

1. As the number of chronic conditions increases, disability rises rapidly, almost exponentially. However, for the few people who are extremely ill, an additional comorbid condition does not significantly contribute to a higher level of limitations and disabilities.
2. The effect of chronic health conditions on the level of functioning depends on both the prevalence of that condition and its relative level of severity. Moreover, the conditions tend to have either (1) high prevalence and low-disability impact or (2) low prevalence and high impact. For example, arthritis is the leading chronic condition for middle-aged and older persons, but it has modest impact compared to cardiovascular disease, osteoporosis, and fracture of the hip, all less common.
3. Health problems are the main cause of limitations and disability. Initial age differences in limitations and disability decline when comorbidity is held constant. However, women continue to have higher levels of limitations and disability than men, and nonwhites have higher levels than whites when comorbidity is held constant.
4. In most cases, the effect of comorbidity, measured as pairs of conditions, has an additive rather than synergistic relationship.
5. There was a synergistic effect on functioning for 16% of the possible pairs (88 of 546). In 38% of those cases (33 of 88), the concurrent conditions were associated with elevated prevalence of limitations and disability.
6. The concurrent conditions that had the most significant effect on functioning determined by both prevalence and severity included cardiovascular disease and fractured hip, diabetes, osteoporosis, fractured hip with osteoporosis or atherosclerosis, visual impairment with osteoporosis, and ischemic heart disease and cancer.

Results from the Cardiovascular Health Study also indicate that the number and types of health problems are associated with particular types of limitations and disabilities (Fried, Borhani, Enright, Furberg, Gardin, Kronmal, Kuller, 1991). Participants in the study reported that arthritis and other musculoskeletal disease were the primary causes of difficulty in performing physical tasks, followed by heart disease, injury, lung disease, and stroke. Whereas arthritis was given as a cause of difficulty in most of the 17 different daily tasks, heart and lung disease were more likely to be reported as causing difficulty with activities requiring high aerobic work capacity such as walking a half mile or doing heavy housework. Stroke was more likely to be reported as causing difficulty with use of the upper extremities and in performing basic ADL.

Not only do the number and types of chronic conditions affect the extent and type of limitations, but they also affect the timing of impairments, limitations, and disability. For example, Guralnik and colleagues (2001) determined from examinations of participants in the EPESE project that those aged 85 years and older or having three or more chronic conditions at baseline were significantly more likely to develop progressive disability than catastrophic disability (defined as no previous walking limitation in the previous two rounds of assessment). Selected health conditions (i.e., stroke, hip fracture, and cancer) were shown to be associated with an elevated risk of catastrophic disability (defined as severe disability of rapid onset). The type of disability (catastrophic versus progressive) did not seem to affect subsequent survival during the first three years. However, after the first three years, those with progressive disability had an elevated risk of death, compared to those with catastrophic disability.

There is also evidence from the Women's Health and Aging Study that particular combinations of concurrent health conditions are associated with particular combinations and types of functional limitations and disabilities (Fried, Bandeen-Roche, Kasper, & Guralnik, 1999). Categories of functioning in this study include the following:

- Mobility difficulty only
- Upper extremity difficulty only
- Mobility and upper extremity difficulty only
- Difficulty in higher functioning but not self-care tasks
- Self-care tasks difficulty but not higher functioning
- Difficulty in both higher functioning and self-care

Specific disease pairs that were associated with the type and severity of functional limitations included arthritis and visual impairments, arthritis and high blood pressure, heart disease and cancer, lung disease and cancer, and stroke and high blood pressure. For example, the independent risks associated with difficulty in mobility and upper-extremity function for people with lung disease alone and for people with cancer alone were 0.9 and 0.4 respectively. However, among people with both lung disease and cancer, the risk was as high as 17.2. This finding is important. The results indicate that the effects of concurrent health conditions on functional limitations can be multiplicative as well as simply additive.

Cardiovascular diseases, including diabetes and stroke, are associated with functional limitations and disability. Recent research from the Women's Health and Aging Study examined the cross-sectional association between diabetes and specific types of physical functioning and physical performance (Volpato, Balum, Resnick, Ferrucci, Fried, & Guralnik, 2002). After adjustment for age, women with diabetes had a greater prevalence of mobility disability, activities of living disability, and severe walking limitation, and their summary mobility performance score was significantly lower than that evident for women without diabetes. In a separate study based on national data from the Third National Health and Nutrition Examination Survey, diabetes was associated with a 2- to 3-fold increase in not being able to perform three basic daily tasks among both men and women, and up to a 3.6-fold increase in slower walking speed, inferior lower-extremity function, decreased balance, and risk of falling (Gregg, Beckles, Williamson, Leveille, Langlois, Engelgau, et al., 2000).

There is also evidence that diagnosis and treatment of cancer are associated with subsequent levels of functional limitations and disability (Given, Given, Azzouz, Stommel, & Kozachik, 2000; Lash & Silliman, 2000; Satariano & Ragland, 1996). For example, research based on a longitudinal study of women with incident breast cancer indicates that cases aged 40–54, 55–64, and 65–74 years were approximately twice as likely as age-matched controls to report upper-body limitations at three months after diagnosis (Satariano & Ragland, 1996). Little difference was found for cases aged 75–84 years between 3 and 12 months. One explanation for the relatively modest case-control difference in the oldest women was that a comparable percentage of the controls aged 75–84 years reported upper-body limitations, suggesting that age processes leading to limitations and disability may mask or mimic limitations related to breast cancer. These results also may help to explain why functional limitations associated with some conditions, such as specific forms of cancer, may be modest or nonexistent in studies based on prevalent conditions; by definition, the length of time since diagnosis will vary among prevalent conditions. Time at diagnosis and timing of the assessment of function must be included in studies of chronic disease and disability. Subsequent studies have confirmed the significance of upper-body limitations among women with breast cancer (Lash & Silliman, 2000).

To summarize, the number and types of acute and chronic health conditions are strongly associated with subsequent levels of limitations and disabilities. In addition, medication use, which is certainly related to the numbers and types of acute and chronic health conditions, is associated with functional limitations and disabilities. For example, Tinetti and colleagues (1995) reported that seniors who were taking five or more medications had poorer functional status than those who were taking fewer medications. Few studies analyzed the types of medications associated with functional status decline. There is evidence, however, that insulin, loop-diuretics, tranquilizers, and antidepressants are associated with reduced functional status.

FALLS AND INJURIES

There is evidence that falls are associated with poor functional outcomes. According to Stuck and colleagues (1999), research from Wolinsky and colleagues (1992) and Dunn and colleagues (1992) indicated that a history of multiple falls is associated with poorer levels of functioning. Stuck (1999) also qualifies these findings with data from Tinetti and colleagues. (1995). If baseline measures of physical performance were included in the model, the association between a history of falls and physical functioning disappeared (Tinetti et al. 1995). This suggests that the history of falls, rather than representing a risk factor for subsequent functional limitations, may be part of a constellation of factors that serves as a marker of functional limitations. These results underscore the complexity of research in this area. It is not completely clear from these results whether a history of falls is an independent predictor of subsequent functional status or whether a history of falls is simply a marker for a generalized reduced level of function.

COGNITIVE FUNCTIONING

There are several studies that indicate an association between cognitive dysfunction or cognitive deficits and subsequent levels of functional limitations. Stuck and colleagues (1999) indicate that seniors with reduced memory and cognitive orientation have significantly lower levels of physical functioning (Gill, Williams, Richardson, Berkman, & Tinetti, 1997). In addition, research by Bruce and colleagues (1994) and Seeman, Charpentiar, and Berkman, (1994) demonstrated an association between reduced cognitive function and subsequent functional limitations, holding constant baseline levels of dementia. Interestingly, the level of cognitive function was shown to account for the association between depression and physical functioning (Gallo, Rebok, Tennsted, Wadley, & Horgas, 2003).

DEPRESSION

Depression is associated with reduced levels of physical functioning. Among older men and women with peripheral arterial disease, those with increasing numbers of depressive symptoms were more likely to demonstrate poor lower-extremity function, as measured by a series of walking tests (McDermott, Greenland, Guralnik, Liu, Criqui, Pearce, et al., 2003). There is also evidence of an association between depressive symptoms, as measured by the Center for Epidemiologic Studies Depression (CES-D) scale and reduced physical functioning at baseline and over time (Callahan et al., 1998). A longitudinal study also revealed an association between depressive symptoms and a subsequent decline in physical performance (Penninx, Guralnik, Ferrucci, Simonsick, Deeg, & Wallace, 1998). In addition, evidence of "emotional vitality" among older disabled women, a summary measure that included absent or low levels of depression as measured by the CES-D scale, was associated with a low risk of the development of subsequent disability (Penninx, Deeg, Van Eijk, Beckman, & Guralnik, 2000).

PHYSIOLOGIC FACTORS

In addition to acute and chronic health conditions, there is evidence that underlying physiologic factors are associated with subsequent levels of functional limitations and disability. Along these lines, there have been attempts to better summarize measures of physical functioning in terms of physiologic factors. Fried and colleagues (1994) proposed a physiologic basis of functional classification to better investigate underlying pathophysiology. Based on data from the Cardiovascular Health study, factor analyses of 17 self-reported tasks of daily life were classified into four groups based on the difficulty in one task being associated with difficulty in the other tasks in the group. The groups were classified as: (1) activities primarily dependent on mobility and exercise tolerance; (2) complex activities heavily dependent on cognition and sensory input; (3) selected basic self-care activities; and (4) upper-extremity activities. These four groups, in turn, were shown to be associated with specific groups of chronic conditions. The researchers conclude that physiologically based functional outcomes may be better suited for research on the causes of disability. In a subsequent study of participants enrolled in the Women's Health and Aging Study, Leveille, Fried, McMullen, and Guralnik (2004) grouped disabilities in terms of five categories, based on the participants' reports of the causes of disabilities. These categories were classified as pain, balance, weakness, endurance, and other symptoms.

Allostatic load, the cumulative biological burden exacted on the body through attempts to adapt to life's demands, also is associated with subsequent decline in physical functioning, as well as an elevated risk of death (Karlamangla, Singer, McEwen, Rowe, & Seeman, 2002). The concepts of allostasis and allostatic load are important, because they represent the physiological centerpiece of a broader ecological model that captures the interplay of a variety of behavioral, social, and environmental factors over the life course. In addition to the summary measure of allostasis, there are a number of specific physiological factors that have been associated with functional activities. These measures include musculoskeletal strength and integrity, lung function, and body mass.

Sacropenia, a loss of muscle mass and decline in muscle quality, has received considerable attention (Roubenoff & Hughes, 2000). There is evidence that those with demonstrated sacropenia are at elevated risk of functional difficulties, including problems with gait and balance, increased fall risk, and loss of functional independence (Kamel, 2003).

Overall body composition, fat and lean mass, has been shown to be associated with functional limitations (Sternfeld, Ngo, Satariano, & Tager, 2002). In an examination of data from the SPPARCS project, higher fat mass was associated with slower walking speed and greater likelihood of functional limitation, while higher lean mass was generally associated only with increased grip strength. A higher ratio of lean mass to fat mass, a relative measure of body composition, was associated with faster walking speed and less limitation. These findings suggest that fat mass negatively impacts some domains of physical performance and overall functioning, while lean mass is less significant in absolute terms but is important relative to body fat. The negative effects of overall fat mass are associated with other studies that suggest that obesity, although less common in the elderly than in middle-aged populations, is strongly associated with poor physical functioning (Sharma, Cahue, Sone, Hayes, Pai, Dunlop, et al., 2003; Stewart et al., 1994).

CONCLUSION

The study of aging, health, and functioning is a key topic in the epidemiology of aging. Current research indicates that patterns and causes of functional limitations and disability are due to a variety of factors that include biologic, behavioral, social, and environmental factors. Levels of cognitive function and depression, topics to which we will turn in Chapters 5 and 6, also affect the extent and course of functional limitations significantly.

REFERENCES

Amarantos, E., Martinez, A., & Dwyer, J. (2001). Nutrition and quality of life in older adults [Special issue]. *Journals of Gerontology: Medical Science, 56*(Spec N 2), 54–64.

Arday, D. R., Milton, M. H., Husten, C. G., Haffer, S. C., Wheeless, S. C., Hones, S. M., et al. (2003). Smoking and functional status among Medicare managed care enrollees. *American Journal of Preventive Medicine, 24*(3), 234–241.

Avlund, K., Vass, M., & Hendriksen, C. (2003). Onset of mobility disability among community-dwelling old men and women: The role of tiredness in daily activities. *Age & Ageing, 32*(6), 579–584.

Balfour, J. L., & Kaplan, G. A. (2002). Neighborhood environment and loss of physical function in older adults: Evidence from the Alameda County Study. *American Journal of Epidemiology, 255*(6), 507–515.

Beckett, L. A., Brock, D. B., Lemke, J. H., Mendes de Leon, C. F., Guralnik, J. M., Fillenbaum, G. C., et al. (1996). Analysis of change in self-reported physical function among older persons in four population studies. *American Journal of Epidemiology, 143,* 766–778.

Berkman, L. F., Seeman, T. E., Albert, M., Blazer, D., Kahn, R., Mohs, R., et al. (1993). High, usual, and impaired functioning in community-dwelling older men and women: Findings from the MacArthur Foundation Research Network on Successful Aging. *Journal of Clinical Epidemiology, 46*(10), 1129–1140.

Boult, C., Kane, R. L., Louis, T. A., Boult, L., & McCaffrey, D. (1994). Chronic conditions that lead to functional limitations in the elderly. *Journals of Gerontology: Medical Sciences, 49,* M28–M36.

Branch, L. G., & Jette, A. M. (1981). The Framingham Disability Study: I. Social disability among the aging. *American Journal of Public Health, 71*(11), 1202–1210.

Branch, L. G., Katz, S., Kniepmann, K., & Papsidero, J. A. (1984). A prospective study of functional status among community elders. *American Journal of Public Health, 74*(3), 266–268.

Branch, L. G., Guralnik, J. M., Foley, D. J., Kohout, F. J., Wetle, T. T., Ostfeld, A., et al. (1991). Active life expectancy for 10,000 Caucasian men and women in three communities. *Journal of Gerontology: Medical Sciences, 46*(4), M145–M150.

Bruce, M. L., Seeman, T. E., Merrill, S. S., & Blazer, D. G. (1994). The impact of depressive symptomatology on physical disability: MacArthur Studies of Successful Aging. *American Journal of Public Health, 84,* 1796–1799.

Callahan, C. M., Wolinsky, F. D., Stump, T. E., Nienaber, N. A., Hui, S. L., & Tierney, W. M. (1998). Mortality, symptoms, and functional impairment in late-life depression. *Journal of General Internal Medicine 13*(11), 746–752.

Cornoni-Huntley, J. C., Brock, D. B., Ostfeld, A. M. Taylor, J. O., & Wallace, R. B. (1986). *Established Populations for Epidemiologic Studies of the Elderly.* Washington, DC: National Institutes of Health (NIH Publication Number: No. 86-2443).

Cress, M. E., Buchner, D. M., Questad, K. A., Esselman, P. C., de Lateur, B. J., & Schwartz, R. S. (1999). Exercise: Effects on physical functional performance in independent older adults. *Journals of Gerontology: Medical Sciences, 54,* M242–M248.

Crimmins, E., Hayward, M. D., & Saito, Y. (1996). Differentials in active life expectancy in the older population in the United States. *Journals of Gerontology: Social Sciences, 51*(3), S111–S120.

Dunn J. E., Rudberg, M. A., Furner, S. E., & Cassel, C. K. (1992). Mortality, disability and falls in older persons: The role of underlying disease and disability. *American Journal of Public Health, 82,* 395–400.

Ferraro, K. F. (1983). The health consequences of relocation among the aged in the community. *Journals of Gerontology, 38*(1), 90–96.

Ferrucci, L., Izmirlian, G., Seveille, S., et al. (1999). Smoking, physical activity, and active life expectancy. *American Journal of Epidemiology, 149,* 645–653.

Frank L. D., Engelke, P. O., & Schmid, T. L. (2003). *Health and Community Design: The Impact of the Built Environment on Physical Activity.* Washington, DC: Island Press.

Fried, L. P., Borhani, N. O., Enright, P., Furberg, C. D., Gardin, J. M., Kronmal, R. A., Kuller, L. H., Manolio, T. A., Mittelmark, M. P., & Newman, A., et al. (1991). The Cardiovascular Health Study: Design and rationale. *Annals of Epidemiology, 1*(3), 263–276.

Fried, L. P., Ettinger, W. H., Lind, B., Newman, A. B., & Gardin, J. (1994). Physical disability in older adults: A physiological approach. Cardiovascular Health Study Research Group. *Journal of Clinical Epidemiology, 47*(7), 747–760.

Fried, L. P., Bandeen-Roche, K., Williamson, J. D., Prasada-Rao, P., Chee, E., Tepper, S., & Rubin, G. S. (1996). Functional decline in older adults: Expanding methods of ascertainment. *Journals of Gerontology: Medical Sciences, 51*(5), M206–M214.

Fried, L. P., Bandeen-Roche, K., Kasper, J. D., & Guralnik, J. M. (1999). Association of comorbidity with disability in older women: The Women's Health and Aging Study. *Journal of Clinical Epidemiology, 52*(1), 27–37.

Fried, L. P., Bandeen-Roche, K., Chaves, P. H., & Johnson, B. A. (2000). Preclinical mobility disbility predicts incident mobility disability in older women. *Journals of Gerontology: Medical Sciences, 55*(1), M43–M52.

Fried, L. P., & Guralnik, J. M. (1997). Disability in older adults: Evidence regarding significance, etiology, and risk. *Journal of the American Geriatric Society, 45*, 92–100.

Gallo, J. J., Rebok, G. W., Tennsted, S., Wadley, V. G., & Horgas, A. (2003). Linking depressive symptoms and functional Disability in late life. *Aging Mental Health, 7*(6), 469–480.

Gill, T. M., Williams, C. S., Richardson, E.D., Berkman, L. F., Tinetti, M. E. (1997). A predictive model for ADL dependence in community-living older adults based on a reduced set of cognitive status items. *Journal of the American Geriatrics Society, 45*, 441–445.

Given, C. W., Given, B., Azzouz, F., Stommel, M., & Kozachik, S. (2000). Comparison of changes in physical functioning of elderly patients with new diagnosis of cancer. *Medical Care, 38*, 482–493.

Gregg, E. W., Beckles, G. L., Williamson, D. F., Leveille, S. G., Langlois, J. A., Engelgau, M. M., et al. (2000). *Diabetes Care, 23*(9), 1272–1277.

Guccione, A., Felson, D., Anderson, J., Anthony, J. M., Zhang, Y., Wilson, P. W., et al. (1994). The effects of specific medical conditions on the functional limitations of elders in the Framingham Study. *American Journal of Public Health, 84*, 351–358.

Guralnik, J. M., LaCroix, A. Z., Abbott, R. D., Berkman, L. F., Satterfield, S., Evans, D. A., et al. (1993). Maintaining mobility in late life. I. Demographic characteristics and chronic conditions. *American Journal of Epidemiology, 137*(8), 845–857.

REFERENCES **165**

Guralnik, J. M., Land, K. C., Blazer, D., Fillenbaum, G. G., & Branch, L. G. (1993). Educational status and active life expectancy among older blacks and whites. *The New England Journal of Medicine, 329*(2), 110–116.

Guralnik, J. M., Ferrucci, L., Balfour, J. L., Volpato, S., & Di Iorio, A. (2001). Progressive versus catastrophic loss of the ability to walk: Implications for the prevention of mobility loss. *Journal of the American Geriatrics Society, 49*(11), 1463–1470.

Guralnik, J. M., Branch, L. G., Cummings, S. R., & Curb, J. D. (1989). Physical performance measures in aging research. *Journals of Gerontology: Medical Sciences, 44*(5), M141–M146.

Hazzard, W. R. (1986). Biological basis of the sex differential in longevity. *Journal of the American Geriatrics Society, 34*(6), 455–471.

House, J. S., Lepkowski, J. M., Kinney, A. M., Mero, R. P., Kessler, R. C., & Herzig, A. R. (1994). The social stratification of aging and health. *Journal of Health and Social Behavior, 35*(3), 213–234.

Hummer, R. A., Benjamins, M. R., & Rogers, R. G. (2004). Racial and ethnic disparities in health and mortality among the U.S. elderly population. In N. B. Anderson, R. A. Bulatao, & B. Cohen (Eds.). *Critical perspectives on racial and ethnic differences in health in late life.* Washington, D.C.: National Academies Press, pp. 53–94.

Jagger, C., Arthur, A. J., Spiers, N. A., & Clarke, M. (2001). Patterns of onset of disability in activities of daily living with age. *Journal of the American Geriatrics Society, 49*(4), 404–409.

Jette, A. M. (2003). Assessing disability in studies on physical activity. *American Journal of Preventive Medicine, 25*(3 Suppl. 2), 122–128.

Jette, A. M., & Branch, L. G. (1981). The Framingham Disability Study: II. Physical disability among the aging. *American Journal of Public Health, 71*(11), 1211–1216.

Jette, A. M., Haley, S. M., Coster, W. J., Kooyoomjian, J. T., Levenson, S., Heeren, T., et al. (2002). Late-Life Function and Disability Instrument: I. Development and evaluation of the disability component. *Journals of Gerontology: Medical Sciences, 57*(4), M209–M216.

Kamel, H. K. (2003). Sarcopenia and aging. *Nutrition Review, 61, 5Pt.1,* 157–167.

Karlamangla, A. S., Singer, B. H., McEwen, B. S., Rowe, J. W., & Seeman, T. E. (2002). Allostatic load as a predictor of functional decline: Macarthur Studies of Successful Aging. *Journal of Clinical Epidemiology, 55*(7), 696–710.

Karnofsky, D. A., Abelmann, W. H., Craver, L. F., & Burchenal, J. H. (1948). The use of nitrogen mustards in the palliative treatment of cancer. *Cancer, 1,* 634–656.

Katz, S., Ford, A. B., Moscowitz, R. W., Jackson, B. A., & Jaffe, M. W. (1963). Studies of illness in the aged: The index of ADL: A standardized measure of biological and psychosocial function. *Journal of the American Medical Association, 185,* 914–919.

Katz, S., Branch, L. G., Branson, M. H., Pasidero, J. A., Beck, J. C., & Greer, D. S. (1983). Active life expectancy. *The New England Journal of Medicine, 309*(20), 1218–1224.

Keysor, J. J., & Jette, A. M. (2001). Have we oversold the benefit of late-life exercise? *Journals of Gerontology: Medical Sciences, 56*(7), M412–M423.

LaCroix, A. Z., Guralnik, J. M., Berkman, L. F., Wallace, R. B., & Satterfield, S. (1993). Maintaining mobility in late life. II. Smoking, alcohol consumption, physical activity, and body mass index. *American Journal of Epidemiology, 137*(8), 858–869.

Land, K. C., Guralnik, J. M., & Blazer, D. G. (1994). Estimating increment-decrement life tables with multiple covariates from panel data: The case of active life expectancy. *Demography, 31*(2), 297–319.

Lash, T. L., & Silliman, R. A. (2000). Patient characteristics and treatments associated with a decline in upper-body function following breast cancer therapy. *Journal of Clinical Epidemiology, 53*(6), 615–622.

Lawton, M. P., & Brody, E. M. (1969). Assessment of older people: Self-maintaining and instrumental activities of daily living. *The Gerontologist, 9*(3), 179–186.

Leveille, S. G., Fried, L. P., McMullen, W., & Guralnik, J. M. (2004). Advancing the taxonomy of disability in older adults. *Journals of Gerontology: Medical Sciences, 59*(1), 86–93.

Markides, Rudkin, Angel, & Espino (1997)

McDermott, M. M., Greenland, P., Guralnik, J. M., Liu, K., Criqui, M. H., Pearce, W. H., et al. (2003). Depressive symptoms and lower extremity function in men and women with peripheral arterial disease. *Journal of General Internal Medicine, 18*(6), 461–467.

McDowell, I., & Newell, C. (1996). *Measuring Health: A Guide to Rating Scales and Questionnaires* (2nd ed.). New York: Oxford University Press.

Mendes de Leon, C. F., Fillenbaum, G. G., Williams, C. S., Brock, D. B., Beckett, L. A., & Berkman, L. F. (1995). Functional disability among elderly blacks and whites in two diverse areas: The New Haven and North Carolina EPESE Established Populations for the Epidemiologic Studies of the Elderly. *American Journal of Public Health, 85,* 994–998.

Mendes de Leon, C. F., Glass, T. A., & Berkman, L. F. (2003). Social engagement and disability in a community population of older adults: The New Haven EPESE. *American Journal of Epidemiology, 157*(7), 633–642.

Mendes de Leon, C. F., Seeman, T. E., Baker, D. I., Richardson, E. D., & Tinetti, M. E. (1996). Self-efficacy, physical decline, and change in functioning in community-living elders: A prospective study. *Journals of Gerontology: Social Sciences, 51,* S183–S190.

Mendes de Leon, C. F., Guralnik, J. M., & Bandeen-Roche, K. (2002). Short-term change in physical function and disability: The Women's Health and Aging Study. *Journals of Gerontology: Social Sciences, 57*(6), S355–S365.

Mor, V., Murphy, J., Materson-Allen, S., Willey, C., Razmpour, A., Jackson M. E., Greer, D., & Katz, S. (1989). Risk of functional decline among well elders. *Journal of Clinical Epidemiology, 42*(9), 895–904.

Moritz, D. J., Kasl, S. V., & Berkman, L. F. (1995). Cognitive functioning and the incidence of limitations in activities of daily living in an elderly community sample. *American Journal of Epidemiology, 141*(1), 41–49.

Nagi, S. Z. (1976). An epidemiology of disability among adults in the United States. *Milbank Memorial Fund Quarterly, 54,* 439–467.

Onder, G., Penninx, B. W., Lapuerta, P., Fried, L. P., Ostir, G. V., Guralnik, J. M., et al. (2002). Change in physical performance over time in older women: The Women's Health and Aging Study. *Journals of Gerontology: Medical Sciences, 57*(5), M289–M293.

Penninx, B. W., Deeg, D. J., ven Eijk, J. T., Beekman, A. T., & Guralnik, J. M. (2000). Changes in depression and physical decline in older adults: A longitudinal study. *Journal of Affective Disorders, 61*(1–2), 1–12.

Penninx, B. W., Leveille, S., Ferrucci, L., van Eijk, J. T., & Guralnik, J. M. (1999). Exploring the effect of depression on physical disability: Longitudinal evidence from EPESE. *American Journal of Public Health, 89*(9), 1346–1352.

Pirlich, M., & Lochs, H. (2004). Nutrition in the Elderly. *Best Practices Research in Clinical Gastroenterology, 15*(6), 869–884.

Pollack, C. E., & von dem Knesebeck, O. (2004). Social capital and health among the aged: Comparisons between the United States and Germany. *Health & Place, 10*(4), 383–391.

Rosow, I., & Breslau, N. (1966). A Guttman scale for the aged. *Journals of Gerontology, 21,* 556–559.

Roubenoff, R., & Hughes, V. A. (2000). Sacropenia: Current concepts. *Journals of Gerontology: Medical Sciences, 55*(12), M716–M724.

Sarwari, A. R., Fredman, L., Langenberg, P., & Magaziner, J. (1998). Prospective study on the relation between living arrangement and change in functional health status of elderly women. *American Journal of Epidemiology, 147*(4), 370–378.

Satariano, W. A., Ragheb, N. E., Branch, L. G., & Swanson, G. M. (1990). Difficulties in physical functioning reported by middle-aged and elderly women with breast cancer: A case-control comparison. *Journals of Gerontology: Medical Sciences, 45*(1), M3–M11.

Satariano, W. A., DeLorenze, G. N., Reed, D., & Schneider, E. L. (1996). Imbalance in an older population: An epidemiological analysis. *Journal of Aging & Health, 8*(3), 334–358.

Satariano, W. A., & Ragland, D. R. (1996). Upper-body strength and breast cancer: A comparison of the effects of age and disease. *Journals of Gerontology: Medical Sciences, 51*(5), M215–M219.

Seeman, T. E., Berkman, L. F., Charpentier, P. A., Blazer, D. G., Albert, M. S., & Tinetti, M. E. (1995). Behavioral and psychosocial predictors of physical performance: MacArthur Studies of Successful Aging. *Journals of Gerontology, 50*(4), M177–M108.

Seeman, T. E., Charpentiar, P. A., & Berkman, L. F. (1994). Predicting changes in physical performance in a high-functioning elderly cohort: MacArthur Studies of Successful Aging. *Journals of Gerontology: Medical Sciences, 49,* M97–M108.

Seeman, T. E., Unger, J. B., McAvay, G., et al. (1999). Self-efficacy beliefs and perceived declines in functional ability: MacArthur studies of successful aging. *Journals of Gerontology: Social Sciences, 4,* S214–S222.

Sharma, L., Cahue, S., Song, J., Hayes, K., Pai, Y. C., & Dunlop, D., et al. (2003). Physical functioning over three years in knee osteoarthritis: Role of psychosocial, local mechanical, and neuromuscular function. *Arthritis & Rheumatism, 48*(12), 3359–3370.

Simonsick, E., Kasper, J. D., Guralnik, J. M., Bandeen-Roche, K., Ferrucci, L., Hirst, R., et al. (2001). Severity of upper and lower extremity functional limitation: Scale development and validation with self-report and performance measures of physical function. *Journals of Gerontology: Social Sciences, 56*(1), S10–S19.

Smith, L. A., Branch, L. G., Scheer, P. A., Wetle, T., & Evans, D. A. (1990). Short-term variability of measures of physical function in older people. *Journal of the American Geriatric Society, 38*(9), 993–998.

Spector, W. D., Katz, S., Murphy, J. B., & Fulton, J. P. (1987). The hierarchical relationship between activities of daily living and instrumental activities of daily living. *Journal of Chronic Diseases, 40*(6), 481–489.

Sprangers, M. A., de Regt, E. B., Andries, F., van Agt, H. M., Bijl, R. V., de Boer, J. B., et al. (2000). Which chronic conditions are associated with better or poorer quality of life? *Journal of Clinical Epidemiology, 53*(9), 895–907.

Sternfeld, B., Ngo, L., Satariano, W. A., & Tager, I. B. (2002). Associations of body composition with physical performance and self-reported functional limitations in elderly men and women. *American Journal of Epidemiology, 156*(2), 110–121.

Stewart, A. L., Hays, R. D., Wells, K. B., Rogers, W. H., Spritzer, K. L., & Greenfield, S. (1994). Long-term functioning and well-being outcomes associated with physical activity and exercise in patients with chronic conditions in the Medical Outcomes Study. *Journal of Clinical Epidemiology, 47*(7), 719–730.

Stuck, A. E., Walthert, J. M., Nikolaus, T., Bula, C. J., Hohmann, C., & Beck, J. C. (1999). Risk factors for functional status decline in community-living elderly people: A systematic literature review. *Social Science & Medicine, 48,* 445–469.

Tager, I. B., Haight, T. J., Hollenberg, M., & Satariano, W. A. (2003). Physical functioning and mortality in older women: Assessment of energy costs and level of difficulty. *Journal of Clinical Epidemiology, 56, 8,* 807–813.

Tager, I. B., Swanson A., & Satariano, W. A. (1998). Reliability of measures of physical performance and self-reported functional measures in an older population. *Journals of Gerontology: Medical Sciences, 53*(4), M295–M300.

Tinetti, M. E., Inouye, S. H., Gill, T. M., & Doucette, J. T. (1995). Shared risk factors for falls, incontinence, and functional dependence. *Journal of the American Medical Association, 273*, 1348–1353.

U.S. Department of Health and Human Services. (2000). *Healthy People 2000.* Washington, DC: Author.

Verbrugge, L. M., Lepkowski, J. M., & Imanaka, Y. (1989). Comorbidity and its impact on disability, *Milbank Quarterly, 67*(3–4), 450–484.

Verbrugge, L. M., & Jette, A. M. (1994). The disablement process. *Social Science & Medicine, 38*, 1–14.

Volpato, S., Balum, C., Resnick, H., Ferrucci, L., Fried, L. P., & Guralnik, J. M. (2002). Comorbidities and impairments explaining the association between diabetes and lower extremity disability: The Women's Health and Aging Study. *Diabetes Care, 25*(4), 678–683.

Waite, L. J., & Hughes, M. E. (1999). At risk on the cusp of old age: Living arrangements and functional status among black, white, and Hispanic adults. *Journals of Gerontology: Social Sciences, 54*(3), S136–S144.

Wallace, R. B. (1992). Aging and disease: From laboratory to community. In R. B. Wallace and R. F. Woolson (Eds.). *The Epidemiologic Study of the Elderly.* New York: Oxford University Press, 3–9.

Wang, L., van Belle, G., Kukull, W. B., & Larson, E. B. (2002). Predictors of functional change: A longitudinal study of nondemented people aged 65 and older. *Journal of the American Geriatrics Society, 50*, 1525–1534.

Wolinsky, F. D., Johnson, R. J., & Fitzgerald, J. F. (1992). Falling health status and the use of health services by older adults: A prospective study. *Medical Care, 30*, 587–597.

Yen, I. H., & Kaplan, G. A. (1999). Poverty area residence and changes in physical activity level: Evidence from the Alameda County Study. *American Journal of Public Health, 88*(1), 1709–1712.

CHAPTER 5

Cognitive Functioning

The last ten years of the 20th century were known as the "decade of the brain." During that period, scientific attention and governmental support focused on the study of aging and cognition, with the objective of developing better strategies to preserve cognitive functioning among a growing aging population. Cognition, of course, has always been considered a special and long-prized human function, summarized well in the early French philosopher, Rene Descartes' famous dictum: "I think; therefore, I am." To be human is to think and to reason—the essence of being. It is not surprising, therefore, that the prospect of age-related losses in cognitive capacities and a dramatic increase in the incidence of Alzheimer's disease and other dementias prompted particular concern in the scientific community and among members of the general public. When commentators then and now give examples of the "failures" associated with the "success" of improvements in life expectancy, they often cite the anticipated, concurrent increases in the prevalence of dementias among a growing number of older people (Gruenberg, 1977). Cognitive function, therefore, represents one of the central topics in the epidemiology of aging.

It is not surprising, given our Cartesian heritage and its dualism between mind and body, that cognitive function is often studied separately from physical function. While this enables us to focus attention on each of these important topics, as we have done by devoting separate chapters to each type of functioning, it also leads us to lose sight of the fact that cognitive functioning and physical functioning are interrelated. Indeed, measures of physical performance, such as gait speed, discussed in the previous chapter, are often used as markers of specific types of cognitive functioning. When we consider the aging population and ask questions about what a continuing increase in life expectancy will mean in terms of patterns of health and well-being, we should think in terms of

171

both cognitive and physical functioning. In fact, researchers with the Baltimore Epidemiologic Catchment Area Program report that estimates of active life expectancy, discussed in the previous chapter, decreased from 9.8 years to 8.9 years at 65 years for men, and from 10 years to 8.4 years for women, when the definition of "inactivity" included measures of cognitive impairment and depression (Gallo, Schoen, & Jones, 2000).

Although the significance of aging and cognitive functioning is clear, it is only recently that a body of research has been established that examines the epidemiology of aging and cognitive function. In fact, as late as 1992, one leading commentator was able to observe quite legitimately that, "Despite recognition that age-associated cognitive dysfunction represents a significant and increasing public health problem, relatively little is known about population distributions of cognitive functions" (Colsher, 1992, p. 130). While cerebrovascular disease, Alzheimer's, and Parkinson's disease focused attention on issues of aging and cognitive function, today there is growing interest in mild cognitive deficits found in the general, nondemented population. In this chapter, we will review the basic themes in this growing area of research. In addition to addressing the measurement and methodological issues, we will describe how the patterns of cognitive function vary by age, gender, race, and ethnicity. Finally, we will observe how these population patterns can be explained in terms of biologic, behavioral, social, and environmental factors.

In keeping with our ecological approach to the study of the epidemiology of aging, it should be noted that the aging brain and cognitive function reflect the interplay of biologic, behavioral, and environmental factors. John Ratey summarizes this point well in a passage from his excellent book, *A User's Guide to the Brain* (2002, p. 17):

> The brain is not a computer that simply executes genetically predetermined programs. Nor is it a passive gray cabbage, victim to the environmental influences that bear upon it. Genes and environment interact to continually change the brain, from the time we are conceived until the moment we die.

Later, he discusses the significance of aging and cognitive function (Ratey, 2002, pp. 34–35) by noting that, "Although the brain's flexibility may decrease with age, it remains plastic throughout life, restructuring itself according to what it learns." This observation is important both for an understanding of the epidemiology of aging and cognitive function and for a later consideration of strategies to preserve and enhance cognition as part of public health interventions. Prior to a consideration of those issues, we will begin by considering, first, the definition and measurement of cognitive function and, then, by addressing the broad demographic patterns of aging and cognition in the general population.

DEFINITION AND MEASUREMENT

Cognitive function is an abstract concept that reflects the integration of a number of different components. These components include attention, concentration, both short-term and long-term memory, abstraction, language, and visospatial skills (Folstein, Anthony, Parhad, Duffy, & Gruenberg, 1985). These components are included in specialized measurements for both clinical diagnosis and epidemiologic research. There has been considerable development over the past 20 years in specialized measures of cognitive and functional impairment that characterize dementias and chart the progression of the disease. The diagnosis of Alzheimer's disease is a diagnosis of exclusion—a process of excluding alternative explanations for behavioral symptoms (Katzman, 1997). The first step in this process is typically the administration of brief, reliable screening tests. Based on the results of the screening test, the patient may undergo more detailed neurologic and health assessments. It is interesting to note that these tests, following Wallace's characterization of the development of the epidemiology of aging (1992), are often included as the standard measures of cognitive function in epidemiologic research. Rather than being used exclusively for the purpose of diagnosis, these screening tests have been adapted for use in population studies to provide an overall assessment of different areas of cognitive function and to identify differences in the population by age, gender, race, and ethnicity, as well as other social and behavioral factors. In addition to covering the basic cognitive areas, the tests are well suited to monitor areas of function over time.

A variety of clinical measures have been developed that include assessments of psychometric intelligence, overall mental status, neuropsychological batteries, and specialized functions, such as memory. In epidemiologic studies, most general measures of cognitive function have been based on the Mini-Mental State Examination (MMSE) and the Short Portable Mental Status Questionnaire (SPMSQ). Each measure, which includes requests for personal and public information, concentration, and memory, has been used to characterize both the current state of cognitive function as well as the change in cognitive function among different population groups.

Mini-Mental State Examination

The MMSE, developed by Marshall Folstein and colleagues (1975), is the most commonly used assessment tool in both clinical and epidemiologic research. It consists of 20 separate items. The items can be organized heuristically into seven categories: (1) orientation to time; (2) orientation to place; (3) immediate recall (registration of three words); (4) attention and calculation; (5) short-term memory (recall of three words); (6) language; and (7) visual construction. The MMSE is based on the total number of correct answers, from a total of 30. A score of 23 or lower is considered to be indicative of some cognitive impairment. Several longitudinal studies indicate that the MMSE is a useful tool in serially documenting changes in subjects who do not have severe cognitive dysfunction. Many studies of community-based older adults find that MMSE scores decline as the age of the patient increases. The items that seem to be most affected by age are repeating "no ifs, ands, or buts," and recall of the three words.

Short-Portable Mental Status Questionnaire

This 10-item test was designed to provide a quick assessment of organic brain deficit in both community-dwelling and institutionalized older adults (Fillenbaum, Landerman, & Simonsick, 1998). The items, most of which were used previously in modified form in other tests, address the subject's orientation and long-term memory. A four-level scoring system was developed to map four levels of intellectual functioning: intact functioning, mild functioning, moderate functioning, and severe functioning. In addition, the scoring system formally takes into account education and racial influences on test performance.

Measurement Issues

The assessment of cognitive function raises a number of unique methodological issues. Two general considerations have been identified. First, performance on cognitive tests is affected by many factors other than the process under study, including educational attainment, cultural experiences, language usage, prior testing experience, emotional and physical states, the testing environment, and measurement error. This, of course, makes it difficult to distinguish between true etiological factors and other factors. Second, in contrast to studies of specialized clinical populations, it is often necessary in epidemiologic studies to consider a wide range of cognition, from the upper end of normal function to the effects of severe diseases. It is difficult for any one test to capture the range of cognitive function in a community population. One of the concerns expressed about the standard tests, such as the MMSE, is that it is designed to assess gross levels of cognitive function. In community studies, it is more difficult to distinguish among people who are determined by the standard tests to have normal cognitive functioning. This is especially problematic in assessment of people with higher levels of education, a point to be discussed in greater detail (Launer, Kinkgreve, Jonker, Hooijer, Lindeboom, 1993). In an effort to address this issue, some researchers have recommended supplementing the MMSE and SPMSQ with measures such as the Trails Test (a neuropsychological assessment) to capture higher levels of cognitive functioning, such as executive function, or the capacity to summarize and organize information for the purpose of making decisions. The Trails Making Test assesses the time required for a subject to connect the dots in sequence, alternating between letters and numbers (Reitan, 1958). There are two versions of the test. In the first version, Trails A, subjects are asked to draw a series of lines in sequence from one number to another. The second version, Trails B, includes both letters and numbers. In this test, the protocol is the same, but the subjects must draw lines in sequence, including both numbers and letters (e.g., 1 to A, A to 2, etc.). The time required to complete the task is recorded. Trails Test A and B can be viewed at http://dop.hawaii.edu/resources/Trail%20Making%20 test.pdf (Accessed: June 15, 2005). There are other tests that are designed to assess executive function. For example, the Mental Alternation Test requires a similar set of tasks, but the test can be administrated orally and does not require the subject to connect letters and numbers with a pencil (Jones, Teng, Folstein, & Harrison, 1993). Subjects are first asked to recite out loud from 1 to 20. They are then asked to say the letters of the alphabet, from A to Z. Finally, they are instructed to alternate numbers and letters in sequence (that is, 1A, 2B, 3C, etc.). The number of correct alternations completed in 30 seconds is recorded (see Figure 5-1).

There also is a need for uniform measurement of cognition across all subjects. Some epidemiological studies are limited in the time and space that can be devoted to any one assessment; there is a need to use the most comprehensive test available.

I am going to ask you to recite a series of numbers and letters. I will be using my stopwatch to time this exercise.

Please count, aloud, from 1 to 20.

1 2 3 4 5 6 7 8 9 10 11 12 13 14 15 16 17 18 19 20

Please say the letters of the alphabet, from A to Z.

A B C D E F G H I J K L M N O P Q R S T U V W X Y Z

Now, please SWITCH between the numbers and the letters, like this:

1-A-2-B-3-C-4-D and so on.

1 2 3 4 5 6 7 8 9 10 11 12 13 14 15 16 17 18 19 20 21 22 23 24 25 26

A B C D E F G H I J K L M N O P Q R S T U V W X Y Z

Number of correct alternations in 30 seconds _____

Source: Jones et al., 1993.

FIGURE 5–1 Protocol for the Mental Alternation Test

The assessment of cognitive change presents some unique challenges. Ideally, to assess change, there should be three or more assessments. As is true of the assessment of other outcomes in epidemiological research, the intervals should be long enough to observe some change but short enough to allow multiple measures within the study period and to minimize sample attrition, especially any that may be due to illness and mortality. There are several specific challenges associated with the measurement of cognitive change. First, tests should include the entire range of cognitive function in the population to be studied, both at the beginning of the study and throughout the study interval. Second, the observed changes in cognitive function that are of interest in a study are generally small in comparison with the entire range of function. This requires that the tests be sufficiently sensitive to modest levels of change and also have high reliability. It is unfortunate, however, that there are relatively few assessments of the reliability of these measures. Third, to measure cognitive change, it is desirable to administer the same test at multiple points in time. However, there is always the danger of a "learning effect." Maintenance or even improvement in test performance may not reflect cognitive status or change, but rather the subject's growing familiarity with the test itself. Finally, terminal drop, or accelerated decline in cognitive function observed prior to death may have a significant impact on estimates of cognitive function among the elderly. By including mortality surveillance, it may be possible to separate the effects of terminal drop from other potential causes of cognitive decline.

This overview should provide a sense of some of the challenges and difficulties associated with the assessment of cognitive function. With this in mind, the greatest challenge is to strike a balance across competing demands, identify a set of measures, and then take to the field. The following sections will summarize some of the current research in the epidemiology of aging and cognitive function.

DEMOGRAPHIC PATTERNS

Age

Overall cognitive function, as measured by the MMSE, is lower in older subjects, especially after age 75, than in younger subjects. In a recent study, researchers assessed the effect of increasing age on cognition in nondemented older people. A decline of MMSE of .4 points every 10 years is considered typical. Although it is fair to say that overall cognitive function declines with age, it is important to realize that there is considerable variation in the extent and type of decline. First, some people are able to maintain much of their cognitive function as they age. Second, some types of cognitive function decline more precipitously than others. A distinction is often made between crystallized intelligence (accumulated knowledge) and fluid intelligence (intellectual potential). There is evidence that fluid intelligence tends to decline with age. Speed in the processing of information, working memory, and complex attention (i.e., being attentive to multiple items) are especially affected by age. On the other hand, crystallized intellectual performance is either stable or shows only minimal decline. In fact, in most cases, vocabulary continues to increase with age (Christensen, 2001). As Troller and Valenzuela (2001, p. 789) write, "While it is important to appreciate the limitations in cognitive processing that are implicated in human aging, it is equally pertinent to remember that older people have access to a unique repository of cultural, historical, and personal information." Consistent with what might be viewed as the more positive aspects of aging, older people also are more likely than the young to demonstrate "wisdom," defined here to mean a combination of flexibility of perspective, compassion, and decision making under conditions of uncertainty (Baltes, 1991, 1993). In fact, several years ago, aging and wisdom were the topics of a popular book, entitled, *America—The Wise* (Roszak, 1998).

There is also evidence that the present cohort of older people may have better overall cognitive function than previous generations (Freedman, Aykan, & Martin, 2001). Using the 1993 Asset and Health Dynamics of the Oldest Old study and the 1998 Health and Retirement Survey, this study examined aggregate changes in the proportion of the noninstitutionalized population aged 70 years and older with severe cognitive impairment. The results indicate that the percentage of older Americans with severe cognitive impairment declined from 6.1% in 1993 to 3.6% in 1998. Although this type of cohort comparison needs to be addressed across other populations, the results from this study could not be accounted for by shifts in demographic and socioeconomic factors. Based on these results, the authors conclude that older persons, especially those well into their eighth decade, appear to have better cognitive functioning today than they did in the early 1990s.

Gender

Unlike the results for aging and physical function, there is no consistent evidence of a gender difference in cognitive function. In a large population-based study of aging and cognitive function, men and women performed similarly on tests of immediate memory, delayed memory, and attention, although men scored slightly higher than did women on the mental status questionnaire (Scherr, Albert, Funenstein, Cook, Hennekens, Branch, et al., 1988). As we will consider later in more detail, it was originally believed that a reduction in estrogen, occurring at the time of menopause, was associated with a reduction in most measures of cognitive function. Recent research suggests, however, that estrogen replacement therapy is not associated with maintenance or improvement in cognitive function (Mulnard, Corrada, & Kawas, 2004). It is important to note, however, that there is some evidence that among the very old—aged 90 and older—men have better cognitive function than women of the same age (Perls, Morris, Ooi, & Lipsitz, 1993). As we noted in Chapter 3, decreased cognitive performance is significantly associated with mortality, especially among men. Men who do survive to old age may be more cognitively fit than women who survive to the same age. This, of course, will have to be addressed in more detail.

Race and Ethnicity

There are relatively few studies that examine the association between race and cognitive function in older populations, with the possible exception of studies of African-Americans. Data from the New Haven component of the Established Populations for Epidemiologic Studies of the Elderly (EPESE) indicate that Caucasian men and women were more likely than men and women of other racial groups (primarily African-American) to receive the highest cognitive function score (Berkman, Singer, & Manton, 1989). In a separate study of participants in the North Carolina EPESE study, Caucasians were more likely than African-Americans to report worsening memory (59% vs. 49%) (Fillenbaum, Heyman, Huber, Woodbury, Leiss, Schmader, et al., 1998). The complaint about memory was positively correlated with age, depressive symptomatology, and physical function but not with level of cognitive function (as measured by the SPMSQ) at baseline. In a controlled analysis of longitudinal data, initial SPMSQ score, age, African-American race, lower education, depressive symptomatology, and physical deficits at baseline, but not memory complaint, predicted a decline in cognitive function as measured by SPMSQ three years later. Although African-American men and women were less likely to complain of memory problems, they were more likely than Caucasians to experience an actual decline in cognitive function.

SOCIOECONOMIC STATUS

Socioeconomic status is associated with cognitive function. In general, those of lower socioeconomic status have lower levels of cognitive function, measured in a variety of ways, than those of higher socioeconomic status. While it is always useful to assess the component parts of socioeconomic status, for example, level of education, family income, and occupational status, to better understand the association between socioeconomic status and health, it is especially the case for an examination of cognitive function. As noted previously, level of education is particularly important for an examination of cognitive function (White, Katzman, Losonczy, Salieve, Wallace, Berkman, et al., 1994). Those with higher levels of education have higher levels of cognitive function and experience a less pronounced decline with age. There is also evidence of an interaction between age and education. In a study of 783 women randomly selected from Baltimore who were 65 years of age and older, researchers found that age and educational attainment interacted, so that younger women with more education had the highest MMSE scores and older women with less education had the lowest scores, but older women with more education scored higher than did younger women with less education (Magaziner, Bassett, & Helul, 1987). In a study of older residents of the Rancho Bernardo Heart and Chronic Disease Study, both men and women with some college education performed better on most tests than men and women with only high-school educations, and the rate of decline with age was sometimes slower in the college-educated group (Wierderholt, Cahn, Butters, Salmon, Kritz-Silverstein, & Barrett-Connor et al., 1993). In a study of residents of East Boston, Massachusetts, aged 70–79 years, low levels of education were associated with poorer psychological function (less mastery, efficacy, and happiness) than those with higher levels of education (Kubzansky, Berkman, Glass, & Seeman, 1998).

Level of education may be associated with cognitive function in several ways (Cagney & Lauderdale, 2002; Stern, Albert, Tang, & Tsai, 1999). Education, together with other indicators of socioeconomic status, has been shown to be associated with health behavior, such as nutrition and physical activity, and environmental exposures, which in turn may be associated with the risk of cognitive dysfunction, as well as other measures of poor health. The effects of physical activity and nutrition on cognitive function will be discussed later in more detail. Results from the EPESE project indicate that low levels of education were associated with poorer psychological function, less optimal health behaviors (increased tobacco consumption and decreased levels of physical activity), poorer biologic conditions (decreased pulmonary function, increased body mass index and waste-to-hip ratio), and larger social networks (increased number of contacts, decreased negative support) (Lee, Kawachi, Berkman, & Grodstein, 2003). In addition, educational level may reflect intellectual stimulation and, following the research of Marion Diamond and colleagues, an increased number of dendritic connections (Diamond & Conner, 1982; Mohammed, Zhu, Darmopil, Hjerling-Leffler, Ernfors, Winblad, et al., 2002). If aging is associated with the loss of such connections, those people with more connections have more to lose before different components of cognition are negatively affected. Put differently, educational attainment may be associated with cognitive reserves and thus better protect against age-associated losses in cognitive function. Along these lines, Barnes and colleagues (2004) recently published the results of a study from the Study of Physical Performance and Age-Related Changes in Sonomans (SPPARCS) cohort that showed that older people who demonstrated higher literacy, measured here by the North American Adult Reading Test, had higher overall cognitive functioning. Based on a list of 61 words with irregular spellings, subjects aged 55 and older were asked to pronounce each word, and pronunciations were scored as correct or incorrect based on a standardized key that takes into account regional differences in pronunciations. Cognitive function was based on a global measure that included standard assessments such as MMSE as well as measures of attention/executive function, verbal learning, memory, and verbal fluency. Literacy was strongly associated with higher levels across a variety of different domains of cognitive functioning. Most important, the relationship between level of education and cognitive functioning was eliminated after adjustment for level of literacy. This suggests that the relationship between education and cognitive function was due to literacy or perhaps other measures that suggest learning or language ability.

The role of educational attainment and cognitive function raises some of the most fascinating and, in many ways, perplexing issues in the epidemiology of aging. Despite the strong and consistent association between education and cognitive function, some commentators have argued that years of education have less to do with the etiology of cognitive function and more to do with the assessment of cognitive functioning (Jones & Gallo, 2001). Consider for a moment, education and MMSE. As noted previously, most studies show that MMSE scores are positively related to the education level of demented and cognitively intact older subjects. Several studies, in fact, found that educational level predicts MMSE scores independently of other social factors and age. It has been suggested that the relationship between education and cognitive function can be explained by differences in the learned resources associated with educational attainment. Subjects with more years of formal education have greater facility with language, as suggested by the results from Barnes and colleagues (2004). However, while this may suggest greater cognitive reserves, it also may suggest, as noted by some commentators, more experience in taking tests, such as the MMSE. In light of these concerns, it has been proposed that test scores be adjusted for level of education. One group of researchers proposes adjustment of MMSE scores based on educational attainment, especially the score that is suggestive of cognitive impairment. For college-educated subjects, a score of 24 is proposed, compared to a score of 23 for subjects with a 12th-grade education, and a score of 21 for those subjects with less than a high school education.

Family income is also associated with cognitive functioning and other measures of health and functioning. In this case, the association may be due less to the establishment of cognitive reserves and perhaps more to the association between family income and health behaviors (such as nutrition and physical activity), as well as social and environmental factors.

Likewise, occupational history may be associated with cognitive function, because of the risk of work-related exposures and injuries. In addition, occupational histories also may be associated with past tobacco exposures and levels of physical activity.

PHYSICAL ENVIRONMENT

There is no consistent evidence of a direct association between characteristics of the physical environment, in particular, the built environment, and levels of cognitive function. There is evidence of an association between characteristics of the environment and the likelihood that memories will be recalled (Evans, Brennan, Skorpanich, & Held, 1984). However, to the extent that the land use and characteristics of the built environment are associated with stressors, such as crime, it is reasonable to expect that residence in such settings is associated with cognitive dysfunction. In fact, a recent study indicated that older Holocaust survivors who suffered from posttraumatic stress disorder (PTSD) were more likely than older survivors who did not suffer from PTSD to demonstrate lower levels of cognitive function (Yehunda, Golier, Halligan, & Harvey, 2004). In addition, as noted previously, land use and the built environment are associated with opportunities for physical activity as well as access to reasonably priced nutritious food—factors, as we shall see, that are associated with cognitive function.

SOCIAL CAPITAL

Although there are no direct assessments of the relationship between social capital and cognitive function in older populations, it is reasonable to hypothesize that such a relationship may exist. There is evidence, for example, that fear and anxiety are associated with poor cognitive performance. To the extent that social capital is associated with trust and confidence, it is reasonable to expect it is associated with positive cognitive function.

LIVING ARRANGEMENTS, SOCIAL NETWORKS, AND SOCIAL SUPPORT

There is evidence that levels of cognitive function are associated with the number and quality of social relationships. Social engagement, defined as the maintenance of social connections and a high level of participation in social activities, has been hypothesized to prevent cognitive decline in elderly persons (Bassuk, Glass, & Berkman, 1999). Based on data from the New Haven EPESE project, a study was conducted to determine the relation between social disengagement and incidents of cognitive decline in community-dwelling elderly. Compared with persons who had five or six social ties, those who had no social ties were at increased risk for incident cognitive decline after adjustment for age, initial cognitive performance, sex, ethnicity, education, income, housing type, physical disability, cardiovascular profile, sensory impairment, and symptoms of depression, smoking, alcohol use, and level of physical activity. It is concluded in this study that social disengagement is a risk factor for cognitive impairment among elderly persons. There also is evidence from previous studies that the social contacts are associated with both physical and cognitive recovery from stroke as well as with the presence of depression. Based on a small sample of 50 subjects with incident stroke, the results indicated that an impaired relationship with a closest friend prior to the stroke was associated with impaired recovery in activities of daily living and cognition at long-term follow-up. Overall, the results suggest that during the first few weeks following a stroke, social supports and contact provide essential resources for stroke patients, whereas over the long run, other factors such as financial security, adequacy of living arrangements, and loss of job satisfaction also become important (Yeh & Liu, 2003). Finally, based on longitudinal data from the MacArthur Study on Successful Aging, it was found that seniors who reported more emotional support at baseline were more likely than others to demonstrate higher levels of cognitive functioning $7\frac{1}{2}$ years later, after adjustment for known social, behavioral, and health factors known to be associated with cognitive functioning (Seeman, Lusignolo, Albert, & Berkman, 2001).

HEALTH BEHAVIORS

Tobacco Exposure

A history of cigarette smoking seems to elevate the risk of cognitive dysfunction in older populations. In a recent study of residents of Gospel Oak electoral ward in London, the risk of cognitive decline was associated with particular health behaviors, including a history of cigarette smoking (Cervilla, Prince, & Mann, 2000). The results indicated that current smoking predicted cognitive impairment, independently of gender, age, alcohol, occupational class, education, handicap, depression, and baseline cognitive functioning. The association between cigarette smoking history and altered cognitive performance was also examined among 3429 Japanese-American participants of the Honolulu Heart program and its extension, the Honolulu-Asia Aging Study (Galanis, Petrovitch, Launer, Harris, Foley, & White, 1997). Compared with people who never smoked, those who had smoked continuously between two exams and those who had quit smoking during that period had significantly lower cognitive scores, after adjustment for age, education, Japanese acculturation, and subsequent alcohol consumption. There was evidence that the association between smoking and cognitive decline was reduced among older people who quit smoking over an extended period. The results indicate that there was a positive association between smoking during middle age and later risk of cognitive impairment. In addition, in a study of health behavior and cognitive function among members of the Rancho Bernardo cohort, the association between a history of cigarette smoking and reduced cognitive function was demonstrated for women, but not for men (Edelstein, Kritz-Silverstein, & Barrett-Connor, 1998). As will be noted in more detail, tobacco exposure is associated with health conditions, such as cardiac disease, stroke, and diabetes, known to be associated with reduced cognitive functioning. In spite of these findings, there is some evidence to suggest that tobacco exposure is associated with reduced risk of conditions, such as Parkinson's disease, that are often associated with cognitive dysfunctions. There is evidence from some epidemiologic studies that smoking is protective against the development of neurodegenerative diseases (Picciotto & Zoli, 2002). One possible explanation is that nicotine and nicotinic agonists are shown to be associated with improvement in cognitive function. It is also reported that activation of neuronal nicotinic acetylcholine receptors maintains cognitive function among aging subjects. It is fair to say that the role of tobacco exposure and cognitive function is presently unclear. It is necessary to determine under what circumstances tobacco exposure is detrimental to cognitive function and under what conditions it is beneficial. The answer to that question will have important implications for the development of programs and interventions to preserve cognitive functioning, a topic to which we will return in later chapters.

Alcohol Consumption

Although most studies in this area show no association between moderate alcohol consumption and cognitive functioning, one study found that that women who drank moderately (2–4 drinks per day) showed superior performance in many cognitive areas, compared to abstainers (Christensen, 2001). In contrast, excessive alcohol consumption can have very detrimental effects on cognitive functioning (Dufouil, Clayton, Brayne, Chi, Dening, Paykel, et al., 2000). Excessive alcohol consumption, like other health behaviors including tobacco exposure, is associated with cardiovascular diseases and diabetes, which in turn, are associated with reduced cognitive functioning. These results are generally consistent with results from the Framingham Heart Study (Elias, Elias, D'Agnostino, Silbershatz, & Wolf, 1999). Compared to abstainers, moderate consumption among women (2–4 drinks per day) was associated with "superior performance" on a set of cognitive function tests. In contrast, the association between alcohol consumption and cognitive function was found for males who consumed 4–8 drinks per day, although most of these relationships were not found to be significant.

Physical Activity

Participation in regular physical activity is associated with health and functioning in older populations (U.S. Department of Health and Human Services, 1996). Two reports from the MacArthur Study on Successful Aging indicate that participation in physical activity was associated with various measures of cognitive functioning (Albert, Jones, Savage, Berkman, Seeman, Blazer, 1995; DiPietro et al., 1996). There are still relatively few longitudinal examinations in this area. One exception is a study from the SPPARCS cohort in Sonoma, California. Results from that study indicate that cardiovascular fitness among healthy older adults protected cognitive function over a 6-year period (Barnes, Yaffe, Satariano, & Tager, 2003).

Diet and Nutrition

A variety of review studies indicate that diet and nutrition are associated with cognitive functioning in older populations (Riedel & Jorissen, 1998). There is evidence, for example, that supplementation with beta-carotene and alpha-tocopherol, substances that promote vitamins A and E, is associated with positive cognitive function. In addition, folate is also associated with positive cognitive functioning (Rampersaud, Kauwell, & Bailey, 2003). Folate-rich foods include orange juice, dark green leafy vegetables, asparagus, strawberries, and legumes. Research on vitamins B_6 and B_{12} also demonstrates an association with positive cognitive functioning (Solfrizzi, Panza, & Capurso, 2003). Results from the Seven Countries Study indicate a cross-sectional relationship between a healthy diet (as defined by the World Health Organization guidelines) and better cognitive function as assessed by the MMSE (Huijbregts, Feskens, Rasaner, Fidauza, Alberti-Fidanza, Nissianev, et al., 1998).

SENSE OF CONTROL, COHERENCE, AND SELF-EFFICACY

Self-efficacy refers to a sense of confidence in being able to complete a specific task. There is evidence that seniors with confidence in their ability to function cognitively will be able to do so (McDougall et al., 1999). Two reports from the MacArthur Study on Successful Aging indicate a positive association between self-efficacy beliefs (in this case, confidence in the ability to complete instrumental tasks) was associated with both high levels of physical and cognitive functioning (Berkman, Seeman, Albet, Blazer, Kahn, Mohs, 1993) and maintenance of difference measures of cognitive functioning (Seeman, McAvay, Merrill, Albert, & Rodin, 1996).

DISEASE AND COMORBIDITIES

The presence of disease and comorbidities is known to affect levels of cognitive functioning. Health conditions can be of two kinds. First, there are those health conditions, such as Alzheimer's disease and Parkinson's disease, which are very closely aligned with cognitive functioning. Indeed, an advanced state of cognitive dysfunction is one of the primary signs for diagnosis of Alzheimer's disease and other dementias. Second, there are conditions, such as cardiovascular diseases and diabetes, which are associated with subsequent cognitive functioning. In this case, impairments and limitations in cognitive functioning can be one of the sequelae of these conditions. Cancer is another example. If a primary cancer progresses to distant sites, such as the brain, it will clearly have negative consequences on cognitive functioning.

Alzheimer's Disease

As noted previously, cognitive dysfunction, such as loss of short- and long-term memory and executive functioning, is one of the signs of Alzheimer's disease. There is evidence of variation in the rate of cognitive decline associated with the onset of the disease. Change in cognitive functioning was assessed over 12 months in 110 subjects with "probable" Alzheimer's disease (Burns, Jacoby, & Levy, 1991). A greater rate of decline in cognitive functioning was observed in subjects whose parents suffered from dementia, in subjects who had moderate dementia, and those who had been ill for less than 24 months. Age, age of onset, and the presence or absence of aphasia or apraxia had no influence on the rate of progression.

Cardiovascular Disease

A number of studies have examined the association between cardiovascular disease and cognitive functioning. Results from the Seattle Longitudinal Study, which examined cognitive function and related psychobehavioral measures, indicated that subjects with specific health conditions, especially cardiovascular disease, were more likely than others to experience a decline in cognitive function (Wang, van Belle, Kukull, & Larson, 2002). Results form the Duke Longitudinal Study also showed an association between the presence of coronary artery disease and untreated hypertension with a decline in cognitive function (Bohannon, Fillenbaum, Pieper, Hanlon, & Blazer, 2002).

There is also concern that the treatment administered for particular cardiovascular conditions may be independently associated with cognitive decline. For example, calcium-channel blockers have been a focus of attention. Research was conducted in a Canadian population to determine whether there was a prospective association between antihypertensive medications and cognitive functioning (Maxwell, Hogan, & Ebly, 1999). The risk of cognitive decline, as indicated by a decline in performance on the MMSE over a 5-year period, was assessed in relation to the use of anti-hypertensive and diuretic drugs by 205 subjects with a history of hypertension and no evidence of dementia at baseline. The results indicated that the subjects taking calcium-channel blockers were over two times more likely to experience a significant decline over the 5-year period, compared to subjects who were taking other antihypertensive drugs.

Cerebrovascular Disease

People with cerebrovascular disease (stroke) are at elevated risk of cognitive decline. In a Swedish study, the risk of dementia associated with stroke was examined. One-third of stroke survivors were diagnosed as demented, which was three times higher than those without stroke (Zhu, Fratiglioni, Guo, Zguero-Torres, Winblad, & Viitanen, 1998). Stroke was also significantly related to cognitive impairment without dementia. In a related Swedish study, researchers examined to what extent the elevated risk associated with stroke was due to atrial fibrillation (Kilander, Andren, Nyman, Lind, Boberg, & Lithell, 1998). Specifically, the study aim was to examine whether atrial fibrillation was associated with low cognitive function in elderly men with and without stroke. The results indicated an association between atrial fibrillation and low cognitive function that was independent of stroke, high blood pressure, and diabetes.

Diabetes

Older people with diabetes are at elevated risk for cognitive decline. In a collaborative study of 9679 women aged 65 and older, those with diabetes had lower baseline scores than those without the condition on three tests of cognitive functioning, including the MMSE and the Trails Test (Gregg, Yaffe, Lauley, Rolka, Blackwell, Narayan, 2000). Diabetic women also experienced an even more precipitous decline than those without diabetes. These results are consistent with other studies in the area. Specifically, prolonged exposure to vascular risk factors such as diabetes mellitus and hypercholesterolemia may lead to atherosclerotic disease, possibly resulting in "silent" infarctions or impaired cerebral blood flow and a decline in cognitive functioning.

FALLS AND INJURIES

Some of the same factors, such as number and types of medications that elevate the risk of falls and injuries, are also associated with cognitive dysfunction. Falls and injuries may be a marker for underlying cognitive dysfunction (Tinetti, Speechley, & Gintur, 1988). It is also reasonable to hypothesize that severe injuries, resulting from either a fall or automobile crash, would be associated with subsequent cognitive and physical dysfunction. Finally, there is evidence that a fear of falling often leads to social isolation and an absence of contact with others. This, in turn, has been associated with a reduction in both cognitive and physical functioning. Although this is a reasonable chain of events, to my knowledge, it has not been investigated as yet.

PHYSICAL FUNCTIONING

There is evidence of an association between physical and cognitive functioning, a part of a general state that is referred to as "healthy aging" (see Chapter 4). With the exception of an examination of the prognostic significance of physical activity, there have been relatively few attempts to examine the exact patterns or mechanisms associated with the cross-sectional and prospective association between physical and cognitive functioning.

DEPRESSION

One of the most intriguing associations is between depression and cognitive dysfunction (Wilson, Mendes de Leon, Bienias, & Evans, 2004). Although the general consensus is that each represents a distinct condition, there are instances of overlap. In fact, some argue that the loss of affect, associated with depression, may be incorrectly interpreted as cognitive dysfunction. In a recent study, the association between depressive disorders and subsequent cognitive decline was assessed. Specifically, the study hypothesis was that older women aged 65 and older without dementia but with depressive symptoms had worse cognitive function and greater cognitive decline than women with few or no symptoms (Yaffe, Blackwell, Gore, Sands, Reus, & Browner, 1999). Cognitive and depressive assessments were conducted at baseline and at a 4-year follow-up. The results indicated that increasing symptoms of depression were associated with worse performance at baseline and follow-up on all three tests of cognitive function. It was concluded that depressive symptoms in older women were associated with both poor cognitive function and subsequent cognitive decline. In a separate study, the relationship between depressive symptoms and incident cognitive decline was examined. The results indicated that an elevated level of depressive symptoms was associated with an increased risk of incident cognitive decline among subjects who received a medium SPMSQ score, but not among subjects who received a high SPMSQ score. It was concluded that depressive symptoms, particularly dysphoric mood, precede future cognitive losses among elderly persons with moderate cognitive impairments. There is no evidence, however, that depressive symptoms are associated with the onset or rate of cognitive decline among cognitively intact older persons.

PHYSIOLOGICAL FACTORS

There are a number of anatomical and functional changes in the brain that occur with chronological aging (Trollor & Valenzuela, 2001). First, there is a reduction or shrinkage of the frontal lobe in normal individuals with age. Second, there is more reduction in white than in grey matter—a process referred to as "demylineation." Third, there is an increase in the presence of senile plaques, primarily in the associated cortices, and not, as is found in the brains of people with dementia, in the primary sensory and motor cortices. Fourth, there is an increase in the presence of neurofibrillary tangles in selected locations in the brain and not widespread, as is the case again in the brains of people with dementia. Fifth, the density of the brain's vascular system changes with age; most notably the degree and number of microvessel deformities begin to increase. Finally, there are minimal changes in choleric activity that aid in the processing of information.

Although these represent the general patterns of anatomical and functional changes associated with brain aging, there is considerable variation in cognitive functioning. There is evidence, for example, of neuroprotective agents and hormonal factors that modify cognitive vulnerability associated with the aging process. This has been described as "brain reserve." According to Stern (2002), "The idea of reserve against brain damage stems from the repeated observations that there does not appear to be a direct relationship between the degree of brain pathology or brain damage and the clinical manifestation of that damage." One suggestion, made by Stern and others, is that cognitive reserve may be based on more efficient utilization of brain networks or of enhanced ability to recruit alternative brain networks as needed. It is suggested that both pathological and protective processes result from the interaction of biologic, behavioral, and environmental factors.

One leading candidate for explaining the pathological process is oxidative damage associated with aging. Oxidation is a process that occurs naturally as part of cellular metabolism. The production of free radicals, a byproduct of oxidation, can interfere with normal aging and functioning. The nature of the oxidation process, coupled with the presence of protective factors, may be due to a variety of biologic, behavioral, and environmental factors (Floyd & Hensley, 2002). Justification for this hypothesis includes the following: The brain has a high content of easily peroxidizable unsaturated fatty acids. The brain requires very high amounts of oxygen per unit weight (about 20% of the total amount used in humans). The brain is not highly enriched in antioxidant protective defenses, and this then adds to the potential for oxidative damage associated with aging.

Genetic factors associated with dementia and cognitive decline are receiving increased attention. Of particular importance is epsiolon4 allele of apoliprotein E (APOE-4). In a Dutch study of elderly men, the baseline prevalence of impaired cognitive function (MMSE score of less than or equal to 25) was higher among carriers of the e4 allele compared with men without the allele. This association was maintained even after adjustment for age, occupation, smoking, alcohol use, and cardiovascular disease. The risk of developing impaired cognitive function during follow-up was significantly increased in allele carriers compared with noncarriers. Finally, in this population of elderly men, it was concluded that 22% of the risk of developing impaired cognitive function was most probably due to APOE-4 (Feskens, Havekes, Kalmign, de Knijff, Launer, & Kromhout 1994). The relationship between APOE-4, as well as age, education, and subclinical and clinical cardiovascular disease on changes in cognitive function was examined in the Cardiovascular Health Study (Kuller, Shemanksi, Manolio, Hau, Fried, Bryan, 1998). The results indicate that APOE-4 genotype, as well as vascular changes on magnetic resonance imaging, measures of brain atrophy, age, education, and race, were associated with low cognitive scores among older individuals.

There is also evidence that signs of future cognitive dysfunction in the senior years may appear early in life. One of the most interesting and compelling demonstrations of this is reported by David Snowdon (2001) in his book, *Aging with Grace*, a chronicle of his research studies with a group of aging Roman Catholic nuns. Snowdon and colleagues determined that those nuns who had spent their years in study and education maintained higher levels of cognitive function and were at lower risk of Alzheimer's disease than those who had lower levels of education and spent most of their time performing more domestic tasks, such as cleaning and cooking. Their research also suggested that signs of differential cognition were evident at the time that the nuns had entered the religious order as very young women. At the time of their admission to the order, all women were required to prepare a short autobiographical essay. Snowdon (2001, p. 106) recalled the point at which he discovered the autobiographies:

> Almost as soon as I discovered the autobiographies in the archives at Mankato, Jim Mortimer and I realized that they were fossils of a sort— miraculously preserved fragments of the past that might help us better understand the sisters' mental function early in life. But Jim and I had few concrete ideas how these fragments might fit together into a recognizable and meaningful form.

Later, Snowdon and Mortimer formulated a plan to analyze the content of the autobiographies. This plan included the use of monosyllabic and multisyllabic words, and the richness of vocabulary and the frequency of rarely used words. To ensure that the review of words reflected the historical period in which the autobiographies were written, Snowdon and colleagues used a database of 10,000 words that had been prepared in 1921 by psychologist Edward Thorndike, the time when the sisters were children or young women. Snowdon and his colleagues later collaborated with Susan Kemper, a psycholinguist, to identify criteria for assessment of the content of the young sisters' writings. Kemper recommended two important dimensions: idea density and grammatical complexity. As Snowdon (2001, p. 109) writes,

> Kemper explained to me that idea density reflects language-processing ability, which in turn is associated with a person's level of education, general knowledge, vocabulary, and reading comprehension. Grammatical complexity, on the other hand, is associated with working memory capacity. In order to write a complex sentence, Kemper pointed out, you have to keep many elements in play, juggling them until they are all properly coordinated.

The results later determined that the nuns who demonstrated greater "idea density" in their autobiographical essays early in life were much more likely to preserve cognitive function and be less likely to develop Alzheimer's disease later in life. These results are in keeping with the widely reported finding in many epidemiologic studies of an association between years of education and the preservation of cognitive function in older populations.

CONCLUSION

Cognitive functioning, together with physical functioning, represents important components of enhanced life expectancy. More important, while cognitive functioning generally declines with age, there is considerable variation in the extent and timing of that decline. In addition, this variation, while strongly associated with the biology of aging, is due to the interplay of behavioral, social, and environmental factors.

REFERENCES

Albert, M. S., Jones, K., Savage, C. R., Berkman, L., Seeman, T., Blazer, D., et al. (1995). Predictors of cognitive change in older persons: MacArthur Studies of Successful Aging. *Psychology of Aging, 10*(4), 578–589.

Baltes, P. B. (1991). Wisdom and successful aging. *Nebraska Symposium on Motivation, 39,* 123–167.

Baltes, P. B. (1993). The aging mind: Potential and limits. *The Gerontologist, 33*(5), 580–594.

Barnes, D. E., Tager, I. B., Satariano, W. A., & Yaffe, K. (2004). The relationship between literacy and cognition in well-educated elders. *Journals of Gerontology: Medical Sciences, 59*(4), M390–M395.

Barnes, D. E., Yaffe, K., Satariano, W. A., & Tager, I. B. (2003). A longitudinal study of cardiorespiratory fitness and cognitive function in healthy older adults. *Journal of the American Geriatrics Society, 51*(4), 459–465.

Bassuk, S. S., Glass. T. A., & Berkman, L. F. (1999). Social disengagement and incident cognitive decline in community-dwelling elderly persons. *Annals of Internal Medicine, 131*(3), 165–173.

Berkman, L., Singer, B., & Manton, K. (1989). Black/white differences in health status and mortality among the elderly. *Demography, 26*(4), 661–678.

Berkman, L. F., Seeman, T. E., Albet, M., Blazer, D., Kahn, R., Mohs, R., et al. (1993). High, usual, and impaired functioning in community-dwelling older men and women. Findings from the MacArthur Foundation Research Network on Successful Aging. *Journal of Clinical Epidemiology, 46*(10), 1129–1140.

Bohannon, A. D., Fillenbaum, G. G., Pieper, C. F., Hanlon, J. T., & Blazer, D. G. (2002). Relationship of race/ethnicity and blood pressure to change in cognitive function. *Journal of the American Geriatrics Society, 50*(3), 424–429.

Burns, A., Jacobs, R., & Levy, R. (1991). Progression of cognitive impairment in Alzheimer's disease. *Journal of the American Geriatrics Society, 39*(1), 39–45.

Cagney, K. A., & Lauderdale, D. S. (2002). Education, wealth, and cognitive function in later life. *Journals of Gerontology: Psychological Sciences, 57*(2), P163–P172.

Cervilla, J. A., Prince, M., & Mann, A. (2000). Smoking, drinking, and incident cognitive impairment: A cohort community-based study included in the Gospel Oak project. *Journal of Neurological Neurosurgery & Psychiatry, 68,* 622–626.

Christensen, H. (2001). What cognitive changes can be expected with normal ageing? *Australian and New Zealand Journal of Psychiatry, 35,* 768–775.

Colsher, P. L. (1992). Epidemiologic studies of the cognitive function in the elderly: Rationale, methods, and findings. In R. B. Wallace & R. F. Woolson (Eds.), *The epidemiologic study of the elderly.* (pp. 130–156). New York: Oxford University Press.

Diamond, M. C., & Connor, J. R., Jr. (1982). Plasticity of the aging cerebral cortex. *Experimental Brain Research, 5* (Suppl.), 36–44.

DiPietro, L. (1996). The epidemiology of physical activity and physical function in older people. *Medical Science, Sports, & Exercise, 28*(5), 596–600.

Dufouil, C., Clayton, D., Brayne, C., Chi, L. Y., Dening, T. R., Paykel, E. S., et al. (2000). Population norms for the MMSE in the very old: Estimates based on longitudinal data: Mini-Mental State Examination. *Neurology, 55*(11), 1609–1613.

Edelstein, S. L., Kritz-Silverstein, D., & Barrett-Connor, E. (1998). Prospective association of smoking and alcohol use with cognitive function in an elderly cohort. *Journal of Women's Health, 7*(10), 1271–1281.

Elias, P. K., Elias, M. F., D'Agnostino, R. B., Silbershatz, H., & Wolf, P. A. (1999). Alcohol consumption and cognitive performance in the Framingham Heart Study. *American Journal of Epidemiology, 150*(6), 580–589.

Evans, G. W., Brennan, P. L., Skorpanich, M. A., & Held, D. (1984). Cognitive mapping and elderly adults: Verbal and location memory for urban landmarks. *Journal of Gerontology, 39*(4), 452–457.

Feskens, E. J., Havekes, L. M., Kalmign, S., de Knijff, P., Launer, L. J., & Kromhout, D. (1994). Apolipoprotein e4 allele and cognitive decline in elderly men. *British Medical Journal, 309*(6963), 1202–1206.

Fillenbaum, G. G., Heyman, A., Huber, M. S., Woodbury, M. A., Leiss, J., Schmader, K. E., et al. (1998). The prevalence and 3-year incidence of dementia in older black and white community residents. *Journal of Clinical Epidemiology, 51*(7), 587–595.

Fillenbaum, G. G., Landerman, L. R., & Simonsick, E. M. (1998). Equivalence of two screens of cognitive functioning: The short Portable Mental Status Questionnaire and the Orientation-Memory-Concentration test. *Journal of American Geriatric Society, 46*(12), 1512–1518.

Floyd, R. A., & Hensley, K. (2002). Oxidative stress in brain aging: Implications for therapeutics of neurodegenerative diseases. *Neurodegenerative Diseases, 23*(5), 795–807.

Folstein, M., Anthony J. C., Parhad, I., Duffy, B., & Gruenberg, E. M. (1985). The meaning of cognitive impairment in the elderly. *Journal of the American Geriatrics Society, 33*(4), 228–235.

Folstein, M. F., Folstein, S. E., & McHugh, P. R. (1975). "Mini-mental state": A practical method for grading the cognitive state of patients for the clinician. *Journal of Psychiatric Research, 12*(3), 189–198.

Freedman, V. A., Aykan, H., & Martin, L. G. (2001). Aggregate changes in severe cognitive impairment among older Americans: 1993 and 1998. *Journals of Gerontology: Social Sciences, 56*(2), S100–S111.

Galanis, D. J., Petrovitch, H., Launer, L. J., Harris, T. B., Foley, D. J., & White, L. R. (1997). Smoking history in middle age and subsequent cognitive performance in elderly Japanese-American men: The Honolulu-Asia Aging Study. *American Journal of Epidemiology, 145*(6), 507–515.

Gallo, J. J., Schoen, R., & Jones, R. (2000). Cognitive impairment and syndromal depression in estimates of active life expectancy: The 13-year follow-up of the Baltimore Epidemiologic Catchment Area sample. *Acta Psychiatric Scand, 101*(4), 265–273.

Gregg, E. W., Yaffe, K., Cauley, J. A., Rolka, D. B., Blackwell, T. L., Narayan, K. M., et al. (2000). Is diabetes associated with cognitive impairment and cognitive decline among older women? Study of Osteoporotic Fractures Research Group. *Archives of Internal Medicine, 160*(2), 141–143.

Gruenberg, E. M. (1977). The failure of success. *Milbank Memorial Fund Quarterly, 55*(1), 3–24.

Huijbregts, P. P., Feskens, E. J., Rasanen, L., Fidanza, F., Alberti-Fidanza, A., Nissinen, A., et al. (1998). Dietary patterns and cognitive function in elderly men in Finland, Italy, and The Netherlands. *European Journal of Clinical Nutrition, 52*(11), 826–831.

Jones, R. N., & Gallo, J. J. (2001). Education bias in the mini-mental state examination. *International Psychogeriatrics, 13*(3), P548–P558.

Jones, B. N., Teng, E. L., Folstein, M. F., & Harrison, K. S. (1993). A new bedside test of cognition for patients with HIV infection. *Annals of Internal Medicine, 119*(10), 1001–1004.

Katzman, R. (1997). The aging brain: Limitations in our knowledge and future approaches. *Archives of Neurology, 54*(10), 1201–1205.

Kilander, L., Andren, B., Nyman, N., Lind, L., Boberg, M., & Lithell, H. (1998). Atrial fibrillation is an independent determinant of low cognitive function: A cross-sectional study in elderly men. *Stroke, 29*(9), 1816–1820.

Kubzanksy, L. D., Berkman, L. F., Glass, T. A., & Seeman, T. E. (1998). Is educational attainment associated with shared determinants of health in the elderly? Findings from the MacArthur Studies of Successful Aging. *Psychosomatic Medicine, 60*(5), 578–585.

Kuller, L. H., Shemanski, L., Manolio, T., Han, M., Fried, L., Bryan, N., et al. (1998). Relationship between ApoE, MRI findings, and cognitive function in the Cardiovascular Health Study. *Stroke, 29*(2), 388–398.

Launer, L. J., Kinkgreve, M. A., Jonker, C., Hooijer, C., & Lindeboom, J. (1993). Are age and education independent correlates of the Mini-Mental State Exam performance of community-dwelling elderly? *Journals of Gerontology, 48*(6), P271–P277.

Lee, S., Kawachi, I., Berkman, L. F., & Grodstein, F. (2003). Education, other socioeconomic indicators, and cognitive function. *American Journal of Epidemiology, 157*(8), 712–720.

Magaziner, J., Bassett, S., & Hebel, J. R. (1987). Predicting performance on the Mini-Mental State Exam: Use of age- and education-specific equations. *Journal of the American Geriatrics Society, 35*(11), 996–1000.

Maxwell, C. J., Hogan, D. B., & Ebly, E. M. (1999). Calcium-channel blockers and cognitive function in elderly people: Results from the Canadian Study of Health and Aging. *Canadian Medical Association Journal, 161*(5), 534–535.

McDougall, G. J. (1999). Cognitive interventions among older adults. *Annual Review of Nursing Research, 17,* 219–240.

Mohammed, A. H., Zhu, S. W., Darmopil, S., Hjerling-Leffler, J., Ernfors, P., Winblad, B., et al. (2002). Environmental enrichment and the brain. *Progress in Brain Research, 138,* 109–133.

Mulnard, R. A., Corrada, M. M., & Kawas, C. H. (2004). Estrogen replacement therapy, Alzheimer's disease, and mild cognitive impairment. *Current Neurology Neuroscience Report, 4*(5), 368–373.

Perls, T. T., Morris, J. N., Ooi, W. L., & Lipsitz, L. A. (1993). The relationship between age, gender, and cognitive performance in the very old: The effect of selective survival. *Journal of the American Geriatrics Society, 41*(11), 1193–1201.

Picciotto, M., & Zoli, M. (2002). Nicotinic receptors in aging and dementia. *Neurobiology, 53,* 641–655.

Rampersaud, G. C., Kauwell, G. P. A., & Bailey, L. B. (2003). Folate: A key to optimizing health and reducing disease risk in the elderly. *Journal of the American College of Nutrition, 22*(1), 1–8.

Ratey, J. J. (2002). *A user's guide to the brain: Perception, attention, and the four theaters of the brain.* New York: Vintage Books.

Reitan, R. M. (1958). Validity of the trail making test as an indicator of organic brain damage. *Perceptual Motor Skills, 8,* 271–276.

Riedel, W. J., & Jorissen, B. L. (1998). Nutrients, age, and cognitive function. *Current Opinion in Clinical Nutritional Metabolic Care, 1*(6), 579–585.

Roszak, T. (1998). *America—The wise: The longevity revolution and the true wealth of nations.* New York: Houghton Mifflin.

Scherr, P. A., Albert, M. S., Funenstein, H. H., Cook, N. R., Hennekens, C. H., Branch, L. G., et al. (1988). Correlates of cognitive function in an elderly community population. *American Journal of Epidemiology, 128*(5), 1084–1101.

Seeman, T. E., McAvay, G., Merrill, S., Albert, M., & Rodin, J. (1996). Self-efficacy beliefs and change in cognitive performance: MacArthur Studies of Successful Aging. *Psychology of Aging, 11*(3), 538–551.

Seeman, T. E., Lusignolo, T. M., Albert, M., & Berkman, L. (2001). Social relationships, social support, and patterns of cognitive aging in healthy, high-functioning older adults: MacArthur Studies of Successful Aging. *Health Psychology, 20*(4), 243–255.

Snowdon, D. (2001). *Aging with grace: What the nun study teaches us about leading longer, healthier, and more meaningful lives.* New York: Bantam Books.

Solfrizzi, V., Panza, F., & Capurso, A. (2003). The role of diet in cognitive decline. *Journal of Neural Transmission, 110*(1), 95–110.

Stern, Y. (2002). What is cognitive reserve? Theory and research application of the reserve concept. *Journal of International Neuropsychological Society, 8*(3), 448–460.

Stern, Y., Albert, S., Tang, M. X., & Tsai, W. Y. (1999). Rate of memory decline in AD is related to education and occupation: Cognitive reserve? *Neurology, 53*(9), 1942–1947.

Tinetti, M. E., Speechley, M., & Ginter, S. F. (1988). Risk factors for falls among elderly persons living in the community. *The New England Journal of Medicine, 319*(26), 1701–1707.

Troller, J. N., & Valenzuela, M. J. (2001). Brain ageing in the new millennium. *Australian/New Zealand Journal of Psychiatry, 35*(6), 788–805.

U.S. Department of Health and Human Services (1996). *Physical activity and health: A Report of the Surgeon General.* Washington, D.C.

Wallace, R. B. (1992). Aging and disease: From laboratory to community. In R. B. Wallace & R. F. Woolson (Eds.), *The epidemiologic study of the elderly.* New York: Oxford University Press: pp. 3–9.

Wang, L., van Belle, G., Kukull, W. B., & Larson, E. B. (2002). Predictors of functional change: A longitudinal study of nondemented people aged 65 and older. *Journal of the American Geriatrics Society, 50*(9), 1525–1534.

White, L., Katzman, R., Losonczy, K., Salieve, M., Wallace, R., Berkman, L., et al. (1994). Association of education with incidence of cognitive impairment in three established populations for epidemiologic studies of the elderly. *Journal of Clinical Epidemiology, 47*(4), 363–374.

Wiederholt, W. C., Cahn, D., Butters, N. M., Salmon, D. P., Kritz-Silverstein, D., & Barrett-Connor, E. (1993). Effects of age, gender and education on selected neuropsychological tests in an elderly community cohort. *Journal of the American Geriatrics Society, 41*(6), 639–647.

Wilson, R. S., Mendes de Leon, C. F., Bienias, J. L., & Evans, D. A. (2004). Depressive symptoms and cognitive decline in a community population of older persons. *Journal of Neurology, Neurosurgery, Psychiatry, 75,* 126–129.

Yaffe, K., Blackwell, T., Gore, R., Sands, L., Reus, V., & Browner, W. S. (1999). Depressive symptoms and cognitive decline in nondemented elderly women: A prospective study. *Archives of General Psychiatry, 56*(5), 432–430.

Yeh, S. C., & Liu, Y. Y. (2003). Influence of social support on cognitive function in the elderly. *BMC Health Services Research, 3*(1), 9.

Yehunda, R., Golier, J. A., Halligan, S. L., & Harvey, P. D. (2004). Learning and memory in Holocaust survivors with posttraumatic stress disorder. *Biological Psychiatry, 55*(3), 291–295.

Zhu, L., Fratiglioni, L., Guo, Z., Zguero-Torres, H., Winblad, B., & Viitanen, M. (1998). Association of stroke with dementia, cognitive impairment, and function disability in the very old: A population-based study. *Stroke, 29*(1), 2094–2099.

CHAPTER 6

Depression

Depression represents one of the leading public health problems facing older populations. As Daniel Blazer, a leading researcher in the epidemiology of aging and depression, has written (2003, p. 249): "Depression is perhaps the most frequent cause of [both] emotional suffering in later life and significantly decreased quality of life in older adults." The World Health Organization has reported that depression represents one of the leading "burdens of disease" in both the developed and in the developing world—truly a global public health problem (Murray & Lopez, 1997). Not only does depression have an independent effect on the quality and duration of life, but it also compounds the course of other conditions, such as heart disease, diabetes, and cancer. Regardless of the health condition, the presence of depression makes it worse, both in terms of functional limitations, disabilities, and elevations in the risk of death. Moreover, depression increases the number and length of hospital stays and associated health costs for people diagnosed with other conditions (Ranga, Krishnan, Delong, Kraemer, Carney, Spiegel, et al., 2002).

In this chapter, we will review the definition and measurement of depression in epidemiologic studies of older population, noting in particular the interplay between depression and cognitive dysfunction (Clayton, 1990a). In addition to noting the demographic and socioeconomic patterns of depression, we will examine the research that addresses the reasons for those patterns.

DEFINITION AND MEASUREMENT

There is an important difference between depressive disorders and depressive symptoms. A depressive disorder is a clinical diagnosis that captures a relatively persistent and severe form of the condition. Depressive disorders are often classified as either unipolar or the more serious, bipolar disorders. There are various forms of unipolar depressive disorders. Symptoms of unipolar disorder include the following:

- Depressed mood
- Diminished interest or pleasure in almost all activities
- Significant changes in appetite or weight
- Insomnia
- Psychomotor agitation or retardation
- Fatigue
- Feelings of worthlessness or excessive or inappropriate guilt
- Diminished ability to think, concentrate, or make decisions
- Recurrent thoughts of death or suicide, often accompanied by a sense of hopelessness.

According to the fourth edition of the American Psychiatric Association, *Diagnostic and Statistical Manual of Mental Disorders (DSM-IV)*, a major depression is present when an older adult exhibits one or both of two correlated symptoms (depressed mood and lack of interest) concurrently with four of more of the following symptoms for at least two weeks. These concurrent symptoms include feelings of worthlessness or inappropriate guilt, fatigue, psychomotor disorder, insomnia or hypersomnia, significant increase or decrease in weight or appetite, and recurrent thoughts of death or suicidal ideation. In addition, there are characteristics that serve to distinguish late-life depression. Melancholia is more likely to be present in older age subjects than in younger adults. Depression in late life is also more likely to appear concurrently with other health conditions. Major depressive episodes may persist for months or even years if left untreated. In contrast to major depressive disorders, minor, subsyndromal, or subthreshold depression is diagnosed as one of the core symptoms in addition to one to three additional symptoms just listed. Other definitions of minor depression include a biogenic depression that does not meet the criteria for major depression, yet responds to the administration of antidepressant medication. Finally, minor depression is classified as a score of 16 or more on the Centers for Epidemiologic Studies Depression (CES-D) scale (Radloff, 1977).

Measures of mild depression, or more appropriately, mild depressive symptoms, are used in a clinical setting as one of the initial steps in the diagnostic process. If the patient displays depressive symptoms, other tests follow to determine whether a major depressive disorder is present. In epidemiologic studies, depressive symptoms, rather than major depressive disorders, are used as a key outcome in general population studies. Often the same measures of depressive symptoms are used in both epidemiologic and clinical areas.

Center for Epidemiological Studies Depression (CES-D) Scale

The CES-D scale, introduced in 1977, is one of the most widely used instruments in epidemiologic studies (Radloff, 1977). The index consists of 20 statements, each describing a positive or depressive symptom associated with morale or mood (e.g., "I enjoyed life" or "I felt sad") (see Table 6–1). The 20 items can be classified into four subsets: depressive affect, positive affect, somatic symptoms, and interpersonal items. Subjects are asked to indicate on a 4-point ordinal scale (ranging from "Rarely or none of the time" to "Most or all of the time") the extent to which the statement reflected their mood during the past week. Options are scored 0 to 3 respectively. For items indicating absence of depressive symptoms, the scoring is reversed. The total scores can range from 0 (absence of symptoms) to 60 (most depressed). Results have been shown to be associated with clinical depression (score of 16 or greater). Shorter versions also have been developed and demonstrated to be associated with the full CES-D scale (Kohout, Berkman, Evans, & Cornoni-Huntley, 1993). Although not originally designed for study in an older population, the CES-D scale is the most often used depression instrument in epidemiologic studies of older populations, including the National Institute on Aging's Established Populations for Epidemiologic Studies of the Elderly (EPESE) project.

Geriatric Depression Scale (GDS)

The GDS was designed specifically for an older population (Yesavage, Brink, Rose, Lum, Huang, Adey, et al., 1983) (see Table 6–2). The items were selected from an initial pool of 100 questions identified by geriatric specialists as potentially distinguishing between depressed and nondepressed elderly people. The 30 items that correlated most highly with the total score were selected. Like the CES-D scale, the subject is asked to assess each item or statement in terms of whether it characterizes the subject's experience or mood during the past week. Unlike the ordinal response categories used in the CES-D scale, the subject answers "yes" or "no" to each statement. The GDS has been used in a variety of studies including studies examining atti-

Table 6-1 Center for Epidemiologic Studies Depression (CES-D) Scale

Instructions: Using the scale below, please circle the number before each statement which best describes how often you felt or behaved this way *during the past week.*

1 = Rarely or none of the time (less than 1 day)

2 = Some or a little of the time (1–2 days)

3 = Occasionally or a moderate amount of time (3–4 days)

4 = Most or all of the time (5–7 days)

During the past week

1 2 3 4 I was bothered by things that usually don't bother me.

1 2 3 4 I did not feel like eating; my appetite was poor.

1 2 3 4 I felt that I could not shake off the blues even with help from my family or friends.

1 2 3 4 I felt that I was just as good as other people.

1 2 3 4 I had trouble keeping my mind on what I was doing.

1 2 3 4 I felt depressed.

1 2 3 4 I felt that everything I did was an effort.

1 2 3 4 I felt hopeful about the future.

1 2 3 4 I thought my life had been a failure.

1 2 3 4 I felt fearful.

1 2 3 4 My sleep was restless.

1 2 3 4 I was happy.

1 2 3 4 I talked less than usual.

1 2 3 4 I felt lonely.

1 2 3 4 People were unfriendly.

1 2 3 4 I enjoyed life.

1 2 3 4 I had crying spells.

1 2 3 4 I felt sad.

1 2 3 4 I felt that people dislike me.

1 2 3 4 I could not get "going."

Scoring: Items are summed after reverse scoring item 4, 8, 12, and 16. Total CES-D scores range from 0–60, with greater scores reflecting higher levels of depression.

Source: Reprinted from the Journal of Psychiatric Research, VIT: 37–49, © 1983 Elsevier Ltd., with permission from Elsevier.

tudes toward life-sustaining therapy, functional dependency, pain, caregivers' burden, psychopharmacologic treatment, memory, and other topics.

Beck Depression Scale (BDS)

The BDS was developed in the 1960s and is used primarily for clinical studies of depression (Beck, Ward, Mendelson, Mock, & Erbaugh, 1961).

Table 6-2 Geriatric Depression Scale (Short Form)

Patient's Name: _____ Date: _____

Instructions: Choose the best answer for how you felt over the past week.

No.	Question	Answer	Score
1.	Are you basically satisfied with your life?	Yes / No	
2.	Have you dropped many of your activities and interests?	Yes / No	
3.	Do you feel that your life is empty?	Yes / No	
4.	Do you often get bored?	Yes / No	
5.	Are you in good spirits most of the time?	Yes / No	
6.	Are you afraid that something bad is going to happen to you?	Yes / No	
7.	Do you feel happy most of the time?	Yes / No	
8.	Do you often feel helpless?	Yes / No	
9.	Do you prefer to stay at home, rather than going out and doing new things?	Yes / No	
10.	Do you feel you have more problems with memory than most?	Yes / No	
11.	Do you think it is wonderful to be alive?	Yes / No	
12.	Do you feel pretty worthless the way you are now?	Yes / No	
13.	Do you feel full of energy?	Yes / No	
14.	Do you feel that your situation is hopeless?	Yes / No	
15.	Do you think that most people are better than you are?	Yes / No	
		TOTAL	

Scoring:

Assign one point for each of these answers:

1. NO	4. YES	7. NO	10. YES	13. NO
2. YES	5. NO	8. YES	11. NO	14. YES
3. YES	6. YES	9. YES	12. YES	15. YES

A score of 0 to 5 is normal. A score above 5 suggests depression.

Source: Reprinted from Journal of Psychiatric Research, 17:37–49, Yesavage, Short-form of the Geriatric Depression Scale, Copyright (1983), with permission from Elsevier.

The scale consists of 21 statements relating to symptoms and attitudes, such as a sense of failure, indecisiveness, and social withdrawal. As is true of the CES-D and GDS, subjects are asked to provide graded responses to statements based on their experiences during the preceding week. The BDS has been used primarily in clinical and gerontological studies of depression.

There is general correspondence in scores across the three major depression scales. Since there are no clear criteria for the selection of scales, most commentators recommend using the instrument that is most often used in their field of study. It should be emphasized again, however, that while the CES-D scale was not designed exclusively for the study of older population, it is used almost exclusively in epidemiologic research. As such, it may be more appropriate for epidemiologic studies in which the objective is to examine depression across a wide spectrum of adult ages.

There are three issues associated with the measurement of depression. First, somatic factors, such as fatigue and loss of appetite, are included in the constellation of depressive symptoms. This has prompted concerns about the specificity of the criteria for depressive symptoms. It is unclear, some have charged, whether the somatic symptoms are reflective of depression or associated physical health problems. This is likely, some charge, since depressive symptoms are strongly associated with leading chronic health conditions, such as coronary heart disease, diabetes, and cerebrovascular disease. Second, questions have been raised about the close association between depressive symptoms, cognitive dysfunction, and leading types of dementia, such as Alzheimer's disease. Third, there is concern that racial and ethnic factors may affect how older people respond to different assessment criteria for depression. For example, Cole and colleagues (2000) evaluated whether there is an item–response bias in the CES-D scale. Based on data from the New Haven EPESE, the likelihood of blacks responding higher on the CES-D items, "People are unfriendly" and "People dislike me" were 2.3 times that of whites matched on overall depressive symptoms. In addition, the odds of women responding higher on the CES-D item "Crying spells" were 2.1 times that of men matched on overall depressive symptoms. The researchers conclude that the CES-D would have greater validity across gender and race and ethnic groups after removal of the more emotional and interpersonal items.

As noted previously, depressive symptoms and clinical depression can occur across the life course. Late-life depression, defined again as that occurring for the first time at age 60 and older, has a number of distinctive characteristics. In addition to often occurring in conjunction with other health conditions, it also can be characterized by a set of distinctive symptoms. It is reported that older people may be more likely than younger people to develop a condition referred to as "depression without sadness," defined as a depletion syndrome manifested by withdrawal, apathy, and lack of vigor (Blazer, 2003, p. 250).

DEMOGRAPHIC PATTERNS

Age

One of the important research questions is whether the incidence and prevalence of depression increases with age. Most research examining age as a risk factor for depression has been based on cross-sectional data. To our knowledge, there is no research that has examined the incidence and prevalence of depression over the life course. It is generally reported that the prevalence of clinically diagnosed major depression in community-dwelling older adults is between 2–5% (Blazer & Williams, 1980; Myers, Lesser, Rodriguez, Mira, Hwang, Camp, et al., 2002). In contrast, depressive symptoms are more frequently found in this population, with a prevalence of 15% consistently reported across studies of community-dwelling older adults (Blazer, 1994). Although late-life depression is defined as the first episode of depression occurring at age 60 and older, it is unclear what proportion of elderly persons with depression have had episodes of depression earlier in life, especially during late childhood and adolescence. This is an important question, given recent evidence that suggests an increase in depressive symptoms in puberty, adolescence, and young adulthood, especially among females (Leon, Klerman, & Wickramaratne, 1993). There also is evidence that depression in old age is associated with emotional abuse and neglect during childhood (Blazer, 2003). In addition, a Finnish study indicates that an early loss of the mother among men and an early loss of the father among women independently predicted the occurrence of depression, after holding constant other predictors of late-life depression (Kivela, Luukinen, Koski, Viramo, & Pahkala, 1998). The researchers conclude that the psychological trauma associated with early parental loss contributes to the development of depression even in old age.

Data on symptoms of major depressive episodes were examined for the 1994 and 1995 cohorts in the Alameda County Study. In addition to age, the effects of gender, marital status, education, financial strain, chronic medical conditions, functional impairment, cognitive problems, life events, neighborhood problems, social isolation, and social support were examined. Depression was measured with 12 items covering DSM-IV diagnostic criteria for major depressive episodes. Among the subjects 60 years of age and older, there was a higher prevalence in 1995. The highest prevalence rates in 1994 and in 1995 were among those 80 years of age and older. Those people who were depressed in 1994 were at greater risk for depression in 1995 (Roberts, Kaplan, Shema, & Strawbridge, 1997). The important question was to determine the reasons for the association between both age and depressive symptoms. It was determined that the effects of age were due in large part to the prevalence of chronic diseases and functional limitations. The evidence from this study suggests that it is not age per se that causes depression but rather the effects of chronic diseases and functional limitations that are often associated with aging. Most important, healthy, normally functioning older adults are at no greater risk for depression than younger adults. In addition to age, chronic health conditions, and functional limitations, it was determined that depressive symptoms were associated with gender, cognitive problems, neighborhood problems, and social isolation. Each of these factors will be described in greater detail.

Gender

Following gender differences noted earlier in the life course, the general consensus is that older women are more likely than older men to display depressive symptoms (Blazer, Burchett, Service, & George, 1991; Kessler, 2000). As with age, the issue is to determine what it is about gender—in this case, being female—that affects the risk of depression. There is evidence that the gender difference in depression is due at least in part to social and psychological factors (Nolen-Hoeksema, Larson, & Grayson, 1999). In a community study of residents age 25 to 75, it was determined that a low sense of mastery control and exposure to chronic strain was associated with depressive symptoms. Moreover, women were more likely than men to have less mastery and experience greater strain. Multivariate analysis indicated that these factors explained in part the gender difference in depressive symptoms. Differences in the presence of chronic disease and functional limitations also have been shown to help account for gender differences in depression.

Blazer (2002, p. 160) summarizes the research on gender and late-life depression:

> Female gender is a risk factor for depression throughout the adult life cycle. Gender differences in the prevalence of major depression, however, appear to narrow as age increases. To date, no one has adequately identified those factors related to gender that may place women at increased risk for depression, regardless of age. If such factors exist (bias

in case identification may contribute significantly to the reported gender differences), those risk factors appear to decrease in late life. Some presumed vulnerability in women, such as multiple roles (e.g., worker and homemaker), social isolation, and childbearing responsibilities disappear with increasing age. Yet older women often face unique social stressors with greater frequency than older men, such as caretaking responsibility and widowhood.

Race and Ethnicity

There is evidence that African-American and Hispanic elderly are more likely than non-Hispanic white elderly to display depressive symptoms, although the research is less consistent than the research that is reported by gender. A series of examinations of racial and ethnic differences in depression have been conducted using data from the Duke EPESE (Blazer, Landerman, Hays, Simonsick, & Saunders, 1998). The Duke study consists of 3401 subjects aged 65 and older, over half (54%) of whom are African-Americans. When comparisons of specific symptoms by race were examined, African-American elderly were more likely to report less hope about the future, poor appetite, difficulty concentrating, the need to exert more effort to accomplish regular tasks, being less talkative, feeling people were unfriendly, feeling disliked by others, and being more "bothered" than usual. Following research reported earlier on age and gender differences, the racial differences in these items disappeared after adjustment for socioeconomic factors (income and education), cognitive impairment, chronic health problems, disability, and other factors. It is important to note, however, that the racial difference in the reports of differences in interpersonal relations (i.e., feeling disliked and feeling people were unfriendly) persisted. Overall, the researchers concluded that the results confirmed earlier findings of minimal overall differences in the frequency of symptoms between African-Americans and non-African-Americans in this community study. In the New Haven EPESE, significant differences in depressive symptoms were found between African-American and non-Hispanic white seniors. In this case, however, it was concluded that if the interpersonal items were excluded, there would be association between race and depressive symptoms in this older population (Cole et al., 2000).

There is evidence that Hispanic elders have a higher prevalence of depressive symptoms than non-Hispanic whites. For example, research from the San Luis Valley Health and Aging Study in rural Colorado

(Swenson, Baxter, Shetterly, Scarbro, & Hamman, 2000) indicate that the age-adjusted odds ratio of depressive symptoms in Hispanic women compared with that of non-Hispanic white women was 2.11. Those Hispanic older women displaying lower levels of acculturation to the American culture displayed higher levels of depressive symptoms than those with higher acculturation scores. In this study, there was no significance difference in the prevalence of depressive symptoms between Hispanic and non-Hispanic white males. A more recent report from the Hispanic EPESE study indicates that older Mexican-Americans who lived in higher density neighborhoods with a higher percentage of Mexican-American residents had lower levels of depression than those who lived in higher density neighborhoods with lower levels of Mexican-Americans (Ostir, Eschbach, Markides, & Goodwin, 2003). This suggests the issue of acculturation needs further study. The results may indicate that level of acculturation to a non-Hispanic society depends on the nature of the seniors' daily life. If a Hispanic senior resides in a Hispanic neighborhood, then low acculturation to non-Hispanic society may be less associated with depression. However, if a Hispanic senior resides in a non-Hispanic neighborhood, then low acculturation to a non-Hispanic society may be more problematic and be more closely associated with depression.

There is also evidence that immigrant status and recency of immigration was associated with depression among Hispanic elders (Black, Goodwin, & Markides, 1998). Moreover, female immigrants were at significantly higher risk for depressive symptoms, compared to male immigrants (Black et al., 1998).

As noted previously, the prevalence of race and ethnicity seems to be due in part to differences in socioeconomic status. As we will see, the patterns of socioeconomic status and depression, in turn, are due to differences in socioeconomic components—family income, education, and level of occupation.

SOCIOECONOMIC STATUS

Lower socioeconomic status (Kessler, 1979, 1982), less education (Blazer et al., 1994) and lower income (Blazer et al., 1991; Townsend, Miller, & Guo, 2001) all have been found to be associated with greater depressive symptoms. As we know from other studies of socioeconomic status and health in older populations, it may be that lower socioeconomic status, represented by lower family income, lower level of education, and lower occupational status, elevates the incidence and prevalence of depression in at least two ways: First, it may increase the likelihood that the person is exposed (perhaps, across the life course) to a variety of social, environmental, and behavioral insults. Second, lower socioeconomic status may provide fewer resources to address the insults or to reduce their effects. Results from the National Black Women's Health Project indicated that African-American women with higher levels of education and higher levels of income were less likely to demonstrate depressive symptoms than African-American women with lower socioeconomic status, regardless of age (Scarinci, Thomas, Brantley, & Jones, 2002). In a multiethnic sample of older women, lower levels of education were significantly associated with elevated prevalence of depressive symptoms (Myers, Lesser, Rodriquez, Mira, Huang, et al., 2002). A report from a British community study of seniors indicates that the Townsend Index, a community-level measure of socioeconomic deprivation, was significantly related to both the incidence and prevalence of depression (Wilson, Chen, Taylor, McCracken, & Copeland, 1999).

THE PHYSICAL ENVIRONMENT

There is evidence that those who live in more stressful environments are more likely to display psychiatric difficulties, including depression (Evans, 2003). Although there is little evidence in older populations, Evans (2003, p. 536) argues that, "Indirectly, the physical environment may influence mental health by altering psychosocial processes with known mental health sequelae. Personal control, socially supportive relationships, and restoration from stress and fatigue are all affected by properties of the built environment." There is evidence that weather patterns may affect the risk of depression (Evans, 2003). Seasonal affective disorder (SAD) has been characterized as a form of depression. The onset of this condition is associated with chronic exposure to shorter hours of daylight. SAD is characterized by sadness, fatigue, and, in some cases, depression.

SOCIAL CAPITAL

There is evidence of an association between a report of low social capital and higher levels of depression among a sample of older residents of Taiwan (Hahn et al., 2004). Kawachi and Berkman (2001), in a review of social ties and mental health, also noted an association between social capital (in this case, defined as social networks embedded in a larger social structure) and depression.

LIVING ARRANGEMENTS, SOCIAL NETWORKS, AND SOCIAL SUPPORT

Depression is a condition that is closely associated with social relationships. Social relations are associated with the incidence of depression in older populations, although, according to some research, not as strongly as found in younger populations (George, 1992). In a sample of North Carolina residents, it was determined that gender, race, place of residence, education, and physical illness all were significant predictors of the onset of depression only for younger respondents. Only marital status—both being married and having never been married—was a stronger predictor of illness onset for older than younger adults. Interestingly, subjective social support was a significant predictor of recovery for middle-aged but not for older respondents. It is suggested that age differences in the association between social factors and depression may indicate that certain social factors have different meaning or salience at different ages or stages of life. For example, marital status may be unrelated to depression at younger ages because it is both common and normatively acceptable for young adults to have not yet established families. There is also evidence that older people who are socially isolated are more likely than those with higher levels of contact and support to be depressed (Krishnan, George, Pieper, Jiang, Arias, Look, et al., 1998; Prince, Harwood, Thomas, & Mann, 1998). This may be one of the possible explanations for recent results that indicate that older people who have stopped driving are more likely to become depressed than those older people who continue to drive, adjusting for health and functional covariates (Ragland, Satariano, & MacLeod, 2005). The cessation of driving may reduce the likelihood that older people will have contact with friends and relatives as well as reduce the opportunities for older people to participate in group and organizational activities.

Older people who participate in groups and organizations are less likely to experience depression than those who are more socially isolated. Along these lines, there is research that indicates that older people who participate in religious organizations and take part in religious activities are less likely to experience depressive symptoms than those who do not belong to such organizations (Blazer, 2003). In this case, church membership may involve both group affiliation as well as a belief system that assists the older person to adapt to stressors and to maintain coherence. More generally, there is evidence that indicates that older people who have difficulty with activities of everyday life, such as Instrumental Activities of Daily Living (recall Chapter 4), are more likely to have depressive symptoms. As is true with other research in this area, it is sometimes difficult to determine whether depression is a cause or consequence of some other set of factors (Alexopoulos, Vrontou, Kakuma, Meyers, Young, Klauser, et al., 1996).

There is also evidence that older people who have lost a spouse through death are at elevated risk for depression (Rosenzweig et al., 1997). There is evidence that nearly one-third of bereaved elderly demonstrate signs of depression one month after the death of the spouse. This drops to one quarter at 2–7 months. Rosenzweig and colleagues (1997, p. 421) summarize current research:

> Spousal bereavement is a common event in later life and, not infrequently, an important cause of psychiatric and medical morbidity. Depression (along with suicide), anxiety, substance abuse, and symptoms of "complicated" grief are among the more important psychiatric sequelae of spousal bereavement. They may represent, in part, forms of abnormal reaction to the stress of loss and the challenges of adaptation to becoming widowed.

Research based on data from the U.S. Asset and Health Dynamics Among the Oldest Old determined that there is a strong association between bereavement and depression for both men and women aged 70 years or older (Turvey, Carney, Arndit, Wallace, & Herzog, 1999). Moreover, the loss of a spouse was associated with subsequent depression at a rate nine times that of those who did not lose a spouse, following adjustment for age, sex, preloss depressive symptoms, and medical illness. In other studies, there is the suggestion that older men may be at elevated risk. Although older women are more likely than older men to lose a spouse, there is evidence that older men are more likely to experience depression. One hypothesized explanation is that since it is relatively uncommon for men to survive their wives, there are fewer supports available to adapt to the loss. Clayton (1990b, p. 34) summarizes some of the research in this area:

The essence of the morbidity of bereavement is the increased use of alcohol, tranquilizers, hypnotics, cigarettes, and other substances during this stressful time. Increased mortality occurs in men aged 75 years or younger in the first year of bereavement, but mortality does not increase in women or parents during that first year.

There are related findings that indicate that stressful caregiving may elevate the risk for depression. Older people who provide care to people who are suffering from a chronic condition, functional limitation, or cognitive impairment are themselves likely to experience depression (Dura, Haywood-Niler, & Kiecolt-Glaser, 1990; Moritz, Kasl, & Berkman, 1989). There are different possible reasons for this association. First, as noted in Chapter 2, there is evidence that stress may adversely affect physiological regulatory systems and lead to allostatic load, the weathering process that is associated with an elevated risk of ill health and poorer cognitive and physical functioning. Second, caregiving may prevent the caregiver from engaging in healthful behavior. Either the caregiver has less time or is simply distracted from his or her own healthful behavior. There is evidence that women who provide care are less likely to engage in leisure physical activity, which, as will be noted later, is independently associated with reduced odds of depression (Satariano, Haight, & Tager, 2002).

There is also a growing body of evidence that indicates that a spouse's health and level of well-being are associated with the health and well-being of the subject. A number of studies have indicated that the physical health and depressive symptoms of a spouse are associated independently with the depressive symptoms of the subject, after adjustment for relevant covariates (McLeod, 1993; Kivela, Luukinen, Viramo, & Koski, 1998). Although these findings are very interesting, most of the studies have been based on clinic populations or have been limited to cross-sectional examinations. There are at least three studies, however, that have examined the longitudinal association between the physical health and depressive symptoms of the spouse and the health and level of depression in the subject, based on samples of men and women from a community sample (Hagnell & Kreitman, 1974; Tower & Kasl, 1996). Tower and Kasl, using data from the New Haven EPESE sample, determined that changes in the depressive symptoms were associated with the level of depression in the subject, adjusting for other relevant covariates. In the Swedish study by Hagnell and Kreitman (1974), the results indicated that there was a gender difference. Following results from studies of caregiving, older women were more likely than men to be influenced by the health and level of depression of their spouses. The most compelling evidence to date has been based on the 1992 and 1994 waves of the US Health and Retirement Survey. After adjustment for the subject's mental and physical health and sociodemographic characteristics, the presence of a spouse with more depressive symptoms was associated with significantly higher levels of depression in the subject (Siegel, Bradley, Gallo, & Kasl, 2004). There are several possible explanations for the concordance of depressive symptoms in the spouse. First, since the spouses share a common environment, they may share a common exposure, such as a stressful event, that jointly elevates the risk of depression. Second, given the intimacy of marriage, the problems and distress that affect one spouse may create problems in the other. As noted previously, the provision of care may be physically and emotionally debilitating. Moreover, the ill or depressed spouse may represent a lost source of support for the other spouse. Third, there is some evidence to suggest that people who marry are likely to share many behavioral, health, and functional characteristics, what some have described as "assortative mating." This leads to a consideration of other factors that have been shown to affect the level of depression.

HEALTH BEHAVIORS

Tobacco Exposure

There have been few examinations of the association between tobacco use and the incidence and prevalence of depression in older populations. It is reasonable, however, to hypothesize that such an association exists. A number of the factors associated with the incidence of depression, such as specific types of health conditions, functional limitations, and disabilities, are associated with tobacco exposure. It may be, therefore, that tobacco exposure does affect depression, and the mechanism for that relationship may operate through those other factors. One study that does demonstrate a more direct association is reported from the Baltimore Epidemiologic Catchment Study (Larson, Booth-Kewley, Merrill, & Stander, 2001). Results from that study indicate that current or past tobacco use is associated with depressive symptoms over a 13-year follow-up period.

Alcohol Consumption

It also may be that alcohol consumption, either in excessive amounts or in conjunction with one or more medications, may elevate the risk for a variety of conditions, such as cognitive dysfunction, health problems, and depression (Atkinson, 1999). Atkinson (1999, p. 907) writes, "Drinking bouts induce depressive symptoms in many primary alcoholics. These symptoms, which may be subsyndromal or meet criteria for major depression, spontaneously remit with abstinence over a few weeks' time in the majority of cases without antidepressant treatment." It is also useful to consider the reasons for alcohol consumption. It may be that some of the social factors shown to be associated with depression, such as social isolation, caregiving, or bereavement, also may be associated with the reasons the older person consumes alcohol. As such, it will be useful to determine whether the consumption of alcohol or for that matter, sedentary behavior, helps to account for the association between social factors and depressive symptoms.

Physical Activity

Sedentary behavior is associated with the risk of subsequent depression. Depressed women enrolled in the Study of Physical Performance and Age-Related Changes in Sonomans (SPPARCS) in Sonoma, California, reported physical activity that was only 60–80% of the level of activity reported by nondepressed women, following adjustment of other factors (Hollenberg, Haight, & Tager, 2003). In a separate study of the Sonoma cohort, it was determined that older men and women with depressive symptoms were less likely than others to engage in any form of physical activity, even the most modest (Satariano et al., 2002). A number of epidemiologic studies have examined the association between physical activity and subsequent levels of depression. In general, those who engaged in physical activity were less likely to demonstrate depressive symptoms later in life. For example, male and female subjects from the Alameda County Study, who reported a low level of physical activity at baseline were at greater risk for depression at the follow-up, compared to those who were more active (Camacho, Roberts, Lazarus, Kaplan, & Cohen, 1991). Among older subjects in the Iowa EPESE study who reported depressive symptoms at baseline, those who indicated an increase in walking in the interim were more likely to report fewer depressive symptoms than those who did not engage in walking in the interim. A recent Finnish study indicated that older people who had reduced their intensity of physical exercise over an 8-year period reported more depressive symptoms than those who remained active or increased their physical activity (Lampinen, Heikinen, & Ruoppila, 2000). Depressive symptoms were predicted by the level of baseline physical exercise, earlier depressive symptoms, older age, gender, having three or more chronic health conditions, and difficulties in performing activities of daily living. It is necessary to examine the reasons for the decline in physical activity to understand more clearly the reasons for the association between reduced physical activity and increased depression. It may be, for example, that those social or behavioral factors may be associated with the decline in physical activity, which, in turn, are associated with the elevation in depressive symptoms.

Diet and Nutrition

There appears to be a strong interaction between undernutrition and depression among older population (Donini, Savine, & Cannella, 2003; Pirlich & Lochs, 2001). As noted previously, undernutrition, as well as obesity, is identified as a significant nutrition problem in older populations. It is well known that depression may lead to loss of appetite (Blazer, 2002). In addition, a poor appetite may lead to reduced consumption of nutritious food and result in a low energy output. This, in turn, may lead to or aggravate a current depressive state.

SENSE OF CONTROL, COHERENCE, AND SELF EFFICACY

In addition to health behaviors, there may be particular psychosocial factors that are associated with depression in older populations. For example, there is evidence that a sense of control and self-efficacy, or confidence in the ability to complete a particular task, is associated with depressive symptoms. There is a report that an overall sense of control is associated with lower prevalence of depression in a sample of residents aged 25–75 years. There is no evidence of a significant difference in the results by age group (Lachman & Weaver, 1998). Blazer (2002) concludes that positive self-efficacy may be the cause and consequence of a variety of activities such as positive health behavior, especially physical activity, and social connections with others, factors that have been shown to be associated with a reduced incidence and prevalence of depression. Blazer goes on to recommend that it will be possible to develop clinical and public health programs in older populations, programs that would reduce the risk of depression in older populations. The development of this and other interventions will be considered later in the book.

DISEASE AND COMORBIDITIES

As noted previously, late-life depression often occurs concurrently with other types of chronic health conditions (Blazer, 2003). While late-onset depression is less likely than depression that occurs earlier in life to have a familial component, late-onset depression is more likely to occur concurrently with other medical conditions as well as cognitive dysfunctions. Leading comorbid conditions include cardiovascular disease, cancer, neurologic disorders, arthritis, sensory loss, and various metabolic disturbances. It is also reported that cerebrovascular disease occurs concurrently with some geriatric depressive syndromes. As reported by Serby and Yu (2003), basal ganglia and left-hemisphere lesions, especially those close to the frontal pole, are most frequently associated with poststroke depression. Blazer (2002, p. 41) reports that "Physical, somatic, or endogenous symptoms are frequently associated with depression in late life." Sleep difficulties are among the most common physical complaints of depressed elderly. Vegetative symptoms are in general more common in the elderly than in younger persons. For persons diagnosed as suffering from a major depressive episode, some symptoms are more common in younger persons (crying spells), whereas others tend to be more common in the elderly (e.g., difficulty concentrating). In contrast to clinical studies, feelings of guilt were just as common in the elderly as in individuals of other stages of life (Blazer, 2002). Suicidal ideation was less common and loss of appetite more common among older persons. In general, however, the similarities in symptom presentation between persons in midlife and late life are more evident than the differences.

Depressive symptoms are very common in patients with coronary heart disease. It is estimated that up to 65% of patients report depressive symptoms following an acute myocardial infarction. There is evidence that depression tends to follow a chronic, somewhat uneven course, following a cardiac event. A number of patients found to be depressed after the clinical onset of coronary heart disease were already depressed prior to the clinical onset. Depression, in turn, increases the risk of a subsequent cardiac event and elevates the risk of death. Interestingly, women with coronary heart disease are more likely than men with the same condition to be depressed. Not surprisingly, the risk of depression increases during the last six months of life among older patients dying of coronary heart disease (Levenson, McCarthy, Lynn, Davis, & Phillips, 2000).

The specific mechanisms for the association between coronary heart disease and depression are presently unclear. It is unclear, for example, whether the association is due to the severity of the heart disease, and to what extent the association is due to cardiac medications. The associations between coronary heart disease and depression also may be affected by the presence of comorbid conditions and associated medications and treatments for those conditions. It has been suggested that avoidance of depression, as well as preventive measures, including physical exercise, mental stimulation, good nutrition, and abstinence from tobacco use, are useful approaches to postpone or ameliorate the consequences of aging and allow patients to tolerate cardiovascular diseases when they become manifest (Friesinger & Ryan, 1999). In a separate study, coronary heart disease patients who were depressed in the hospital were at higher risk of adverse psychological and quality-of-life outcomes over the course of the subsequent year (Mayou, Black, & Bryant, 2000). A recent Finnish study examined in more detail the factors that elevated the risk of depression among patients with coronary heart disease (Ahto, Isoaho, Puolijoki, Laippala, Romo, & Kivela, 1997). Among men, the occurrence of coronary heart disease, physical disability, widowhood or being divorced, and among women with previous depression, physical disability and the use of angiotensin-converting enzyme inhibitors, were associated with depression. It is concluded that coronary heart disease is not an independent factor in the etiology of depression among the elderly. Moreover, the association of coronary heart disease and depression among men is explained by the acute or chronic psychic stress caused by the heart disease. Finally, it is concluded that the more complicated the patient's coronary heart disease, the greater the likelihood for the onset of depression. There is also some evidence that physical dysfunction may aggravate the association between coronary heart disease and depression in the elderly, from a 1-year prospective cohort study of 198 health maintenance organization members who had elective cardiac catheterization for coronary artery diseases (Sullivan, LaCroix, Baum, Grothaus, & Katon, 1997). At the time of catheterization, patients' self-reported physical function differed significantly by number of main coronary vessels stenosed greater than 70%, by anxiety quartiles, and by depression quartiles. At one year, physical function was no longer associated with the number of main coronary vessels stenosed at baseline, but still was significantly associated with baseline anxiety and depression. The results indicated that anxiety and depression have a significant and persistent effect on physical dysfunction in patients with coronary artery disease. In contrast to other research on coronary heart disease, there is evidence that low rather than high blood pressure is associated with the onset of depression (Prisant, Spruill, Fincham, Wade, Carr, & Adams, 1991). Based on other studies that suggest that depression is a potential side effect of antihypertensive drug therapy, the risk of depression was examined in a prospective study of older patients from four hypertension groups. The treatment groups included 466 patients, each receiving one of the following four protocols: (1) no drug therapy, (2) diuretics only, (3) diuretics plus reserpine, and (4) diuretics plus beta-blockers. Demographic data including age, sex, and race were collected. The results indicated that 35.4% of the hypertensive population was depressed, based on the Zung Self-Rating Depression Scale. Age and sex were not significant factors in the frequency of depression. Blacks scored higher than whites in all drug treatment groups except those treated with high lipophilic beta-blockers, but the depression was not higher. The rate of depression among those taking reserpine or beta-blockers was not different than that among those receiving either no treatment or diuretics. It was concluded, therefore, that reserpine or beta-blockers therapy did not cause any more depression than any other antihypertensive treatment. Interestingly, in a separate study of 143,253 Medicaid recipients, there was a significant association between beta-blockers and tricylic antidepressants. It is concluded that beta-blocker use may be an important cause of iatrogenic depression among hypertensive patients (Avorn, Everitt, & Weiss, 1986). Finally, there is evidence that the absence of social support may elevate the risk of depression among older patients with coronary heart disease (Krishnan, George, Pieper, Jiang, Arias, Look, et al., 1998). There is evidence, for example, that negative life events and social support are important factors in the development and outcome of depression. Patients with coronary artery disease were assessed with the Duke

Depression Evaluation Schedule for the Elderly. It was determined that the presence of major depression was associated with increased negative life events and lowered subjective social support after accounting for age, sex, and race. Overall, the research suggests that the association between coronary disease and depression may be due to a variety of factors including previous depression, severity of coronary heart disease, type of treatment, and perceived social support.

Cerebrovascular disease is also associated with the onset of depression in older populations. In fact, it is argued that stroke and depression, together with a series of other factors—most notably, lower extremity fracture, dementia, and comorbid medical conditions—should be thought of as constituting a common cluster or syndrome of geriatric conditions (Mast, MacNeill, & Lichtenberg, 1999). In a recent review of the literature in this area (Rao, 2000), the relationship between depression and cerebrovascular disease was examined in three distinct settings: depression in established cerebrovascular disease, cerebrovascular disease in established depression, and erosion in vascular dementia. Overall, the prevalence of depression is higher than controls only within the first year after stroke, but most studies did not include a control group. The prevalence of depression in vascular dementia compared with Alzheimer's disease is higher in most studies, but matching for sociodemographic factors and severity cognitive impairments has been inconsistent. Research has determined an association between frontal or subcortical cerebrovascular lesions and depression in later life. It is recommended that these results be viewed with caution, given the possibility of methodological flaws. The following conclusions are made: First, there is some evidence that cerebrovascular disease has an etiological role in late-life depression. Second, the increased likelihood of damage to frontal or subcortical brain circuitry following stroke, transient ischemia, and hypertension may explain the high prevalence of depression in older people with vascular risk factors. More valid definitions of lesion location and the use of appropriately matched control groups should be employed to clarify this issue. Finally, the high prevalence of depression accompanying cerebrovascular disease and the prolongation of disability in depressed people with stroke suggests the need for closer collaboration between geriatric psychiatrists, neurologists, and physicians caring for the elderly.

Diabetes is a relatively common condition that is reported to be associated with subsequent depression. A comprehensive review of symptoms and complications of adult diabetic patients found that the occurrence of symptoms of depression, anxiety, panic, and forgetfulness were unexpectedly common and, more important, may adversely affect the ability of diabetic patients to comply with the intended therapy (Konen, Curtis, & Summerson, 1996). It is unclear from this research, however, whether the risk of depression increases significantly among older diabetic patients. In an Italian study (Amato, Polisso, Cacciatore, Ferrara, Canonico, Rengo, & Varricchio, 1996), diabetes was found to be independently associated with depression independently of age, gender, loneliness, cognitive impairment, chronic obstructive lung disease, degenerative joint disease, heart diseases, cancer, kidney disease, cirrhosis of the liver, and cholelithiasis. It is concluded that non-insulin-dependent diabetes is significantly associated in the elderly. It is further concluded that this may have clinical implications for the goal of blood glucose control in older populations.

There is also evidence that depression is associated with dementia-related conditions, such as Alzheimer's disease and Parkinson's disease. It is estimated that depression is present in 50% of older people with some type of dementia-related conditions. Some depressed elderly patients develop a dementia syndrome that resolves either completely or partially after remission of depression. In addition, depressed elderly patients who have only partial cognitive improvement after the amelioration of depression usually have an early-stage dementing disorder. Moreover, cognitive dysfunction associated with dementia may be exacerbated by the presence of depression.

Since depression is, in most cases, a chronic condition, it is often difficult to determine whether the health condition preceded the onset of depression or vice versa. It has been reported (Carney, Freedland, Eisen, Rich, & Jaffe, 1995) that some depressive episodes are reactions to the physical dysfunction or discomfort associated with medical illness, but many depressed patients have depressive episodes before they develop any medical problems. Depression also may occur later in the course of the disease and be an outcome of the condition, even if the depressive episode began as a reaction to the medical illness.

FALLS AND INJURIES

There is evidence, as we shall see in Chapter 7, that depression is identified as a risk factor for falls and injuries. Given that older people that fall are at elevated risk for subsequent falls, it is reasonable to assume that there may be a complex interaction of depression and falling over time. Moreover, older people that fall are at risk for developing a fear of falling, the characteristics of which may overlap with depressive symptoms.

PHYSICAL FUNCTIONING

Physical functioning is associated with depressive symptoms. Specifically, those older people with depressive symptoms are also likely to have physical functional limitations and disabilities (Blazer et al., 1991; Hybels, Blazer, & Pieper, 2001). It was concluded from a systematic review and meta-analysis of the research on the epidemiology of depression among the elderly that preexisting disability was one of the recognized risk factors for depression in this population (Cole & Dendukuri, 2003).

COGNITIVE FUNCTIONING

In addition to be associated with dementia-related conditions, older people with depressive symptoms are also more likely to have cognitive limitations. In fact, the lack of affect associated with depression is also evidence of cognitive dysfunction. This, of course, raises some intriguing issues regarding the overlapping etiologies of both conditions. Schweitzer and colleagues (2002, p. 999) summarize the epidemiological research in this area:

> Epidemiological data support a close association of depressive symptoms and cognitive decline or the development of dementia in the elderly. The majority of available studies either support, or do not contradict, the proposition that a depressive syndrome in many instances is a prodrome to the development of dementia. They further indicate that cognitive decline may accompany the depressive syndrome rather than depression necessarily predating the onset of cognitive decline. The data are inconclusive, however, concerning depression as a risk factor for dementia, that is, whether depression predisposes the individual to the later development of dementia. The differences in findings are most likely due to the many methodologies that have been applied.

At a practical level, it also is associated with misdiagnosis. A person with depression may be misdiagnosed with a cognitive deficit, and vice versa.

PHYSIOLOGICAL FACTORS

There are no pathological criteria for the diagnosis of late-life depression. As noted previously, the assessment of depression is based on a set of behavioral symptoms. There is evidence, however, that certain types of depression are associated with specific pathological characteristics. For example, vascular depression, defined here to mean depression due to vascular lesions in the brain, may be more common with late-onset depression than for depression occurring earlier in life. Symptoms associated with this type of depression include impairment in verbal fluency, psychomotor speed, recognition memory, and executive cognitive function, defined in the previous chapter as impairment in being able to plan. There is evidence that vascular lesions in selected regions of the brain may contribute to a subset of late-life depression.

Although there are no pathological criteria for the diagnosis of late-life depression, it is associated with a variety of brain abnormalities, such as a reduction in brain volume, white-matter hyperintensities, and ventriculomegaly, defined here to mean. Late-life depression also has been associated with reductions in global cortical cerebral blood flow and cerebral metabolic rate (Serby & Yu, 2003). There is also evidence that serotonin dysregulation is associated with geriatric major depression disorder. Accordingly, selective serotonin reuptake inhibitors (SSRIs) represent the recommended treatment for older patients. Unlike other standard treatments for depression, such as tricyclic antidepressants, SSRIs have fewer cardiovascular side effects and are less likely to adversely affect cognition (Serby & Yu, 2003).

There is increasingly an interest in a determination of genetic susceptibility to depression and mood disorders across the life span (Blazer, 2003). Although familial association of depression has been reported, a genetic susceptibility to depression seems to be reduced with chronological age. Despite the association between depression and a various cardiovascular diseases, there is no apparent association between depression and APOE-E allele.

Research from the SPPARCS study in Sonoma, California, determined that there was a relationship between depressive symptoms and reduced cardiorespiratory fitness (Hollenberg, Haight, & Tager, 2003). This result, in turn, suggests some interesting physiological pathways. As Hollenberg and his colleagues report (2003, p. 1116):

Many investigators have suggested that depression is caused by chronic hyperactivity of the hypothalamic-pituitary-adrenal axis and the locus coeruleus-norepinephrine system. Because these systems coordinate behavioral and neuroendocrine responses, chronic hyperactivity could well lead to autonomic adaptations (with possible down regulation of adrenergic receptors) that would influence cardiorespiratory performance. One of the neurohormonal systems involved in the physiology of depression involves corticotrophin-releasing hormone, which, by stimulating ACTH secretion, regulates glucocorticoid levels. Depressed patients have been shown to have raised plasma levels of cortisol, which, by its catabolic actions, could potentially decrease muscle mass.

CONCLUSION

Depression is one of the leading public health problems in older populations. The etiology of late-life depression implicates a variety of factors, including chronic health conditions as well as physical and cognitive health conditions. In addition, social, behavioral, and environmental factors are associated with the incidence and prevalence of depression. These results highlight the significance of an ecological model to understand more clearly the causes of depression in this population. The study of depression also underscores the difficulty in understanding the interactions of what we are characterizing as the causes and consequences of depression. Rather than thinking of these topics as discrete conditions, it is perhaps more appropriate to consider them as clusters of conditions, better defined as "geriatric syndromes." The significance of this view becomes clear as we consider subsequent topics, such as falls, injuries, and automobile crashes.

REFERENCES

Ahto, M., Isoaho, R., Puolijoki, H., Laippala, P., Romo, M., & Kivela, S. L. (1997). Coronary heart disease and depression in the elderly—A population-based study. *Family Practice, 14,* 436–445.

Alexopoulos, G. S., Vrontou, C., Kakuma, T., Meyers, B. S., Young, R. C., Klauser, E., et al. (1996). Disability in geriatric depression. *American Journal of Psychiatry, 153*(7), 877–885.

Amato, L., Polisso, G., Cacciatore, F., Ferrara, N., Canonico, S., Rengo, F., et al. (1996). Non-insulin-dependent diabetes mellitus is associated with a greater prevalence of depression in the elderly. The Osservatorio geriatrico of Campania Region Group. *Diabetes Metabolism, 22*(5), 314–318.

Atkinson, R. (1999). Depression, alcoholism and ageing: A brief review. *International Journal of Geriatric Psychiatry, 14,* 905–910.

Avorn, J., Everitt, D. E., & Weiss, S. (1986). Increased antidepressant use in patients prescribed beta-blockers. *Journal of the American Medical Association, 255*(3), 357–360.

Beck, A. T., Ward, C. H., Mendelson, M., Mock, J., & Erbaugh, J. (1961). An inventory for measuring depression. *Archives of General Psychiatry, 4,* 561–571.

Black, S. A., Goodwin, J. S., & Markides, K. S. (1998). The association between chronic diseases and depressive symptomatology in older Mexican Americans. *Journals of Gerontology: Medical Sciences, 53*(3), M188–M194.

Blazer, D., Burchett, B., Service, C., & George, L. K. (1991). The association of age and depression among the elderly: An epidemiological exploration. *Journal of Gerontology, 46*(6), M210–M215.

Blazer, D. G., Landerman, L. R., Hays, J. C., Simonsick, E. M., & Saunders, W. B. (1998). Symptoms of depression among community-dwelling elderly African-American and white older adults. *Psychology of Medicine, 28*(6), 1311–1320.

Blazer, D. G., Kessler, R. C., McGonagle, K. A., & Swartz, M. S. (1994). The prevalence and distribution of major depression in a national community sample: the National Comorbidity Survey. *American Journal of Psychiatry, 151*(7), 979–986.

Blazer, D. (1994). Dysthymia in community and clinical samples of older adults. *American Journal of Psychiatry, 151,* 1567–1569.

Blazer, D. G. (2003). Depression in late life: Review and commentary. *Journals of Gerontology: Medical Sciences, 58A,* 249–265.

Blazer, D. G., & Williams, C. D. (1980). The epidemiology of dysphoria and depression in a elderly population. *American Journal of Psychiatry, 137,* 439–444.

Camacho, T. C., Roberts, R. E., Lazarus, N. B., Kaplan, G. B., Cohen, R. D. (1991). Physical activity and depression: Evidence from Alameda County Study. *American Journal of Epidemiology, 134*(20), 220–231.

Carney, R. M., Freedland, K. E., Eisen, S. A., Rich, M. W., & Jaffe, A. S. (1995). Major depression and medication adherence in elderly patients with coronary artery disease. *Health Psychology, 1995, 14*(1), 88–90.

Clayton, P. J. (1990a). The comorbidity factor: Establishing the primary diagnosis in patients with mixed symptoms of anxiety and depression. *Journal of Clinical Psychiatry, 51*(Suppl.), 35–39.

Clayton, P. J. (1990b). Bereavement and depression. *Journal of Clinical Psychiatry, 51*(Suppl.), 34–38.

Cole, M. G., & Dendukuri, N. (2003). Risk factors for depression among elderly community subjects: A systematic review and meta-analysis. *American Journal of Psychiatry, 160*(6), 1147–1156.

Cole, S. R., Kawachi, I., Maller, S. J., & Berkman, L. F. (2000). Test of item-response bias in the CES-D scale: Experience from the New Haven EPESE study. *Journal of Clinical Epidemiology, 53*(3), 285–289.

Donini, L. M., Savine, C., & Cannella, C. (2003). Eating habits and appetite control in the elderly: The anorexia of aging. *International Journal of Psychogeriatrics, 15*(1), 73–87.

Dura, J. R., Haywood-Niler, E., & Kiecolt-Glaser, J. K. (1990). Spousal caregivers of persons with Alzheimer's and Parkinson's disease dementia: A preliminary comparison. *The Gerontologist, 30*(3), 332–336.

Evans, G. W. (2003). The built environment and mental health. *Journal of Urban Health, 80*(4), 536–555.

George, L. K. (1992). Social factors and the onset and outcome of depression. In K. W. Schaie, D. Blazer, & J. S. House (Eds.). *Aging, health behaviors, and health outcomes.* Hillsdale, New Jersey: Lawrence Erlbaum Associates Publishers, 137–160.

Hognell, O., & Kreitman, N. (1974). Mental illness in married pairs in a total populations. *British Journal of Psychiatry,* 125, 293–302.

Hahn, C. Y., Yang, M. J., Shih, C. H., & Lo, H. Y. (2004). Religious attendance and depressive symptoms among community dwelling elderly in Taiwan. *International Journal of Psychiatry, 19*(12), 1148–1154.

Hollenberg, M., Haight, T., & Tager, I. B. (2003). Depression decreases cardiovascular fitness in older women. *Journal of Clinical Epidemiology, 56*(11), 1111–1117.

Hybels, C. F., Blazer, D. C., & Pieper, C. F. (2001). Toward a threshold for sub-threshold depression: An analysis of correlates of depression by severity of symptoms. Using data from an elderly community sample. *The Gerontologist, 41*(3), 357–365.

Kawachi, I., & Berkman, L. F. (2001). Social ties and mental health. *Journal of Urban Health, 78*(3), 458–467.

Kessler, R. C. (1979). Stress, social status, and psychological distress. *Journal of Health and Social Behavior, 20*(3), 259–272.

Kessler, R. C. (1982). A disaggregation of the relationship between socioeconomic status and psychological distress. *American Sociological Review, 47*(6), 752–764.

Kessler, R. C. (2000). The epidemiology of pure and comorbid generalized anxiety disorder: A review and evaluation of recent research. *Acta Psychiatric Scandinaven, 406* (Suppl.), 7–13.

Kivela, S. L., Luukinen, H., Koski, K., Viramo, P., & Pahkala, K. (1998). Early loss of mother or father predicts depression in old age. *International Journal of Geriatric Psychiatry, 13*(8), 527–530.

Kohout, F. J., Berkman, L. F., Evans, D. A., & Cornoni-Huntley, J. (1993). Two shorter forms of the CES-D (Center for Epidemiological Studies Depression) Depression Symptoms Index. *Journal of Aging & Health, 5*(2), 179–193.

Krishnan, K. R., George L. K., Pieper, C. F., Jiang, W., Arias, R., Look, A., et al. (1998). Depression and social support in elderly patients with cardiac disease. *American Heart Journal, 136*(3), 491–495.

Lachman, M. E., & Weaver, S. L. (1998). Sociodemographic variation in sense of control by domain: Findings from the MacArthur Studies of Midlife. *Psychology of Aging, 13*(4), 553–562.

Lampinen, P., Heikinen, R. L., & Ruoppila, I. (2000). Changes in intensity of physical exercise as predictors of depressive symptoms among older adults: An eight-year follow-up. *Preventive Medicine, 30*(5), 371–380.

Larson, G. E., Booth-Kewley, S., Merrill, L. L., & Stander, V. A. (2001). Physical symptoms as indicators of depression and anxiety. *Military Medicine, 166*(9), 796–799.

Leon, A. C., Klerman, G. L., & Wickramaratne, P. (1993). Continuing female predominance in depressive illness. *American Journal of Public Health, 83*(5), 754–757.

Levenson, J. W., McCarthy, E. P., Lynn, J., Davis, R. B., & Phillips, R. S. (2000). The last six months of life for patients with congestive heart failure. *Journal of American Geriatrics Society, 48*(5 Suppl.): S101–S109.

Mast, B. T., MacNeill, S. E., & Lichtenberg, P. A. (1999). Geropsychological problems in medical rehabilitation: Dementia and depression among stroke and lower extremity fracture patients. *Journals of Gerontology: Medical Sciences, 54*(12), M607–M612.

Mayou, R. A., Black, J., & Bryant, B. (2000). Unconsciousness, amnesia, and psychiatric symptoms following road traffic accident injury. *British Journal of Psychiatry, 177,* 540–545.

McLeod, J. D. (1993). Spouse concordance for depressive disorders in a community sample. *Journal of Affective Disorders, 27*(1), 43–52.

Moritz, D. J., Kasl, S. V., & Berkman, L. F. (1989). The health impact of living with a cognitively impaired elderly spouse: Depressive symptoms and social functioning. *Journal of Gerontology, 44*(1), S17–S27.

Myers, H. F., Lesser, J., Rodriquez, N., Mira, C., B., Huang, W. C., Camp, C., et al. (2002). Ethnic differences in clinical presentation of depression in adult women. *Cultural Diveristy Ethnic Minority Psychology, 8*(2), 138–156.

Nolen-Hoeksema, S., Larson, J., & Grayson, C. (1999). Explaining the gender difference in depressive symptoms. *Journal of Personality and Social Psychology, 77*(5), 1061–1072.

Ostir, G. V., Eschbach, K., Markides, K. S., & Goodwin, J. S. (2003). Neighborhood composition and depressive symptoms among older Mexican Americans. *Journal of Epidemiology and Community Health, 57*(12), 987–992.

Pirlich, M., & Lochs, H. (2004). Nutrition in the Elderly. *Best Practices Research in Clinical Gastroenterology, 15*(6), 869–884.

Prince, M. J., Harwood, R. H., Thomas, A., & Mann, A. H. (1998). A prospective population-based cohort study of the effects of disablement and social milieu on the onset and maintenance of late-life depression: The Gospel Oak Project VII. *Psychological Medicine, 28*(2), 337–350.

Prisant, L. M., Spruill, W. J., Fincham, J. E., Wade, W. E., Carr, A. A., Adams, M. A., et al. (1991). Depression associated with antihypertensive drugs. *Journal of Family Practice, 33*(5), 481–485.

Radloff, L. S. (1977). The CES scale: A self-report depression scale for research in the general population. *Applied Psychological Measurement,* 1, 385–401.

Ragland, D. R., Satariano, W. A., & MacLeod, K. E. (2005). Driving cessation and depression in an older population. *Journals of Gerontology: Medical Sciences.*

Rao, R. (2000). Cerebrovascular disease and late life depression: An age old association revisited. *International Journal of Geriatric Psychiatry, 15*(5), 419–433.

Roberts, R. E., Kaplan, G. A., Shema, S. J., & Strawbridge, W. J. (1997). Does growing old increase the risk for depression? *American Journal of Psychiatry, 154*(10), 1384–1390.

Rosenzweig, A., Prigerson, H., Miller, M.D., & Reynolds, III, C.F. (1997). Bereavement and late-life depression: Grief and its implications in the elderly. *Annual Review of Medicine, 48,* 421–428.

Satariano, W. A., Haight, T. J., & Tager, I. B. (2002). Living arrangements and participation in leisure-time physical activities in an older population. *Journal of Aging & Health, 14*(2), 427–451.

Scarinci, I. C., Thomas, J., Brantley, P. J., & Jones, G. N. (2002). Examination of the temporal relationship between smoking and major depressive disorder among low-income women in public primary care clinics. *American Journal of Health Promotion, 16*(6), 323–330.

Schweitzer, I., Tuckwell, V., O'Brien, J., & Ames, D. (2002). Is late onset depression a prodrome to dementia? *International Journal of Geriatric Psychiatry, 17*(11), 997–1005.

Serby, M., & Yu, M. (2003). Overview: Depression in the elderly. *Mt. Sinai Journal of Medicine, 70*(1), 38–44.

Siegel, M. J., Bradley, E. H., Gallo, W. T., & Kasl, S. V. (2004). The effect of spousal mental and physical health on husbands' and wives' depressive symptoms, among older adults: Longitudinal evidence from the Health and Retirement Survey. *Journal of Aging & Health, 16*(3), 398–425.

Sullivan, M. D., LaCroix, A. Z., Baum, C., Grothaus, L. C., & Katon, W. J. (1997). Functional status in coronary artery disease: A one-year prospective study of the role of anxiety and depression. *American Journal of Medicine, 103*(5), 348–356.

Swenson, C. J., Baxter, J., Shetterly, S. M., Scarbro, S. L., & Hamman, R. F. (2000). Depressive symptoms in Hispanic and non-Hispanic white rural elderly: The San Luis Valley Health and Aging Study. *American Journal of Epidemiology, 152*(11), 1048–1055.

Tower, R. B., & Kasl, S. V. (1996). Depressive symptoms across older spouses: Longitudinal influences. *Psychology of Aging, 11*(4), 683–697.

Townsend, A. L., Miller, B., & Guo, S. (2001). Depressive symptomology in middle-aged and older married couples: Dyadic analysis. *Journals of Gerontology: Psychological Sciences, 56*(6), S352–S364.

Turvey, C. L., Carney, C., Arndit, S., Wallace, R. B., & Herzog, R. (1999). Conjugal loss and syndromal depression in a sample of elders aged 70 years or older. *American Journal of Psychiatry, 156*(10), 1596–1601.

Wilson, K. C., Chen, R., Taylor, S., McCracken, C. F., & Copeland, J. R. (1999). Socio-economic deprivation and the prevalence and prediction of depression in older community residents: The MRC-AlPHA Study. *British Journal of Psychiatry, 175,* 549–553.

Yesavage, J. A., Brink, T. L., Rose, T. L., Lum, O., Huang, V., Adey, M. B., et al. (1983). Development and validation of a geriatric depression screening scale: A preliminary report. *Journal of Psychiatric Research, 17,* 37–49.

CHAPTER 7

Falls, Injuries, and Automobile Crashes

Fatalities and injuries associated with falling and automobile crashes are considered to be significant public health problems in older populations. Falls represent the leading cause of nonfatal injury and the second leading cause, following automobile crashes, of accidental death in populations aged 65 years and older (Duthie, 1989; Rubenstein, Robbins, Schulman, Rosado, Osterweil, & Josephson, 1988), even though many commentators charge that the number of fall-related deaths may be under-reported on the death certificates (Berg & Cassells, 1992). Automobile- and pedestrian-related injuries are attracting both scientific and public attention. Most recently, in Santa Monica, California, an older driver lost control of his car and killed a number of people at an outdoor market. With the aging of the population, we can expect more of these tragic events and more soul-searching in their aftermath. Driving in older populations represents a classic public policy issue. On one hand, there is concern about public safety. And on the other hand, there is recognition that new restrictions of driving in older populations may lead to reductions in access to goods and services and, perhaps, an increase in social isolation as it becomes more difficult to have regular contact with friends and relatives.

In this chapter, we will examine the causes of falls, injuries, and automobile crashes. In addition to representing leading causes of disability and death, falls, injuries, and crashes are important for other reasons as well. First, unlike diagnosed conditions, falls, injuries, and crashes represent "geriatric syndromes," meaning they are caused by a variety of concurrent factors. Mary Tinetti and colleagues (Tinetti, Inouye, Gill, & Doucette, 1995, p. 1348) define geriatric syndromes as "experienced by older—

229

particularly frail—persons, occur intermittently rather than either continuously or as single episodes, may be triggered by acute insults, and often are linked to subsequent functional decline." As such, falls are considered to be a marker of frailty, immobility, and acute and chronic health impairments. Falls, in turn, reduce function by causing injury, activity limitations, fear of falling, and loss of mobility. Second, there are other unique methodological issues associated with the definition, measurement, and assessment of falls, injuries, and automobile crashes. Third, research in this area is paradigmatic for the use of an ecological model. The independent and joint effects of physical capacity and environmental demands are fundamental for a consideration of research in this area (Gill, Williams, & Tinetti, 2000). Indeed, in research on falls, a distinction is often made between "intrinsic" (functional capacity) and "extrinsic" (social and physical environment) risk factors (Cwikel & Fried, 1992; Tinetti, Doucette, & Claus, 1995). In addition, public health interventions to reduce the incidence and severity of falls and injuries are based on enhancing the capacity of individuals and populations, as well as reducing hazards and barriers associated with the person's or population's environment. Finally, technological interventions to reduce hazards associated with mobility, especially with regard to housing, transportation, and environmental design, are most developed in this area of research and practice.

DEFINITION AND MEASUREMENT OF FALLS AND FALL-RELATED DISORDERS

The Institute of Medicine, in a report titled *The Second Fifty Years: Promoting Health and Preventing Disability* (Berg & Cassells, 1992), defined a fall as follows: "A fall is an unintentional event that results in the person coming to rest on the ground or another lower level (p. 263)." The report further characterized falls as consisting of three components (pp. 263–264):

> Falls can be described in terms of three phases. The first phase is an initiating event that displaces the body's center of mass beyond its base of support. Initiating events involve extrinsic factors such as environmental hazards; intrinsic factors such as unstable joints, muscle weakness, and unreliable postural reflexes; and physical activities in progress at the time of the fall. The second phase of a fall involves a failure of the systems for maintaining upright posture to detect and correct this dis-

placement in time to avoid a fall. This failure is generally due to factors intrinsic to the individual, such as loss of sensory function, impaired central processing, and muscle weakness. The third phase is an impact of the body on environment surfaces, usually the floor or ground, which results in the transmission of forces to body tissue and organs. The potential for injury is a function of the magnitude and direction of the forces and the susceptibility of tissues and organs to damage.

The assessment of falls raises a number of interesting methodological issues. First, the assignment of a fall as a cause of death means that either the decedent's fatal fall was observed or the circumstances of the death led to the assignment as the underlying cause of death. Second, for someone who is unable to report the fall, such as a long-term care resident with dementia, the report of a fall is based on an observation or a conclusion drawn from the circumstances of an injury. Finally, a person may report the timing and circumstances of his or her own fall. With regard to self-reported falls, there is evidence that recall of falls is highest if the recalled periods are not greater than six months (Cummings, Nevitt, & Kidd, 1988). Not surprisingly, the more serious the fall, the more likely it will be recalled. The following explanations are most often used to account for the circumstances or "reasons" for the fall: sudden drop, a slip, trip, bump, or dizziness.

Although the risk of falling is commonly ascertained and measured in terms of a single event, it is difficult to identify risk factors for a single fall (Nevitt, Cummings, Kidd, et al., 1989). Multiple falls, however, are more predictable. This raises the intriguing issue of whether the outcome of "falling" should be really restricted to "two or more falls." It is only at that point, some commentators note, that it is even possible (or perhaps appropriate) to take notice. Multiple falls also have the most serious effect on health and functioning. The risk of a decline in basic activities of daily living increases progressively among older people with the following profiles: one noninjurious fall, at least two noninjurious falls, and at least one injurious fall (Tinetti, Williams, & Mayeski, 1986).

As noted previously, falls are related to the risk of fractures, functional limitations, and death. It is not surprising, therefore, that older people are fearful of falling. A fear of falling is likely to be expressed by older people who have experienced one or more falls (Kressig, Wolf, Sattin, O'Grady, Greenspan, Curns et al., 2001). Interestingly, there is evidence that people who have not had a previous fall also may report a fear of falling (Arfken,

Lach, Birge, & Miller, 1994; Fessel & Nevitt, 1997; Howland, Peterson, Levin, Fried, Pordon, & Bak, 1993). Observing a fall or simply knowing someone who has fallen may cause their fear, yet another example of the significance of the health effects of a social network. A fear of falling has been shown to be associated with the physical limitations associated with falling. Specifically, a fear of falling may lead to inactivity and associated muscle atrophy or deconditioning. This, in turn, may contribute to sarcopenia, or age-related reduction in lean muscle mass. Fear of falling also may have a negative effect on quality of life and contact with friends and relatives (Arfken et al., 1994; Fessel & Nevitt, 1997; Howland et al., 1993). It is reported that older people are likely to become inactive in an effort to reduce the likelihood of falling. In a study of older people in Sonoma, California, a fear of falling was one of five leading reasons older people gave for the limitation or avoidance of physical activity (Satariano, Haight, & Tager, 2000). Fear of falling was especially salient as a leading reason for not engaging in physical activity among men and women aged 75 years and older. Ironically, as will be described in more detail, physical inactivity associated with fear of falling is associated with the risk of subsequent falls.

DEMOGRAPHIC PATTERNS

Age

Falls are relatively common in older populations (Gregg, Pereira, & Caspersen, 2000). Each year, approximately 30% of community-dwelling older people in developed countries fall at least once, and 10% to 20% fall twice or more. The risk of falling increases dramatically with age, as shown in Table 7–1. For example, most national studies in this area indicate that 25% of persons aged 65 to 74 years and a third or more of those aged 75 years and older report a fall in the previous year (Berg & Cassells, 1992). Moreover, about half of those older people who report falling the previous year fall two or more times. The rate is even higher in health care institutions (Berg & Cassells, 1992).

Gender

There are gender differences in the risk of falls, although it depends on the circumstances and location of the fall. Although women are more likely than men to fall in general, gender differences seem to be due in

Table 7-1 Unintentional Fall Mortality Crude Rates per 100,000, by Gender and Race for People Aged 65+, United States, 2002

Age	Males		Females	
	White	Black	White	Black
65-69	10.8	9.2	10.7	5.8
70-74	19.3	15.4	10.3	7.8
75-79	36.3	22.0	22.5	10.4
80-84	71.3	28.4	48.5	12.8
85+	168.1	77.5	125.6	38.7

Source: Centers for Disease Control and Prevention, 2004.

part to the location of the fall. Men are more likely than women to fall out of doors; women are more likely than men to fall indoors. Although the gender differences may reflect where men and women spend most of their time, the differences also may reflect level of functional limitations. As will be described later in more detail, older people who fall indoors are generally in poorer health and are more likely to be frail than are those who fall out of doors.

Race and Ethnicity

There is relatively little information on racial and ethnic differences in the incidence and severity of falls in the United States. One national study of cause-specific mortality in the United States does indicate, however, that Caucasian adults aged 65 and older were more likely than African-American, Hispanic, or Asian/Pacific Islander seniors to have a fatal fall between 1990–98 (Stevens & Dellinger, 2002). There is also evidence from studies of seniors in individual states that reflect the same racial and ethnic patterns. For example, in a study of seniors who were hospitalized for a fall in California, Caucasians were almost twice as likely as African-Americans, Hispanics, and Asian/Pacific Islanders to be hospitalized (Ellis & Trent, 2001). It is also reported that the falls experienced by older Caucasians were more severe and resulted in a poorer outcome, as measured by discharge to a long-term care facility rather than to the patient's home. Of course, differential discharge may simply reflect differences in access to care. If two people sustain an equally serious fall and the first person is discharged to a long-term care facility and the second person is sent home, the first person may be receiving better care. For example, Grisso and colleagues (1992) conducted a study of the impact of falls among African-American women aged 65 and older who were admitted to emergency departments in Western Pennsylvania for fall-related injuries. The results indicate that a significant proportion of these women reported continued pain and restriction of everyday activities. Grisso and colleagues (1992) recommended that follow-up programs to address the needs of African-American women should be developed. Finally, a study of falls among older people in Hawaii determined that Japanese residents in Japan and Hawaii have a lower incidence of hip fractures than Caucasians in Hawaii or the continental United States (Davis, Ross, Novitt, & Wasnich, 1997). In this study, although there were differences in the incidence of falls, there was no racial or ethnic difference in the level of injury sustained by the fall. Although the racial and ethnic differences may be partially due to differences in assessment and measurement, the reasons for these racial and ethnic differences in falls and fall-related injuries are not completely clear. In fact, it would be reasonable to hypothesize that non-Hispanic white persons would be at reduced risk for both falls and fall-related disability and mortality. They tend to be in better health, exhibit higher levels of functioning, and live in safer areas. There is evidence, however, that older African-American women are less likely to be injured in a fall because they have greater levels of bone density and lower-extremity fat. Additional research in this area is needed.

SOCIOECONOMIC STATUS

To my knowledge, there have been no direct examinations of the association between socioeconomic status and the risk of falls and injuries. It is reasonable to hypothesize, however, that those of lower socioeconomic status would be at elevated risk for falls and for sustaining a serious injury associated with the fall. Many of the known intrinsic factors (e.g., multiple chronic health conditions, reduced muscle strength, poor cognitive functioning) and extrinsic factors (e.g., poorly maintained stairs, broken sidewalks, poor lighting, clutter) for falls and injuries have been shown to be associated with lower socioeconomic status. This suggests that the study of falls and injuries has not truly been examined within a community health context. This is an area of needed research.

PHYSICAL ENVIRONMENT

Indoor and outdoor environmental factors have been implicated in the etiology of falls and injuries. These extrinsic factors include poor stairway design and disrepair, inadequate lighting, clutter, slippery floors, unsecured mats and rugs, and a lack of nonskid surfaces in bathtubs (Carter, Campbell, Sanson-Fisher, Redman, & Gillespie, 1997). Although it is often difficult to completely isolate the effects of environmental factors, nearly 33% of older people who fall report that an environmental factor contributed to their fall. It is also difficult to assess the risk associated with an environmental factor without taking into account how older people actually live in that environment (i.e., "make their way in the world," "a day in the life"), especially in a home setting. An outside observer may classify a home as being hazardous for individual mobility. However, such an "objective" observation does not take into account how long people have lived in a particular setting and, most important, what strategies they have developed to adapt to life in that setting. Linda Fried and colleagues (1996) remind us that people develop "compensatory strategies" to adjust to difficult situations. To be more specific, people are likely to know the location of the clutter and how to walk around it. This observation underscores the point that we must study the interaction between the individual and the environment. The process of interaction and adaptation provides useful information, not based on study protocols that assess "intrinsic" and "extrinsic" factors as separate and mutually exclusive. Such an examination also should examine the interactions between the individual and the environment over time. It has been recommended that environmental assessment and modification should be based on the way the individual actually uses his or her own setting, referred to in architecture as "way finding" (Studenski, Duncan, Chandler, Samsa, Prescott, Hougue, et al., 1994). There may be, in fact, situational factors that affect the interaction between the individual and the environment and, as a result, the risk of falls and injuries. If people are impaired, they may be less able to navigate areas that they have no trouble traveling when they are not impaired. One recent study of falls among healthy, community-dwelling, older women in Australia determined that many of the falls occurred during nonthreatening activities such as walking, often under altered situational factors, such as altered sensory or environmental conditions (Hill, Schwarz, Flicker, & Carroll, 1999). Acute situational factors, including the force of movement, body position, location of impact, and protective responses during a fall also influence whether an injury will occur. Imbalance is initially situational and is present when the righting reflexes cannot meet the demands of a challenging environment, such as a slippery surface. As the functional degradation progresses, the imbalance occurs during everyday activities, and independent ambulation becomes difficult and the likelihood of falls increases. Finally, when instability is constant, the individual resorts to the use of a cane, a walker, or a wheelchair.

Differential risk factor profiles have been identified between older people who fall indoors versus those older people who fall outdoors, another reason why the environmental factors are so important when considering the etiology of falls and injuries (Bath & Morgan, 1999). In general, people aged less than 75 years were more likely to fall outdoors than people aged 75 and over. Indoor falls were associated with frailty, while outdoor falls were associated with compromised health or overexertion in more active people.

Despite this promising research, the independent and joint effects of individual capacity and the characteristics of the built environment on the risk of falling are not always immediate apparent. Northridge and colleagues (1995) examined whether environmental hazards elevated the risk of falls among both vigorous and frail older people. This was a 1-year prospective study of 325 community residents aged 60 to 93 years who had reported a fall at least once during the previous year. The results indicated that frail individuals were twice as likely as vigorous individuals to have fallen during the previous year. Home hazards were not strongly associated with the risk of falling and seemed to depend on the older person's functional capacity. Interestingly, it was discovered that home hazards seemed to elevate the risk of falling primarily among vigorous individuals rather than frail individuals. This may suggest that frail individuals are more attuned and cautious about the hazards in their homes. In contrast, among vigorous individuals, higher levels of physical activity and movement may put them at greater risk of a fall in an unsafe environment. In another study, an attempt was made to determine whether environmental hazards related to transfers, balance, and gait were less prevalent in the homes of older persons with specific limitations in functional capabilities than in the home of older persons without the same limitations (Gill, Robison, Williams, & Tinetti, 1999). The study was based on data from 1088 residents of New Haven, Connecticut, aged 72 and older. The results indicated there was little association between individual functional capacity and the presence of environmental hazards, with the exception of grab bars in the tub and shower. Specifically, environmental hazards were as common in the homes of seniors with functional limitations as they were in the homes of seniors without those limitations. Finally, it is recommended that more precise research will be required to assess the association between environmental characteristics and individual functional capacity. Consistent with this recommendation, a systematic review of effect of home interventions on the incidence of injuries concluded that there is presently insufficient evidence to establish the effects of interventions to reduce environmental home hazards (Lyons, Sander, Weightman, Patterson, Jones, Rolfe, et al., 2003).

SOCIAL CAPITAL

There is no direct examination of the association between the level of social capital and the risk of falls and injuries. However, as with socioeconomic status, it is reasonable to hypothesize that higher levels of social capital are associated with a reduced risk of falls and injuries. Recall that measures of social capital include perceptions of reciprocity and safety in environmental areas. Given the rather extensive research on environmental factors associated with falls and injuries, it is reasonable to assume that if an area is safe and is perceived as being safe, older people are less likely to experience a fall or injury. We also would expect that if people fall or are injured, they are likely to receive aid, perhaps reducing the ill effects of a fall or injury.

LIVING ARRANGEMENTS, SOCIAL NETWORKS, AND SOCIAL SUPPORT

Older people who live alone or who are unmarried are at elevated risk for falling (Faulkner, Cauley, Zmuda, Griffin, & Nevitt, 2003; Huang, Gau, Lin, & Kernohan, 2003; Tromp, Smit, Deeg, Bouter, & Lips, 1998). It is hypothesized that people who are at an elevated risk of falling (e.g., those with reduced lower-body function and multiple health conditions and who consume multiple medications) are less likely to actually experience a fall if others are present. Household members are likely to assist someone who is impaired. In addition, if they do fall, they are more likely to receive assistance, thus reducing the likelihood of a more serious injury.

HEALTH BEHAVIORS

Tobacco

There is little direct evidence that past and current use of tobacco is directly associated with the risk of falls and injuries. However, tobacco use elevates the risk of many factors, which, in turn, have been shown to be associated with falls and injuries. These factors include cognitive and physical functional limitations, multiple health conditions, and depression. It seems, therefore, if researchers expanded their "web of causation," tobacco exposure would probably figure more prominently in the etiology of falls and injuries. There is evidence, for example, that older smokers in Marin County were more likely to have poor postural balance than nonsmokers or people who never smoked (Satariano, DeLorenze, Reed, & Schneider, 1996).

Alcohol Consumption

Although the frequency and amount of alcohol consumption tends to decline with age, there is evidence that alcohol increases the risk of falls and fall-related injury in older populations (Edelberg, 2001; Hingson & Howland, 1993; Stenbacka, Jansson, Leifman, & Romelsjo, 2002). The consumption of a specific amount of alcohol may have a more dramatic effect on an older person than it would have on a younger person. There are two reasons for this effect. First, as noted previously, functional and sensory capacity, for example, gait and balance and visual function, tends to be reduced with age. The consumption of alcohol may aggravate this reduced function, thus elevating the risk of sustaining a fall or injury. Second, older people are likely to be affected by multiple health conditions and, as a result, likely to be taking a variety of different medications. The consumption of alcohol, in conjunction with these multiple health problems and multiple medications, therefore, may elevate the risk of a fall and injury.

Physical Activity

The most extensive literature on health behaviors and falls and injuries is found for physical activity. Physical activity has been identified as a lifestyle factor that may influence the risk of falls and fractures among older adults (Gregg et al., 2000). There is a growing body of evidence that indicates that physical activity serves to maintain mobility, physical functioning, bone mineral density, muscle strength, and balance. Thus, physical activity may reduce the risk of falls and fractures. Physical activity, whether conducted in the form of programmed exercise, daily leisure, or household and occupational activities, exerts its effects through several attributes, including amount of energy expenditure, and cardiorespiratory, musculoskeletal, and neuromuscular involvement. These attributes are influenced by the type of physical activity and specific factors such as the muscle groups involved, rate and intensity of muscular contraction, and the physical work and power generated by such behaviors. The most basic attribute of physical activity is the amount of energy expended, which affects obesity, diabetes, and cardiovascular disease risk. It is reported that physical activity is more likely to directly influence the risk for falls and osteoporotic fractures through the musculoskeletal and neuromuscular systems, which can be measured by performance in strength, balance, postural stability, gait, and mobility.

A recent review of physical activity and the risk of falls and osteoporotic fractures included three conclusions about the research in this area (Gregg et al., 2000). First, neither leisure-time physical activity nor participation in exercise programs has been consistently associated with prevention or increased risk of falls. On the other hand, many of these studies have lacked adequate statistical power, and results from some recent larger trials have found beneficial effects of particular types of physical activity (e.g., balance and lower-extremity strength) on risk for falls. Indeed, more recent evaluation concludes that on the basis of nine randomized, controlled studies conducted since 1996, exercise appears to reduce the incidence of falls in older populations (Carter, Kannus, & Khan, 2001). It is also important to be aware of potential disadvantages. For example, some activities, particularly those of higher intensity or duration, may put some women at increased risk of falls. It is reported that increasing activity in a nonambulatory person could possibly transiently increase the risk of falls (Studenski et al., 1994). Second, there is strong evidence from observational studies that a physically active lifestyle reduces the risk of hip fracture. Several prospective and case-control studies suggest physical activity protects against hip fracture. Randomized clinical trials would be required to ensure that this association is not confounded by preexisting health status, but the sample size requirements would make a trial extremely costly and probably impractical. Third, it is reported that it is unclear whether physical activity is associated with the risk of osteoportic fractures at sites other than the hip. Few studies have examined this issue and findings have been equivocal.

It is reported that physical activity can affect each of the three components of a fall: (1) reduce the likelihood that the body will experience an initiating event, such as unstable joints and muscle weakness; (2) reduce the likelihood the person will fail to detect and reestablish equilibrium; and (3) reduce the likelihood that the body will sustain an injury as a result of the fall.

Intense physical activity also can elevate the risk of falls and injuries (Kallinen & Markku, 1995). The safety margin of an exercise tends to decline with aging. Exertional injuries are common among the elderly and are associated with reduced functional reserves associated with aging. It is reported that acute injuries are common in those elderly people participating in sports activities that demand high coordination, reaction time, and balance capabilities, such as ball games, downhill skiing, and gymnastics. The lower extremities are the most susceptible to injury. Although it is reported that many acute injuries are mild, some of the injuries are long term and cause disability not only during training and competition, but also in the normal activities of daily life.

Diet and Nutrition

Research indicates that particular dietary practices over the life course can reduce bone density and lean fat mass in older populations (Pirlich & Lochs, 2001). Osteoporosis (reduced bone density) and sarcopenia (reduced lean muscle mass) are risk factors for falls and injuries in older populations. Not only will these conditions contribute to instability and imbalance, which may precipitate a fall, but they also reduce the likelihood that the person will absorb the trauma of that fall (Kinney, 2004). In other words, these conditions may both precipitate a fall and elevate the risk of injury associated with that fall. There is also growing concern about the prevalence of malnutrition in older populations. In addition to not consuming nutritious foods, there is also an increase with age in the body's inability to absorb nutrients. Malnutrition may be due to a variety of factors. For example, older people may simply have a poor appetite. This may be caused, in turn, by a reduction in the sense of taste and smell, associated generally with aging as well as the use of particular types of medication. Poor oral health, decayed teeth, missing teeth, and ill-fitting dentures also can contribute to poor dietary practices. In addition, to the extent that older people live alone, especially men, there may be less incentive to prepare full meals. As noted previously, living alone is associated with poorer dietary practices in older populations.

SENSE OF CONTROL, COHERENCE, AND SELF-EFFICACY

Mary Tinetti and colleagues (1994) developed a fall-efficacy scale to assess whether an older person's level of confidence in mobility and avoidance of a fall is associated with a history of falling as well as associated with the likelihood of a subsequent fall. It was determined that those older people with low fall efficacy were more likely than others to have experienced a fall, more likely to be more sedentary, and more likely to experience a subsequent fall. Interestingly, there is also evidence that falls and injuries are likely to occur among older people who are physically fit and active (Hill et al., 1999). As noted previously, these falls and injuries tend to be different from those experienced by those who are frail. Moreover, as noted by Northridge and colleagues (1995), the physically active people may be especially vulnerable, while performing regular tasks under altered or unsafe environment conditions. This may suggest that, at least in some cases, their perceived capacity may exceed their actual capacity to meet the demands of the environment. Thus, there may be situations in which an ill-conceived or exaggerated level of self-efficacy may lead to a fall.

DISEASE AND COMORBIDITIES

The number and types of diagnosed health conditions are associated with the risk of falls and injuries. As with studies of survival and physical and cognitive functioning, it is especially important to identify and distinguish the effects of the disease pathology from the effects of the medications to treat that pathology. In addition to the absolute number of multiple morbidities, the health conditions that are most associated with the risk of falls and injuries include diabetes; coronary heart disease; Parkinson's disease;

dementias, including, most notably, Alzheimer's disease; and incontinence (Koepsell, Wolf, McCloskey, Buchner, Louis, Wagner, et al., 1994; Tromp et al., 1998). There is also evidence that falls, as well as infections, are two major complications associated with a stroke (Langhorne, Stott, Robertson, Macdonald, Jones, McAlpine, et al., 2000). The use of sedatives and hypnotics, as well as the absolute number of medications, is associated with the risk of falls. There is a small, but consistent, association between the use of most classes of psychotropic drugs and falls (Leipzig, Cumming, & Tinetti, 1999a). A second study determined that older adults taking more than three or four medications were at increased risk of recurrent falls (Leipzig, Cumming, & Tinetti, 1999b).

PHYSICAL FUNCTIONING

There is extensive research that indicates an association between limitations in physical functioning and the risk of falls (Cesari, Landi, Torre, Onder, Lattanzio, & Bernabei, 2002; De Rekeneire, Visser, Peila, Nevitt, Cauley, Tylavsky, et al., 2003; Kosorok, Omenn, Diehr, Koepsell, & Patrick, 1992; Tinetti & Williams, 1998). Although reduced functional capacity is associated with an elevation in the risk of falls, falls, in turn, are associated with the risk of subsequent functional decline. It is difficult to simply indicate that falls represent a marker of frailty. Instead, it is perhaps more accurate to think in terms of a "cascading" of the interrelationship between falls and functional limitations. In addition to restrictions in Activities of Daily Living, other measures of physical performance associated with falls include gait abnormalities, reduced walking speed, impaired balance, and difficulty rising from a chair. It is reported, for example, that gait variability was significantly greater in older fallers compared with both older non-fallers and younger fallers (Hausdorff, Rios, & Edelberg, 2001). Reduced knee, hip, or ankle strength and reduced grip strength have been identified as risk factors as well. There is also evidence that foot problems reduce gait speed and contribute to an elevated risk of falls (Menz & Lord, 2001). Of the variety of sensory impairments, impaired visual acuity is most strongly associated with falls. In one study, hip fractures in persons aged 40 years and older were significantly related to all measures of visual function, such as measures of near and distant vision, contrast sensitivity, and visual sensitivity (Klein, Moss, Klein, Lee,

& Cruickshanks, 2003). It is estimated that poor vision accounts for nearly a quarter to a half of all falls (Harwood, 2001). It is further estimated that visual impairment in 70% or more of elderly people is remediable with relatively simple interventions, such as correcting refractive errors and cataract surgery (Harwood, 2001).

COGNITIVE FUNCTIONING

As noted previously, those with dementia are more likely than others to experience a fall. There is also evidence that older people with reduced cognitive function are at risk of falling as well (Tinetti, Speechley, & Ginter, 1988). This may be caused by a variety of factors. For example, cognitive function is essential for coordination and processing of information and movement, task memory, and executive function or effective decision making. The result may be to underestimate or overestimate capacity to complete a daily task. In either case, the result may be a fall or injury.

DEPRESSION

Older people with depressive symptoms are also at elevated risk for falls and injuries (Whooley, Kip, Cauley, Ensrud, Nevitt, & Browner, 1999). Depression is associated with loss of appetite, inability to sleep, and anxiety. Each of these symptoms may be associated with falls and injuries. As we know, older people with depression are less likely to engage in physical activities and to consume regular meals. This, in turn, is likely to render the older person increasingly sedentary and weak. Depression is also associated with a fear of falling, which, as we know, can elevate the risk of falling.

PHYSIOLOGICAL FACTORS

As noted previously, the risk of falls and injuries is associated with a variety of factors, including poor overall health, poor vision, and reduced physical and cognitive functioning (Lord, Menz, & Tiedemann, 2003). In addition, sarcopenia, osteoporosis, and overall frailty are associated with the risk of most falls, specifically those that occur indoors, in older populations. While those older persons who fall outdoors are typically more fit and in better health, they are still likely to be at reduced functional capacity, especially, in this case, relative to the demands of the outside environment.

DEFINITION AND MEASUREMENT OF AUTOMOBILE- AND PEDESTRIAN-RELATED INJURIES

Automobile- and pedestrian-related crashes and injuries, as with falls and injuries, represent a leading cause of accidental disabilities and death (Evans, 2000; Stevens & Dellinger, 2002). This area of study, although not as well developed as research on falls and injuries, is conceptually and methodologically related. Interestingly, some of the same individual and environmental factors affecting the risk of falls and injuries are associated with the risk of driving and pedestrian-related injuries (Lyman, McGwin, & Sims, 2001). Indeed, it is reported that a history of falls is associated with difficulty driving (Lyman et al., 2001). A car crash, like a fall, represents, in many ways, a "misalignment" between the individual's capacity and the demands of the environment. There are also some notable differences. In the case of automobile- and pedestrian-related crashes, the causal pathway is expanded to include technology. The car, therefore, is not part of the environment, but rather a technological device that is designed to enhance and extend personal mobility in the environment.

The study of aging and transportation, especially the use of the private automobile, is important for a variety of reasons. First, in the United States and many other industrialized nations, it represents the primary means by which older people are able to get to places beyond walking distance to obtain goods and services and to maintain contact with friends and relatives. Data from the 1995 U.S. Nationwide Personal Transportation Survey indicate that over 90% of daily trips taken by people aged 65 and older were made by privately owned automobile (Collia, Sharp, & Giesbrecht, 2003; Waldorf, 2003). Moreover, in three fourths of those cases, the older person was the driver (Waldorf, 2003). With the aging of the population, it is anticipated that there will be increasing numbers of older drivers on the road. This is not only the result of the aging of the population per se, but also the result of the aging of a cohort of people that has relied on the automobile as its primary means of transportation for much of its adult years. There are also global changes in transportation. In countries such as China, the private automobile is becoming increasingly popular as a primary source of transportation. We can predict that crash-related disability and mortality will become more of a global health issue in the years to come (Wang, Chi, Jing, Dong, Wu, & Li, 2003). Second, the study of driving and transportation is important because the ability to get to places beyond walking distance is considered to be one of the basic measures of everyday functioning, in other words, one of the Instrumental Activities of Daily Living, as discussed in Chapter 4. Third, transportation (in particular, the use of the private car) represents one of the few tasks that requires the coordination and execution of a variety of functional capacities, including cognition, vision, and upper- and lower-body strength (Korteling, 1994). Fourth, as noted previously, automobile crashes represent one of the leading causes of accidental death in older populations, especially among older men (Evans, 2000; Stevens & Dellinger, 2002). The risk of crashes, in turn, is associated with a variety of physical, cognitive, and visual functioning (Koepsell et al., 1994; Lundberg, Hakamies-Blomqvist, Almkvist, & Johansson, 1998; McGwin, Chapman, & Owsley, 2000).

Although the definition of a "crash" may vary, in the United States, a reportable "crash" involves a death, injury, or damage. Damage is defined in terms of a monetary cost for repair (e.g., $500 in California) or, as is the case in Pennsylvania, sufficient to require a car to be towed from the scene.

Deaths or injuries associated with a crash can refer to the driver, occupants or passengers, and pedestrians. It is reported that for all age groups, driver deaths represent the most common category (Dellinger, Langlois, & Li, 2002). In general, case-injury and case-fatality rates associated with crashes increase with the person's chronological age. This underscores the point that injuries and fatalities are not completely due to the extent of force or the level of trauma, but also the vulnerability of the person (Dellinger et al., 2002). Therefore, the health and functional status of the person can affect both the likelihood of the crash as well as the effect of that crash on both quality and duration of life.

DEMOGRAPHIC PATTERNS

Age

The effect of older drivers on overall traffic safety is not completely clear and seems to depend on how "traffic safety" is defined. For example, based on US data from 1994–1996, Evans (2000) estimated the risk drivers posed to other road users, estimated by driver involvement in pedestrian fatality crashes. The results indicated that renewing the license of a 70-year-old male driver for another year poses, on average, 40% less threat to other road users than renewing the license of a 40-year-old male driver. In a separate analysis of US data, Dellinger and colleagues (Dellinger, Kresnow, White, & Sehgal, 2004) report that crashes among drivers ages 16 to 19 and among drivers aged 75 and older were associated with more deaths to others than were crashes among drivers aged 20 to 74, based on deaths to others per 100 million miles driven. In addition, the number of injuries among others per 100 million miles driven also was highest among drivers aged 16 to 19 and among drivers aged 85 and older.

It is clear that the risk of death that drivers themselves face generally increase as they age, with the increase in risk due in large part to their increased vulnerability to survive the impact of a crash. In other words, holding the magnitude of the crash constant, mortality increases a function of chronological age (Evans, 2000). Data are represented from Dellinger and colleagues (2002) that crash fatality involvement increases with age (see Table 7–2).

Gender

As noted previously, older women are less likely than older men to drive, due perhaps in larger part, to the particular cohort of older drivers. Older women of this generation were less likely to learn to drive and more likely to be in situations in which their male partners drove. In addition, older women seem to be more likely than older men to reduce or cease driving as health and functional problems increase (Campbell, Bush, & Hale, 1993; Ragland, Satariano, & MacLeod, 2004; Stewart, Moore, & Marks, 1993). It will be important to determine whether these particular patterns are different among newer cohorts of older drivers. Interestingly, although older women tend to have lower functional capacity than older men and would seem to be a greater risk for serious injury or death from a crash, the crash fatality risk is greater for older men than older women (Stevens & Dellinger, 2002). Although the reasons for the differences in crash-related mortality between older men and older women are not completely clear, it may be caused, at least in part, to the fact that older men are more likely than older women to drive. To our knowledge, it is unknown whether older men are more likely than older women to drive alone.

Table 7–2 Fatal Crash Involvement Rate, Crash Fatality Rate, Crash Incidence Density, and Exposure Prevalence by Age Group and Year, United States, 1990 and 1995

Age (years)	No. of fatal crashes	No. of total crashes	No. of drivers	No. of miles driven*	Fatal crash involvement rate†	Crash fatality rate‡	Crash incidence density§	Exposure prevalence¶
1990								
55-64	4,067	711,041	18,285,251	155,796,734,323	2.22	5.72	4.56	8,520
65-74	3,161	562,486	13,821,802	79,796,455,476	2.29	5.62	7.05	5,773
75-84	1,932	215,665	5,799,075	22,013,026,706	3.33	8.96	9.80	3,796
≥85	408	39,746	859,796	1,736,210,804	6.18	10.27	22.88	2,631
1995								
55-64	4,079	775,484	18,364,048	201,162,338,318	2.22	5.26	3.86	10,054
65-74	3,251	537,854	16,537,228	133,188,361,196	1.97	6.04	4.04	8,054
75-84	2,380	283,045	6,709,000	35,084,651,539	3.56	8.41	8.07	5,229
≥85	609	54,144	960,176	3,733,976,418	6.34	11.25	14.50	3,889

*1990 miles adjusted upward 22% (1 mile = 1.61 km).
†Rate per 10,000 drivers.
‡Rate per 1,000 crashes.
§Number of crashes per million miles driven.
¶Average annual miles driven.

Source: Dellinger et al., 2002.

Race and Ethnicity

There is evidence from national US data that African-American, Hispanic, and Asian/Pacific Islander seniors are more likely than Caucasian seniors to experience crash-related injury and mortality (Schlundt, Warren, & Miller, 2004; Stevens & Dellinger, 2002). In a separate study of seniors in Alabama, there was a six-fold increase in the likelihood of at-fault crashes for older African-American drivers (Sims, Owsley, Allman, Ball, & Smoot, 1998). These results are interesting, in light of research that indicates that racial and ethnic minority seniors are less likely than Caucasian seniors to drive or to rely on a private automobile for transportation (Waldorf, 2003). Although racial/ethnic and age differences in crash-related injury and mortality have not been studied extensively, there are some possible hypotheses. First, as noted previously, injury and mortality are not only due to the circumstances and impact of the crash, but to the relative levels of functional limitations and vulnerabilities of the driver and passengers as well. As noted previously, racial and ethnic minority seniors are more likely than Caucasian seniors to be in ill health and experience functional limitations and disabilities. This, in turn, may increase the relative impact of the crash. Second, it may be that the cars driven or occupied by racial and ethnic minority seniors are less safe and have more mechanical difficulties and worn equipment, thus increasing the likelihood that the car will malfunction, resulting in a crash. Third, driving performance and safety, such as the presence and use of seat belts, may be different by race and ethnicity. Finally, racial and ethnic minority seniors may drive in areas that have more unsafe drivers as well as more environmental hazards and distractions (e.g., visual clutter) that could elevate the risk of a crash.

SOCIOECONOMIC STATUS

To our knowledge, there has not been a systematic examination of socioeconomic status and automobile crashes, injuries, and mortality in older populations. There is evidence from at least one study, however, that seniors with low family income are more likely than those seniors with higher family income to limit or avoid driving (Ragland et al., 2004). In general, it is reasonable to assume that the racial and ethnic differences in injuries and mortality noted previously are associated with racial and ethnic differences in individual (for example, family income, years of education, and occupational position) and aggregate (for example, mean levels of census block or neighborhood family income and nature and quality of neighborhood streets) indicators of socioeconomic status. Moreover, the specific hypotheses noted previously to explain the elevated risk of injury and death for racial and ethnic minority seniors also could account for differences in socioeconomic status. This should be examined in more detail.

PHYSICAL ENVIRONMENT

The physical environment figures prominently in a consideration of automobile- and pedestrian-related crashes. Older drivers are more likely than younger drivers to drive on surface streets and more likely to avoid major highways and freeways. In addition, older drivers are less likely to drive after dark or during periods of peak traffic volume (Janke, 1991). The time of day that crashes occur also varies significantly as drivers age. Older drivers are less likely to be involved in crashes during the morning and afternoon commute periods as well as after dark. The primary times for older drivers to be involved in crashes are from 9 a.m. to 4 p.m. In fact, changes in the location and timing of driving represent primary strategies by older drivers to modify and regulate their own driving patterns (Ball, Owsley, Stalvey, Roenker, Sloane, & Graves, 1998; Gilhotra, Mitchell, Ivers, & Cumming, 2001; Marottoli, Ostfeld, Merrill, Perlman, Foley, & Cooney, 1993). These findings underscore two important points. First, the risk of crashes depends on exposure—this can be the volume and timing of driving. Although it may be an obvious point, crashes are most likely to occur during those times when older drivers are most likely to be operating an automobile. Second, both driving time and the risk of crashes depend on the need to drive. Since older people typically have more flexible schedules than do younger adults, they have more discretion in deciding when and under what circumstances they should drive.

There is evidence that older drivers are involved in different types of crashes. Compared to younger drivers, a larger share of the accidents of older drivers are collisions between vehicles, as opposed to single-vehicle accidents (Hakamies-Blmquist, 1993, 1994). They also tend to be legally responsible parties in their collisions (Cooper, 1990; Viano, Culver, Evans, Frick, & Scott, 1990; Hakamies-Blomqvist, 1993). In the typical intersection accident situation in which the older driver is attempting to complete a left turn, research suggests that older drivers are less likely to notice oncoming drivers, and fail to give the right-of-way as they attempt to complete their turn (Daigneault, Joly, & Frigon, 2002). It is suggested that older drivers, as a group, have more difficulty judging the speed of oncoming vehicles. For older drivers, the increase of intersection crashes has been a salient finding that less attention often is paid to the fact that older drivers are less likely to be involved in single-vehicle accidents that are caused by a loss of control, or collisions due to speeding or risking overtaking of another car.

SOCIAL CAPITAL

There is no research that directly examines the association between social capital and automobile- and pedestrian-related crashes. However, there is evidence, as noted previously, that older drivers are likely to modify the timing and location of driving for considerations of safety. Since social capital is based on perceptions of trust and safety, it is reasonable to hypothesize that older drivers would be more likely to drive in settings that are characterized by high social capital, following adjustment for other factors.

LIVING ARRANGEMENTS, SOCIAL NETWORKS, AND SOCIAL SUPPORT

There is no direct evidence of an association between living arrangements, social networks, and support and the risk of crashes and pedestrian-related injuries. Again, however, it is reasonable to hypothesize a possible interaction between social networks, functional capacity, driving behavior, and the risk of crashes and injuries. As noted previously, the extent, timing, and location of driving depend on the individual's functional capacity, environmental points of origin and destination, and need to reach that destination by automobile, in other words the need to drive. It is reasonable to hypothesize that living arrangements, social networks, and social support are likely to be associated with crash risk in situations in which an older person has functional limitations, needs to drive, and needs to drive in an area and at a time that is challenging. Studies do not investigate that possible interaction. There is some evidence, however, that the presence of another person in the car is associated with a lower crash risk for older drivers (Hing, Stamatiadis, & Aultman-Hall, 2003). One possible explanation is that the passenger assists the older driver in giving directions and calling attention to hazards. On the other hand, the presence of a passenger has the opposite effect for younger drivers (Chen, Baker, Braver, & Li, 2000). The presence of a passenger, especially a younger passenger, is associated with a higher crash risk for the younger driver. One explanation is that the presence of a younger passenger encourages the younger driver to engage in risky behavior (Grabowski & Morrisey, 2001).

HEALTH BEHAVIORS

Tobacco

There is no evidence that cigarette smoking is associated with the risk of crashes and injuries among older drivers. However, it is reasonable to hypothesize that tobacco, in fact, does affect crash risk through its effect on the development of health problems and functional limitations, factors with a known association with crash risk.

Alcohol Consumption

The study of the association between alcohol consumption and driving performance and the risk of crashes has focused primarily on younger drivers. There is evidence, however, that consumption of alcohol is implicated in the risk of crashes among older drivers (Koepsell et al., 1994). As noted previously in reference to falls, older people may be more sensitive than younger people to the effects of alcohol. This may be due to reduced capacity, as well as the presence of multiple, comorbid health conditions and the consumption of associated, multiple medications.

Physical Activity

Older drivers who are physically active, either in the form of everyday walking or leisure-time activities, are more likely to drive and less likely to be involved in an automobile crash (Sims et al., 1998). Physical activity may affect driving frequency and performance in at least two ways. First, as we have described in some detail, involvement in physical activity has been shown to be associated with a variety of positive health outcomes, including reduced risk of chronic health conditions and depression as well as positive physical and cognitive functioning. Each of these health and functional outcomes has been shown to be associated with driving frequency and performance. Second, those who are physically active are more likely than sedentary older people to have developed more social networks and to have greater involvement in everyday activities. As such, those who are physically active also have more reasons and are better able to get to places outside of walking distance to obtain goods and services and maintain contacts with friends and relatives.

Diet and Nutrition

To our knowledge, there has been no direct examination of the association between diet and nutrition and driving frequency and performance in older populations. However, many of the points made earlier about nutritional factors and the risk of falls apply here. To the extent that nutritional factors are associated with health and cognitive and physical functioning, nutritional factors can affect the complex and coordinated acts of functioning that are required to operate an automobile (Kinney, 2004; Pirlich & Lochs, 2001). In addition, body mass and, more specifically, muscle mass would seem to be associated with the likelihood that an older person would be able to withstand the impact of a crash. Diet and nutrition and driving performance need to be examined in more detail.

SENSE OF CONTROL, COHERENCE, AND SELF-EFFICACY

There is evidence that older drivers limit or avoid driving as they age for a variety of health and non-health-related reasons (Ragland et al., 2004). Concern about visual deficits is by far the most common reason for the limitation, avoidance, or cessation of driving (Ragland et al., 2004; Satariano, MacLeod, Cohn, & Ragland, 2004; Stalvey & Owsley, 2003). Other reasons include concerns about being in a traffic accident and, for older women in particular, a general concern about crime (Ragland et al., 2004). In most cases, older people modify their driving to accommodate these perceived limitations. These modifications include reducing the timing, location, and circumstances of driving to daytime hours, fair weather, and surfaced streets (Ball et al., 1998; Gallo, Rebok, & Lesikar, 1999). There is also evidence that older drivers tend to reduce their car speed, when confronted with a difficult or demanding driving situation. Although there is no driving self-efficacy scale, there are programs in place to improve skills and confidence in driving for older drivers (Stalvey & Owsley, 2003).

DISEASE AND COMORBIDITIES

There are a number of health conditions that have been associated with driving outcomes, including driving frequency, cessation, and crashes. These conditions include arthritis, seizure disorders, diabetes, coronary heart disease, cerebrovascular disease, cataracts, and early-stage dementia associated with Alzheimer's disease (Hansotia, 1993; Koepsell et al., 1994; Lyman et al., 2001; Owsley, Stalvey, Wells, & Sloane, 1999; Roberts & Roberts, 1993). Although these associations have been noted, it is important to emphasize again that a specific diagnosis often does not provide complete information about the effect of that condition on driving frequency or performance. It is necessary to consider the severity of conditions, the multiplicity of conditions, and the effects of medications used to manage those conditions.

PHYSICAL FUNCTIONING

As noted previously, driving an automobile reflects the complex, coordination of multiple physical, sensory, and cognitive functional capacities. With regard to physical functioning, upper- and lower-body functioning is associated with driving performance (Ball et al., 1998; Sims, McGwin, Allman, Ball, & Owsley, 2000). One of the most common errors made by older drivers is to not look over their shoulder prior to making a lane change (DiStefano & MacDonald, 2003). Failure to perform this maneuver may be due to reduced upper-body flexibility and mobility. As noted previously, both researchers and older drivers themselves have identified visual function as one of the most important types of driving-related capacities (Ragland et al., 2004; Satariano et al., 2004). Contrast sensitivity, depth perception, and peripheral vision are visual functions most likely to affect driving performance in older drivers. It is ironic, therefore, that visual acuity, the visual function that is most likely to be assessed as part of driving licensure, is less strongly associated with driving performance (Koepsell et al., 1994). It has been suggested that rather than examining the independent effects of single functional limitations, it may be more productive to consider effects of multiple functional limitations (McKnight & McKnight, 1999). Of course, the characteristics of the automobile itself affect the extent to which a specific limitation is associated with driving performance.

COGNITIVE FUNCTIONING

As noted previously, seniors with early-stage dementia associated with early Alzheimer's disease have been shown to be at elevated risk for automobile crashes, especially involving inability to function at an intersection (Reinach, Rizzo, McGehee, 1997; Foley, Masaki, Ross, & White, 2000; Rizzo, McGehee, Dawson, & Anderson, 2001). There is also evidence that reduced levels of cognitive functioning are associated with poor driving performance. Types of cognitive functioning that are most associated with driving performance include memory, attention, systematic scanning of the environment, processing speed, decision making, and problem solving (Ball, Owsley, & Sloane, 1991; Colsher & Wallace, 1993; Foley, Wallace, & Eberhard, 1995; Stutts, Stewart, & Martell, 1998; Lundberg et al., 1998). When considering particular driving behaviors, the role of specific abilities becomes more evident. For example, finding one's way and some parking tasks (e.g., parallel parking) are likely to involve spatial ability, the ability to mentally rotate and visualize automobiles and roadways in two- and three-dimensional space. In contrast, interpreting road signs may be affected significantly by verbal ability and experimental knowledge. Completing a left turn in traffic involves skills such as inductive reasoning and judgment of distance and "rate of closure." Executive functioning, or, as we discussed earlier, higher levels of cognitive functioning necessary to make complex decisions, deserves special attention. This important, higher level cognitive functioning, is necessary to plan a route in an unfamiliar environment as well as to cope with a demanding or stressful traffic situation.

DEPRESSION

Depressive symptoms have been associated with driving outcomes in older populations. Sims and colleagues (2000) report that seniors with depressive symptoms, as measured by the Geriatric Depression Scale, were over two times more likely to be involved in a subsequent vehicle crash over a five-year period, following adjustment for other health and functional indicators. Since depressive symptoms are often associated with fatigue and difficulty in the ability to focus attention, it seems reasonable that such symptoms would be associated with poor driving performance. In addition to depressive symptoms, the medications that are often prescribed to manage depression in older populations are also associated with poor depressive symptoms (McGwin, Sims, Pulley, & Roseman, 2000; Ramaekers, 2003). There is also evidence that older people who have stopped driving are at elevated risk for depressive symptoms (Fonda, Wallace, & Herzog, 2001; Ragland, Satariano, & MacLeod, 2005).

PHYSIOLOGICAL FACTORS

Driving frequency, performance, and crashes are associated with a variety of factors, health status, and overall physical and cognitive functional capacity. In this way, the factors associated with driving outcomes are very similar to factors associated with falls and injuries. Although research in this area is still relatively undeveloped, it is reasonable that the study of aging and driving performance will provide a unique opportunity to assess physiological factors associated with the coordination of multiple factors. Not only are older people required to function in the environment, but they are also required to manage sophisticated technological equipment to undertake this function. In addition to representing an important public health issue, driving in older populations will represent a laboratory for understanding the age-related coordination of higher human functioning.

CONCLUSION

Falls, injuries, and automobile crashes represent one of the significant public health problems facing older populations. To date, it represents the best exemplar for public health research that involves the intersection of biologic, behavioral, social, and environmental factors. As noted previously, the study of automobile crashes, although not as well developed as research on falls and injuries, is conceptually and methodologically related. Indeed, many of the same factors that elevate the risk for falls and injuries are also strongly implicated in the causes of automobile crashes.

REFERENCES

Arfken, C. L., Lach, H. W., Birge, S. J., & Miller, J. P. (1994). The prevalence and correlates of fear of falling in elderly persons living in the community. *American Journal of Public Health, 84*(5), 565–570.

Ball, K., Owsley, C., Stalvey, B., Roenker, D. L, Sloane, M. E., & Graves, M. (1998). Driving avoidance and functional impairment in older drivers. *Accident Analysis Prevention, 30*(3), 313–322.

Ball, K., Owsley, C., & Sloane, M. (1991). Visual and cognitive predictors of driving problems in older adults. *Experimental Aging Research, 17*(2), 79–80.

Bath, P. A., & Morgan, K. (1999). Differential risk factor profiles for indoor and outdoor falls in older people living at home in Nottingham, UK. *European Journal of Epidemiology, 15*(1), 65–73.

Campbell, M. K., Bush, T. L., & Hale, W. E. (1993). Medical conditions associated with driving cessation in community-dwelling, ambulatory elders. *Journal of Gerontology, 48*, 4, S230–S234.

Carter, N. D., Kannus, P., & Khan, K. M. (2001). Exercise in the prevention of falls in older people: A systematic literature review examining the rationale and the evidence. *Sports Medicine, 31*(6), 427–438.

Carter, S. E., Campbell, E. M., Sanson-Fisher, R. W., Redman, S., & Gillespie, W. J. (1997). *Age and Ageing, 26*(3), 195–202.

Cesari, M., Landi, F., Torre, S., Onder, G., Lattanzio, F., & Bernabei, R. (2002). Prevalence and risk factors for falls in an older community-dwelling population. *Journal of Gerontology: Medical Sciences, 57*(11), M722–M726.

Chen, L. H., Baker, S. P., Braver, E. R., & Li, G. (2000). Carrying passengers as a risk factor for crashes fatal to 16- and 17-year-old drivers. *Journal of the American Medical Association, 283*(12), 1578–1582.

Collia, D. V., Sharp, J., & Giesbrecht, L. (2003). The 2001 National Household Travel Survey: A look into the travel patterns of older Americans. *Journal of Safety Research, 34*, 461–470.

Colsher, P. L., & Wallace, R. B. (1993). Geriatric assessment and driver functioning. *Clinics in Geriatric Medicine, 9*(2), 365–375.

Cooper, P. J. (1990). Differences in accident characteristics among elderly drivers and between elderly and middle-aged drivers. *Accident Analysis and Prevention, 22*(5), 499–508.

Cummings, S. R., Nevitt, M. C., & Kidd, S. (1988). Forgetting falls. The limited accuracy of recall of falls in the elderly. *Journal of the American Geriatrics Society, 36*(7), 613–616.

Cwikel, J., & Fried, A. V. (1992). The social epidemiology of falls among community-dwelling elderly: Guidelines for prevention. *Disability and Rehabilitation, 14*(3), 113–121.

Daigneault, G., Joly, P., & Frigon, J. Y. (2002). Executive function in the evaluation of accident risk of older drivers. *Journal of Clinical Experimental Neuropsychology, 24,* 2, 221–238.

Davis, J. W., Ross, P. D., Nevitt, M. C., & Wasnich, R. D. (1997). Incidence rates of falls among Japanese men and women living in Hawaii. *Journal of Clinical Epidemiology, 50*(5), 589–594.

Dellinger, A. M., Langlois, J. A., & Li, G. (2002). Fatal crashes among older drivers: Decomposition of rates into contributing factors. *American Journal of Epidemiology, 155,* 3, 231–241.

Dellinger, A. M., Kresnow, M. J., White, D. D., & Sehgal, M. (2004). Risk to self versus risk to others: How do older drivers compare to others on the road? *American Journal of Preventive Medicine, 26*(3), 217–221.

De Rekeneire, N., Visser, M., Peila, R., Nevitt, M. C., Cauley, J. A., Tylavsky, F. A., et al. (2003). Is a fall just a fall: Correlates of falling healthy older persons. The Health, Aging, and Body Composition Study. *Journal of the American Geriatrics Society, 51,* 841–846.

Di Stefano, M., & Macdonald, W. (2003). Assessment of older drivers: Relationships among on-road errors, medical conditions and test outcome. *Journal of Safety Research, 34,* 415–429.

Duthie, E. H., Jr. (1989). Falls. *Medicine Clinical North America, 73*(6), 1321–1336.

Edelberg, H. K. (2001). Falls and function: How to prevent falls and injuries in patients with impaired mobility. *Geriatrics, 56*(3), 41–45.

Ellis, A. A., & Trent, R. B. (2001). Hospitalized fall injuries and race in California. *Injury Prevention, 7*(4), 316–320.

Evans, L. (2000). Risks older drivers face themselves and threats they pose to other road users. *International Journal of Epidemiology, 29,* 315–322.

Faulkner, K. A., Cauley, J. A., Zmuda, J. M., Griffin, J. M., & Nevitt, M. C. (2003). Is social integration associated with the risk of falling in older community-dwelling women? *Journals of Gerontology: Medical Sciences, 58*(10), M954–M959.

Fessel, K. D., & Nevitt, M. C. (1997). Correlates of fear of falling and activity limitation among persons with rheumatoid arthritis. *Arthritis Care Research, 10*(4), 222–228.

Foley, D. J., Masaki, K. H., Ross, G. W., & White, L. R. (2000). Driving cessation in older men with incident dementia. *Journal of the American Geriatrics Society, 48*(8), 928–930.

Foley, D. J., Wallace, R. B., & Eberhard, J. (1995). Risk factors for motor vehicle crashes among older drivers in a rural community. *Journal of the American Geriatrics Society, 43*(7), 776–781.

Fonda, S. J., Wallace, R. E., & Herzog, A. R. (2001). Changes in driving patterns and worsening depressive symptoms among older adults. *Journals of Gerontology: Social Sciences, 56*(6), S343–S351.

Fried, L. P., Bandeen-Roche, K., Williamsom, J. D., Prasada-Rao, P., Chee, E., Tepper, S., et al. (1996). Functional decline in older adults: Expanding methods of ascertainment. *Journals of Gerontology: Medical Sciences, 51*(5), M206–M214.

Gallo, J. J., Rebok, G. W., & Lesikar, S. E. (1999). The driving habits of adults aged 60 years and older. *Journal of the American Geriatric Society, 37*(3), 335–341.

Gilhotra, J. S., Mitchell, P., Ivers, R., & Cumming, R. G. (2001). Impaired vision and other factors associated with driving cessation in the elderly: The Blue Mountains Eye Study. *Clinical Experiment Ophthalmology, 29*(3), 104–107.

Gill, T. M., Robison, J. T., Williams, C. S., & Tinetti, M. E. (1999). Mismatches between the home environment and physical capabilities among community-living older persons. *Journal of the American Geriatric Society, 47,* 88–92.

Gill, T. M., Williams, C. S., & Tinetti, M. E. (2000). Environmental hazards and the risk of nonsyncopal falls in the homes of community-living older persons. *Medical Care, 38*(12), 1174–1183.

Grabowski, D. C., & Morrisey, M. A. (2001). The effect of state regulations on motor vehicle fatalities for younger and older drivers: A review and analysis. *The Milbank Quarterly, 79*(4), 517–545.

Gregg, E. W., Pereira, M. A., & Caspersen, C. J. (2000). Physical activity, falls, and fractures among older adults: A review of the epidemiologic evidence. *Journal of the American Geriatric Society, 48*(8), 883–893.

Grisso, J. A., Schwarz, D. F., Wolfson, V., Polansky, M., & LaPann, K. (1992). The impact of falls in an inner-city elderly African-American population. *Journal of the American Geriatrics Society, 40*(7), 673–678.

Hakamies-Blomqvist, L. (1993). Fatal accidents of older drivers. *Accident Analysis & Prevention, 25,* 1, 19–27.

Hakamies-Blomqvist, L. (1994). Compensation in older drivers as reflected in their fatal accidents. *Accident Analysis & Prevention, 26,* 1, 107–112.

Hansotia, P. (1993). Seizure disorders, diabetes mellitus, and cerebrovascular disease: Considerations for older derivers. *Clinics in Geriatric Medicine, 9*(2), 323–339.

Harwood, R.H. (2001). Visual problems and falls. *Age & Ageing, 30,* Suppl 4, 13–18.

Hausdorff, J. M, Rios, D. A., & Edelberg, H. K. (2001). Gait variability and fall risk in community-living older adults: A 1-year prospective study. *Archives of Physical and Medical Rehabilitation, 82*(8), 1050–1056.

Hill, K., Schwarz, J., Flicker, L., & Carroll, S. (1999). Falls among healthy, community-dwelling, older women: A prospective study of frequency, circumstances, consequences and prediction accuracy. *Australian and New Zealand Journal of Public Health, 23,* 41–48.

Hing, J. Y., Stamatiadis, N., & Aultman-Hall, L. (2003). Evaluating the impact of passengers on the safety of older drivers. *Journal of Safety Research, 34*(4), 343–351.

Hingson, R., & Howland, J. (1993). Alcohol and non-traffic unintended injuries. *Addiction, 88*(7), 883.

Howland, J., Peterson, E. W., Levin, W. C., Fried, L., Pordon, D., & Bak, S. (1993). Fear of falling among the community-dwelling elderly. *Journal of Aging & Health, 5*(2), 229–243.

Huang, H. C., Gau, M. L., Lin, W. C., & Kernohan, G. (2003). Assessing risk of falling older adults. *Public Health Nursing, 20*(3), 399–411.

Janke, M. K. (1991). Accidents, mileage, and exaggeration of risk. *Accident Analysis and Prevention, 23*(2–3), 183–188.

Kallinen, M., & Markku, A. (1995). Aging, physical activity and sports injuries: An overview of common sports injuries in the elderly. *Sports Medicine, 20*(1), 41–52.

Kinney, J. M. (2004). Nutritional frailty, sarcopenia, and falls in the elderly. *Current Opinion in Clinical Nutrition and Metabolic Care, 7,* 15–20.

Klein, B. E., Moss, S. E., Klein, R., Lee, K. E., & Cruickshanks, K. J. (2003). Associations of visual function with physical outcomes and limitations 5 years later in an older population: The Beaver Dam Eye Study. *Ophthalmology, 110*(4), 644–650.

Koepsell, T. D., Wolf, M. E., McCloskey, L., Buchner, D. M., Louis, D., Wagner, E. H., et al. (1994). Medical conditions and motor vehicle collision injuries in older adults. *Journal of the American Geriatrics Society, 42*(7), 695–700.

Korteling, J. E. (1994). Effects of aging, skill modification, and demand alternation on multiple-task performance. *Human Factors, 36*(1), 27–43.

Kosorok, M. R., Omenn, G. S., Diehr, P., Koepsell, T. D., & Patrick, D. L. (1992). Restricted activity days among older adults. *American Journal of Public Health, 82*(9), 1263–1267.

Kressig, R. W., Wolf, S. L., Sattin, R. W., O'Grady, M., Greenspan, A., Curns, A. L., et al. (2001). Associations of demographic, functional, and behavioral characteristics with activity-related fear of falling among older adults transitioning to frailty. *Journal of the American Geriatrics Society, 49*(11), 1456–1462.

Langhorne, P., Stott, D. J., Robertson, L., Macdonald, J., Jones, L., McAlpine, C., et al. (2000). Medical complications after stroke: A multicenter study. *Stroke, 31*(6), 1223–1229.

Leipzig, R. M., Cumming, R. G., & Tinetti, M. E. (1999a). Drugs and falls in older people: A systematic review and meta-analysis: II. Cardiac and analgesic drugs. *Journal of the American Geriatrics Society, 47*(10), 40–50.

Leipzig, R. M., Cumming, R. G., & Tinetti, M. E. (1999b). Drugs and falls in older people: A systematic review and meta-analysis: I. Psychotropic drugs. *Journal of the American Geriatrics Society, 47*(1), 30–39.

Lord, S. R., Menz, H. B., & Tiedemann, A. (2003). A physiological profile approach to falls risk and prevention. *Physical Therapy, 83*(3), 237–252.

Lundberg, C., Hakamies-Blomqvist, L., Almkvist, O., & Johansson, K. (1998). Impairments of some cognitive functions are common in crash-involved older drivers. *Accident Analysis and Prevention, 30*(3), 371–377.

Lyman, J. M., McGwin, G., Jr., & Sims, R. V. (2001). Factors related to driving difficulty and habits in older drivers. *Accident Analysis and Prevention, 33*(3), 413–421.

Lyons, R. A., Sander, L. V., Weightman, A. L., Patterson, J., Jones, S. A., Rolfe, B., et al. (2003). Modification of the home environment for the reduction of injuries. *Cochrane Database System Review, 2003*(4), No. CD003600.

Marottoli, R. A., Ostfeld, A. M., Merrill, S. S., Perlman, G. D., Foley, D. J., & Cooney, L. M., Jr. (1993). Driving cessation and changes in mileage driven among elderly. *Journal of Gerontology, 48*(5), S255–260.

McGwin, G. Jr., Chapman, V., & Owsley, C. (2000). Visual risk factors for driving difficulty among older drivers. *Accident Analysis & Prevention, 32,* 735–744.

McGwin, G. Jr., Sims, R. V., Pulley, L., & Roseman, J. M. (2000). Relations among chronic medical conditions, medications, and automobile crashes in the elderly: A population-based case-control study. *American Journal of Epidemiology, 152*(5), 424–431.

McKnight, A. J., & McKnight, A. S. (1999). Multivariate analysis of age-related driver ability and performance deficits. *Accident Analysis and Prevention, 31,* 445–454.

Menz, H. B., & Lord, S. R. (2001). The contribution of foot problems to mobility impairment and falls in community-dwelling older people. *Journal of the American Geriatrics Society, 49,* 1651–1656.

Nevitt, M. C., Cummings, S. R., Kidd, S., & Black, D. (1989). Risk factors for recurrent nonsyncopal falls. A prospective study. *Journal of the American Medical Association, 261,* 2663.

Northridge, M. E., Nevitt, M. C., Kelsey, J. L., & Link, B. (1995). Home hazards and falls in the elderly: The role of health and functional status. *American Journal of Public Health, 85*(4), 509–515.

Owsley, C., Stalvey, B., Wells, J., & Sloane, M. E. (1999). Older drivers and cataracts: Driving habits and crash risk. *Journals of Gerontology: Medical Sciences, 54*(4), M203–M211.

Pirlich, M., & Lochs, H. (2001). Nutrition in the elderly. *Best Practice Research Clinical Gastroenterology, 15*(6), 869–884.

Ragland, D. R., Satariano, W. A., & MacLeod, K. E. (2005). Driving cessation and increased depressive symptoms. *Journals of Gerontology: Medical Sciences, 60A*, 3, 399–403.

Ragland, D. R., Satariano, W. A., & MacLeod, K. E. (2004). Reasons given by older people for limitation or avoidance of driving. *The Gerontologist, 44*(2), 237–244.

Ramaekers, J. G. (2003). Antidepressants and driver impairment: Empirical evidence from a standard on-the-road test. *Journal of Clinical Psychiatry, 64*(1), 20–29.

Reinach, S. J., Rizzo, M., & McGehee, D. V. (1997). Driving with Alzheimer disease: The anatomy of a crash. *Alzheimer's Disease Associated Disorders, 11*, Suppl 1, 21–27.

Rizzo, M., McGehee, D. V., Dawson, J. D., & Anderson, S. N. (2001). Simulated car crashes at intersections in drivers with Alzheimer's disease. *Alzheimer's Disease Associated Disorders, 15*(1), 10–20.

Roberts, W. N., & Roberts, P. C. (1993). Evaluation of the elderly driver with arthritis. *Clinics in Geriatric Medicine, 9*(2), 311–322.

Rubenstein, L. Z., Robbins, A. S., Schulman, B. L., Rosado, J., Osterweil, D., & Josephson, K. R. (1988). Falls and instability in the elderly. *Journal of the American Geriatrics Society, 36*, 266–278.

Satariano, W. A., DeLorenze, G. N., Reed, D., & Schneider, E. L. (1996). Imbalance in an older population: An epidemiologic analysis. *Journal of Aging & Health, 8*(3), 334–358.

Satariano, W. A., Haight, T. J., & Tager, I. B. (2000). Reasons given by older people for limitation or avoidance of leisure-time physical activity. *Journal of the American Geriatrics Society, 48*(5), 505–512.

Satariano, W. A., MacLeod, K. E., Cohn, T. E., & Ragland, D. R. (2004). Problems with vision associated with limitations or avoidance of driving in older populations. *Journals of Gerontology: Social Sciences, 59B*, 5, S281–S286.

Schlundt, D., Warren, R., & Miller, S. (2004). Reducing unintentional injuries on the nation's highways: A literature review. *Journal of Health Care for the Poor and Underserved, 15*(1), 76–98.

Sims, R. V., McGwin, G., Jr., Allman, R. M., Ball, K., & Owsley, C. (2000). Exploratory study of incident vehicle crashes among older drivers. *Journals of Gerontology: Medical Sciences, 55*(1), M22–M27.

Sims, R. V., Owsley, C., Allman, R. M., Ball, K., & Smoot, T. M. (1998). A preliminary assessment of the medical and functional factors associated with vehicle crashes by older adults. *Journal of the American Geriatrics Society, 46*(5), 556–561.

Stalvey, B. T., & Owsley, C. (2003). The development and efficacy of a theory-based educational curriculum to promote self-regulation among high-risk older drivers. *Health Promotion Practice, 4*(2), 109–119.

Stenbacka, M., Jansson, B., Leifman, A., & Romelsjo, A. (2002). Association between use of sedatives of hypnotics, alcohol consumption, or other risk factors and a single injurious fall or multiple injurious falls: A longitudinal general population study. *Alcohol, 28,* 9–16.

Stevens, J. A., & Dellinger, A. M. (2002). Motor vehicle and fall-related deaths among older Americans 1990–98: Sex, race, and ethnic disparities. *Injury Prevention, 8*(4), 272–275.

Stewart, R. B., Moore, M. T., & Marks, R. G. (1993). *Driving cessation and accidents in the elderly: An analysis of symptoms, diseases, cognitive dysfunction and medications.* Washington, DC: AAA Foundation for Traffic Safety.

Studenski, S., Duncan, P. W., Chandler, J., Samsa, G., Prescott, B., Hougue, C., et al. (1994). Predicting falls: The role of mobility and nonphysical factors. *Journal of the American Geriatrics Society, 42*(3), 297–302.

Stutts, J. C., Stewart, J. R., & Martell, C. (1998). Cognitive test performance and crash risk in an older driver population. *Accident Analysis and Prevention, 30*(3), 337–346.

Tinetti, M. E., Doucette, J. T., & Claus, E. B. (1995). The contribution of predisposing and situational risk factors to serious fall injuries. *Journal of the American Geriatrics Society, 43*(11), 1207–1213.

Tinetti, M. E., Inouye, S. K., Gill, T. M., & Doucette, J. T. (1995). Shared risk factors for falls, incontinence, and functional dependence: Unifying the approach to geriatric syndromes. *Journal of the American Medical Association, 273,* 1348–1353.

Tinetti, M. E., Mendes de Leon, C. F., Doucette, J. T., & Baker, D. I. (1994). Fear of falling and fall-related efficacy in relationship to functioning among community-living elders. *Journal of Gerontology: Medical Sciences, 49,* M140.

Tinetti, M. E., Speechley, M., & Ginter, S. F. (1988). Risk factors for falls among elderly persons living in the community. *New England Journal of Medicine, 319,* 1701–1707.

Tinetti, M. E., & Williams, C. S. (1998). The effect of falls and fall injuries on functioning in community-dwelling older persons. *Journal of Gerontology: Medical Sciences, 53A*(2), M112–M119.

Tinetti, M. E., Williams, T. F., & Mayewski, R. (1986). Fall risk index for elderly patients based on number of chronic disabilities. *American Journal of Medicine, 80,* 429–434.

Tromp, A. M., Smit, J. H., Deeg, D. J., Bouter, L. M., & Lips, P. (1998). Predictors for falls and fractures in the Longitudinal Aging Study Amsterdam. *Journal of Bone Mineral Research, 13*(12), 1932–1939.

Viano, D. C., Culver, C. C., Evans, L., Frick, M., & Scott, R. (1990). Involvement of older drivers in multivehicle side-impact crashes. *Accident Analysis and Prevention, 22*(2), 177–188.

Waldorf, B. (2003). Automobile reliance among the elderly: Race and spatial context effects. *Growth and Change, 34*(2), 175–201.

Wang, S. Y., Chi, G. B., Jing, C. X., Dong, X. M., Wu, C. P., & Li, L. P. (2003). Trends in road traffic crashes and associated injury and fatality in the People's Republic of China, 1951–1999. *Injury Control Safety Promotion, 10*(1–2), 83–87.

Whooley, M. A., Kip, I. E., Cauley, J. A., Ensrud, K. E., Nevitt, M. C., & Browner, W. S. (1999). Depression, falls, and risk of fracture in older women. Study of Osteoporotic Fractures Research Group. *Annuals of Internal Medicine, 159*, 5, 484–490.

CHAPTER 8

Disease and Comorbidities

Our examination of the epidemiology of aging has focused to this point on the extent to which aging and disease affect a variety of outcomes, including survival; physical and cognitive functioning; depression; and falls, injuries, and automobile crashes. In this chapter, we will examine the epidemiology of aging and disease itself, including a review and examination of the risk of specific diseases, and, in particular, the extent and manner in which age and aging affect the number, type, and severity of etiological factors; the timing of the onset of disease; and, indeed, the nature, severity, and course of the disease itself. In keeping with the ecological model, our task is to determine to what extent these disease processes are affected by the interplay among biologic, behavioral, social, and environmental factors, an interplay that occurs over the life course of individuals, families, neighborhoods, and communities. In addition, we will consider the epidemiology of comorbidity and multimorbidities.

The risk, onset, and course of disease associated with aging are central issues in both epidemiology and gerontology. Recall, for the moment, the epidemiological transition theory discussed in Chapter 1. Just to repeat, the theory posits that demographic transitions in human populations, in particular, the aging of populations, are characterized by the prevalence of different types of disease—initially, a transition from infectious to chronic conditions, to disabling conditions, to a combination of infectious, chronic, and disabling conditions.

Despite the interrelationship between aging and disease, it is important to emphasize again that they are distinct processes. Indeed, the identification of the conceptual and analytical distinctions between the aging

265

process and the disease process has been identified as the primary task in gerontological research (Timiras, 2003). As Wallace (1992, p. 7) writes, aging is characterized by "universal biological processes; generally slowly paced but always progressive; ultimately deleterious; emphasizing molecular, physiologic levels; clinical impact often not easily discernible; and rarely treatable." Disease, on the other hand, is characterized by the following: "selective in species, tissues; varying rates of progression, some regression; varying harm to host; almost always anatomically disruptive; impact is usually discernible; and it is often treatable" (1992, p. 7). Elsewhere, disease is defined as "anything that an individual (or population) experiences that causes, literally, 'dis-ease,' that is, anything that leads to discomfort, pain, distress of all sorts, disability of any kind, and death, constitutes disease from whatever cause, including injuries or psychiatric disabilities" (Hyder & Morrow, 2001, p. 1).

It is clear that the relationship between aging and disease involves more than just the joint association between the incidence and prevalence of disease on the one hand, and increasing chronological age on the other. This is captured well in the following observation and recommendation: "Just as we should not consider children to be simply young adults, we should not consider the elderly to be simply old adults" (Rowe, 1985, p. 827). This means that the study of aging, health, and disease requires an understanding of the special physiologic, psychosocial, and pathologic characteristics of aging.

In this chapter, we will consider some of the underlying biologic, behavioral, social, and environmental factors associated with the risk, onset, presentation, and course of disease in general, as well as the factors associated with specific health outcomes. Leonard Syme and Claudine Torfs (1978) underscored the importance of these two distinct, yet related, issues in an article on hypertension: "This inquiry could be organized around two central questions: (1) while all of us are exposed to noxious agents all the time, why do only some of us become ill? (2) Having become susceptible, why do we become ill with one disease rather than with another?" This can be thought of as overlapping circles. The overlapping parts of the circle represent those factors that are common across specific health outcomes and common to the generic disease process. Those parts that are not overlapping are not necessarily generic to the disease process, but evident in one or more conditions.

There is another issue, which is important, but not unique to the study of older populations, that is, the distinction between individual health and population health. At one level, population health is, in fact, the aggregation of health outcomes among individuals. This is best represented by the disease rate, simply put, the number of people with a condition divided by the number of people in the population, over a designated time period, multiplied by some constant (such as 100,000). The incidence rate represents the number of newly diagnosed conditions in a year per 100,000 in the population at that time. If illness represents a disruption in normal functioning, then it may be useful to also consider "population health" as a disruption in the functioning of the population at large. In this case, the concept of "population health" depends on population itself, and not on the aggregation of individual states of health. Population health and illness also may be thought of as population functioning, in this case, the interplay of groups in the population or the adaptation of those groups to environmental changes. If we think of population health in this way, then it assumes more the idea of evolutionary health. We will return to these points in subsequent chapters.

AGING AND THE COMPLEXITY OF DISEASE

The risk, onset, presentation, and course of disease often differ by chronological age. To paraphrase Gertrude Stein, a disease is not a disease is not a disease. The timing of disease, meaning when it occurs in the life course, is a critical issue. As noted earlier, differences in the timing of disease may be due to differences in the timing of exposure to the same set of risk factors, such as age at the time of exposure to tobacco smoke, and/or a different set of risk factors, such as weight gain (obesity) and the risk of postmenopausal breast cancer (Kelsey, 1979). There also may be differences in the interrelationship between genetic factors and the timing and extent of exposure to one or more environmental factors (NIA Aging and Genetic Epidemiology Working Group, 2000). In addition to genetic susceptibility, age at onset may be affected by a "weathering" associated with the timing and extent of environmental exposures, the aging process itself, and the history of other diseases. Past diagnosed diseases and conditions deserve special attention. As noted previously, older people are not only at elevated risk for specific diseases, but for multiple, concurrent diseases as well (Gijsen, Hoeymans, Schellevis, Ruwaard, Satariano, & van den Bos, 2001). As people age, they are likely to develop a series of health conditions. The presence of multiple conditions, including the treatment for those conditions, may affect the risk of subsequent diseases as well as the presentation of the symptoms of those diseases. The presence of previously diagnosed conditions, including their past and current treatments and monitoring, may affect the nature and interpretation of symptoms for current conditions. As Ouslander and Beck (1982, p. 61) write:

> Clinical signs of disease are often deceiving in the elderly. Myocardial infarction or a perforated ulcer may occur without pain and pneumonia and other infections may be present without fever. Or specific conditions, such as falls, confusion and urinary incontinence may be the representing manifestations of a variety of treatable diseases. Many physical and emotional disorders often coexist in an elderly individual, and can be extremely difficult to attribute accurately a given symptom to a physical disease, psychopathology, a drug side effect, or a combination of these.

The standard medical model may not accurately reflect the complexity of disease in older populations (Fried, Storer, King, & Lodder, 1991). This model is based on the proposition that a standard set of presenting symptoms and signs is associated with a diagnosis of a single pathological condition. In contrast to this somewhat idealized model, Fried and colleagues (1991) propose a set of four alternative models to provide a more accurate assessment of illnesses in older patients through the incorporation of information on comorbidity, function, and psychosocial factors.

Synergistic Morbidity Model

This model captures situations in which a person presents with a history of multiple, generally chronic, diseases, each of which contributes to a uniform, cumulative morbidity. Over time, these diseases cause functional decrements. Eventually, the decrements reach a point at which medical assistance is sought. In this case, the diagnostic strategy is similar to the medical model. In both models, a collection of potentially disparate appearing problems is aggregated to explain a common condition. The disparate problems, however, are not discrete symptoms but rather unrelated specific diseases or conditions and the outcome is the cumulative functional effect. This situation also may require treatments directed at the multiple comorbid conditions as well as the resulting disability.

The Attribution Model and the Facilitating Complaint

In this case, a decline in functional status and well-being is attributed to a previously diagnosed condition. An examination of the symptoms typically reveals, however, that the declining health and functioning is due to one or more new health conditions.

Causal Chain Model

The third alternative model characterizes a situation in which there is an interaction between medical and psychiatric factors. In this case, the major complaint is often the latest symptom in a progression of factors, not unlike the synergistic model. In the causal chain model, one physical ailment can precipitate a chain of events that could lead to the current state of illness. According to Fried and colleagues (1991, p. 121), "This Causal Chain is characterized by all symptoms being connected to an initial event and by multiple points of interaction and feedback loops among symptoms."

The Unmasking Event Model

This final model characterizes a situation in which an external event, such as the death of a spouse, reveals an "underlying, stable or slowly progressing chronic condition," a condition that was not previously apparent. It may be, for example, that a spouse had previously compensated or assisted in masking a condition, symptoms, or functional limitations. With the loss of the spouse, the condition became apparent.

It is argued that these alternative models complement the traditional medical model and expand the presentation of illnesses in older populations to include "interactions and cumulative burden of multiple physical diseases, psychiatric illness, and compromised function." In addition, the models also take into account the social and environmental context. Moreover, an examination of a series of older patients treated at the Johns Hopkins Geriatric Assessment Center revealed that conditions of most patients were better characterized by one of the four alternative models than they were by the traditional medical model. While the alternative models were developed to facilitate assessment and treatment of geriatric patients, the models have important implications for the assessment of disease for epidemiological studies. This will be described in greater detail later in this chapter as well as in a subsequent discussion of the conduct of epidemiological studies in older populations in Chapter 10.

AGE AT ONSET IN POPULATIONS: REVISITING THE DOUBLE-JEOPARDY HYPOTHESIS

Age at onset is one of the key issues in the epidemiology of aging. Why do some people develop disease earlier in life than others? What are the factors, for example, behavioral and environmental, that occur at different points in the early and middle years and, as a result, come to affect the subsequent risk and timing of health conditions later in life? These questions have important implications for understanding the effect of human development and the life course on the onset, presentation, and course of disease. It also has significant implications for understanding the incidence and impact of disease in everyday life. While there is significant variability among individuals, at the level of the population, there is evidence that many chronic diseases occur earlier in life and are diagnosed at a more severe stage for underrepresented racial and ethnic minorities (e.g., African-Americans and Latino populations) and for people of lower socioeconomic status (SES) than occur among non-Hispanic whites and among people of higher SES. Among adults, the middle years between age 40 and 65 are characterized by the greatest difference in the incidence and severity of leading chronic conditions (House, Kessler, & Herzog, 1990). One study of age-specific patterns of cancer incidence in the Detroit metropolitan area (Satariano & Swanson, 1988) determined that African-American men aged 40 to 64 were more likely than non-Hispanic white men of the same age to develop cancer, especially those cancer sites, lung and bronchus, esophagus, and stomach, that are associated with tobacco exposure. However, among men diagnosed with cancer in their later years (aged 65 and older), the racial difference was much less pronounced. Although these race-age patterns of cancer incidence were less pronounced among female residents of the Detroit metropolitan area, the results seem to suggest that the middle years may represent a "watershed." The accumulation of insults, coupled with reduced age-related physiological resistance, may make the middle years critical for determining who will develop disease and who will not (Satariano, 1986). While this is an intriguing hypothesis, these cross-sectional results, of course, are only suggestive. With cross-sectional data, we cannot isolate age, period, or cohort effects. Moreover, we cannot legitimately posit a temporal pattern. However, with those qualifications in mind, it may be that African-American and Latino men who survive their middle years without developing cancer may have a subsequent risk profile that is similar to non-Hispanic white men of the same age. As noted in Chapter 3, these cross-sectional results may provide evidence, however indirect, of a survivor effect and support for a leveling hypothesis rather than a double-jeopardy hypothesis.

AGE AT ONSET IN POPULATIONS: RECUPERATION AND RECURRENCE

Just as aging is associated with the risk of developing multiple, concurrent conditions, there is evidence that aging also may be associated with the recurrence of a condition following its initial diagnosis, course of treatment, and a symptom-free period, a period in which the condition is thought "cured." The most notable example of this phenomenon is Post-polio syndrome (Aston, 1992; Trojan, Cashman, Shapiro, Tansey, & Esdaile, 1994). Poliomyelitis, originally described in 1875, was quite common during the 1940s and 1950s in the United States. It is estimated that over 500,000 people in this country contracted the disease during that period. As of late, a growing number of former polio patients have begun to experience symptoms of weakness, fatigue, and joint pain 20 to 40 years following their acute illness (Aston, 1992). It is proposed that the loss of muscle strength results from a loss of muscle fibers that have become detached from their adopted axon (Aston, 1992). Interestingly, it is further proposed by some investigators that normal aging may contribute to the effects of the damaged motor unit (Bromberg & Waring, 1991). In a case-control study of post-polio syndrome, increased age, together with severity of weakness at acute polio, muscle pain with exercise, recent weight gain, and reported join pain were associated with an increased likelihood of post-polio syndrome (Trojan et al., 1994). The researchers conclude that the degree of initial motor unit involvement as measured by weakness at acute polio, and possibly the aging process and overuse, are important in predicting post-polio syndrome (Trojan et al., 1994). While post-polio syndrome is characterized by a specific disease process, this syndrome may reflect, in fact, a more generic process associated with aging and disease. As more longitudinal studies of aging and disease are conducted, other examples of recurrent disease and the symptoms of that disease may become apparent. It may be that in some cases the diagnosis of a condition, although asymptomatic following treatment, may impose a vulnerability that becomes manifest only with increasing age. If this is the case, then the disease and disability burden of segments of the aging population may be greater than initially estimated. This is clearly an area for future research, a topic to which we will return in Chapter 12.

AGING AND DISEASE: FOUR EXEMPLARS

Aging is associated with the risk of a variety of acute and chronic conditions (McQueen, McKenna, & Sleet, 2001). In this section, we will focus on a set of four exemplars—key health conditions—that reflect significant issues associated with the epidemiology of aging and disease. Criteria for the selection of these exemplars include the following: (1) strong age-related incidence and/or prevalence; (2) significant effect on the risk of disability and/or death; and (3) pronounced effect on health care costs. In short, these are the conditions that we have considered in the previous chapters, that is, the leading conditions that are associated with an elevated risk of death, physical and cognitive limitations and disabilities, depression, and falls, injuries, and crashes.

Four categories of age-related conditions will be reviewed. First, there are highly prevalent chronic conditions, such as coronary heart disease (CHD), stroke, cancer, and diabetes, which are also characterized by elevated rates of disability and death. Second, there are also highly prevalent chronic conditions, such as osteoarthritis and cataracts, which are associated with elevated disability, but are not leading causes of death. Third, infectious conditions, such as influenza and more recently, human immunodeficiency virus (HIV)/acquired immune deficiency syndrome (AIDS) and severe acute respiratory syndrome (SARS), are associated with a relatively short course and can be fatal. Fourth, chronic cognitive and motor-neuron diseases—the dementias, such as Alzheimers disease (AD) and Parkinson's disease (PD)—are characterized by late-onset with a typically degenerative course that renders the person at risk for opportunistic infections or other comorbid conditions, which, in turn, lead to death.

Leading Chronic Conditions: High Disability and High Mortality

Coronary Heart Disease

CHD is the leading cause of death in the United States, among the general population and specifically among both men and women aged 65 and older. The incidence of CHD and CHD-related death increases steadily with age (Mittelmark, Psaty, Rautaharju, Fried, Borhani, Tracy, et al., 1993). CHD is a leading cause of death, even among people newly diagnosed with other significant chronic conditions. For example, approximately 50% of decedent prostate cancer patients die of a disease other than prostate cancer. CHD is the second leading cause of death of men diagnosed with prostate cancer (Satariano, Ragland, & Van Den Eden, 1998). CHD is also a leading cause of disability. CHD was second only to musculoskeletal disorders as a primary cause of disability in a national survey of older subjects (Ettinger, Fried, Harris, Shemanski, Schultz, & Robbins, 1994).

Although the incidence and prevalence of CHD is greatest in middle-aged and older populations, the development of CHD often occurs earlier in life (Schocken, 2000). Labarthe (1998) outlines the significance of CHD-related factors at different points in the life course. It is reported, for example, the fetal and neonatal period may be important for the establishment of subsequent risk of adult-onset CHD. Low birth weight and limited weight gain during the first year have been associated with CHD death among a British cohort of men born in the early 1900s. Additional evidence from familial aggregation studies demonstrates a significant concordance in CHD risk factors between parents and children. These results, coupled with other studies on the significance of childhood prevention, indicate the importance of childhood behavior and exposures for the development of subsequent risk of CHD. During the middle and senior years, the incidence and prevalence of CHD become most pronounced. Indeed, it is reported that older people may survive an initial myocardial infarction to develop chronic ischemic heart disease and congestive heart failure and the associated levels of significant disabilities (Labarthe, 1998).

A number of studies have compared the factors associated with early-adult onset versus late-adult onset of CHD (Corti, Guralnik, & Bilato, 1996). As noted previously, there is a strong interest in determining whether the risk associated with CHD found in middle-aged populations, the source of much of our information about the epidemiology of CHD, is similar in CHD that occurs in older populations. With the growing number of studies of older populations, including the Cardiovascular Health Study (Fried, Borhani, Enright, Furberg, Gardin, Kronmal, et al., 1991), there will be more definitive research in this area. The Cardiovascular Health Study is a population-based, longitudinal study of CHD and stroke in adults aged 65 and older. The main objective of the study is to identify factors related to the onset and course of CHD and stroke. It is specifically designed to determine the importance of such conventional cardiovascular disease factors as tobacco, blood pressure, diet, and physical activity, in older adults, and to identify new risk factors in the older population.

Despite clear evidence of the association between cigarette smoking and CHD incidence and mortality in middle-aged populations, fewer studies examined the association in older populations. There also was evidence from the Framingham study that suggested that there was no association in older populations (Corti et al., 1996). More recent evidence from the Established Populations for Epidemiologic Studies of the Elderly (EPESE) indicated, however, that current smokers aged 65 and older had a significantly higher risk of all-cause and cardiovascular mortality, after adjustment for other cardiovascular risk factors (Weintraub, Klein, Seelaus, Agarwal, & Helfact, 1985). It is generally accepted at this point that current cigarette smoking is associated with CHD mortality among older men and women, although the association is reduced somewhat among people aged 75 and older (Corti et al., 1996).

Hypertension is relatively common among older populations, and it is a significant risk factor for CHD. Hypertension is typically defined as a systolic blood pressure (SBP) greater than 140, or a diastolic blood pressure (DBP) greater than 90. The question again is whether the association between blood pressure and the risk of CHD is the same for middle-aged and older populations. It is important to realize that the mean SBP tends to increase with age, while DBP tends to decline after age 55. Although both SBP and DBP are associated with CHD risk, it has been generally assumed that DBP is a more significant risk factor and, in fact, the objective of most treatment strategies has been to reduce the level of DBP. Interestingly, recent studies have demonstrated that for people aged 45 and older, SBP is a more significant risk factor (Kannel, Wolf, McGee, Dawber, McNamara, & Castelli, 1981). Results from the East Boston component of the EPESE project demonstrated a strong association between SBP and DBP with both total mortality and CHD mortality (Glynn, Brock, Harris, Havilik, Chrischilles, Ostfeld, et al., 1995). There is also evidence from several clinical trials, including the Systolic Hypertension in the Elderly Program, that pharmacological interventions can reduce the risk of death from both stroke and CHD in older populations (Hypertension Detection and Follow-up Program Cooperative Group, 1984).

Based on increasing evidence from studies of older populations, traditional risk factors, such as smoking, hypertension, and physical activity, are shown to be associated with CHD incidence and mortality in both middle-aged and elderly populations (Corti et al., 1996). Moreover, there is evidence that the risk factors can be modified through interventions in older as well as younger populations. This is a significant issue, since involvement in leisure-time physical activity tends to decline with age for both men and women (U.S. Department of Health & Human Services, 1996). Epidemiologic studies do suggest that modifying a sedentary lifestyle is associated with a reduction in the risk of CHD (Berlin & Colditz, 1990). Research from the Cardiovascular Health Study (Siscovick, Fried, Millelmark, Rutan, Bild, & O'Leary, et al., 1997) also provides evidence of the significance of physical exercise in older populations. In this study, the association between intensity of exercise in later life and CHD risk factors and subclinical disease was examined among 2274 men and women, aged 65 years and older. Subjects were free of prior clinical cardiovascular disease or impairment of physical functioning. After adjustment for age, education, and postmenopausal hormone therapy (among women), there was an inverse dose-response relationship of exercise intensity with selected risk factors. Intensity of exercise in later life was associated with favorable coronary disease risk factor levels and a reduced prevalence of several markers of subclinical disease, such as lower-extremity arterial disease by percent with ankle-arm index (Siscovick et al., 1997).

There is evidence that the risk factor profile associated with CHD may vary between older African-American and Caucasian males (Kuller, Fisher,

McClelland, Fried, Cushman, Jackson, & Manolio, 1998). Data from the Cardiovascular Health Study indicate that age, SBP, low-density lipoprotein cholesterol, smoking, and family history of myocardial infarction were independently associated with subclinical disease among both African-American and Caucasian women, while for Caucasian men, SBP, use of antihypertensive medication, smoking, body mass index, and DBP were related to subclinical disease. In contrast, among African-American men, blood triglyceride level, use of antihypertensive medications, and family history of myocardial infarction were associated with subclinical disease. These results suggest that the association between aging and CHD may vary by other demographic and social factors.

Stroke

Cerebrovascular disease, together with CHD, constitute the two major types of cardiovascular disease. Whereas "heart attack" refers to an acute event associated with CHD, a "brain attack" or stroke is the comparable acute event associated with cerebrovascular disease (Labarthe, 1998).

There are two major types of stroke, each defined in terms of its etiology: ischemic stroke and hemorrhagic stroke. An ischemic stroke is due to an obstruction of cerebral blood. In contrast, a hemorrhagic stroke is due to a rupture to a vessel associated with transmission of blood to either the brain or spinal cord.

Ischemic stroke is the most common type of cerebrovascular accident, accounting for between 75% and 85% of the cases (Boden-Albala & Sacco, 2004). While the incidence of the cerebrovascular disease increases with age and is more common in men than women, the prevalence is higher in women. This seems to suggest that while women are less likely than men to have a stroke, they are more likely to live with the disease, meaning women are more likely than men to survive. Although there are no definitive age-specific incidence data by race and ethnicity, results from studies of stroke mortality indicate that African-American men and women have a higher stroke mortality rate than non-Hispanic white populations. There has been limited research on the stroke rate in Hispanic populations. There is evidence, however, from one study of Hispanic migrants from the Dominican Republic to New York City indicating nearly a two-fold higher stroke mortality rate, compared to non-Hispanic white populations (Sacco, Boden-Albala, Gan, Chen, Kargman, Shea, et al., 1998). Although Chinese and

Japanese have very high stroke incidence rates, those who migrated to the United States, most notably to Hawaii and California, have reduced rates, especially over several generations (Boden-Albala & Sacco, 2004). In addition to demographic factors, there is evidence that those of lower SES are at elevated risk for the disease (Galobardes, Lynch, & Davey-Smith, 2004; Kunst, del Rios, Groenhoff, & Mackenbach, 1998). There is also evidence of specific geographic patterns in the United States. The southeastern portion of the United States has been identified as the "stroke belt." Residents in this area have an elevated risk for the disease, reflecting in large part the compositional characteristics noted previously, especially race and socioeconomic characteristics (Howard, 1999). As we shall see, however, there may be contextual factors, associated with the customs, policies, sale and distribution, exposure, and consumption of products and practices associated with particular behavioral factors that have been shown to be associated with the risk of stroke. These factors include tobacco exposure and consumption, dietary and nutritional practices, and opportunities, practices, and customs. The behavioral factors most closely associated with the risk of stroke include direct and secondary tobacco exposure; high alcohol consumption; increased consumption of high-fat foods and reduced consumption of folate, leading to high homocysteine levels; and sedentary behavior (Boden-Albala & Sacco, 2000). Obesity, associated with both high-fat consumption and sedentary behavior, is associated with the risk of stroke (Sacco, Gan, Boden-Albala, Lin, Kargman, Hauser, et al., 1998). There is also evidence that ischemic stroke is associated with particular types of health conditions, meaning a history of particular types of conditions will elevate the risk for subsequent stroke. These conditions include hypertension, CHD, and diabetes. Given the latency associated with the appearance of these conditions, it is reasonable to hypothesize that risks associated with comorbidity would be more common in elderly populations. Although there is a familial pattern associated with stroke, it is difficult to establish to what extent the familial pattern is due to a genetic component and to what extent it is due to shared familial behavior patterns and exposures. It is reported that potential genetic risk factors include APOE-4 as well as a genetic marker of thrombosis (Rubattu, Giliberti, & Volpe, 2000).

Hemorrhagic stroke is less common than ischemic stroke, accounting for only 15% to 20% of the cases. According to Boden-Albala and Sacco

(2004), this form of stroke is less amenable to treatment and has a higher case-fatality rate. The demographic pattern is very similar. The incidence and mortality rates increase with age, and the condition is more common among men and among African-Americans. It is unclear whether hypertension and alcohol consumption elevate the risk for this form of cerebrovascular disease as they do for ischemic strokes. Moreover, unlike diet and nutrition, tobacco exposure is clearly associated with this form of the disease. Hormones have received particular attention. Oral contraceptives of any kind were once thought to elevate the risk of hemorrhagic stroke. Later research suggests that risk for this disease was only associated with consumption of higher dosage of estrogens.

Cancer

Cancer (malignant neoplasm) refers to a general class of disease that is characterized by unrestricted cell growth that invades and destroys adjacent normal tissue and ultimately may spread through the lymphatic or blood systems to distant sites, compromising normal functions at those sites (Ruddon, 1995). Cancers are generally classified by the primary site of origin, such as cancers of the lung and bronchus, breast, prostrate, and colon or rectum. As noted in Chapter 3, cancer is the second leading cause of death. Like CHD and stroke, cancer also affects levels of functioning and disability. The risk of limitation and disability is associated with the primary site, stage of disease at diagnosis, and invasiveness of treatment. Most important, the incidence of most forms of cancer, especially cancers of the prostate and colon and rectum, increase markedly with chronological age. Cancer, viewed as a "wasting disease," also carries special significance, a significance captured in a history of the cultural interpretation of cancer in the United States (Patterson, 1987, p. vii):

> Cancer has evoked population fears that transcend its deadliness. Invested with feral personalities, cancers have been seen as "insidious," "mysterious," "lawless," "savage," and above all "relentless" . . . Cancerphobia is deeply rooted in American culture.

In the United States, cancer is the second most frequent cause of death (Devesa & Hunter, 2000). The most frequent cause of death due to cancer was lung cancer, followed by prostate cancer among males and breast cancer among females. The risk of death associated with cancer increases dramatically with age.

Between 1973 and 1994, the cancer incidence rates in men rose 33% for all cancers combined, 3% for lung cancer, and 110% for prostate cancer (Yancik, 1997). Among women, the incidence rates increased 13% for all cancers combined, 122% for lung cancer, and 23% for breast cancer. Sixty-three percent of all new cancers in 1990 occurred in men and women aged 65 and older, a group that represents, as we know, approximately 12.8% of the US population.

As will be explained in more detail in Chapter 10, the most definitive population-based data on disease incidence are available for cancer. The National Cancer Institute's Surveillance, Epidemiology, and End Results program represents a network of population-based registries around the United States. Although the number of cancer registries has expanded over the years, regular cancer surveillance has been conducted continuously among residents in specific areas of the country since 1973. The most sophisticated system of surveillance may have been developed for cancer because of the significance of the disease. In addition, the criteria for the pathological and clinical diagnosis of cancer are well established.

Lung Cancer

Cancer of the lung and bronchus represents the leading form of cancer for men and women combined (Grunberg & Bibawi, 2000). The most definitive risk factor for lung cancer is direct and indirect tobacco exposure (Osann, 1998). The early increase in the incidence of lung cancer among men—and later after World War II among women—in the United States can be directly attributable to increases in the prevalence of cigarette smoking. Other factors, such as exposure to air pollution and asbestos, are associated with the elevated risk for the disease, although far less pronounced than found for those exposed to tobacco. Recent evidence suggests that there are familial patterns of lung cancer that are not directly attributable to direct or indirect exposure to tobacco smoke (Schwartz, 2004). Cancer of the lung and bronchus is also noteworthy because the likelihood of survival is poor, especially for those diagnosed with regional or remote disease. With the exception of those with a family history of lung cancer, the age-specific incidence rate increases markedly in the middle years and peaks in the 60s and 70s. The onset of the disease is very strongly associated with the latency between the initiation of tobacco exposure and the onset of the disease (generally, about 20 years). As is true of many other forms of cancer, men have a higher incidence rate than women, and the incidence and mortality rates are higher in African-Americans than non-Hispanic whites.

Breast Cancer

Cancer of the breast is the leading form of cancer in women, accounting for approximately one-third of all malignancies. The risk of breast cancer increases markedly with age. Results from surveillance studies in the United States indicate that breast cancer occurs in 60 per 100,000 aged less than 65 years old; 322 per 100,000 women aged over 65 years; and 375 per 100,000 over 85 years of age (Kimmick, 2000). Today, almost half of all newly diagnosed breast cancers in the United States occur in women over age 65 years, and it is estimated that, by 2030, two-thirds of patients with breast cancer will be 65 years of age or older (Kimmick, 2000). Women age 65 and older are more likely than younger women to be diagnosed with advanced breast cancer, thus elevating the risk of disability and death (Satariano, Belle, & Swanson, 1986). Older women, especially African-American women with later stage disease and comorbidity, are more likely than younger women to report severe upper-body limitations one year after diagnosis (Satariano, Ragland, & DeLorenze, 1996).

Despite the clinical and public health significance of breast cancer, especially for older women, there is relatively little information about the cause of the disease. Those risk factors that have been identified to date are not readily modifiable. In addition to gender and age, these factors include a personal history of breast cancer, a family history of the disease, most notably, among first-degree relatives. Other suspected risk factors, such as high dietary fat and sedentary behavior, are still unclear, although obesity has been shown to elevate the risk for the disease among postmenopausal women. Other factors implicated in the etiology of breast cancer include alcohol consumption. There is evidence that alcohol exposure, especially in regular, high dosage, is associated with tumor proliferation. There is evidence, for example, in one study of older women with breast cancer that those women with a history of heavy alcohol consumption were more likely than women with moderate consumption to be diagnosed with a later-stage disease (Vaeth & Satariano, 1998). Unfortunately, the results are somewhat difficult to interpret. Either heavy consumption is associated with rapid tumor proliferation associated with late disease, or those older women who are heavy drinkers are also the same women who are less likely to be screened for breast cancer, meaning it is a joint behavioral pattern. There is also concern that environmental exposures, most notably pesticide exposures, are associated with an elevated risk. Although there has been no clear evidence for such an association, it remains a persistent hypothesis, especially among advocacy groups, to account for "breast cancer clusters" in the community. Such an association is certainly biologically plausible, given that toxins have been shown to accumulate in breast fluid and in breast milk. It may be that the clustering of behavioral risk factors, perhaps in combination with familial patterns and even environmental factors that occur at particular points in the life course, will ultimately provide insight into the etiology of this disease.

Of particular significance for the epidemiology of aging, there is evidence that some risk factors may vary by age at onset, classified in most cases as premenopausal and postmenopausal breast cancer (Kelsey, 1979). In general, a family history of breast cancer is more strongly associated with premenopausal breast cancer, although family history is nevertheless implicated in postmenopausal disease as well. There is strong evidence that the BRCA gene is implicated in the etiology of the disease. Obesity, on the other hand, as noted previously, is more likely to be associated with postmenopausal breast cancer than premenopausal breast cancer (Kelsey, 1979). One explanation is that obesity elevates the level of circulating estrogens among postmenopausal women, thus increasing the risk for the disease. The risk of early- versus late-onset breast cancer needs to be examined in greater detail.

In terms of demographic and socioeconomic patterns, breast cancer is somewhat of an anomaly. Unlike other leading forms of cancer, non-Hispanic white women are more likely than African-American, Hispanic white, and Asian women to develop the disease. Moreover, women of higher SES are more likely than women of lower SES to be at risk. These demographic and socioeconomic patterns are typically explained in terms of some of the known risk factors. These risk factors include delayed childbirth. Women who have not had a full-term delivery or did not have a full-term birth until after the age of 30 are at increased risk. These birthing practices are more common among women of higher SES who have advanced levels of education and professional occupational positions. It is important to remember two things. First, the risks associated with birthing practices as well as early age at menarche and later age at menopause explain only a modest variation in the occurrence of breast cancer. Second, although ethnic minorities and those of lower SES are at lower risk, when compared to the risk for non-Hispanic white women and women of higher SES, breast cancer remains the leading form of cancer for all women, regardless of race, ethnicity, and SES.

It is important to note that men, especially older men, can develop breast cancer (Thomas, Rosenblatt, Jimenez, McTiernan, Stalsberg, Thompson, et al., 1994). There have been several large collaborative studies to examine the epidemiology of breast cancer in men. In addition to advanced age, men share family history as a common risk factor. In fact, the family pedigrees with evidence of female breast cancer also are likely to include males with the disease. There is evidence as well that men who consume high-fat diets have an elevated risk for the disease. Studies of male breast cancer also have contributed to our understanding the potential role of occupational exposures on breast cancer. Men, especially older cohorts of men, assume a wider variety of occupations than women. By studying breast cancer in men, it is possible, therefore, to investigate a wider range of possible occupational exposures, especially those jobs that are employing larger numbers of women. The results of one study revealed that men with a history of exposure to electromagnetic fields, such as telephone linemen, were at elevated risk for the disease (Thomas et al., 1994). The results of that study add credence to the hypothesis that risk of breast cancer in women may be due, in part, to environmental exposures.

Prostate Cancer

Prostate cancer is the leading form of cancer in men in the United States with incidence rates of 140 per 100,000, representing nearly 30% of all new cancers (Gronberg, 2003). The age-adjusted incidence rate in men under the age of 65 is only 22.7 per 100,000, compared to 884.1 per 100,000 in men ages 65 and older. Prostate cancer is also the second leading cause of cancer death among older men. While the age-adjusted mortality rate in men under the age of 65 is only 2.9 per 100,000, it increases to a rate of 227.1 per 100,000 for men ages 65 and older. Relatively little is known about the disease. Dietary fat and elevated levels of male hormones (especially testosterone) have been implicated. Unlike many other cancers, prostate cancer can be relatively slow growing (Gronberg, 2003). Autopsy studies reveal that up to one-half of all elderly men autopsied had some form of prostate cancer. As noted earlier, one study revealed that 50% of decedent prostate cancer patients die of a cause other than prostate cancer (Satariano et al., 1998). Those most likely to die of a cause other than prostate cancer include men aged 75 and older and men with comorbid conditions (Satariano et al., 1998). African-American men are more likely than non-Hispanic white men to develop the cancer earlier in life, be diagnosed with advanced disease, and die from the disease. Although there is presently little information about early- versus late-onset disease, it may be that familial patterns and circulating levels of testosterone may be implicated.

Diabetes

With the aging of the population, it is anticipated that the incidence and prevalence of diabetes will increase (Jack, Boseman, & Vinicor, 2004). It is reported that diabetes among older adults is a complex chronic disease that affects a variety of psychologic, behavioral, social, health, and functional domains. Diabetes is a type of metabolic disorder. The pathogenesis of diabetes is associated with a deficiency in the pancreas and is reflected in the inability to secrete adequate amounts of insulin. In terms of a life course perspective, diabetes is classified as either type 1 diabetes, also referred to as juvenile-onset diabetes (insulin dependent), or type 2 diabetes, also referred to as adult-onset (non-insulin dependent) diabetes. Type 1 is characterized by immune destruction of the cells of the pancreas that secrete insulin. Type 1 is strongly influenced by genetic factors. Non-insulin-dependent diabetes is important for several reasons. First, it is the most common form of the disease. Second, it is the form of the disease that is most strongly associated with aging. In fact, one commentator speculates whether the disease, in fact, is a phenomenon of aging (Heine, 1991). Third, one of the startling statistics is that more and more children are being diagnosed with the adult form of the disease. Fourth, diabetes is itself a risk factor for other chronic conditions, such as CHD, stroke, and specific forms of cancer, such as cancer of the colon and rectum. It is one of the most common and most significant comorbid conditions in older populations. Obesity is one of the most common risk factors for diabetes. There are distinctive demographic patterns. Although not associated with gender, African-Americans and Hispanic white Americans are at elevated risk for the disease. In fact, among Hispanic white Americans, a group that generally has a fairly healthy profile, diabetes is one of the most significant health conditions.

Leading Chronic Conditions: High Morbidity and Low Mortality

Osteoarthritis

Osteoarthritis is the leading form of arthritis. The overall incidence and prevalence increase with age (Felson, Lawrence, Dieppe, Hirsch, Helmich, Jordan, et al., 2000). The site of the arthritis, for example, hip or knee, affects the extent and severity of functional limitations and disability (NIH Conference, 2000). Gender differences in the prevalence of arthritis seem to differ by age (Verbrugge, 1995). Prior to the age of 50, osteoarthritis is more common among men than women. After the age of 50, women have higher rates of arthritis than men. This gender-age pattern suggests that estrogen deficiency is associated with the risk of the disease. There is evidence from cohort studies that estrogen deficiency may be associated with the development of the condition, despite inconsistent results from case-control studies. There is also evidence that women with high bone mineral density are at elevated risk for osteoarthritis. The irony, however, is that while it is associated with the incidence of the condition, it may protect against disease progression. African-American women are at elevated risk for osteoarthritis. In addition to higher bone mineral density, African-American women are more likely to have a higher body mass, another risk for the chronic condition.

Biomedical factors affect the development of the condition through previous injury, as well as persistent age-associated stress and wearing of the joints. That is one of the hypothesized reasons that obesity is associated with higher prevalence of the condition, especially arthritis of the knee and hip. It also helps to account for associations with a history of employment in occupations that require repetitive joint-related tasks. In addition, people who have joint injuries in their adult years are at elevated risk for the development of arthritis at those sites.

Behavioral factors are also associated with the risk of osteoarthritis. Dietary practices that are deficient in antioxidants are associated with an elevated risk. In addition, tobacco exposure is associated with the risk of osteoarthritis.

There is also a strong association with genetic factors. The NIH consensus panel (2000, p. 638) on osteoarthritis reported "At least 50% of cases of osteoarthritis occur in the hands and hips and a smaller percentage in the knees." The candidate genes for common types of osteoarthritis "include the vitamin D receptor gene (which influences bone density and is near the locus for type II collagen, the major form of collagen in hyaline articular cartilage), insulin-like growth factor I genes, cartilage oligomeric protein genes, and the HLA region" (NIH Conference, 2000, p. 638).

It is also important to note that the factors associated with the incidence of the disease are not necessarily the same factors that are associated with the severity or progression of the disease. This important point is summarized very well by the NIH Conference on Osteoarthritis (NIH Conference, 2000, p. 642):

> Whereas osteoarthritis is associated with increasing age, obesity, injury, previous deformity, and ligamentous laxity, the broader clinical problem of musculoskeletal pain and disability is predicted by increasing age; osteoarthritis; obesity; lack of exercise; low personal self-efficacy; comorbid conditions caused by smoking, alcohol, and other risk factors; depression; low educational level; and poor socioeconomic status.

Cataracts

Cataract is one of leading conditions affecting older populations (Hodge, Witcher, & Satariano, 1995; Taylor, 1999). Senile cataract, the most common type of cataract in older populations, develops as a thickening and yellowing of the lens (Hodge et al., 1995). Although nuclear cataracts are the most common type, senile cataracts can also occur in the cortical and posterior subcapsular regions (Hammond, Snieder, Spector, & Gilbert, 2000; Taylor, 1999). Each of these conditions occurs in separate areas of the lens, and each is due to a different set of risk factors (Taylor, 1999). Although not associated with high mortality, cataracts represent one of the leading causes of blindness in both the developed and developing world. There is evidence from studies of twins that cataracts are heritable (Hammond et al., 2000). In addition to chronological age, females are at greater risk than men (Hodge et al., 1995). Those of lower SES have a higher risk of cataracts (Klein, Klein, Lee, & Meuer, 2003). Other risk factors associated with age-related cataracts include diabetes, exposure of ultraviolet light, light-colored eyes, and exposure to tobacco smoke (Hodge et al., 1995; Taylor, 1999). It is unknown whether the timing of these risk factors, for example, the extent and timing of cigarette smoking, is associated with the timing of age-related cataracts. Interestingly, myopia, i.e., characterized by elongated corneal shape, also known as "being near-sighted," is associated with the risk of age-related cataracts (McCarty, 2002). Both myopia and cataract are familial conditions with a significant heritable component (Hammond et al., 2000; Zadnik, Satariano, Mutti, Sholtz, & Adams, 1994). These results suggest the potential value of examining the development of age-related cataracts from a life course perspective.

Late-Onset Neurological Conditions: High Morbidity and High Mortality

Alzheimer's Disease

It is fair to say that AD, one of the leading forms of dementia, is assuming the stature of a "dread disease," previously reserved for cancer (Sloane, Zimmerman, Suchindran, Reed, Wang, Boustani, et al., 2002). Just as cancer is thought to be a wasting disease, so too is AD. Alzheimer's disease is characterized by a number of distinctive pathological signs, including neurofibrillary tangles and neuritic plaques. Although these signs have also been identified in the brains of older people without symptoms of dementia, the quantity and location of these tangles and plaques are distinctive among persons with AD. Neutrophil threads are also consistent with AD pathology. In fact, it is reported that the density of these threads is more likely than plaques or tangles to be associated with reduced cognitive function (Graves, 2004). Clinical symptoms include a progressive loss of cognitive function, beginning with long-term memory, coupled with purposeful movement (apraxia), language (aphasia), and the ability to execute tasks in everyday life. Clinical symptoms also include evidence of poor judgment as well as some feelings of paranoia. Over time, individuals become incontinent and may lose the ability to speak. In addition, individuals with the disease lose the ability to recognize family members and close friends. In the end, the person may experience seizures and the inability to walk. The last days are typically spent in a vegetative state, and the immediate cause of death is pneumonia. Four subtypes of AD have been identified (Mayeux, Stern, & Spanton, 1985). Each type differs in terms of its clinical profile and, most notably how quickly a person is likely to decline from normal to impaired cognitive function. Although AD can only be confirmed through pathologic examination, there is a strong correlation between clinical assessment and pathological diagnosis. In fact, the correspondence is as high as 80% to 90% in a specialized AD clinic, but somewhat less pronounced in general medical practice.

Estimates of the prevalence of AD vary considerably. The incidence of the disease increases significantly with age (Hebert, Scherr, Beckett, Albert, Pilgrim, Chown, et al., 1995). It is reported that the prevalence of dementia and AD doubles every 5.1 years (Jorm, Korten, & Henderson, 1987). Chronological age figured significantly in the original characterization of the disease. The first published report of this condition by Dr. Alois Alzheimer was of a woman in her 40s. Given that a number of the symptoms were akin to what might be expected in a much older person, the condition was first referred to as "presenile dementia." Today, a distinction is made, as it is with other conditions, between early-onset and late-onset disease. As we will see, the risk factors for the two conditions seem to differ, especially with regard to the role of familial and genetic factors. There is also a growing interest in examining risk and protective factors that may affect the occurrence and severity of disease across the life course. This will be examined in more detail when we discuss specific risk and protective factors.

In addition to age, gender is an important factor. Research from epidemiology indicates that women are more likely than men to develop the disease. There is also evidence that the disease is more common among African-Americans than non-Hispanic whites (Graves, 2004). Socioeconomic status is also associated with the incidence and prevalence of AD. In general, those of lower SES are more likely than those of higher SES to be diagnosed with AD. Interestingly, when people of higher SES are diagnosed with AD, it tends to be more advanced. It is hypothesized that people of higher SES are more likely to have protective factors, such as greater cognitive reserves. If this is the case, either the reserves serve to moderate the connection between pathology and symptomatic presentation, or the connection between pathology and presentation are just as pronounced, but the reserves enable the person to better compensate or, in fact, hide the loss of cognitive function.

Research has examined the relationship between risk and protective factors for AD. Dementia and AD may be prevented either through slowing of the rate of accumulation of lesions or through the preservation of brain reserve. As Graves (2004, p. 113) writes:

> Factors that enhance brain reserve (good childhood environment and nutrition, adult mental stimulation) and interventions that interrupt the cascade of events leading to clinical presentation of disease (estrogen

replacement therapy, nonsteroidal anti-inflammatory drugs, antioxi-dant therapy) are promising candidates for prevention.

There is a growing appreciation of the role of factors that have been previously referred to as "cardiovascular risk factors." Most notably, people with APOE-4 allele are at elevated risk for the development of AD. As noted previously, this allele is also associated with the development of cardiovascular disease. This also underscores the hypothesized connection between vascular dementia and AD. In addition, research indicates that high SBP, hypercholesterolemia, plasma homocysteine, and, interestingly, diabetes mellitus are at elevated risk for AD. Indeed, associated risk of those factors is increased among people with the APOE-4 allele. Other suspected risk factors include head injury and exposure to neurotoxic elements, such as aluminum, although the latter association remains controversial. Cigarette smoking has an interesting pattern. Among people with the APOE-4 allele, smoking seems to be protective. However, among those without the allele, smoking elevates the risk. In addition, alcohol seems to be protective, when the dosage is moderate, and aggravates the risk when the dosage is high.

There are a number of protective factors. These factors include uterine, infant, and childhood nutrition; environmental stimulation; and number of years of education (Haan & Wallace, 2004). In addition, there is evidence that nonsteroidal anti-inflammatory drugs are associated with reduced risk. Among women, hormone replacement therapy has been shown to be protective in case-control studies, but there is no evidence in longitudinal studies. Associated with the risk associated with high cholesterol, patients on statin drugs are at reduced risk for AD. Finally, there is a growing body of research that suggests that consumption of antioxidants (Vitamin E and C, especially in combination) and folate is associated with reduced risk.

Parkinson's Disease

PD is one of the most common age-related neurodegenerative movement disorders (Tanner, 1992). It has a distinctive clinical profile that includes bradykinesia, resting tremor, cogwheel rigidity, and postural reflect impairment. In some cases, PD patients may have comorbid dementia. There is no diagnostic test for PD. Diagnosis depends on neurological history and examination. The pathological signs of PD include loss of pigmented neurons, typically in the substantia nigra with evidence of distinctive characteristics called Lewy bodies.

In addition to chronological age, gender is an important factor. Men are almost twice as likely as women to be diagnosed with PD. This has led some commentators to speculate that PD may be associated with male-associated environmental exposures or X chromosome-linked genetic susceptibility factors.

There is evidence that environmental factors affect the risk and course of the disease. For example, in 1983, researchers identified a cluster of parkinsonism in northern California. Young men and women were presenting at a hospital in San Jose, California, with symptoms of parkinsonism. It was determined that these young adults had been injecting a designer drug that contained a neurotoxicant 1-methyl-4-phenyltetrahydropyridine (MPTP). Although MPTP is uncommon, it is similar to paraquat, a neurotoxicant that has been shown to produce parkinsonism in animals. This finding, in turn, is associated with other studies that suggest an association with pesticide exposures (Butterfield, Valanis, Spencer, Lindeman, & Nutt, 1993). There is evidence that residents of rural and farm areas are at elevated risk for the disease.

Like AD, head trauma is associated with an elevated risk of PD. Often the head trauma occurs decades before the appearance of PD. Inverse relationships are noted for smoking, alcohol, and coffee and caffeine.

Since PD is a late-life condition without a definitive clinical diagnosis, it is difficult to conduct familial and genetic studies (Tanner & Marder, 2004). In spite of these difficulties, there are promising findings. As is true of other conditions, people with earlier onset of PD are likely to be from families in which other first-degree relatives have the condition. In addition, studies of twins suggest a genetic contribution to early-onset PD. No evidence is reported for late-onset disease.

Leading Infectious Diseases: High Morbidity and High Mortality

Influenza and Pneumonia

There are two common forms of pneumonia—community-acquired pneumonia (CAP) and nursing home-acquired pneumonia (NHAP) (Reingold & Phares, 2001). Although the pathophysiology does not differ significantly between the two types of pneumonia, NHAP tends to be more severe, perhaps in large part because immune competence of older people in nursing home is worse than the competence of people in community settings. Susceptibility to influenza and pneumonia is associated with age-associated changes in the lung. These changes include a decrease in the elastic recoil of the lung, a decrease in the strength of respiratory muscles, and calcification of the rib cage. Together these factors make it more difficult to breath, especially during periods of exertion. CAP is a leading condition affecting older populations in the general community (Loeb, 2003). *Streptococcus pneumoniae*, or pneumococcus, is the most common cause of CAP in older adults. The risk of pneumonia is elevated by the presence of multiple, comorbid conditions as well as the therapies for those conditions (Niederman & Fein, 1986). "Gram-negative colonization of the oropharynx, followed by the spread of bacteria to the tracheobronchia tree, commonly precedes the development of pneumonia" (Niederman & Fein, 1986, p. 241). Factors that affect the colonization of the lower-respiratory tract and upper-respiratory tract include antibiotic therapy, endotracheal intubation, smoking, malnutrition, surgery, and any other serious medical condition (Janssens & Krause, 2004). In addition, decreased salivation, associated with administration of antidepressants, antiparkinsonian medications, diuretics, antihypertensives, and antihistamines, also stimulate this colonization. Some researchers contend that lower SES, poor nutrition, and exposure to tobacco smoke, air pollution, and other pollutants elevate the risk for CAP. It also may be that the absence of immunization with influenza or pneumococcal vaccine may be more common in older people of lower SES.

Following the points made earlier, the presenting symptoms for pneumonia and influenza in the elderly are different than in younger populations. Falls, injuries, and confusion are presenting symptoms for pneumonia and influenza in older populations. It is understandable that recognition and treatment for this condition are sometimes delayed.

SARS is a recent manifestation of the influenza virus. In 2002 and 2003, a new infectious disease—SARS—developed among residents of China. Travelers from China also were infected, initiating a new network of infectious cases in their own countries, most notably travelers returning to Canada. The disease was eventually traced to people who had come in contact with civet cats (Lai, 2003). The case-fatality rate was especially high among the elderly, a pattern consistent with other infectious diseases. Although there were more fatal cases of seasonal influenza virus, SARS is noteworthy for a number of reasons. First, the SARS virus illustrates how a new condition can appear and risk the lives of many people, especially the very young and the very old. Second, given extensive global travel patterns, there is now the likelihood that an infectious disease of this kind can be spread very rapidly. Third, SARS illustrated that the global public health system used to identify and address an infectious disease of this kind is limited.

Human Immunodeficiency Virus (HIV) and Acquired Immune Deficiency Syndrome (AIDS)

HIV/AIDS represents a significant public health problem. Even though HIV/AIDS is typically viewed as a condition that primarily affects young adults as well as infants infected during pregnancy, there seems to be a growing appreciation that the elderly are also at risk. It is reported, for example, that between 1990 and 2001, the cumulative number of AIDS cases in the United States reported to the Centers for Disease Control and Prevention in adults aged 50 years or older quintupled from 16,288 to 86,875 (Levy, Ory, & Crystal, 2003). According to Mack and Ory (2003, S69), "This increase could stem from several sources: (1) an actual increase in incident AIDS cases; (2) better case reporting of the older population than earlier in the epidemic; or (3) a delayed progression to AIDS because effective antiretroviral therapy prolongs the period from HIV infection to AIDS."

It is fair to say that there have been three stages in the study of HIV/AIDS in older populations. In the first stage, older people were viewed as caregivers for their children and, in some cases, their partners who became HIV positive and subsequently developed AIDS. In that stage, the people who were perceived to be at greatest risk were injection drug users who developed the disease through previously infected needles. In addition, there were men who developed the condition through specific sexual practices with other men. In the second stage, there were reports of older people who had developed the diseases, in most case, through transfusion of infected blood plasma between 1978 and 1983 (Chen, Ryan, Ferguson, Yataco, Markowitz, & Raksis, 1998; Linsk, Fowler, & Klein, 2003). In the third stage, many older people with HIV/AIDS share the same risk profile as younger people with the disease (Levy, Holmes, & Smith, 2003).

As Linsk and colleagues (2003, S243) report:

"Risk behaviors for HIV infection for older people are the same as those for people of any age: being sexually active and practicing unprotected sex with a partner of the opposite or the same sex; not knowing your sexual partner's (or partners') sexual and drug history; and injecting drugs and sharing needles or syringes with other people." Older people with the disease could become infected at age 50 or could have become infected at an earlier age and are living longer before progression to AIDS (Mack & Ory, 2003).

Today, there are older people with the condition as well as older people who are serving as caregivers for their children or partners with the condition. According to Levy and colleagues (2003, S62), "Although HIV is found among people aged 50 years or older throughout the world, the greatest impact of the epidemic on such persons has been through their relationship with children, grandchildren, and family members who are infected." Other researchers concur with this assessment. Knodel, Watkins, and VanLandingham (2003, S153), for example, report, "Although older persons represent a non-negligible minority of the reported global caseload, a far larger number of older persons are affected through the illness and death of their adult children and younger generation relatives who contract AIDS."

Even though older and younger people share many of the same risk factors for HIV/AIDS, it is important to realize that there are some important differences. First, it is reported that older people are less likely than younger people to use condoms during sexual activities (Chiao, Ries, & Sande, 1999). One explanation for this behavior is that many older people view the use of condoms as a strategy to prevent pregnancy rather than as a technique to prevent sexually transmitted diseases. Since unwanted pregnancies are of little concern at that age, condoms are less likely to be used. Second, since older people are generally not thought of as being at risk for HIV/AIDS, even among primary physicians, older people are less likely to be screened for HIV (Chiao et al., 1999; Gordon & Thompson, 1995). Third, older people are likely to have a variety of concurrent, health conditions. As noted by Ouslander and Beck (1982), the presence of comorbidity may confound the diagnosis of a new condition. In this case, the symptoms for an index condition, such as HIV/AIDS, may be obscured by the presence of a pre-existing comorbid condition (Zelenetz & Epstein, 1998). Fourth, the presence of comorbid conditions, coupled with reduced immunological status, accelerate the transition from HIV to AIDS (Adler & Nagel, 1994; Levy, Holmes, & Smith, 2003). Finally, most of the current treatments and services for HIV/AIDS have been developed from research on younger populations. It is unknown whether conventional therapy is equally effective in older populations (Alder & Nagel, 1994; Chiao et al., 1999).

Four Exemplar Conditions: Summary

The four exemplary sets of conditions are associated with an elevation of risk for either high functional limitations and disabilities or high mortality or both. Although there are some distinctive risk profiles, the sets of conditions share some factors in common. For example, the incidence and prevalence of each set of conditions increase with age. An elevation of risk also was greater among African-American elders and among those of lower SES. The reasons for those socioeconomic, race, and ethnic patterns may differ, however, across the conditions. It also was noteworthy that so-called cardiovascular risk factors played an important role in the etiology of the dementias. These factors include high blood pressure and high cholesterol. The generalized effect of APOE-4 allele deserves special attention. This allele is associated with both cardiovascular diseases and the late-life dementias. In both sets of conditions, APOE-4 allele is associated more strongly with early-onset conditions. Moreover, one condition, diabetes, serves as a risk factor for other conditions. In the future, research may suggest a common set of genetic, behavioral, social, and environmental factors that are associated with a variety of age-related conditions. Research in this area relates to the first question raised by Syme and Torfs (1978): Why do some people become ill, while others do not? The topic of common risk factors also leads us to a consideration of comorbidity and multiple morbidities.

COMORBIDITIES AND MULTIMORBIDITIES

We have previously noted that there is a growing body of research that examines the topic of aging and comorbidity and multiple morbidities. Although there is clear evidence that the number and types of multiple, concurrent conditions are associated with an elevation in the risk of both disability and death, there are fewer studies designed to examine the epidemiology of the multiple occurrence of conditions (Gijsen et al., 2001). In addition, most studies in this area have used summary measures alone (multimorbidity) or in combination with a single index disease (comorbidity). The incidence and prevalence of co-occurrence of conditions increase with age. Overall, research in the United States indicates that non-Hispanic whites are more likely to develop multiple chronic health conditions. This may be caused by a survivor effect. One has to survive to develop multiple conditions. As noted in Chapter 2, evidence for the concept of allostasis, the summary measure of physiological disregulation, was based on the presence of multiple, comorbid conditions in older populations. As noted by Seeman and colleagues, since multiple morbidity is so varied, it is reasonable to assume that there is a generic underlying physiological process (Seeman, McEwen, Rowe, & Singer, 2001). In addition, the same behavioral factors that are associated with the risk of single conditions, such as cigarette smoking, physical inactivity, and specific diet factors, are also associated with the risk of multiple conditions. In addition, there is evidence that the treatment for some health conditions may initiate or aggravate the course of other conditions. For example, some chemotherapeutic agents for cancer, most notably, doxorubicin, have cardiac side effects (Satariano, 2000). Some health conditions, such as diabetes, may elevate the risk of other conditions, such as cataracts and colorectal cancer.

Most research on comorbidity and multimorbidity has focused on the co-occurrence of specific diagnosed conditions. Recent research and commentary have noted the importance of examining the multiple, interactions of underlying physiological processes and "preclinical" conditions. Attention also has been directed to the co-occurrence of impairments and functional limitations. Regardless of the "unit of investigation," whether it is a set of diagnosed conditions, underlying physiological processes, impairments, or functional limitations, the important observation is the significance of "multiplicity." In other words, it is important to examine the middle ground between single entities on the one hand and summary measures on the others. Just as it is important to understand why some older persons develop a single condition, while others do not; it is also important to understand why some older persons have specific multiple, comorbid conditions, and others do not.

CONCLUSION

The study of the causes and consequences of single or multiple health conditions is a core area of study in the epidemiology of aging. In general, the risk for disease increases with chronological age. This may be caused by a variety of factors. In addition to reduced host resistance, aging may be associated with increased exposure to a common set of risk factors. In some cases, however, the risk of late-onset disease may be caused by factors that are different than the factors associated with early-onset disease.

REFERENCES

Adler, W. H., & Nagel, J. E. (1994). Acquired immunodeficiency syndrome in the elderly. *Drugs & Aging, 4*(5), 410–416.

Aston, J. W. Jr. (1992). Post-polio syndrome: An emerging threat to polio survivors. *Postgraduate Medicine, 92*(1), 249–256, 260.

Berlin, J. A., & Colditz, G. A. (1990). A meta-analysis of physical activity in the prevention of coronary heart disease. *American Journal of Epidemiology, 132*(4), 612–628.

Boden-Albala, B., & Sacco, R. L. (2000). Lifestyle factors and stroke risk: Exercise, alcohol, diet, obesity, smoking, drug use, and stress. *Current Atheroscleric Report, 2,* 160–166.

Boden-Albala, B., & Sacco, R. L. (2002). Lifestyle factors and stroke risk: Exercise, alcohol, diet, obesity, smoking, drug use, and stress. *Current Atheroscleric Report, 2,* 160–166.

Boden-Albala, B., & Sacco, R. L. (2004). Stroke. In L. M. Nelson, C. M. Tanner, S. K. Van Den Eeden, & V. M. McGuire (Eds.), *Neuroepidemiology: From Principles to Practice.* New York: Oxford University Press, 223–253.

Butterfield, P. G., Valanis, B. G., Spencer, P. S., Lindeman, C. A., & Nutt, J. G. (1993). Environmental antecedents of young-onset Parkinson's disease. *Neurology, 43*(6), 1150–1158.

Bromberg, M. B., & Waring, W. P. (1991). Neurologically normal patients with suspected postpoliomyelitis syndrome: Electromyographic assessment of past denervation. *Archives of Physical and Medical Rehabilitation, 72*(7), 493–497.

Chen, H. X., Ryan, P. A., Ferguson, R. P., Yataco, A., Markowitz, J. A., & Raksis, K. (1998). Characteristics of acquired immunodeficiency syndrome in older adults. *Journal of the American Geriatrics Society, 46*(2), 153–156.

Chiao, E. Y., Ries, K. M., & Sande, M. A. (1999). AIDS and the elderly. *Clinical Infectious Disease, 28*(4), 740–745.

Corti, M. C., Guralnik, J. M., & Bilato, C. (1996). Coronary heart disease risk factors in older persons. *Aging (Milano), 8*(2), 75–89.

Devesa, S. S., & Hunter, C. P. (2000). The burden of cancer in the elderly. In C. P. Hunter, K. A. Johnson, & H. B. Muss (Eds.), *Cancer in the Elderly.* New York: Marcel Dekker, Inc., 1–24.

Ettinger, W. H., Jr., Fried, L. P., Harris, T., Shemanski, L., Schultz, R., & Robbins, J. (1994). Self-reported causes of physical disability in older people. The Cardiovascular Health Study, CHS Collaborative Research Group. *Journal of the American Geriatrics Society, 42*(10), 1035–1044.

Felson, D. T., Lawrence, R. C., Dieppe, P. A., Hirsch, R., Helmich, C. G., Jordan, J. M., et al. (2000). Osteoarthritis: New insights. Part 1: The disease and its risk factors. *Annals of Internal Medicine, 133*, 635–646.

Fried, L. P., Borhani, N. O., Enright, P., Furberg, C. D., Gardin, J. M., Kronmal, R. A., et al. (1991). The Cardiovascular Health Study: Design and rationale. *Annals of Epidemiology, 1*(3), 263–276.

Fried, L. P., Storer, D. J., King, D. E., & Lodder, F. (1991). Diagnosis of illness presentation in the elderly. *Journal of the American Geriatrics Society, 39*(2), 117–123.

Galobardes, B., Lynch, J. W., & Davey-Smith, G. (2004). Childhood socioeconomic circumstances and cause-specific mortality in adulthood: Systematic review and interpretation. *Epidemiologic Reviews, 26*, 7–21.

Gijsen, R., Hoeymans, N., Schellevis, F. G., Ruwaard, D., Satariano, W. A., & van den Bos, G. A. (2001). Causes and consequences of comorbidity: A review. *Journal of Clinical Epidemiology, 54*(7), 661–674.

Glynn, R. J., Brock, D. B., Harris, T., Havilik, R., Chrischilles, P. A., Ostfeld, A. M., et al. (1995). Use of anti-hypertensive drugs and trends in blood pressure in the elderly. *Annals of Internal Medicine, 155*(17), 1855–1860.

Gordon, S. M., & Thompson, S. (1995). The changing epidemiology of human immunodeficiency virus infection in older persons. *Journal of the American Geriatrics Society, 43*, 7–9.

Graves, A. B. (2004). Alzheimer's disease and vascular dementia. In L. M. Nelson, C. M. Tanner, S. K. Van Den Eeden, & V. M. McGuire (Eds.), *Neuroepidemiology: From Principles to Practice.* New York: Oxford University Press, 102–130.

Gronberg, H. (2003). Prostate cancer epidemiology, *Lancet, 361*(9360), 859–864.

Grunberg, S. M., & Bibawi, S. E. (2000). Lung cancer. In C. P. Hunter, K. A. Johnson, & H. B. Muss (Eds.), *Cancer in the Elderly.* New York: Marcel Dekker, 345–360.

Haan, M. N., & Wallace, R. (2004). Can dementia be prevented? Brain aging in a population-based context. *Annual Review of Public Health, 25*, 1–24.

Hammond, C. J., Snieder, H., Spector, T. D., & Gilbert, C. E. (2000). Genetic and environmental factors in age-related nuclear cataracts in monozygotic and dizygotic twins. *The New England Journal of Medicine, 343*, 1786–1790.

Hebert, L. E., Scherr, P. A., Beckett, L. A., Albert, M. S., Pilgrim, D. M., Chown, M. J., et al. (1995). Age-specific incidence of Alzheimer's disease in a community population. *Journal of the American Medical Association, 273*(17), 1354–1359.

Heine, R. J. (1991). Non-insulin dependent diabetes mellitus: A phenomenon of ageing? *International Journal of Epidemiology, 20*(Suppl 1), S18–S24.

Hodge, W. G., Whitcher, J. P., & Satariano, W. A. (1995). Risk factors for age-related cataracts. *Epidemiologic Reviews, 17*(2), 336–346.

House, J. S., Kessler, R. C., & Herzog, A. R. (1990). Age, socioeconomic status, and health. *The Milbank Quarterly, 68*(3), 381–411.

Howard, G. (1999). Why do we have a stroke belt in the southeastern U.S.? A review of unlikely and uninvestigated potential causes. *American Journal of Medicine, 317*(3), 160–167.

Hyder, A. A., & Morrow, R. H. (2001). Disease burden measurement and trends. In M. H. Merson, R. E. Black, & A. J. Mills (Eds.), *International Public Health: Diseases, Programs, Systems, and Policies*. Gaithersburg, MD: Aspen Publishers, 1–52.

Hypertension Detection and Follow-Up Program Cooperative Research Group (1984). The effect of antihypertensive drug treatment on mortality in the presence of resting electrocardiographic abnormalities at baseline: The HDFP experience. *Circulation, 70*(6), 996–1003.

Jack, L. Jr., Boseman, L., & Vinicor, F. (2004). Aging Americans and diabetes: A public health and clinical response. *Geriatrics, 59*(4), 14–17.

Janssens, J. P., & Krause, K. H. (2004). Pneumonia in the very old. *The Lancet: Infectious Diseases, 4*(February), 112–124.

Jorm, A. F., Korten, A. E., & Henderson, A. S. (1987). The prevalence of dementia: A quantitative integration of the literature. *Acta Psychiatric Scandinavia, 76*, 465–479.

Kannel, W. B., Wolf, P. A., McGee, D. L., Dawber, T. R., McNamara, P., & Castelli, W. P. (1981). Systolic blood pressure, arterial rigidity, and risk of stroke: The Framingham Study. *Journal of the American Medical Association, 245*(12), 1225–1229.

Kelsey, J. (1979). A review of the epidemiology of human breast cancer. *Epidemiologic Reviews, 1*, 74–109.

Kimmick, G. (2000). Breast cancer. In C. P. Hunter, K. A. Johnson, & H. B. Muss (Eds.), *Cancer in the Elderly*. New York: Marcel Dekker, 233–265.

Klein, B. E., Klein, R., Lee, K. F., & Meuer, S. M. (2003). Socioeconomic status and lifestyle factors and the 10-year incidence of age-related cataracts. *American Journal of Ophthalmology, 136*(3), 506–512.

Knodel, J., Watkins, S., & Vanlandingham, M. (2003). AIDS and older persons: An international perspective. *Journal of Acquired Immune Deficiency Syndromes, 33*, S153–S165.

Kuller, L., Fisher, L., McClelland, R., Fried, L., Cushman, M., Jackson, S., & Manolio, T. (1998). Differences in the prevalence of and risk factors for subclinical vascular disease among black and white participants in the Cardio-vascular Health Study. *Arterioscleroic Thrombosis Vascular-Biology, 18*(2), 283–293.

Kunst, A. E., del Rios, M., Groenhof, F., & Mackenbach, J. P. (1998). Socio-economic inequalities in stroke mortality among middle-aged men: An inter-national overview. European Union Working Group on Socioeconomic Inequalities in Health. *Stroke, 29*(11), 2285–2291.

Labarthe, D. R. (1998). *Epidemiology and Prevention of Cardiovascular Diseases: A Global Challenge.* Gaithersburg, MD: Aspen Publishers.

Lai, M. M. (2003). SARS virus: The beginning of the unraveling of a new coro-navirus. *Journal of Biomedical Science, 10*(6), Pt.2, 664–675.

Levy, J. A., Ory, M. G., & Crystal, S. (2003). HIV/AIDS interventions for midlife and older adults: Current status and challenges. *Journal of Acquired Immune Deficiency Syndrome, 33, Suppl 2,* S59–S67.

Linsk, N. L., Fowler, J. P., & Klein, S. J. (2003). HIV/AIDS prevention and care services and services for the aging: Bridging the gap between service systems to assist older people. *Journal of the Acquired Immune Deficiency Syndromes, 33,* S243–S250.

Loeb, M. B. (2003). Community-acquired pneumonia in older people: The need for a broader perspective. *Journal of the American Geriatrics Society, 51,* 539–543.

Mack, K. A., & Ory, M. G. (2003). AIDS and older Americans at the end of the Twentieth Century. *Journal of the Acquired Immune Deficiency Syndromes, 33,* S68–S75.

Mayeux, R., Stern, Y., & Spanton, S. (1985). Heterogeniety in dementia of the AD type: Evidence of subgroups. *Neurology, 35*(4), 453–461.

McCarty, C. A. (2002). Cataract in the 21st century: Lessons from previous epidemiologic research, *Clinical and Experimental Optomology, 85*(2), 91–96.

McQueen, D. V., McKenna, M. T., & Sleet, D. A. (2001). Chronic diseases and injury. In M. H. Merson, R. E. Black, & A. J. Mills (Eds.), *International Public Health: Diseases, Programs, Systems, and Policies.* Gaithersburg, MD: Aspen Publishers, 293–330.

Mittelmark, M. B., Psaty, B. M., Rautaharju, P. M., Fried, L. P., Borhani, N. O., Tracy, R. P., et al. (1993). Prevalence of cardiovascular diseases among older adults. The Cardiovascular Health Study. *American Journal of Epidemiology, 137*(3), 311–317.

National Institutes of Health. (2000). Osteoporosis Prevention, Diagnosis, and Therapy. NIH Consensus Statement Online 2000 March 27–29, *17*(1), 1–36.

NIA Aging and Genetic Epidemiology Working Group. (2000). Genetic epi-demiologic studies on age-specific traits. *American Journal of Epidemioogy, 152*(11), 1003–1008.

Niederman, M. S., & Fein, A. M. (1986). Pneumonia in the elderly. *Clinics in Geriatric Medicine, 2*(2), 241–268.

Osann, K. E. (1998). Epidemiology of lung cancer. *Current Opinion in Pulmonary Medicine, 4*(4), 198–204.

Ouslander, J. G., & Beck, J. C. (1982). Defining the health problems of the elderly. *Annual Review of Public Health, 3,* 55–83.

Patterson, J. T. (1987). *The Dread Disease: Cancer and Modern American Culture.* Cambridge, MA: Harvard University Press.

Reingold, A. L., & Phares, C. R. (2001). Infectious diseases. In M. H. Merson, R. E. Black, & A. J. Mills (Eds.), *International Public Health: Diseases, Programs, Systems, and Policies.* Gaithersburg, MD: Aspen Publishers, 139–206.

Rowe, J. (1985). Health care of the elderly. *The New England Journal of Medicine, 312,* 826–835.

Rubattu, S., Giliberti, R., & Volpe, M. (2000). Etiology and pathophysiology of stroke as a complex trait. *American Journal of Hypertension, 13,* 1139–1148.

Ruddon, R. W. (1995). *Cancer Biology,* 3rd ed. New York: Oxford University Press.

Sacco, R. L., Boden-Albala, B., Gan, R., Chen, X., Kargman, D. E., Shea, S., et al. (1998). Stroke incidence among white, black, and Hispanic residents of an urban community: The Northern Manhattan Stroke Study. *American Journal of Epidemiology, 147,* 259–268.

Sacco, R. L., Gan, R., Boden-Albala, B., Lin, I. F., Kargman, D. E., Hauser, W. H., et al. (1998). Leisure-time physical activity and ischemic stroke risk: The Northern Manhattan Stroke Study. *Stroke, 29,* 380–387.

Satariano, W. A. (2000). Comorbidities and cancer. In C. P. Hunter, K. A. Johnson, & H. M. Muss (Eds.), *Cancer in the Elderly.* New York: Marcel Dekker, 477–499.

Satariano, W. A. (1986). Race, socioeconomic status, and health: A study of age differences in a depressed area. *American Journal of Preventive Medicine, 2*(1), 1–5.

Satariano, W. A., Belle, S. H., & Swanson, G. M. (1986). The severity of breast cancer at diagnosis: A comparison of age and extent of disease in black and white women. *American Journal of Public Health, 76*(7), 779–782.

Satariano, W. A., Ragland, K. E., & Van Den Eeden, S. K. (1998). Cause of death in men diagnosed with prostate carcinoma. *Cancer, 83*(6), 1180–1186.

Satariano, W. A., & Swanson, G. M. (1988). Racial differences in cancer incidence: The significance of age-specific patterns. *Cancer, 62,* 2640–2653.

Satariano, W. A., Ragland, D. R., & DeLorenze, G. N. (1996). Limitations in upper-body strength associated with breast cancer: A comparison of black and white women. *Journal of Clinical Epidemiology, 49*(5), 535–544.

Schocken, D. D. (2000). Epidemiology and risk factors for heart failure in the elderly. *Clinics in Geriatric Medicine, 16*(3), 407–418.

Schwartz, A. G. (2004). Genetic predisposition to lung cancer. *Chest, 125,* 5 *Suppl,* 86S–89S.

Seeman, T. E., McEwen, B. S., Rowe, J. W., & Singer, B. H. (2001). Allostatic load as a marker of cumulative biological risk: MacArthur studies of successful aging. *Proceedings of the National Academy of Sciences, 98*(8), 4770–4775.

Siscovick, D. S., Fried, L., Millelmark, M., Rutan, G., Bild, D., & O'Leary, D. H. (1997). Exercise intensity and subclinical cardiovascular disease in the elderly: The Cardiovascular Health Study. *American Journal of Epidemiology, 145*(11), 977–986.

Sloane, P. D., Zimmerman, S., Suchindran, C., Reed, P., Wang, L., Boustani, M., et al. (2002). The public health impact of Alzheimer's disease, 2000–2050: Potential implication of treatment advances. *Annual Review of Public Health, 23*, 213–231.

Syme, S. L., & Torfs, C. P. (1978). Epidemiologic research in hypertension: A Critical appraisal. *Journal of Human Stress, 4*(1), 43–48.

Tanner, C. M. (1992). Epidemiology of Parkinson's disease. *Neurologic Clinics, 10*(2), 317–329.

Tanner, C. M., & Marder, K. (2004). Movement disorders. In L. M. Nelson, C. M. Tanner, S. K. Van Den Eeden, & V. M. McGuire (Eds.), *Neuroepidemiology: From Principles to Practice.* New York: Oxford University Press, 131–161.

Taylor, H. R. (1999). Epidemiology of age-related cataract. *Eye, 13*(Pt 3b), 445–448.

Thomas, D. B., Rosenblatt, K., Jimenez, L. M., McTiernan, A., Stalsberg, A., Thompson, W. D., et al. (1994). Ionizing radiation and breast cancer in men (United States). *Cancer Causes & Control, 5*(1), 9–14.

Timiras, P. S. (Ed.). (2003). *Physiological Basis of Aging and Geriatrics.* New York: CRC Press.

Trojan, D. A., Cashman, N. R., Shapiro, S., Tansey, C. M., & Esdaile, J. M. (1994). Predictive factors for post-poliomyelitis syndrome. *Archives of Physical Medicine and Rehabilitation, 75*, 770–777.

U.S. Department of Health and Human Services. (1996). *Physical Activity and Health: A Report of the Surgeon General.* Atlanta, GA: U.S. Department of Health and Human Services, Centers for Disease Control and Prevention, National Center for Chronic Disease Prevention and Health Promotion.

Vaeth, P. A., & Satariano, W. A. (1998). Alcohol consumption and breast cancer stage at diagnosis. *Alcohol Clinics and Experimental Research, 22*(4), 928–934.

Wallace, R. B. (1992). Aging and disease: From laboratory to community. In R. B. Wallace & R. F. Woolson (Eds.), *The Epidemiologic Study of the Elderly.* New York: Oxford University Press, 3–9.

Weintraub, W. S., Klein, L. W., Seelaus, P. A., Agarwal, J. B., & Helfact, R. H. (1985). Importance of total life consumption of cigarettes as a risk factor for coronary artery disease. *American Journal of Cardiology, 5596*, 669–672.

Yancik, R. (1997). Cancer burden in the aged: An epidemiologic and demographic overview. *Cancer, 80*(7), 1273–1283.

Zadnik, K., Satariano, W. A., Mutti, D. O., Sholtz, R. I., & Adams, A. J. (1994). The effect of parental history of myopia on children's eye size. *Journal of the American Medical Association, 271*(17), 1323–1327.

Zelenetz, P. D., & Epstein, M. E. (1998). HIV in the elderly. *AIDS Patient Care STDS, 12*(4), 255–262.

CHAPTER 9

General Health, Frailty, and Successful Aging

It is clear that health and functioning, together with mortality and survival, represent the major outcomes in the epidemiology of aging. Although it may be convenient to speak in terms of overall "health and functioning," one may legitimately question, especially after reading the preceding chapters, whether it is really possible to summarize in a single term all that health and functioning entails, that is, the independent and joint effects of past and current health conditions; physical, cognitive, and psychological functioning; as well as the effects of past injuries and collisions.

In this chapter, we will review recent attempts to do just that, that is, to provide overall assessments of health and functioning. Although work in this area is motivated in part by a desire to obtain a clear, parsimonious assessment of health and functioning, it is also driven by the notion of *sui generis*, the belief that the whole is somehow greater than the sum of its parts. Research in this area includes work on general health, frailty, and successful aging. Although each area of research is relatively distinct, we will consider the common themes.

DEFINITION AND MEASUREMENT OF GENERAL HEALTH

The preamble of the World Health Organization (WHO) defines "health" as "a state of complete physical, mental, and social well-being and not merely the absence of disease or infirmity." Although this definition was generally praised when it was first published, concern was soon expressed about whether it would be possible to measure such an abstract, although laudatory, term. Researchers at the Human Population Laboratory in California initiated the Alameda County Study, a community-based study of health and well-being in 1965 (Berkman & Breslow, 1983). The purpose of this study was in part to give substance to the WHO definition of health. The mailed questionnaire included questions that were designed to measure physical, mental, and social well-being. Although separate scales were developed for each of the three areas, it also was possible to include the three subscales to establish an overall assessment of health.

Physical Health

Physical health was defined in terms of general states of being well or sick, in addition to specific diseases, discomforts, or disabilities (Berkman & Breslow, 1983). Physical health indicators included energy level, compared with peers; recurrent symptoms, such as headaches, coughing, and pains in the stomach; chronic conditions, such as cancer, heart trouble, and arthritis; impairments, including difficulty in seeing or hearing, or a missing limb; and disability, defined as a reported restriction of movement, work capacity, or other activity. The final physical health scale consists of seven categories:

- Disability
- Less disability
- Two or more chronic conditions
- One chronic condition
- One or more symptoms
- Low to medium energy level without complaints
- High energy level (see Table 9–1)

It is important to note that the scale does not simply range from disability to what many might consider an average state, "low to medium energy level without complaints," but rather to "high energy level." This is very much in keeping with the WHO definition of health as not simply being the absence of disease.

Psychological Health

Psychological or mental health was based on indicators of ego resiliency, the presence of neurotic traits, a sense of alienation or isolation, and report of or medical visits for emotional or mental illness. The items were

Table 9–1 Physical Health Index, Human Population Laboratory, Alameda County Study of Health and Well-Being, 1965

Physical Health

Severe disability	Reported trouble with feeding, dressing, climbing stairs, or getting outdoors, or inability to work for six months or longer
Less disability	None of the above, but reported changing hours or type of work or cutting down on other activities for six months or longer
Chronic conditions Level 1	No disability, but reported two or more impairments or chronic conditions in the past 12 months
Chronic conditions Level 2	No disability, but reported one chronic condition or impairment in the past 12 months
Symptomatic	No disability, impairment, or chronic condition, but reported one or more symptoms in the past 12 months
Without complaints Level 1	No disability, impairment, or chronic condition and report of fewer than three high-energy responses in questionnaire
Without complaints Level 2	No disability, impairment, or chronic conditions and report of at least three high-energy responses in questionnaire

Source: Adapted from Berkman & Breslow, 1983, 37–42.

derived in large part from the Bardburn-Baplovitz index of position and negative feelings.

Social Health

The scale of social health assesses the extent to which a person lived with his or her family, and whether happily or not; the number of relatives and close friends, and the strength of connection with them; whether employed or not and other aspects of occupational adjustment; and the degree of relationship maintained with social and community organizations, such as in church, fraternal, union, and political groups. As evidence of the interrelationship of physical, psychological, and social health, these items also were adapted for inclusion in the Berkman and Syme Social Network Index (Berkman & Syme, 1979). As noted previously, social isolation, as reflected by minimal participation in social networks, often assessed in terms of this index, has been shown to be associated with an elevated risk of death among adults and, in particular, the elderly.

Results from the Alameda County Study indicate a decline in physical, mental, and social health with increasing health problems (Berkman & Breslow, 1983). Declines are also associated with lower socioeconomic status and among women and racial and ethnic minorities.

Overall Health. General measures of health are also based on single overall assessment of health reported by subjects. Unlike scales in which overall assessments are based on answers to a series of individual questions, these measures are based on the subjects' single, overall assessment of their general health. For example, in most cases, subjects are asked to assess their overall health (excellent, good, fair, or poor) over some period of time, typically over the past month or past six months. Another version asks subjects to evaluate their overall health in comparison to other people (men or women) their age (better than most, same as most, worse than most). Subjects also may be asked to rate their overall health, compared to their health one year earlier (better, same, worse).

Self-rated health has been determined to be multifactorial in nature, with demographic, biological, functional, social, and psychological correlates. It is reported that the criteria people use in rating their health are complex and multilayered. Although most people use physical health, such as the number of health problems, in evaluating their health, others also assess their health in terms of function, meaning what their bodies can do, their involvement in social activities, or emotional or spiritual well-being (Benyamini, Idler, Leventhal, & Leventhal, 2000). Moreover, research indicates that when people use criteria such as functional status, participation in social activities, and emotional and spiritual well-being, it may result in a more positive assessment of health than would be obtained if the assessment was based solely on the number and severity of health conditions. This also suggests that these other factors, such as a sense of psychological well-being, may, in fact, moderate the effects of physical health conditions. Krause and Jay (1994) indicate that the criteria for assessment vary by age, gender, race, and ethnicity. Older people tend to base their assessment primarily on functional criteria or how well they do in the completion of everyday activities.

Although overall assessments of health are quite simple, they have been shown to be associated with a variety of outcomes, including mortality, survival, functional status, health care utilization, and institutionalization (Idler & Benyamini, 1997; Idler & Kasl, 1995; Idler, Russell, & Davis,

2000). The results, in general, are similar to those reported from the Alameda County study.

Predictors of Overall Health. Those who report poorer overall health tend to be older, of lower socioeconomic status, women, and racial and ethnic minorities. Results from the Follow-up Study of the National Health and Nutrition Examination Survey indicate that self-assessed health among African-Americans declined at a faster rate than it did for white adults (Ferraro, Farmer, & Wybraniec, 1997). A report of poor health also is related to the presence of symptoms, the presence of comorbid conditions, and number of medications. Self-rated health is also associated with psychological variables such as assessments of life satisfaction, life chances, and depression. Despite these results, these variables only explain approximately 30% of the variance in self-rated health. Clearly, assessments of overall health reflect items not included in more traditional assessments of health and functioning. There is also evidence that older people living in poorer and more physically debilitated neighborhoods are more likely than older people living in better neighborhoods to report poorer overall health (Krause, 1996). In a comparative study of older people in Germany and the United States, the results indicate that older people who reported poorer overall health were most likely to be mistrustful of civic authority and most likely to report an absence of norms of reciprocity (Pollack & von dem Knesebeck, 2004). The national Social Capital Community Benchmark Survey, a US survey of 21,456 residents, revealed that reports of individual trust (e.g., "extent to which people in the neighborhood can be trusted") and measures of community trust (aggregate measure of individual responses) were associated with reports of overall health. Those who report greater trust and reside in areas of higher community trust are most likely to report better health. Moreover, the association between individual trust and positive reported health was greatest for those people who resided in areas of highest community trust (Subramanian, Kim, & Kawachi, 2002).

DEFINITION AND MEASUREMENT OF FRAILTY

Frailty is considered to be a geriatric syndrome, more specifically, "a wasting syndrome" that elevates the risk for a variety of health events and conditions, including falls, functional decline, morbidity, and premature mortality (Bortz II, 2002; Brown, Renwick, & Raphael, 1995; Hammerman, 1999; Ory, Schechtman, Miller, Hadley, Fiatarone, Province, et al., 1993; Walston & Fried, 1999). Frailty or "a failure to thrive" represents a vulnerable state that includes a constellation of characteristics that are reminiscent in some ways of allostatic load, discussed in Chapter 2. Along those lines, Fried and colleagues (2004, p. 256) define frailty "as a physiologic state of increased vulnerability to stressors that results from decreased physiologic reserves, and even dysregulation of multiple physiological systems." This concept represents a summary of physiologic factors (weight loss), impairments or limitations (reduced walking speed and grip strength), symptoms (reports of reduced energy), and functioning in everyday life (reports of limited physical activity), key components of the disablement model (Verbrugge & Jette, 1994). It is similar to the HPL general measures of health in that it represents a summary of different, yet interrelated factors.

The specific measures of frailty vary in epidemiologic research. For example, Fried and colleagues (2001) have proposed a set of specific measures to capture the "phenotype" of frailty. Specifically, frailty for them is defined as a clinical syndrome in which three or more of the following criteria are present: Unintentional weight loss (10 pounds in the past year), self-reported exhaustion, weakness (grip strength), slow walking speed, and low physical activity. Other researchers, such as Strawbridge and colleagues (1998), define frailty simply as two or more problems or difficulties in physical, nutritive, cognitive, or sensory domains (see Table 9–2).

There has been some discussion of the relationship between frailty, comorbidity, and disability. While some researchers tend to see these concepts as overlapping, Fried and colleagues (2004) indicated that frailty should be viewed as a summary pathway between comorbidity on the one hand and disability on the other. As noted previously, comorbidity typically refers to the presence of one or more health conditions among persons with an index health condition. The related concept of multimorbidity refers to the presence of two or more conditions within the same individual, without the designation of one of those conditions as an index condition. Disability, on the other hand, is used to refer to the inability to complete a social role because of a functional impairment or limitation. It is also useful to recall how social and environmental demands affect whether a functional limitation becomes a disability. In

Table 9-2 Examples of Measures of Frailty in Epidemiologic Studies

Fried et al., 2001	Three or more of the following characteristics:
	Unintentional weight loss (10 pounds in past year)
	Self-reported exhaustion
	Weakness (grip strength)
	Slow walking speed
	Low physical activity
Strawbridge et al., 1998	Two or more problems or difficulties in the following domains:
	Physical
	Nutritive
	Cognitive
	Sensory

Source: Adapted from Fried et al., 2001 and Strawbridge et al., 1998.

Fried's view, frailty should be defined primarily as a summary physiological measure. Along these lines, Ferrucci and colleagues (2002) contend that special attention should be given to the identification of biomarkers of frailty, including markers associated with macronutrients, micronutrients, and inflammatory response.

As noted previously, frailty prevents a person from responding or adapting to changes in the environment and renders the person at elevated risk for immobility, depression, disease, disability, and death. In fact, some researchers (Pressley & Patrick, 1999) have referred to a "frailty bias" as a situation in which differential susceptibility to adverse health outcomes are due to frailty but attributed to other factors. In one recent study (Corti, Guralnik, Salive, Harris, Ferrucci, Glynn, et al., 1997), results indicate that previous reports of an absence of an association between cholesterol and the risk of heart disease in older populations may be caused by a failure to adjust or hold constant levels of frailty. Specifically, after adjustment for established risk factors of coronary heart disease and markers of poor health (including chronic conditions, low serum iron and albumin levels) and exclusion of deaths from coronary heart disease that occurred within the first year, results indicate that elevated total cholesterol levels predicted increased risk for death from coronary heart disease, and the risk for death from coronary heart disease decreased as cholesterol levels decreased. Low blood pressure also has been associated with increased mortality in older people. It is unclear, however, whether the hypotension is independently associated with mortality, or is instead a marker of disease. In a study of 782 New Zealand residents aged 70 and older, established cardiovascular disease and frailty only partially explained the presence of hypotension (Busby, Campbell, & Robertson, 1994).

There is also evidence that the "frailty process" is aggravated by disease, injury, immobility, depression, and the use of medications. In fact, results indicate that depressed mood was associated with increased risk of a decline in strength, in particular in older men with low body weight (Rantanen, Penninx, Masaki, Lintunen, Foley, & Guralnik, 2000). Low body weight in combination with depressed mood may be an indicator of frailty or severe disease status that leads, in turn, to accelerated loss of strength, and, ultimately, to disability. Not surprisingly, frailty complicates the treatment of other conditions, such as coronary heart disease and cancer (Balducci & Stanta, 2000; McGann, 2000). Ferrucci and colleagues (2003, pp. 133–134) also address the issue of this frailty process:

> An appealing hypothesis on the development of frailty is that disease, disuse, and age per se trigger a mechanism that exhausts the redundancy of muscular and nervous backup systems and, when the damage goes beyond the threshold of possible compensation, leads to a measurable decline in physical performance. To some extent, once this mechanism is activated, its progression becomes independent of the nature and the persistence of the triggering cause. The entry points that can trigger the activation of this circular pathological process are many.

Predictors of Frailty. The demographic and social patterns of frailty are similar to that reported for individual health conditions, functional limitations, and disability. Results from the Cardiovascular Health Study indicate that those manifesting the frailty phenotype were characterized by the following (Fried et al., 2001): female, African-American, lower education and income, poorer health, and higher rates of comorbid chronic diseases and disability. It is hypothesized that differences in the dysregulation of the HPA axis with the resultant prolonged elevations of cortisol and its negative effect on both lean body mass and bone mineral density may explain the gender difference in frailty. Specific neuroendocrine and hormonal factors that may make men less likely to develop frailty than women include testosterone and growth hormone, which may provide advantages in muscle mass maintenance and cortisol, which is less likely to be dysregulated in older men than in older women. There is also evidence of immune system dimorphism, perhaps making men more vulnerable to sepsis and infection and women more vulnerable to chronic inflammatory conditions and loss of muscle mass. The net effect of the hormonal dysregulation and immune system dysfunction, then, is an accelerated loss of muscle mass. As noted previously, this is a cyclic process. The gender difference is also due to the fact that adult men typically have more initial muscle mass. Since men have grater reserves of muscle mass, they have more to lose. Higher baseline levels of muscle mass may protect men from reaching a threshold of weakness and muscle mass loss and resultant frailty.

Unplanned weight loss, as noted previously, is an indicator of frailty. Although unplanned weight loss, associated with loss of lean muscle mass, is more likely to occur in women than men, such loss is also an important determinant of hip fracture and frailty in men. For example, a weight loss of 10 percent or more beginning at age 50 years increases the risk of hip fracture in older white men; weight gain of 10 percent or more decreases the risk of hip fracture (Langlois, Visser, Davidovic, Maggi, Li, & Harris, 1998). It is concluded, then, that the relationship between extreme weight loss and poor health suggests that weight loss is a marker of frailty that may increase the risk of hip fracture in older men.

Molecular epidemiologic studies indicate a familial component to frailty. In an examination of Danish, Swedish, and Finnish male and female twins, there is evidence of the presence of genetic influences on individual frailty and longevity (Iachine, Holm, Harris, Begun, Iachina, Laitinen, et al., 1998). There is also evidence that APOE-4 alleles are associated with the development of an "inherited frailty" (Corder, Basun, Fratiglioni, Guo, Lannfelt, Viitanen, et al., 2000).

Behavioral risk factors also have been implicated (Strawbridge et al., 1998). Results from the Alameda County Study examined the predictors of frailty over a 30-year period among 574 residents aged 65 and older. To recall, in this study, frailty was defined as involving problems or difficulties in two or more functional domains (physical, nutritive, cognitive, and sensory). Frail persons reported reduced activities, poorer mental health, and lower life satisfaction. Predictors of frailty included heavy drinking, cigarette smoking, physical inactivity, depression, social isolation, fair or poor perceived health, prevalence of chronic symptoms, and prevalence of chronic conditions. As noted previously, frailty leads to immobility.

However, there is also evidence that lower levels of physical activity, coupled with lower caloric intake, in women may further aggravate the natural history of frailty, thus elevating the risk for falls, disability, and death.

In keeping with the tenets of an ecological model, Raphael and colleagues (1995) and Markle-Reid and Browne (2003) contend that frailty should be thought of in a broader context that includes social and environmental factors. They note that environmental factors can initiate events that lead to frailty as well as either aggravating or moderating the severity of frailty. Just as the process of disablement can be affected by the social and physical environmental context, so too can environmental factors affect the risk and severity of frailty.

DEFINITION AND MEASUREMENT OF SUCCESSFUL AGING

Although frailty is associated with increasing age, there are many older people who are able to avoid major chronic conditions, maintain high levels of cognitive and physical functioning, and remain socially engaged. Frailty can be thought of as the polar opposite of hardiness or vitality (Markle-Reid & Browne, 2003). Rowe and Kahn (1998, p. 38) originally characterized older people who age healthfully or successfully as having "the ability to maintain three key behaviors or characteristics: low risk of disease and disease-related disability; high mental and physical function; and active engagement with life." The characterization of successful aging simply underscored the significance of the heterogeneity of aging. Some older people have difficulty as they age; others, however, do not. In fact, some older people are able to maintain the physiological profile of people who are chronically younger (Seeman, 2000). Analysis of data from the Baltimore Longitudinal Study, for example, has shown that there are older individuals whose physiologic functioning is similar to that of much younger subjects (Shock et al., 1984). Norephinephrine response to maximum treadmill exercise for some older subjects was equivalent to the values for much younger subjects as was the rate of left ventricular filling (Gerstenblith, Fredericksen, Yin, Fortuin, Lakatta, & Weisfeldt, 1977; Tzankoff & Norris, 1979). Similar findings have also been reported for blood pressure, serum cholesterol, and body mass index from the Honolulu Heart Study (Benfante, Reed, & Brody, 1985), the Framingham Study (Harris, Cook, Kannel, & Goldman, 1988), and the Systolic Hypertension in the Elderly program (Siegel, Kuller, Lazarus, Black, Feigal, Hughes, et al., 1987). In each case, substantial subgroups of the older subjects were found to exhibit levels for these physiological parameters commensurate with mean scores for younger age groups.

Differences in aging/health outcomes were summarized in a typology, originally proposed by Rowe and Kahn (1987): "disease/disabled," a trajectory characterized by the presence of pathology and/or disability; "usual aging," a trajectory characterized by absence of overt pathology but the presence of nonpathologic declines in some aspects of functioning (e.g., hearing, glucose tolerance, renal function), the types of declines that have traditionally been attributed to "normal" (i.e., nondisease) aging; and "successful aging," a trajectory characterized by minimal (or absence) of the physiologic losses and seen in the "usual aging" group. Therefore, while "successful" may represent the opposite state from "frailty," the two concepts are similar in that they both reflect summary measures of health and functioning.

While the idea of "successful aging" as originally proposed by Rowe and Kahn (1998) included the avoidance of common age-related diseases, broader views of "successful aging" have subsequently included recognition that many older adults with existing chronic diseases continue to maintain high levels of functioning and could reasonably be considered to be aging "successfully." In fact, in a recent review, Rowe and Kahn (2000) reported that "resilience" and "wisdom" also could be considered to be indicators of successful aging.

Nearly all of the definitions of successful aging have been based upon measurements originally intended to capture older individuals functioning at the higher end of the spectrum (see Table 9–3). These included activities of daily living (ADL), independent activities of daily living, gross mobility (e.g., waking a half mile and doing heavy housework), and range of motion and strength (e.g., stooping, kneeling, and lifting ten pounds). While the intent of the studies was to differentiate between usual and successful agers, these measurement tools were not designed to accomplish this task. In part, the choice of measurements for the majority of the studies was a result of the secondary nature of the analysis. For example, in one of the early studies of successful aging (Guralnik & Kaplan, 1989) among 496 Alameda County residents ages 65–89 years over a 19-year period, successful aging was defined as those subjects who performed in the top 20% of a summative score. The score was based on

---

Table 9–3 Examples of Measures of Successful Aging

Guralnik & Kaplan, 1989	Top 20% of a summative score based on the following:

Guralnik & Kaplan, 1989   Top 20% of a summative score based on the following:

- Activities of daily living
- Rosow-Breslau items
  - Climbing stairs
  - Walking one half mile
- Nagi items
  - Pushing or pulling a large object
  - Stooping, crouching, kneeling
  - Lifting or carrying objects over 10 lbs.
- Instrumental activities of daily living
  - Gardening
  - Meal preparation
  - Heavy housework
  - Getting to places beyond walking distance
  - Shopping
- Physical exercise
  - Any sports exercise
  - Calisthenics or stretching
  - Walking for exercise
  - Exercising to a sweat
  - Swimming
  - Any vigorous activity

Roos & Havens, 1991   All of the following:

- Alive in 1983
- Nonresident of a nursing home in 1983
- Did not receive more than 59 days of home care
- Rated health excellent
- Not dependent in activities of daily living
- No need of help in going outdoors
- Able to walk outdoors
- Scored 7 or more correctly on a standard mental status exam

Berkman et al., 1993   All of the following:

- Overall cognitive function (6+ correct on 9-item assessment)
- Delayed recall (3 or more of 6 items recalled)
- Not dependent in activities of daily living

continues

Table 9-3 continued

Not more than 1 disability in measures of gross mobility
and performance measures
Rosow-Brelau Items
  Climbing stairs
  Walking one-half mile
Nagi Items
  Pushing or pulling heavy objects
  Lifting or carrying objects over 10 lbs.
  Maintaining a semitandem stand for at least
  20 seconds
  Ability to stand from a seated position 5 times within
  20 seconds

Source: Adapted from Guralnik & Kaplan, 1989; Ruos & Havens, 1991; and Berkman et al., 1988.

ADL, ability to walk across a room, climbing stairs, walking one-half mile, pushing or pulling a large object, stooping, crouching, kneeling, lifting and carrying weights over 10 pounds, gardening, meal preparation, heavy housework, difficulty getting places, shopping, any sports exercise, walking for exercise, exercising to sweat, calisthenics or stretching, swimming, and vigorous exercise. In a separate study conducted approximately at the same time (Roos & Havens, 1991), successful aging was assessed as follows: Alive in 1983, nonresident of a nursing home in 1983, did not receive more than 59 days of home care during the period, rated health excellent to fair, not dependent in any ADL, did not use a wheelchair, no need of help in going outdoors, able to walk outdoors, and scored well on a standard mental status examination. As recently as 1992, discussion on how to best assess functioning in older populations was underway. Even more recently, in 1994, performance-based measures were shown to be valid measures of high-functioning older persons (Guralnik, Seeman, Tinetti, Nevitt, & Berkman, 1994). The measurement tools used in most of these studies, therefore, represent, in part, the evolution of the study of successful aging.

Only the MacArthur aging studies were designed with the intention of studying successful aging; in their definition, performance-based measures were included. As noted in Chapter 2, the MacArthur cohort consisted of older people aged 70–79 years, selected from the National Institute on Aging's Established Populations for Epidemiologic Studies of the Elderly (EPESE) sites of East Boston, New Haven, and Iowa, who scored in the top one-third of each of the standard measures of cognitive and physical functioning. The purpose was then to examine the etiology of successful aging as well as the factors associated with differences in subsequent health and functioning in this aging cohort. One of the objectives was to determine whether members of this group, in fact, would experience a compression of morbidity as they approached death (Guralnik et al., 1994).

Research in this cohort and other cohorts of this kind has been conducted to determine the factors associated with successful aging. Work in this area is reminiscent of efforts to understand "salutogenesis" in human populations (Antonovsky, 1979). Antonovsky argued that the paradigm in the health sciences should be expanded from its exclusive focus on "pathogenesis" (causes of illness) to include a focus on "salutogenesis," an examination of the causes of health.

The MacArthur studies indicate that cross-sectional, baseline data from the EPESE project could be used to identify a cohort of high-functioning seniors aged 70–79 years. In doing so, the results underscored the extensive level of diversity that exists in people of that age (Berkman, Seeman, Albert, Blazer, Kahn, Mohs, et al., 1993). Moreover, the level and range of variability were evident across a number of different domains: Physical and cognitive functioning, psychosocial factors, leisure and other productive activities, and health status (Berkman et al., 1993).

There have been two standard ways to assess "successful aging" in the MacArthur project. One strategy used a combination of self-reported functioning and direct measures of performance that reflected cognitive and physical dimensions. In this measure (Berkman et al., 1993), "successful aging" was assessed in terms of scores of 6 or more correct on a 9-item Short Portable Mental Status Questionnaire; memory and reporting of 3 or more of 6 elements on a delayed recall of a story; report of no disability on a 7-item ADL; reports of no more than one disability on 8 items tapping gross mobility and physical performance (e.g., walking one-half mile, climbing stairs, pushing heavy objects, lifting groceries); and able to hold a semitandem balance for at least 10 seconds and able to stand from a seated position 5 times within 20 seconds. A second strategy is based exclusively on direct measures of performance (Guralnik, et al., 1994). For this measure, "successful aging" was based on the highest summative score from a scale that included assessments of the following performance items: standing balance, gait, lower-extremity strength, upper-extremity strength, hand performance, and lower-extremity coordination.

A recent review of the literature in this area revealed that there were six basic elements included in the definitions of successful aging: life satisfaction, longevity, freedom from disability, mental growth, active engagement with life, and freedom from chronic illness (Phelan & Larson, 2002). It is important to note that no one definition included all of these elements.

Predictors of Successful Aging. Studies of successful aging have been based on the identification of older people who have higher levels of health and functioning than their age peers. Efforts are then made to determine how the older people who perform at a higher level are different from those who function at a lower level. All of the well-known demographic, social, and behavioral risk factors associated with the risk of disease have been implicated. With the introduction of the MacArthur Study, attempts were made to examine the extent of variation in health and functioning among this high functioning group at baseline and over time. Longitudinal examinations have focused specifically on the predictors of "success" in maintaining the subjects' relatively high levels of functioning. Results indicate that only a minority of subjects shows declines in physical or cognitive functioning over time (Albert, Jones, Savage, Berkman, Seeman, Blazer, et al., 1995; Seeman, Charpentier, Berkman, Tinetti, Guralnik, Albert, et al., 1994). For example, functional decline among members of this cohort was associated with low concentration of albumin and cholesterol (Reuben, Ix, Greendale, & Seeman, 1999). On the other hand, analyses of factors that predict "successful" maintenance or improvement in physical functioning include younger age, higher income, lower relative weight, better lung function, absence of diabetes or hypertension, higher cognitive performance, and the absence of incident conditions or hospitalizations during the 2.5-year period (Seeman et al., 1994). More recent analyses have shown additional behavioral and psychosocial predictors, including participation in moderate or strenuous exercise and receiving more emotional support (Seeman, Berkman, Charpentier, Blazer, Albert, & Tinetti, 1995). Similar analysis of the maintenance or improvement in cognitive function have identified predictors of better performance such as younger age, being white, higher education, better lung function, higher physical performance, and engaging in more strenuous activity (Albert et al., 1995). As with physical functioning, social relationships and the support they provide also appear to promote better cognitive functioning. While successful aging has been used as a summary term, a variety of health and functional outcomes have been examined. Indeed, in both the MacArthur and Alameda County studies on successful aging, subjects, either in the top 33% or top 20% on a variety of measures, have been selected. Longitudinal studies have been conducted to then determine the epidemiology of subsequent patterns in health and functioning among that successful aging cohort (Seeman, 1994).

It has been argued by some that evidence of successful aging reported in studies as those based on the MacArthur cohort, do not, in fact, reflect differences in the aging process itself. Rather, it is argued that the factors that are known to affect longevity do so by their effect on disease development, which is part of secondary aging (Holloszy, 2000). Preventive strategies against secondary aging are aimed at maintaining health and functional capacity and rectangularizing, rather than extending, the survival curve, as suggested originally by Fries (1980). Suggested interventions in this area include a low-fat, low-energy diet supplemented with fruits and vegetables, exercise, and hormone replacement (Holloszy, 2000).

As noted previously, physical activity has attracted significant attention in this area. Some commentators argue that ill health and disabilities associated with aging are due in large part to "disuse" (Bortz, 1982). Moreover, engagement in physical and cognitive activities can serve to restore levels of health and functioning. Although evidence for the health effects of exercise are reported in the recent Surgeon General's Report on Physical Activity, it is useful to summarize some key points (Galloway & Jokl, 2000). Recent studies indicate that health gains can be achieved with relatively low volumes of exercise. Indeed, the greatest benefit is seen among sedentary people who begin to engage in some physical activity, however modest. Current data suggest that a cumulative total of 30 to 50 minutes of aerobic exercise a day performed 3 to 5 days a week and one set of resistance exercises targeting the major muscle groups twice a week can produce significant health benefits.

Genetic factors also have been examined. It has been proposed that since APOE, especially the e4 allele, is associated with a number of different outcomes, including decreased longevity, increased plasma cholesterol levels, and increased prevalence for cardiovascular disease and particularly for Alzheimer's disease, common genetic variation in the APOE gene may be associated with successful aging (Smith, 2000).

There is also evidence that alterations in the location of brain activity may be associated with the maintenance of cognitive and successful aging

(Hazlett, Buchsbaum, Mohs, Speigel-Cohen, Wei, Azueta, et al., 1998). Positron emission tomography and magnetic resonance imaging were used to characterize brain function in 70 volunteers, aged 20–87 years, during a verbal memory task. Frontal activity showed an age-related decline that remained significant after adjustment for other variables. Analysis of young and old subgroups matched for memory scores revealed that young performers who performed well activated frontal regions, whereas old performers who performed well relied on other regions of the brain. Although activating different cortical regions, good performers of all ages used the same cognitive strategy semantic clustering. Age-related functional change may reflect dynamic reallocation in a network of brain areas, not merely anatomically fixed neuronal loss or diminished capacity to perform.

Successful Aging or Healthy Aging? Two related concerns have been expressed about the work on successful aging. Although most commentators accept the concept of successful aging, there is disagreement about how it should be measured. Most measures of successful aging, even those that are based on both self-reports and physical performance measures, are used in most studies of older populations. The difference is that those who are classified as "successful agers" are those at the other end of the continuum. The list of factors associated with "successful aging" are, then, simply the mirror image of the factors associated with ill health and functional limitations, indeed, as we have seen in this chapter, the factors associated with frailty. Some commentators are concerned that the definitions of successful aging may not take into account how older people themselves may define "success" (Bergstrom & Holmes, 2000; Phelan & Larson, 2002). Other commentators have speculated whether this exclusive definition of "successful aging" is too restrictive and whether it, in fact, results in a form of "victim blaming." If you are not completely healthy or psychologically and socially engaged, then you are somehow not successful (Holstein & Minkler, 2003). It is for that reason that some researchers avoid the use of the term, "successful aging," preferring instead the term, "healthy aging" or "productive aging" (Holstein & Minkler, 2003).

Antonovsky's (1979) discussion of "salutogenesis," described earlier, may be instructive. As noted previously, salutogenesis refers to the factors that sustain health (the causes of health), a concept similar to that of successful aging. In his discussion of this concept, Antonovsky argued that it implied more than simply shifting attention from one end of the disease-health continuum to the other. Instead, the essence of the concept implies that research studies focus on factors associated with the maintenance of health and well-being in the face of factors that are associated with ill health, limitations, and disability. It also implies that investigators should focus on variables that are not necessarily linked to physical and cognitive functioning. These variables include wisdom, as suggested recently by Rowe and Kahn (2000), and emotional vitality, as suggested by Penninx and her colleagues (1998; 2000). Emotional vitality is defined as having a high sense of personal mastery, being happy, and having low depressive symptomatology and anxiety. Emotional vitality has been associated with a reduced risk of disability and death. It is important to note that these results were not due simply to the absence of depression. Protective health effects remained when emotionally vital women were compared with women who were not emotionally vital and not depressed (Penninx et al., 2000). Along these lines, Fried's (1996) concept of "compensatory strategies" may represent an important component of "successful aging." Compensatory strategies refer to a form of strategic thinking used to adapt to a given situation, even situations associated with isolation, ill health, limitations, and disability. An example of this form of successful aging is contained in a report of older African-American women (Shenk, Zablotsky, & Croom, 1998). The report is based on the findings of small-group discussions with self-defined successful African-American women ages 60 years and over in Charlotte, North Carolina. These women, who lived for many years in a segregated society, play active roles in their families, churches, and communities. They report that they seek meaning in their lives by sharing the key values of education, religion, work, and volunteerism. The authors conclude that mentoring is an important concept for understanding the lives of African-American women in later life. These results also suggest, as indicated by the authors, that nontraditional definitions of success need to be considered in studies of successful aging. With this expanded definition in mind, it may be possible to examine successful aging among older people who reflect all of the indicators of frailty, noted previously. Therefore, while the MacArthur study has contributed useful information about successful aging, it may be studies such as the Women's Health and Aging Study consisting of women with moderate or severe disability that will complete the picture of successful or healthy aging, those older people who do well in the face of adversity, indeed, in the face of frailty.

Finally, it is useful to conclude by citing a recent definition of healthy aging proposed by the Centers for Disease Control and Prevention Healthy Aging Research Network, a definition that reflects a broad, ecological perspective (https://depts.washington.edu/harn/), accessed April 6, 2005):

> Healthy aging is the development and maintenance of optimal physical, mental and social well-being and function in older adults. It is most likely to be achieved when physical environments and communities are safe, and support the adoption and maintenance by individuals of attitudes and behaviors known to promote health and well-being; and by the effective use of health services and community programs to prevent or minimize the impact of acute and chronic disease on function.

CONCLUSION

The summary measures of general health, frailty, and successful aging contribute to our understanding of the epidemiology of aging. In each case, the concept was designed to summarize across a number of biologic, behavioral, and social variables. In addition to providing a summary of data from different sources, each concept points to perhaps an underlying foundation for aging, health, and functioning. It is clear that the concepts of general health, frailty, and successful aging are based in large part on the health and capacity of the individual. It is unknown, however, to what extent social and environmental resources enhance a person's or population's "success" or "health" as it ages. For example, a frail person, in fact, may live well and successfully with adequate social and environmental resources. Finally, we learned that although on the surface the variables of frailty and successful or healthy aging may appear to be two ends of the spectrum, it is only by integrating the two that we come to appreciate the meaning of both concepts. Subsequent chapters will address strategies for conducting studies in older populations and methods for application of that information to promote health and well-being in older populations.

REFERENCES

Albert, M. S., Jones, K., Savage, C. R., Berkman, L., Seeman, T., Blazer, D., et al. (1995). Predictors of cognitive change in older persons: MacArthur Studies of Successful Aging. *Psychology of Aging, 10*(4), 578–589.

Antonovsky, A. (1979). *Health, stress, and coping.* San Francisco, CA: Jossey-Bass.

Balducci, L., & Stanta, G. (2000). Cancer in the frail patient. A coming epidemic. *Hematology Oncology Clinical North America, 14*(1), 235–250.

Benfante, R., Reed, D., & Brody, J. (1985). Biological and social predictors of health in an aging cohort. *Journal of Chronic Diseases, 38,* 385–395.

Benyamini, Y., Idler, E. L., Leventhal, H., & Leventhal, E. A. (2000). Positive affect and function as influences on self-assessments of health: Expanding our view beyond health and disability. *Journal of Gerontology: Psychological Sciences, 55*(2), P107–P116.

Bergstrom, M. J., & Holmes, M. E. (2000). Lay theories of successful aging after the death of a spouse: A network text analysis of bereavement advice. *Health Communication, 12*(4), 377–406.

Berkman, L. F., & Breslow, L. (1983). *Health and ways of living: The Alameda County Study.* New York: Oxford University Press.

Berkman, L. F., Seeman, T. E., Albert, M., Blazer, D., Kahn, R., Mohs, R., et al. (1993). High, usual, and impaired functioning in community dwelling older men and women: Findings from the MacArthur Foundation Research Network on Successful Aging. *Journal of Clinical Epidemiology, 46*(10), 1129–1140.

Berkman, L. F., & Syme, S. L. (1979). Social networks, host resistance and mortality: A nine year follow-up study of Alameda Country residents. *American Journal of Epidemiology, 109,* 186–204.

Bortz, W. M. (1982). Disuse and aging. *Journal of the American Medical Association, 248,* 1203–1208.

Bortz II, W. M. (2002). A conceptual framework of frailty: A Review. *Journals of Gerontology: Medical Sciences, 57A*(5), M283–M288.

Brown, I., Renwick, R., & Raphael, D. (1995). Frailty: Constructing a common meaning, definition, and conceptual framework. *International Journal of Rehabilitation Research, 18*(2), 93–102.

Busby, W. J., Campbell, A. J., & Robertson, M. C. (1994). Is low blood pressure in elderly people just a consequence of heart disease and frailty? *Age & Ageing, 23*(1), 69–74.

Corder, E. H., Basun, H., Fratiglioni, L., Guo, Z., Lannfelt, L., Viitanen, M., et al. (2000). Inherited frailty. ApoE alleles determine survival after a diagnosis of heart disease or stroke at ages 85+. *Annals of the New York Academy of Science, 908,* 295–298.

Corti, M. C., Guralnik, J. M., Salive, M. E., Harris, T., Ferrucci, L., Glynn, R. J., et al. (1997). Clarifying the direct relation between total cholesterol levels and death from coronary heart disease in older persons. *Annals of Internal Medicine, 126*(2), 753–760.

Ferraro, K. F., Farmer, M. M., & Wybraniec, J. A. (1997). Health trajectories: Long-term dynamics among black and white adults. *Journal of Health and Social Behavior, 38*(1), 38–54.

Ferrucci, L., Cavazzini, C., Corsi, A., Bartali, B., Russo, C. R., Lauretani, F., et al. (2002). Biomarkers of frailty in older persons. *Journal of Endocrinological Investigations, 25*(10 Suppl), 10–15.

Ferrucci, L., Guralnik, J. M., Cavazzini, C., Bandinell, S., Lauretani, F., Bartali, B., et al. (2003). The frailty syndrome: A critical issue in geriatric oncology. *Critical Reviews in Oncology/Hematology, 46,* 127–137.

Fried, L. P., Bandeen-Roche, K., Williamson, J. D., Prasada-Rao, P., Chee, E., Tepper, S., & Rubin, G. S. (1996). Functional decline in older adults: Expanding methods of ascertainment. *Journals of Gerontology: Medical Sciences, 51*(5), M206–M214.

Fried, L. P., Ferrucci, L., Darer, J., Williamson, J. D., & Anderson, G. (2004). Untangling the concepts of disability, frailty, and comorbidity: Implications for improved targeting and care. *Journals of Gerontology: Medical Sciences, 59*(3), 255–263.

Fried, L. P., Tangen, C. M., Walston, J., Newman, A. B., Hirsch, C., Gottdiener, J., et al. for the Cardiovascular Health Study Collaborative Research Group. (2001). Frailty in older adults: Evidence for a phenotype. *Journals of Gerontology: Medical Sciences, 56A*(3), M146–M156.

Fries, J. F. (1980). Aging, natural death, and the compression of morbidity. *The New England Journal of Medicine, 303*(3), 130–135.

Galloway, M. T., & Jokl, P. (2000). Aging successfully: The importance of physical activity in maintaining health and function. *Journal of the American Academy of Orthopedic Surgery, 8*(1), 37–44.

Gerstenblith, G., Fredericksen, J., Yin, F. C., Fortuin, N. J., Lakatta, E. G., & Weisfeldt, M. L. (1977). Echocardiographic assessment of a normal adult aging population. *Circulation, 56*(2), 273–278.

Guralnik, J. M., Seeman, T. E., Tinetti, M. E., Nevitt, M. C., & Berkman, L. F. (1994). Validation and use of performance measures of functioning in non-disabled older population: MacArthur Studies of Successful Aging. *Aging (Milano), 6*(6), 410–419.

Guralnik, J. M., & Kaplan, G. A. (1989). Predictors of healthy aging: Prospective evidence from the Alameda County Study. *American Journal of Public Health, 79,* 703–708.

Hammerman, D. (1999). Toward an understanding of frailty. *Annals of Internal Medicine, 130*(11), 945–950.

Harris, T., Cook, E. F., Kannel, W. B., & Goldman, L. (1988). Proportional hazards analysis of risk factors for coronary heart disease in individuals aged 65 or older. The Framingham Heart Study, *36*(11), 1023–1028.

Hazlett, E. A., Buchsbaum, M. S., Mohs, R. C., Speigel-Cohen, J., Wei, T. C., Azueta, R., et al. (1998). Age-related shift in brain region activity during successful memory performance. *Neurobiology of Aging, 19*(5), 437–445.

Holloszy, J. O. (2000). The biology of aging. *Mayo Clinic Process, 75*(Suppl), S3–8.

Holstein, M. B., & Minkler, M. A. (2003). Self, society, and the "new gerontology." *The Gerontologist, 43*(6), 787–796.

Iachine, I. A., Holm, N. V., Harris, J. R., Begun, A. Z., Iachina, M. K., Laitinen, M., et al. (1998). How heritable is individual susceptibility to death? The results of analysis of survival data on Danish, Swedish, and Finnish twins. *Twin Research, 1*(4), 196–205.

Idler, E. L., & Benyamini, Y. (1997). Self-rated health and mortality: A review of twenty-seven community studies. *Journal of Health and Social Behavior, 38*(1), 21–37.

Idler, E. L., & Kasl, S. V. (1995). Self-ratings of health: Do they also predict change in functional ability? *Journals of Gerontology: Social Sciences, 50*(6), S344–S353.

Idler, E. L., Russell, L. B., & Davis, D. (2000). Survival, functional limitations, and self-rated health in the NHANES I Epidemiologic Follow-up Study, 1992. *American Journal of Epidemiology, 152,* 874–883.

Krause, N. (1996). Neighborhood deterioration and self-rated health in later life. *Psychology and Aging, 11*(2), 342–352.

Krause, N. M., & Jay, G. M. (1994). What do global self-rated health items measure? *Medical Care, 32*(9), 930–942.

Langlois, J. A., Visser, M., Davidovic, L. S., Maggi, S., Li, G., & Harris, T. B. (1998). Hip fracture risk in older white men is associated with change in body weight from age 50 years to old age. *Archives of Internal Medicine, 158*(9), 990–996.

Markle-Reid, M., & Browne, G. (2003). Conceptualization of frailty in relation to older adults. *Journal of Advanced Nursing, 44*(1), 58–68.

McGann, P. E. (2000). Comorbidity in heart failure in the elderly. *Clinics in Geriatric Medicine, 16*(3), 631–648.

Ory, M. G., Schechtman, K. B., Miller, J. P., Hadley, E. C., Fiatarone, M. A., Province, M. A., et al. (1993). Frailty and injuries in later life: The FICSIT trials. *Journal of the American Geriatrics Society, 41*(3), 283–296.

Penninx, B. W., Guralnik, J. M., Bandeen-Roche, K., Kasper, J. D., Simonsick, E. M., Ferrucci, L., & Fried, L. P. (2000). The protective effect of emotional vitality on adverse health outcomes in disabled older women. *Journal of the American Geriatrics Society, 48*(11), 1359–1366.

Penninx, B. W., Guralnik, J. M., Simonsick, E. M., Kasper, J. D., Ferrucci, L., & Fried, L. P. (1998). *Journal of the American Geriatrics Society, 46*(7), 807–815.

Phelan, E. A., & Larson, E. B. (2002). "Successful aging"—Where next? *Journal of the American Geriatrics Society, 50,* 1306–1308.

Pollack, C. E., & von dem Knesebeck, O. (2004). Social capital and health among the aged: Comparisons between the United States and Germany. *Health & Place, 10*(4), 381–391.

Pressley, J. C., & Patrick, C. H. (1999). Frailty bias in comorbidity risk adjustments of community-dwelling elderly populations. *Journal of Clinical Epidemiology, 52*(8), 753–760.

Rantanen, T., Penninx, B. W., Masaki, K., Lintunen, T., Foley, D., & Guralnik, J. M. (2000). Depressed mood and body mass index as predictors of muscle strength decline in old men. *Journal of the American Geriatrics Society, 48*(6), 613–617.

Raphael, D., Cava, M., Brown, I., Rnewick, R., Heathcote, K., Weir, N., et al. (1995). Frailty: A public health perspective. *Canadian Journal of Public Health, 86*(4), 224–227.

Reuben, D. B., Ix, J. H., Greendale, G. A., & Seeman, T. E. (1999). The predictive value of combined hypoalbuminemia and hypocholesterolemia in high functioning community-dwelling older persons: MacArthur Studies of Successful Aging. *Journal of the American Geriatrics Society, 47*(4), 402–406.

Roos, N. P., & Havens, B. (1991). Predictors of successful aging: A twelve-year study of Manitoba elderly. *American Journal of Public Health, 81*(1), 63–68.

Rowe, J. W., & Kahn, R. L. (1998). *Successful aging.* New York: Pantheon Books.

Rowe, J. W., & Kahn, R. L. (2000). Successful aging and disease prevention. *Advances in Renal Replacement Therapy, 7*(1), 70–77.

Rowe, J. W., & Kahn, R. L. (1987). Human aging: Usual and successful. *Science, 237,* 143–149.

Seeman, T. E. (1994). Successful aging: Reconceptalizing the aging process from a more positive perspective. *Facts and Research in Gerontology,* 61–73.

Seeman, T. E. (2000). Health promoting effects of friends and family on health outcomes in older adults. *American Journal of Health Promotion, 14*(6), 362–370.

Seeman, T. E., Berkman, L. F., Charpentier, P. A., Blazer, D. G., Albert, M. S., & Tinetti, M. E. (1995). Behavioral and psychosocial predictors of physical performance: MacArthur Studies of Successful Aging. *Journals of Gerontology: Medical Sciences, 50*(4), M177–M183.

Seeman, T. E., Charpentier, P. A., Berkman, L. F., Tinetti, M. E., Guralnik, J. M., Albert, M., et al. (1994). Predicting changes in physical performance in a high functioning elderly cohort: MacArthur Studies of Successful Aging. *Journals of Gerontology, 49*(3), M97–M108.

Shenk, D., Zablotsky, D., & Croom, M. P. (1998). Thriving older African American women: Aging after Jim Crow. *Journal of Women Aging, 10*(1), 75–95.

Shock, N. W., Greulich, R. C., Andres, R., Arenberg, D., Costa, P. T., Lahatta, E. G., et al. (1984). *Normal human aging: The Baltimore Longitudinal Study.* NIH Publication No. 84-2450. Washington, DC: US Government Printing Office.

Siegel, D., Kuller, L., Lazarus, N. B., Black, D., Feigal, D., Hughes, G., et al. (1987). Predictors of cardiovascular events and mortality in the Systolic Hypertension in the Elderly Program pilot project. *American Journal of Epidemiology, 126*(3), 385–399.

Smith, J. D. (2000). Apolipoprotein E4: An allele associated with many diseases. *Annals of Medicine, 32*(2), 118–127.

Strawbridge, W. J., Shema, S. J., Balfour, J. L., Higby, H. R., & Kaplan, G. A. (1998). Antecedents of frailty over three decades in an older cohort. *Journals of Gerontology: Social Sciences, 53*(1), S9–S16.

Subramanian, S. V., Kim, D. J., & Kawachi, I. (2002). Social trust and self-rated-health in U.S. communities: A multilevel analysis. *Journal of Urban Health, 79*(4), suppl 1, S21–S24.

Tzankoff, S. P., & Norris, A. H. (1979). Age-related differences in lactate distribution following maximal exercise. *European Journal of Applied Physiology, 42*(1), 35–40.

Verbrugge, L. M., & Jette, A. M. (1994). The disablement process. *Social Science & Medicine, 38*(8), 1–14.

Walston, J., & Fried, L. P. (1999). Frailty and the older man. *Medical Clinics of North America, 83*(5), 1173–1193.

CHAPTER 10

Conducting Epidemiologic Studies in Older Populations

There are unique challenges associated with conducting epidemiologic studies in older populations. As Kelsey and colleagues (1989, p. 857) observe, studies of older populations are "beset by many difficulties encountered to a much more limited extent in studies of younger adults." These difficulties are associated with the location and recruitment of older subjects, as well as difficulties associated with the design of studies and interviews that enhance the likelihood of obtaining accurate information from older subjects who, as we know, are sometimes at elevated risk for cognitive impairments, sensory and physical limitations, and fatigue. These difficulties are compounded by new studies that require direct measures of physical performance, biological specimens, and assessment of the household and neighborhood environments. Finally, by definition, studies of *aging* typically require repeated assessments of people over time.

In this chapter, we will review issues associated with conducting epidemiologic studies in older populations. It is not enough to be familiar with the results of epidemiologic research in this population. It is important to be knowledgeable about research methods and design in general and, most important, how those methods and designs need to be fashioned to conduct studies in this area. Put differently, we not only need to be conversant with *what* we know, but also *how* we know it. As part of this discussion, we will consider the implications of these methodological issues for the interpretation of the research.

IDENTIFICATION OF OLDER POPULATIONS

With all of the talk about the aging of the population, it is sometimes difficult to fully appreciate how difficult it is to actually locate older people for research studies. Even people aged 55 and older still represent a minority in most populations. There are three basic studies—studies of older people in the general population, older people residing in long-term care facilities, and older people diagnosed with particular types of medical conditions. Each type of study contributes important information about aging, health, and functioning, and each study poses special challenges.

General Population Surveys

Most epidemiologic studies are based on information obtained from a sample of individuals that ideally represent the characteristics of the target population. In many European communities and a limited number of places in the United States, it is possible to obtain a current list of community residents, together with information about their age and gender and, most important, their address. With this information, a sample of people of a particular age can be identified and contacted. In most cases, however, such lists are not available for studies in the United States. Although the US census reports the age distribution of residents at different levels of geographic specificity (i.e., the census tract and the smaller, more homogeneous census block), there are no published data available for specific households. Such information is considered to be privileged and its release, a violation of a citizen's right to privacy. Other strategies are required. One strategy is to conduct a special census. These special surveys are often conducted by canvassing specific neighborhoods household by household. The demographic characteristics (age, gender, often race and ethnicity) are obtained for each household. With this information, a sample can be selected for particular areas. If there is more than one eligible person in a household, procedures are in place to randomly select one subject per household. It is not surprising that such surveys are expensive and time consuming. It is possible to obtain a listing of addresses for particular areas from the post office. In some cases, it is also possible to obtain the name of the last known resident of a particular household from a so-called reverse directory designed primarily for marketing purposes. A census form can be mailed to the household with a return, posted envelope. Typically, however, this does not result in a suitable response rate, and a return visit either in person or by telephone (if the telephone number is available) is required (Satariano, Smith, Swanson, & Tager, 1998). Although some commentators (Kohout, 1992) have recommended improving the yield of older subjects by restricting the study to neighborhoods with high concentrations of older residents, there may be limitations in generalizing from the results of such studies to a wider population of seniors that reside in areas with a greater diversity of age groups. Older people in these communities may be different from older people in the general population.

Computerized Medicare records may represent one of the best sources of national data for people aged 65 in the United States (Kelsey et al., 1989). These files include a list of seniors who are currently eligible to receive funds through Medicare. Social security number, name, gender, race, and address are included in the files. Given concerns about confidentiality, these files are not readily available. In most cases, the files are available only to researchers who are conducting scientific studies funded by an agency of the federal government. The researcher must prepare a special request to obtain the files for the purpose of selecting a sample of residents for the study. If the request is approved, the files are released to the researcher's federal project officer who, in turn, releases the data to the researcher. It is important to emphasize again that there are very strict confidentiality guidelines associated with obtaining and using these records for scientific studies. The researcher also must include a letter from the US government in any communication that is sent to a prospective study participant indicating the reasons and procedures of subject selection as well as the person's rights of refusal without penalty. Although there may be some variability by geographic area, it is reported that the data in the files are current within six months.

Telephone random-digit dialing (RDD) is an alternative procedure for the identification of eligible participants. As the term implies, sequences of 10-digit numbers (3-digit area code, 3-digit prefix, and 4-digit suffix) are randomly generated, and those numbers called until a private residence is reached. When a private residence is reached, a household census is conducted to determine the number of eligible residents in the household. Of course, multilingual interviewers need to be available to ensure representative coverage of a geographic area. Since this is a very time-consuming process, different strategies have been introduced to make the procedure more efficient. In most cases, the 3-digit numbers for the area code and prefix are restricted to working numbers for the target geographic area. In addition, some RDD techniques are based on a "working stem" that consists of 8-digit sequences that include working area codes, prefixes, and the first two digits of the 4-digit suffix (Figure 10–1). When a working number at a private residence is located, the working stem for that number is included for subsequent calls. Based on the assumption that working stems of published numbers should not be significantly different from the working stems of unpublished numbers, some researchers rely on the stems available in published listings. With these working stems, the last two digits of the suffix are randomly generated. Although this procedure has improved the likelihood of locating working private numbers, the identification of older people is still a difficult task. Other generic problems associated with RDD include the widespread use of telephone-answering machines, mobile cell telephones, and automated procedures to screen incoming calls. In addition, there is growing public discontent and hostility to anything that resembles telephone marketing. Many people, especially recent immigrants, may be suspicious and resistant to a request by telephone for a household census, no matter how legitimate the reason and source of the request. Finally, it is very difficult to target RDD to specific geographic areas. Telephone area codes cover wide geographic areas and the prefix and suffix are not necessarily assigned by geographic area. In addition to these generic difficulties, there are particular problems associated with the identification of an older population. First, there is evidence that indicates that older people are especially suspicious of telephone solicitation and concerned about being victimized. Second, sensory and mobility difficulties may prevent older people from reaching and answering the telephone. Kelsey and colleagues (1989) also caution that some older people may have difficulty using the telephone given problems with hearing. Others contend that this may be less of a problem, now that most telephones are equipped with devices to enhance sound.

FIGURE 10–1 Sample of Stems for Telephone Random-Digit Dialing

Other methods have been suggested for the identification of older populations. For example, the computerized lists of the state departments of motor vehicles include the name, address, and date of birth of people with either a motor vehicle license or a state identification card (Funkhouser, Macaluso, & Wang, 2000). Since these records include those people with only state identification records, it is not necessarily biased toward people with higher levels of functioning, as may be the case for those who drive. Nevertheless, this is not a standard method for the identification of participants, and states may vary in their willingness and capability to generate such lists for scientific study. In some cases, the reluctance may be based on the growing concern about the litigation associated with the release of personal information, even to other state agencies, such as researchers at a state university. These state agencies typically do not have protocols or, for that matter, human subjects committees in place to address these issues. In other cases, the reluctance may be based on limited financial resources. In a climate of reduced funding for essential governmental services, some state agencies may be reluctant to dissipate resources by complying with a request to assist in a scientific study.

It also may be necessary to identify special populations of older residents, such as members of particular racial and ethnic groups. Some researchers have successfully used listings of common surnames of specific ethnic groups to identify potential participants (Cockburn, Hamilton, Zadnick, Cozen, & Mark, 2001; Hage, Oliver, Powles, & Wahlqvist, 1990; Tijam, 2001).

Membership files of large health organizations, such as health maintenance organizations (HMOs), may be useful to identify prospective samples of older subjects. Of course, the more representative the membership, the more effective this is as a source of prospective subjects. For example, studies of the Kaiser health system in California indicate that the members are generally representative of the racial and age distribution of the larger San Francisco Bay Area (Krieger, Chen, Waterman, Rehkopf, & Subramanian, 2003). However, in terms of socioeconomic status, the very affluent and the very poor are underrepresented. With this system, it is possible to supplement interview data with information from medical records, such as health histories and use of health services, and data from geographic information systems on the participant's neighborhood. Computerized records of HMOs also are useful for the selection of prospective older people who have been diagnosed with particular health conditions.

Because more attention is being given to the effects of neighborhood characteristics and the built environment on health and functioning in older populations, ascertainment and recruitment strategies that take that environmental information into account may be especially valuable. Special surveys of specific neighborhoods, as noted previously, represent one such strategy. The use of membership records from large HMO facilities represents another. Other strategies are possible. For example, it may be possible to identify and recruit older people through senior centers. First it would be necessary to identify senior centers by location throughout a city or region of a city. On the assumption that most seniors attending a particular center reside in the surrounding area, it may be possible to stratify seniors geographically, first by the location of the center and then by the senior's own residence. (Of course, there may be situations in which seniors will travel from outside the area to be with older friends or to take advantage of a particular center activity.) This multilevel approach provides different opportunities for recruitment. If the center has a list of the names and addresses of its members, it may be possible to recruit by mail. Alternatively, it may be possible to schedule an information meeting at the center to describe the study and recruit participants in person. This has the added potential benefit of the center endorsing the study, thus improving the odds that center members will participate.

Older Residents of Long-Term Care Facilities

Levels of health and functioning can vary significantly among older residents of long-term care facilities. Seniors in skilled nursing homes, in general, will be more limited than those who reside in assisted-living facilities (Regnier, Hamilton, & Yatable, 1995). If the study is designed to focus on older people with a specific level of functioning or a particular geriatric syndrome, a long-term facility may be an appropriate setting in which to conduct the study. Of course, another advantage is that potential participants can be located and recruited in a cost-efficient manner. There are disadvantages as well. Since residents in long-term care facilities may have particular limitations, they may not be able to complete the study protocol (Schneider, 1985). The administrators of such facilities often have strict guidelines that outline the potential participation of their residents. Relatives of residents often must serve as proxies to obtain permission for their family members to participate. In assisted-living facilities, residents are in relatively good health and are functionally fit to participate in a study. In this case, however, the concern may be that the residents are not sufficiently heterogeneous and may not be representative of a general population of seniors.

Older People with Specific Health Conditions

Epidemiologic studies also are designed to investigate the risks of particular health conditions in older populations. Other studies examine the risks of limitations, disability, or death associated with the diagnosis of particular conditions in older populations. Although the risk of disease may be based on longitudinal examinations of samples of people who are disease free at baseline, the more common case-control study is based on the identification of cases that are newly diagnosed with an index condition, such as a stroke or cancer. Likewise, epidemiologic studies of functional limitations, disability, and mortality associated with particular conditions also require the identification of patients with the disease of interest. As noted previously, depending on the condition, HMOs or other large health care facilities may provide a source of older patients for investigation. In other cases, it may be possible to identify cases through a disease registry. Although there are disease registries for conditions such as diabetes and Alzheimer's disease, cancer registries represent the most well-developed and sophisticated systems for case ascertainment.

In the United States, the National Cancer Institute maintains the Surveillance, Epidemiology, and End Results (SEER) program, a network of 12 population-based cancer registries. Initiated in 1973, the SEER program identifies residents in particular geographic areas, newly diagnosed with cancer. Data are maintained on clinical characteristics of the cancer (i.e., date of diagnosis, cancer type, histology, stage at diagnosis, physician of record, first course of treatment, and treating facility) as well as characteristics of the patient (name, address, age at diagnosis, gender, race/ethnicity, marital status at diagnosis). The SEER registries also maintain a system of following each patient to monitor vital status. For decedents, data from the death certificate, e.g., cause and date of death, are maintained in the system. In addition to cancer surveillance (i.e., monitoring cancer incidence and survival for specific geographic areas), the system was designed to identify newly diagnosed patients for special studies, including the National Institute on Aging/National Cancer Institute

Study of Cancer in the Elderly (Yancik, Havlik, Wesley, Ries, Long, Rossi, et al., 1996). For both studies of cancer incidence and cancer survival, the prospective participant is typically identified soon after diagnosis. In fact, the standard protocol for SEER special studies is that the participant must be identified and interviewed within six months of diagnosis. This time period was instituted to increase the likelihood that the information collected from the patient is associated with the incident cancer. The longer the time interval between the date of diagnosis and the date of the interview, the greater the likelihood that events that occur in the interim will affect the reporting of information. In addition, depending on the type and stage of cancer, the longer the interval, the more likely that the participant will die or be too ill to participate. Following the identification of the prospective participant, the physician of record is contacted to determine whether there is any reason that the cancer patient should not be contacted to determine whether he or she is able to participate.

RECRUITMENT OF OLDER POPULATIONS

The recruitment of older people to participate in a research study depends on a variety of factors. These factors include the perceived importance of the study, the style and language of the introductory presentation, and the extent to which the participants are compensated for time and effort. Increasingly, in studies of aging, recruitment involves strategies for follow-up and agreement to participate in subsequent interviews, as well as the baseline assessment. Recruitment of older people represents one of the most significant challenges. Not only has the general participation rate been declining over time, but the decline is especially precipitous among older people. The recruitment of seniors of color may be especially challenging (Cabral, Napoles-Springer, Miike, McMillan, Sison, Wrensch, et al., 2003).

Importance of the Study

Agreement to participate in a project depends, of course, on the perceived importance or value of that project. There is a growing recognition that community-based studies should involve the active collaboration of community residents in the design and administration of the study. The residents' endorsement of the study is critical for the success of the project. It is important to emphasize that the participation of community residents in the design and administration of the study is not recommended as simply a ploy or inducement to participate. Rather, it is based on the proposition that the active collaboration of community residents will result in a more useful study. Increasingly, researchers will include the endorsement of reputable organizations in the community, e.g., community senior centers and religious organizations. In studies being conducted in more restricted geographic areas, e.g., small towns, descriptions of the study may be included in newspaper articles or radio announcements (Anderson, Fogler, & Dedrick, 1995).

Style and Language of Presentation

The purpose of the study must be presented clearly and succinctly. If a prospective participant is identified through an RDD household census, the telephone interviewer typically will briefly describe the purpose of the study and indicate to the informant that the person so identified meets the eligibility criteria for becoming a subject and may be contacted to determine whether he or she is interested in participating in the study. The name and address of the person are requested, so that a letter can be sent detailing the purpose of the study. Needless to say, it is sometimes difficult to persuade the person being interviewed to supply that information over the telephone. If the prospective subject is identified thorough other means, a letter is sent to the subject that describes the purpose of the study. In addition to a description of the study, the letter should include what is expected of the subject and other information that ensures that the prospective subject's human rights will be protected.

Human Subjects Protection

The protocols of all research studies must be reviewed to ensure that the rights of prospective subjects are protected. Given the potential vulnerability of older subjects, these issues are of particular concern (Barron, Duffey, Byrd, Campbell, & Ferrucci, 2004; Colsher, 1992). Prior to contacting a subject to participate in a research study, the study protocol is reviewed by an institutional review board at the research institution. Human subjects issues are included as part of the scientific review of grant proposals to governmental agencies, both at the state and federal levels. Although the participant's signature is required on a separate human subject's form prior to the interview or any other type of acquisition of data, the introductory letter also should include a brief description of the following: First, the letter should include a clear statement of what the subject will be required to provide or do as a study participant and how the subject was identified for possible participation. Second, it must be noted that if the subject agrees to participate, he or she has the right to refuse to answer any question and the right to terminate the interview at any time. Third, procedures to ensure the reasonable protection of privacy and confidentiality are enclosed. Along these lines, it is typically reported that personal identifiers, e.g., name or address, will not be included in any subsequent presentation or report. Fourth, it is necessary to indicate how the subject may benefit from participation. In most epidemiologic studies, it is typically reported that the subject will not benefit directly, but that it is expected that the results from the study will improve understanding of the topic in question and, in some cases, will lead to programs or treatments to improve the health and well-being, in this case, of aging populations. Finally, if the subject is selected through his or her membership in a long-term care facility, health care organization, or disease registry, it must be clearly stated that the subject's decision to participate in the study will not alter or jeopardize in any way the receipt of care or services.

In studies of older populations, especially among impaired seniors, a representative of the prospective subject will sometimes serve as a "gate-keeper." As the term implies, this person, often a spouse or adult child, will be the first contact of the research team. Special consideration should be taken in approaching a gatekeeper about the participation of his or her family member. As will be explained later, this person also may be called upon to serve as a "proxy respondent" to supply information that the older participant may not be able to provide (Magaziner, 1992).

Compensation

One of the important issues currently facing researchers is participant compensation. There are several reasons why this issue is attracting so much attention. First, study protocols are becoming more demanding. As research is focusing increasingly on a variety of issues, from the biological to the behavioral, social, and environmental, more information is required. Calls for compensation are based, therefore, on an increase in time and effort required of participants, especially studies that require multiple interviews over time, direct assessment of physical performance, environmental audits, and, increasingly, biological specimens (Guralnik, Branch, Cummings, & Curb, 1989). Second, there is growing concern that participation rates are declining, especially among elderly subjects. Third, other studies are providing compensation. To not provide compensation in this type of situation puts a researcher at a competitive disadvantage. Although there may be general agreement that compensation should be provided, there are strong disagreements about what form that compensation should take and, more specifically, whether subjects should be compensated monetarily and, if so, by what standard. What is the formula for the calculation of a just monetary compensation? Some commentators have expressed concern that compensation, especially monetary compensation, changes the nature of the relationship from a researcher and participant to an employer and employee. As such, there is concern that the participants may feel more compelled to provide answers that they feel the researchers may want to receive. Others are concerned that the prospect of some types of compensation, again, especially monetary compensation, may induce or even coerce someone to participate who might decline if no compensation was provided. It becomes even more complicated when the amount of monetary compensation is considered. A specific monetary amount may represent a form of coercion for a lower-income participant, but not for someone with a higher income. This is a problem. Certainly, it would not be appropriate to institute a graduated scale of compensation based on the participant's level of income. Given these problems, some commentators have recommended that monetary compensation not be used, other than cases in which such compensation is provided for mileage if travel is required. Indeed, they argue that adequate monetary compensation, i.e., comparable to an hourly wage, would be financially prohibitive for most research studies. Instead, it is recommended that a "token of appreciation" be provided. Such tokens may include coffee cups, calendars, refrigerator magnets, or shirts with the study logo. In studies that involve laboratory tests, such as cardiopulmonary assessments, researchers have offered to make the results available to the participant's private physician as a courtesy and form of compensation. A number of years ago, Meredith Minkler, Carol Langhauser, and I were involved in a study of older participants from two senior centers in Berkeley, California (Satariano, Minkler, & Langhauser, 1984). Since our funds were limited, even for the purchase of respectful tokens of appreciation, we decided to make an overall monetary contribution to each center. As part of our recruitment of subjects, we indicated our intention and explained that we would make the contribution in the name of each participant. In addition, if a participant wished, we would include his or her name with the group. Most participants appreciated this gesture, and a number of the people indicated that it was the first opportunity they had to contribute to the senior center. The subject of compensation will continue to be an important topic of discussion among researchers, members of human subjects committees, and prospective participants.

Follow-up

Associated with the topic of recruitment is the issue of follow-up. Follow-up refers to the maintenance of contact with the participant for the purpose of requesting additional interviews and other information as part of longitudinal studies. At the conclusion of the baseline interview, it is useful to remind the participants that the researcher would like to contact them in the future to inquire about their health and functioning. As such, the researcher should request that the participant inform by telephone or postcard about any changes in residence or telephone number. Another procedure to facilitate follow-up is to ask the subject at the conclusion of the baseline interview to provide the name and telephone number of someone who is likely to know his or her location in the future in the event that the researcher cannot locate the subject. It is also useful in studies conducted in the United States to request the subject's social security number and, in some cases, driver's license number. In addition to improving follow-up, these identification numbers will facilitate linkage with other sources of information, such as vital status. Some projects publish a study newsletter that is distributed to the participants on a regular basis. In addition to keeping the participants informed of the study results, it helps to ensure that the subjects remain engaged in the project. Increasingly, study participants have access to e-mail and the Internet. In the future, it will be useful to evaluate the potential for using e-mail for communication with subjects and, perhaps, even for the administration of follow-up interviews. Finally, it is worthwhile to consider sending a card to each participant on the date of his or her birthday. In addition to keeping the participants engaged in the study, it is simply a very nice gesture to people who have contributed to the success of the study.

PROXY INTERVIEWS

Because the risk of functional limitations and disability increase with age, older subjects may be less likely than younger subjects to participate. A nonresponse of this kind may potentially result in a systematic bias in the analysis. Put differently, if a legitimate study outcome, in this case, functional limitations, negatively affects the likelihood of the participation of subjects, a systematic bias is introduced—the "healthy participant effect." One strategy to ensure a more representative sampling of subjects is to include the possibility of proxy respondents as sources of information about persons who are unable to respond (Magaziner, 1992).

One of the issues associated with the use of proxy respondents is deciding what types of information will be legitimately requested of the proxy. Although there is some disagreement in the literature, the general rule is that proxy respondents are better able to provide factual information, e.g., the number of years of education and past medical diagnoses, than information about the subject's beliefs, fears, opinions, and experiences of pain and discomfort.

Another issue is deciding who represents the best source of proxy information. Some commentators have argued that the selection of the best proxy depends on the type of information that is being requested. For example, an older sibling may be better able to provide information about the subject's childhood experiences than a spouse or an adult child. On the other hand, a spouse or partner may be better able to report about contemporary, daily events. Because it would be difficult to consult multiple proxies in a given interview, the general rule is to select someone who has had everyday contact with the person for the longest period of time. In most cases, the first choice is a spouse, partner, or other housemate. In any event, a priority list of acceptable proxies should be identified prior to the initiation of the study. Not surprisingly, it will be easier to identify a legitimate proxy for some respondents than for others. Because older women are more likely than older men to live alone, it may be more difficult to locate a proxy for older women than for older men. The potential bias that this introduces should not be neglected.

In addition to any bias that might be introduced by the type of proxy, it is also important to consider the bias that may be introduced by the type of information that is requested. Research indicates that there is a greater concordance between subjects and proxies on general measures of functioning than in more specific measures, such as assessments of depression (Magaziner, Zimmerman, Gruber-Baldini, Hebel, & Fox, 1997). In addition, in a longitudinal study of the same population, it was determined that proxies tend to overstate improvement and understate deterioration, when compared to a standard criterion (Yasuda, Zimmerman, Hawkes, Gruber-Baldini, Hebel, & Magaziner, 2004). Research on proxy bias needs to be expanded.

RESEARCH DESIGN AND INTERVIEW

There has been considerable discussion about the design of studies involving older populations. Issues include the length and timing of interviews, the inclusion of direct measures of physical performance, and the acquisition of biologic specimens.

Because older people are at elevated risk for sensory impairments, such as difficulties with memory, vision, or fatigue, commentators have recommended that studies of older populations be designed to reduce the potentially negative effects of those factors on administration of the study protocol (Kelsey et al., 1989; Kohout, 1992). With regard to the issue of fatigue, it has been recommended that the study protocol, for example, the interview, not be excessively long or demanding. It is difficult to say, as some have written, that an interview should not exceed 60 to 90 minutes. If the topic is engaging and the questions are carefully prepared, an interview may proceed more quickly than the total time would necessarily indicate. Moreover, our experience has been that the placement of direct measures of physical performance, for example, measures of upper- and lower-body strength, balance and fine dexterity, at the midpoint of the interview serves to refresh older participants. Again, the interview may proceed more quickly than the total time would indicate. It is also possible to include the option of allowing the participant to complete the interview in segments. For example, a participant may complete an interview on a second day. In addition, it is also recommended that "fast-track" questions be identified. These are questions that are judged to be critical for the completion of the interview. If a participant indicates or shows signs of wanting to end the interview, the interviewer is trained to administer these key questions. This is certainly preferable to completing only the questions that appear at the first part of the interview and neglecting those that are asked at the end.

There are a number of strategies to improve memory. For example, some studies include "time posts." Prior to asking about past exposures or practices, the interviewer will attempt to bring the participant back in time by asking about the dates associated with key events, such as birthdays, graduations, or anniversaries. Using these events as "time posts," the interviewer then may ask about past exposures or activities taking place at that time. In other cases, the interviewer may not rely simply on the participant's memory, e.g., recalling the names of current medications. In many epidemiologic studies, the participant is informed prior to the interview that information about medications will be requested and that the participant should make available his or her current medications at the time of the interview. The interviewer will then ask the participant during the course of the interview to display each medication so that the name and dosage can be recorded. In other cases, "show cards" are made available to participants to ensure that they can recall the full range of response categories to a set of questions.

The timing of the interview is also important. This is especially the case in studies of functional status. As noted previously, unlike the discrete occurrence of many health outcomes (e.g., presence or absence of a diagnosis), level of functioning can vary over time (Mendes de Leon, Guralnik, & Bandeen-Roche, 2002). In addition, some studies of the epidemiology of functional limitations and disability following the diagnosis and treatment of particular conditions require that interviews be conducted at particular times (Satariano & Ragland, 1994; Yancik et al., 1996). For example, the protocol may require that interviews be conducted at 3, 12, and 24 months following diagnosis of colorectal cancer. Although it has been recommended that investigators be flexible in the timing of interviews of older patients, it is sometimes difficult when the amount of time passed since diagnosis may affect the level of functional outcome.

As noted previously, direct measures of physical performance are being used increasingly in epidemiologic studies of older populations. Although these assessments can be demanding, they can be administered easily and safely in the home (Reed, Satariano, Gildengorin, McMahon, Fleshman, & Schneider, 1995; Simonsick, Maffeo, Rogers, Skinner, Davis, Guralnik, et al., 1997). I have been directly involved in two large population-based studies that included direct assessments of physical performance in over 5000 seniors over extended periods of time. There was never a serious injury to either participants or interviewers in the administration of those direct assessments. Special studies of older populations may require particular types of testing devices. For example, studies of older drivers incorporate the use of driving simulators to standardize the assessment of performance across a variety of driving situations (Rizzo, Reinach, McGehee, & Dawson, 1997; Hancock & de Ridder, 2003).

Although true of all studies of this kind, it is particularly important that questions and response categories be presented clearly and carefully. It is also critical that studies include multilingual interviewers so that the interview can be conducted in the participant's native tongue. Along those lines, the general rule is that the interview should be translated from English to the other language and then translated back into English to ensure that the translation has been done properly.

It is also useful to conclude the home interview in a manner that will be pleasing and satisfying to the participant and improve the likelihood that the participant will consent to subsequent interviews. One technique is to conclude the interview with a series of open-ended questions that provides closure and also provide an opportunity for the participant to provide information that may not have been asked for previously. In our studies, we have used the following questions: "I would like to conclude by asking you some general questions about your health and functioning. First, please tell me what is the worse thing about being your age? Now, tell me what is the best thing about being your age? What is the best advice that you can give to someone who has just turned 25? Finally, is there anything that you would like to add about your health and functional status "that we have not discussed?"

In addition to the home interview, some epidemiologic studies require more detailed laboratory assessments. This too is in keeping with an ecological model in which one of the objectives is to assess the health and functional effects of biologic factors independently and in conjunction with behavioral, social, and environmental factors. For example, the Study of Physical Performance and Age-Related Changes in Sonomans protocol includes a laboratory assessment to collect detailed information on cardiorespiratory fitness and vision (Hollenberg & Tager, 2000). The study laboratory has been established at the local hospital in Sonoma, California. Participants without any health contraindications, e.g., current heart disease, are invited to the laboratory to complete the assessment protocol. Although the study population is restricted to a limited geographic area, transportation is provided to those who request it. A separate preliminary assessment is completed prior to the assessment to ensure that it is safe for the participant to complete the protocol. A physician is always present during the completion of the assessments. A "crash cart" is also available in case of an emergency.

ASSESSMENTS OF THE ENVIRONMENT

In addition to the home interview, it is possible to conduct assessments of the home and neighborhood environments. As noted earlier, assessments of the home environment have been conducted in studies of falls and injuries. Protocols have been established to systematically examine the home environment to determine the number and types of hazards that elevate the likelihood of falls and injuries. Increasingly, researchers are developing similar procedures to assess the characteristics of the home environment to determine in particular to what extent the environment may either enhance or impede everyday functioning (Moudon & Lee, 2003; Saelens, Sallis, Black, & Chen, 2003; Shumway-Cook, Patla, Stewart, Ferrucci, Ciol, & Guralnik, 2002). It is also important to obtain information that clarifies the manner in which the subjects use the home environment. Similar procedures can be used to assess the objective characteristics of the immediate environment. This may include a determination of the distance as well as the nature and condition of the route between the participant's place of residence and the location of goods and services in the community. Environmental audit measures are now being used to systematically assess the characteristics of the built environment, often in terms of street segments (Moudon & Lee, 2003). Other techniques involve the use of devices to monitor the volume of automobile traffic in adjacent streets as well as the lighting levels of streetlights and the quality of the sidewalks. Again, in addition to obtaining these objective assessments, it is important to determine the extent and manner in which the subjects use the environment. This will include "compensatory strategies" used by the participant to adapt to the environment. As Fried and colleagues (1996) note, compensatory strategies can include modifications of the environment or modifications in the extent or manner in which a subject engages in particular types of behavior. In the future, this type of assessment may require the use of portable devices that track movement in the environment through global positioning satellite systems (Schutz & Chambax, 1997).

INTERVIEWER QUALIFICATIONS

The selection and training of qualified interviewers are critical for the conduct of a successful study. An interviewer should be personable, engaging, and focused. In some cases, an older person, especially someone who lives alone, may want to engage in an extended conversation with the interviewer. Although the interviewer must always be polite, the interviewer must remain focused and ensure that the interview itself stays on schedule and is completed according to the protocol.

There has been considerable discussion about the ideal age of an interviewer for a study of aging and health. Although the selection of an interviewer should not be based solely on age, a middle-aged to late middle-aged interviewer may be best suited to put the participant at ease and elicit information. Likewise, given concerns of safety, most commentators agree that a female interviewer is more likely than a male interviewer to be invited into the participant's home.

Given the complexity of most epidemiologic studies, training and regular recertification procedures are important to maintain the quality of the study. As part of the training protocol, it is recommended that a videotape of a complete interview be prepared. The trainees can view the interview and individually record the subject's responses. Following a viewing of the taped interview, the instructor can review each interviewer's completed interviews. Discrepant recordings can be discussed. Consistent scoring is also critically important in the administration of the direct performance measures. The supposed simple process of starting and stopping a stopwatch, an important piece of equipment, requires consistent procedures of operation.

SECONDARY SOURCES OF EPIDEMIOLOGIC DATA

There is a rich resource of available data to conduct secondary analyses in the epidemiology of aging. Some of the most important findings in this field have been obtained from an examination of large, often longitudinal, data. Given the time and effort that is expended to conduct a large epidemiologic study, it is only appropriate that data sets from such studies be used by a variety of investigators for different research objectives. These studies include the Framingham Study, the Alameda County Study, the Honolulu Heart (now Aging) Study, and the Tecumseh Study. In addition, there are several national data sets that have been used for a variety of research investigations. These US studies include the National Health Interview Survey, the National Long-Term Care Surveys, and the Established Populations for Epidemiologic Studies of the Elderly. There also are a number of national data sets from other countries. These include the Beijing Aging Study, the Bonn Longitudinal Study of Aging, and the Longitudinal Aging Study of Amsterdam. In this section, we will review the three national studies from the United States.

The National Health Interview Survey

The National Health Interview Survey was established in 1957. It is designed to record the annual incidence of acute conditions, the prevalence of selected chronic conditions, and the prevalence of functional limitations. Each year a probability sample of approximately 50,000 households is generated and typically includes approximately 130,000 persons. The public use tape has been available since 1982.

The National Long-Term Care Survey

This survey, established in 1982, is based on a nationally representative sample of subjects aged 65 years or more that are eligible for Medicare benefits. Follow-up surveys have been conducted in 1984, 1989, 1994, and 1999. In addition to longitudinal assessments of the preexisting cohort, an additional cross-sectional sample of subjects aged 65 and older is generated at each wave. The sample includes both institutionalized and noninstitutionalized subjects. The data set includes information on health and disability, service utilization, socioeconomic factors, and health care costs.

The Established Populations for Epidemiologic Studies of the Elderly

This study, initiated in 1982, was the first interview study conducted by the federal government on an elderly population. The original sample consists of residents aged 65 years and older from three geographic areas in the United States: East Boston, Massachusetts; New Haven, Connecticut; and selected counties in the state of Iowa. Later, in an effort to increase the sample of African-Americans, selected counties of North Carolina were included. Baseline home interviews were conducted and included a core set of questions of health and functional status. In addition, measures of physical performance, including assessments of upper- and lower-body strength, balance, fine dexterity, and walking speed were included for the first time. The protocol that was developed for this national study was later to become the core protocol for most subsequent population-based studies in aging.

THE EFFECTS OF AGE AND AGING ON ANALYTIC STRATEGIES

Conducting epidemiologic studies in older populations raises a number of significant challenges, challenges associated with the design and administration of study protocols. As the integration of biologic, behavioral, and environmental factors becomes more and more central to the understanding of the epidemiology of aging, the design and conduct of epidemiologic studies will become even more challenging.

Along these lines, there are a number of analytic strategies that are affected by age and aging. Although it is beyond the scope of this chapter to provide a comprehensive overview of these analytic strategies and issues, we will focus on brief discussions of age adjustment; age, period, and cohort analysis; and multilevel analysis.

Age Adjustment

Age adjustment refers to the standardization of age distributions and is often used to compare the distribution of a health outcome among different populations. Because age is so strongly associated with chronological age, it is necessary to standardize the age distribution across the population. Without age standardization, it would not be possible to obtain an unbiased assessment of whether the populations truly differ in the incidence of the disease. This, in turn, may lead researchers to hypothesize that there is something about residence in a particular area, either a particular exposure or a specific characteristic of the members of the populations that might account for the difference in the incidence of the disease. Instead, it may be that one population is simply older than the other population. There are direct and indirect methods to adjust for age.

Direct age adjustment or standardization involves the application of the age-specific incidence rates (in this case) from the populations that are being compared to the age distribution of a standard population, often the general population of a larger geographic area, such as the United States. This entails multiplying the age-specific rates from the different populations by the number of people in the age category for the standard population, in this case, the US population. That calculation provides an expected number of people with that incident condition in the standard-ized population. The expected numbers are then added and divided by the total standardized population. This provides a summary, age-adjusted incident rate for each population, if they shared the same standard age distribution. By comparing the age-adjusted incidence rates among the population, it is possible to view the differences in the incidence of the disease outcome without the confounding effects of age.

The indirect measure is similar. However, in this case, the age-specific rates from the standardized population are applied to the age-specific populations for the populations in question. By multiplying the disease increases by the population totals, it is possible to calculate the expected number of incident cases for each population, if those populations shared the incidence rate of the standardized population. The age-specific expected incident cases are added and compared to the observed number of cases. The expected number divided by the observed number multi-plied by some number, often 100 or 1000, results in a standardized inci-dence ratio (SIR). If the purpose was to examine and compare mortality rates, the resulting statistic would be a standardized mortality ratio (SMR). If the final statistic (either SIR or SMR) is greater than 100, it exceeds the expected incidence. If it is less than 100, it is less than the expected number. For a more detailed discussion of the direct and indi-rect methods of age adjustment, consult a standard introductory text in either epidemiology or biostatistics, such as Szklo and Nieto (2000, pp. 265–276) or Lilienfeld and Stolley (1994, pp. 68–72).

Age, Period, and Cohort Analysis

In Chapter 2, we introduced age, period, and cohort effects. To recall, age differences in an outcome may be affected by different factors that include factors associated with chronological age, characteristics of a spe-cific generation or cohort, and factors associated with a specific period of time. Graphical displays have been used to describe and characterize age, period, and cohort effects. Analytic strategies also have been used to determine the independent effects of age, period, and cohort effects.

Questions have been raised, however, about whether it is, in fact, possible to assess the independent effects of the three factors, since, by definition, the three factors are interrelated, or not independent. It is possible to derive a third factor with information about the other two. This is known as "the identifiability problem." Xiping Xu and colleagues (1995, p. 562) have proposed a solution by using two-factor models to examine the association between age and pulmonary function:

> The age effects estimated from the age-cohort model can be interpreted as the longitudinal age effects when the cohort is fixed. Conversely, the age effects from the age-period model represent the cross-section age effects when the period holds constant.

The results indicate that there were significant period and cohort effects, which the researchers explained in terms of changes in air pollutants, respiratory infections, vaccinations, type of cigarettes, diet, and lifestyles over time (Xu et al., 1995, p. 554).

Multiple Level Analysis

Multiple level analysis is a technique used in an examination of the independent and joint effects of individual, group, and environmental factors on a health outcome (Greenland, 1999; Subramanian, Jones, & Duncan, 2002). In short, this analysis provides a systematic strategy for examining the intersection across multiple levels from the individual to the environment. Environmental factors can be either contextual or compositional. Contextual factors refer to the physical characteristics of the environment. Examples of these contextual factors include types and density of housing, retail, sidewalk, and roadway systems. Compositional factors, on the other hand, refer to characteristics of the population (e.g., age and gender distribution) that resides in a specific geographic area. Although not unique to the study of aging, there are several aspects of multilevel analysis that are important to a consideration of the epidemiology of aging. First, the past and current age distributions of a population may affect the behavioral and health patterns of individuals. These patterns, in turn, may be affected by the chronological age of individuals under study. An individual's level of physical activity may be affected by his or her age as well as the age distribution of fellow residents. A person may be more likely to exercise and more likely to have age-appropriate exercise facilities in situations in which he is close in age to most of the people in his area.

Second, over the life course, a person is likely to reside in a variety of different geographic areas. A comprehensive multilevel analysis should incorporate the string of places where the person lived as he or she aged. As S. V. Subramanian and colleagues (2002, p. 68) write:

> Contexts change over time, as do the circumstances and health of people. Simultaneously incorporating time and space dimensions involves asking the following research question: "While the prevalence of poor health may have declined over time, have neighborhood contextual disparities declined, and, if so, for which type of population groups?"

Multilevel analysis assumes that individual residents of a particular geographic area are not completely independent. In other words, it is assumed that the people who share residence in a particular area, such as a neighborhood, are more alike than people who do not share some geographic area. The mechanism for that similarity may be due to one or both of the following factors. First, people may select to live in the same area because they share similar values, attitudes, and behaviors with others in that area. Second, residence in a common area may make people more alike. For example, there may be common customs and exposures that may causes people to be more alike.

CONCLUSION

Research in the epidemiology of aging presents a number of unique challenges. In this chapter, we addressed the issues of recruitment, interview design and administration, and analytic issues, including age adjustment; age, period, and cohort analysis; and multilevel analysis.

REFERENCES

Anderson, L. A., Fogler, J., & Dedrick, R. F. (1995). Recruiting from the community: Lessons learned from the diabetes care for older adults project. *The Gerontologist, 35*(3), 395–401.

Barron, J. S., Duffey, P. L., Byrd, L. J., Campbell, R., & Ferrucci, L. (2004). Informed consent for research participation in frail older persons. *Aging Clinical Experimental Research, 16*(1), 79–85.

Cabral, D. N., Napoles-Springer, A., Miike, R., McMillan, A., Sison, J. D., Wrensch, M. R., et al. (2003). Population- and community-based recruitment of African Americans and Latinos: The San Francisco Bay Area Lung Cancer Study. *American Journal of Epidemiology, 158*(3), 272–279.

Cockburn, M. G., Hamilton, A. S., Zadnick, J., Cozen, W., & Mark, T. M. (2001). Development and representativeness of a large population-based cohort of native Californians. *Twin Research, 4*(4), 242–250.

Colsher, P. L. (1992). Ethical issues in conducting surveys of the elderly. In R. R. Wallace & R. F. Woolson (Eds.), *The epidemiologic study of the elderly.* New York: Oxford University Press, 39–45.

Fried, L. P., Bandeen-Roche, K., Williamson, J. D., Prasada-Rao, P., Chee, E., Tepper, S., & Rubin, G. S. (1996). Functional decline in older adults: Expanding methods of ascertainment. *Journals of Gerontology: Medical Sciences, 51*(5), M206–M214.

Funkhouser, E., Macaluso, M., & Wang, X. (2000). Alternative strategies for selecting population controls: Comparison of random-digit dialing and targeted telephone calls. *Annals of Epidemiology, 10*(1), 59–67.

Greenland, S. (1999). Multilevel modeling and model averaging. *Scandinavian Journal of Work and Environmental Health, 25,* Suppl 4, 43–48.

Guralnik, J. M., Branch, L. G., Cummings, S. R., & Curb, J. D. (1989). Physical performance measures in aging research. *Journals of Gerontology: Medical Sciences, 44*(5), M141–M146.

Hage, B. H., Oliver, R. G., Powles, J. W., & Wahlqvist, M. L. (1990). Telephone directory listings of presumptive Chinese surnames: An appropriate sampling frame for a dispersed population with characteristic surnames. *Epidemiology, 1*(5), 405–408.

Hancock, P. A., & de Ridder, S. W. (2003). Behavioural accident avoidance science: Understanding response in collision incipient conditions. *Ergonomics, 46*(12), 1111–1135.

Hollenberg, M., & Tager, I. B. (2000). Oxygen uptake efficiency slope: An index of exercise performance and cardiopulmonary reserve requiring only submaximal exercise. *Journal of the American College of Cardiology, 36*(1), 194–201.

Kelsey, J. L., O'Brien, L. A., Grisso, J. A., & Hoffman, S. (1989). Issues in carrying out epidemiologic research in elderly. *American Journal of Epidemiology, 130,* 857–866.

Kohout, F. J. (1992). The pragmatics of survey field work among the elderly. In R. R. Wallace & R. F. Woolson (Eds.), *The epidemiologic study of the elderly.* New York: Oxford University Press, 91–119.

Krieger, N., Chen, J. T., Waterman, P. D., Rehkopf, D. H., & Subramanian, S. V. (2003). Race/ethnicity, gender, and monitoring socioeconomic gradients in health: A comparison of area-bed SES measures—the public health disparities geocoding project. *American Journal of Public Health, 93*(10), 1655–1671.

Lilienfeld, D. E., & Stolley, P. D. (1994). *Foundations of epidemiology,* 3rd ed. New York: Oxford University Press.

Magaziner, J. (1992). The use of proxy respondents in health surveys of the aged. In R. R. Wallace & R. F. Woolson (Eds.), *The epidemiologic study of the elderly.* New York: Oxford University Press, 120–129.

Magaziner, J., Zimmerman, S. I., Gruber-Baldini, A. L., Hebel, J. R., & Fox, K. M. (1997). Proxy reporting in five areas of functional status: Comparison with self-reports and observations of performance. *American Journal of Epidemiology, 146*(5), 418–428.

Mendes de Leon, C., Guralnik, J. M., & Bandeen-Roche, K. (2002). Short-term change in physical function and disability: The Women's Health and Aging Study. *Journals of Gerontology: Social Sciences, 57*(6), S355–S365.

Moudon, A. V., & Lee, C. (2003). Walking and bicycling: An evaluation of environmental audit instruments. *American Journal of Health Promotion, 18*(1), 21–37.

Reed, D., Satariano, W. A., Gildengorin, G., McMahon, K., Fleshman, R., & Schneider, E. (1995). Health and functioning among the elderly of Marin County, California: A glimpse of the future. *Journals of Gerontology: Medical Sciences, 50*(2), M61–M69.

Regnier, V., Hamilton, J., & Yatable, S. (1995). *Assisted living for the aged and frail: Innovations in design, management, and financing.* New York: Columbia University Press.

Rizzo, M., Reinach, S., McGehee, D., & Dawson, J. (1997). Simulated car crashes and crash predictors in drivers with Alzheimer's disease. *Archives of Neurology, 54*(5), 545–551.

Saelens, B. E., Sallis, J. F., Black, J. B., & Chen, D. (2003). Neighborhood-based differences in physical activity: An environment scale evaluation. *American Journal of Public Health, 93*(9), 1552–1558.

Satariano, W. A., Minkler, M. A., & Langhauser, C. A. (1984). The significance of an ill spouse for assessing health differences in an elderly population. *Journal of the American Geriatrics Society, 32*(3), 187–190.

Satariano, W. A., & Ragland, D. R. (1994). The effect of comorbidity on 3-year survival of women with primary breast cancer. *Annals of Internal Medicine, 120*(2), 104–110.

Satariano, W. A., Smith, J., Swanson, A., & Tager, I. B. (1998). A census-based design for the recruitment of a community sample of older adults: Efficacy and costs. *Annals of Epidemiology, 8*(4), 278–282.

Schneider, E. L. (1985). *Teaching nursing home: A new approach to geriatric research, education, and clinical care.* New York: Lippincott, Williams, & Wilkins Co.

Schutz, Y., & Chambax, A. (1997). Could a satellite-based navigation system (GPS) be used to assess the physical activity of individuals on earth? *European Journal of Clinical Nutrition, 51*(5), 338–339.

Shumway-Cook, A., Patla, A. E., Stewart, A., Ferrucci. L., Ciol, M. A., & Guralnik, J. M. (2002). Environmental demands associated with community mobility in older adults with and without mobility disabilities. *Physical Therapy, 82*(7), 670–681.

Simonsick, E. M., Maffeo, C. E., Rogers, S. K., Skinner, E. A., Davis, D., Guralnik, J. M., et al. (1997). Methodology and feasibility of a home-based examination in disabled older women: The Women's Health and Aging Study, *Journals of Gerontology: Medical Sciences, 52*(5), M264–M274.

Subramanian, S. V., Jones, K., & Duncan, C. (2002). Multilevel methods for public health research. In I. Kawachi & L. P. Berkman (Eds.), *Neighborhoods and health*. New York: Oxford University Press, 65–111.

Szklo, M., & Nieto, F. J. (2000). *Epidemiology: Beyond the basics*. Gaithersburg, MD: Aspen Publishers.

Tijam, E. Y. (2001). How to find Chinese research participants: Use of a phonologically-based surname search method. *Canadian Journal of Public Health, 92*(2), 138–142.

Xu, X., Laird, N., Dockery, D. W., Schouten, J. P., Rijcken, B., & Weiss, S. T. (1995). Age, period, and cohort effects on pulmonary function in a 24–year longitudinal study. *American Journal of Epidemiology, 141*(6), 554–566.

Yancik, R., Havlik, R. J., Wesley, M. N., Ries, L., Long, S., Rossi, W. K., et al. (1996). Cancer and comorbidity in older patients: A descriptive profile. *Annals of Epidemiology, 6*(5), 399–412.

Yasuda, N., Zimmerman, S., Hawkes, W. G., Gruber-Baldini, A. L., Hebel, J. R., & Magaziner, J. (2004). Concordance of proxy-perceived change and measured change in multiple domains of function in older persons. *Journal of the American Geriatrics Society, 52*(7), 1157–1162.

CHAPTER 11

Healthy Aging and Its Implications for Public Health

One of the important themes in the epidemiology of aging (indeed, aging research in general) is that the "aging process" and the "disease process" are certainly related, but in many ways distinct (Timiras, 2003). This means that aging is not associated uniformly with the risk of disease, disability, and death. One of the main objectives of the epidemiology of aging, then, is to describe those differences and, ideally, explain the reasons why they exist. Increasingly, attention is being directed to older people who seem to do well—those who seem to be in better health and demonstrate higher levels of functioning than most people in their age group. As noted in a previous chapter, these people, those who age "healthfully," hold the promise for both the development of a clearer understanding of aging, health, and functioning, as well as the establishment of a new generation of programs and policies that enhance health and functioning and reduce the likelihood of disease, disability, and premature death. The objective is to identify factors in the lives of these people and the places where they live that can serve as the basis for programs and policies to enrich the lives of the general population of older people (Anetzberger, 2002; Stokols, Grzywacz, McMahan, & Phillips, 2002; Syme, 2003). Indeed, as we have seen, many of the factors associated with differences in health outcomes are modifiable, such as tobacco exposure, diet, and physical activity (Hazzard, 1997; Omenn, Beresford, Buchner, LaCroix, Martin, Patrick, et al., 1997). As such, there is the possibility of promoting health and well-being in older populations. Research indicates that the older people with the highest levels of health and functioning are those who have avoided the major age-related conditions, limited exposure to tobacco, maintained an ideal weight, engaged in physical activity, and remained socially connected or engaged.

The ecological model, which has served as the basis for our examination of aging and public health, assumes, to repeat yet again, that differences in levels of health and well-being in populations are due to a dynamic interplay among biologic, behavioral, social, and environmental factors, a broad interplay of multilevel factors that unfolds over the life course of individuals, families, neighborhoods, and communities. Most important for our purposes here, this model also serves to identify multiple points of possible intervention, from the microbiologic to the environmental, that may postpone the onset of disease, disability, and premature death and enhance the chances for health, mobility, and longevity (Smedley & Syme, 2000). Just as the ecological model assumes that health and functional outcomes are due to the joint influence of multiple factors, the model also suggests that conjoint programs and policies may be especially effective for addressing these age-related issues.

In this chapter, we will review issues associated with public health interventions and the ecological model. These issues include the objective, level, and timing of public health interventions. In addition, attention will be given to the criteria for translating research into practice as well as a consideration of the role of the individual and community in the establishment, administration, and evaluation of the intervention. Three types of representative interventions will be reviewed. First, we will consider physical activity interventions as an exemplar for behavioral interventions in public health. Second, we will examine interventions that foster social involvement, a key component of healthy aging. The Experience Corps is a prime example of this type of intervention. Finally, we will review recommendations to enhance environmental design. Although not directed specifically toward the elderly, this type of intervention could have a significant impact on patterns of health and functioning in older populations.

PUBLIC HEALTH INTERVENTIONS AND THE ECOLOGICAL MODEL

Although life extension is an area of significant research, according to the National Institute on Aging, the primary objective of public health interventions should be to add life to years rather than years to life. The objective, therefore, is to postpone the onset of disease, disability, and death into the later years. Although the research itself remains controversial, there is consensus regarding the goal of "compressing morbidity" into the later years (Fries, 1997). This is achieved in a variety of ways. In addition to preventing or postponing the onset of disease, an important objective is to develop strategies to identify disease before it occurs (preclinical conditions) or to moderate the course of the disease by diagnosing it at an early stage. It is important to emphasize again that functional limitations and disability may occur independently of the number and types of chronic and infectious conditions. Accordingly, the prevention and moderation of physical and cognitive functional limitations and disability are identified as primary geriatric outcomes. Interventions also can address specific behaviors (e.g., smoking, diet, and physical activity), social factors (social support or social capital), and characteristics of the environment (e.g., chemical exposures, radiation, and barriers to walking).

Time is an important factor. In public health, practitioners often speak of upstream and downstream approaches to population health. The distinction between upstream and downstream is based on a story, often told in public health circles, of a group of people standing on the banks of a river. Cries for help are heard from a drowning man in the river. Several people jump in the water and pull the man to shore. After getting the person safely to shore, other cries for help are heard. Members of the group jump in again and those people are saved. After this happens several more times, a few of the people standing on the shore decide to run upstream to investigate. There, they discover that the railing on a bridge has broken loose. The bridge is repaired, thus preventing additional people from falling in and requiring rescue downstream. By addressing the problem at its source, so the story goes, it is possible to prevent more of the problems later downstream. This story is used to support the rationale for primary prevention. Rather than expending most of our resources downstream, presumably after diseases have occurred and people have fallen into the river, we could spend time upstream addressing the primary causes more effectively and at lower cost. Of course, the stream metaphor should be extended to include the prevention, diagnosis, and treatment of functional limitations and disabilities as well. Even after diseases have been diagnosed, there is much that can be done "upstream" to reduce the likelihood of subsequent functional limitations and disabilities.

Time also provides special meaning for interventions directed at older people in general. Increased attention is being given to a life-course perspective to better understand the likelihood of health outcomes in the middle and senior years (Kuh & Ben-Shlomo, 2004). Although much of the attention in the epidemiology of aging has been focused on the last chapters of life, it is becoming increasingly clear that the content and length of those chapters are due in large part to the content, length, and quality of the preceding chapters. Previous experiences and exposures, coupled with particular salient periods of development (i.e., windows of vulnerability and resiliency), affect the subsequent risk of disease, disability, and death. With this in mind, it is appropriate to consider whether programs and policies that are directed to younger people also can be thought of as indirectly benefiting future cohorts of older people—planting seeds that will bear fruit in the future. It is worthwhile, then, to consider whether there are particular points in the life course at which interventions would be the most effective in sustaining health and functioning into the later years.

Time is also important in considering the readiness of people to respond to an intervention. For example, the transtheoretical or stages-of-change model indicates that the likelihood that people will respond to a particular intervention depends on their stage of readiness to accept the message of the intervention (Prochaska & DiClemente, 1983). This model is based on the proposition that people proceed through specific changes prior to taking health-related action. The stages consist, first, of a period of *precontemplation* in which the person is disinterested or unaware of the necessity of undertaking a particular change. This is followed by the period of *contemplation*, that is, the point at which the person is considering some type of change. This, in turn, is followed by the decision to take action, referred to here as *preparation*. Finally, there is the point at which *action* is taken. Although there is some disagreement about the viability of this transition from one stage to another (Committee on Health and Behavior, 2001), the model underscores the recognition that not all people may be equally responsive to a message to change behavior to enhance health. They are at different points in the stages of change. Some are ready to change; some have not even thought of it. The likelihood and timing of behavioral change, in turn, is due to a variety of factors.

The ecological model is important because it underscores the important point that behavior occurs within a social and environmental context. Indeed, John McKinlay (1995) has noted that many public health interventions fail because they have been "decontextualized," to put it differently, designed with the assumption that one type of intervention will be equally effective across different groups in the population—one size fits all. However, just as health outcomes are not distributed randomly within and among populations, so too are health behaviors. Differences in health behaviors are associated with differences in geography, age, gender, race and ethnicity, socioeconomic status, living arrangements, social networks, and a host of other factors. It is reasonable, therefore, to assume that these factors need to be addressed as part of the design of public health interventions. As Karen Emmons (2000, p. 251) writes, "An ecological framework recognizes that behavior is affected by multiple levels of influence, including intrapersonal factors, interpersonal processes, institutional factors, community factors, and public policy." With this in mind, a public health intervention could be based at one of those levels with an appreciation of the interaction across the different levels, or that the intervention itself could be multilevel, such as, a nutritional intervention that addresses both health information about the nutritional content of foods as well as the location and access to inexpensive and nutritious food in the neighborhood.

TRANSLATION OF RESEARCH INTO PRACTICE: GENERAL ISSUES

There are several general issues that should be discussed in any consideration of the translation of research into practice. It cannot be assumed that solid research leads necessarily to solid practice. Put differently, we cannot assume that once a research study is completed, much of the "heavy lifting" has been completed and that now it is just a matter of applying those findings in the population. Instead, the translation of research into practice should be thought of as a specific area of study. Although there are many possible issues, we consider, here, the following:

- "Sick individuals" and "sick populations"
- Arenas of intervention
- Evidence-based community interventions
- The RE-AIM Framework
- Health impact assessment

- Health perceptions and self-care in later life
- Establishment of partnerships

Sick Individuals and Sick Populations

In Chapter 1, we discussed the important distinction made by Geoffrey Rose (1985) between "sick individuals" and "sick populations". To recall, Rose indicated that the assessment of risk is often based on a comparison between individuals with the condition (i.e., "sick individuals") with individuals without the condition, often in the same population. In this type of comparison, any difference, so says Rose, is often due to differences in individual susceptibility. Both the cases and controls are exposed to many of the same factors in the environment. "If everyone smoked 20 cigarettes a day, then clinical, case-control and cohort studies alike would lead us to conclude that lung cancer was a genetic disease" (Rose, 1985, p. 32). This approach differs from the assessment of the relative incidence of a health condition in a population (i.e., "sick populations"), which requires a comparison with other populations. Here, we will consider the implications of the distinction between "sick individuals" and "sick populations" for a consideration of public health interventions. Rose argues that the typical strategy to prevent sickness among individuals is to identify those people at greatest risk for the condition. This means directing the intervention to the small number of people who are most likely to benefit from the intervention. On the other hand, interventions to improve the health of sick populations are designed to change the entire distribution of the population toward the healthier end of the spectrum. Rather than focusing on a relatively few number of people at high risk, this strategy is designed to address the larger number of people at a more moderate risk. Although Rose contends that both types of interventions are important, the population-based intervention is most likely to affect the largest number of people. Consider, for example, the implications of the two approaches for enhancing physical activity in older populations. A high-risk approach would be designed to improve levels of physical activity among the most sedentary older people as a way of reducing the risk of functional impairments and disabilities. In contrast, a population-based approach would be designed to enhance physical activity, for example, an extra ten minutes a day, among the large number of older people who are already engaged in some form of activity. Although Rose (1985, p. 38) argues that addressing the causes of underlying incidence should be a primary focus in public health, he concludes with the observation that "Many diseases will long continue to call for both approaches, and fortunately, competition between them is usually unnecessary."

Arenas of Intervention

Although there are a large number of biologic, behavioral, social, and environmental factors associated with aging, disease, disability, and death, not all of these factors can be readily modified and included as part of a public health intervention. For example, Leonard Syme (1998) writes that one of the most consistent findings in epidemiologic research is the relationship between socioeconomic status and health, a finding that is found across the life course and in all societies. People of lower socioeconomic status, almost regardless of how it is conceptualized and measured, are more likely to develop health problems, suffer a more negative course, experience greater limitations and disabilities, and die prematurely than those of higher socioeconomic status. What, then, are the implications for public health interventions? While the findings certainly suggest the negative health effects of inequality, it may not be practicable to recommend for public policy a complete reordering of the socioeconomic system. While we may debate the merits of that type of policy, it is probably reasonable to assume that such a policy will not be introduced in the short term. Syme (1998, p. 2003) agrees and suggests that the best and most immediate strategy may be to understand more clearly what it is about social class that is associated so strongly with measures of health and functioning. In his review of the research in this area, Syme (1998, p. 498) concludes that "control of destiny" is one of the factors that accounts for the association between socioeconomic status and health:

> The possibility that inequalities can be traced not to difference in money, in social, economic, and political context, or in relative deprivation, but, rather, to differences in problem-solving skills and ability to access resources, would open *a path to intervention*. This view suggests that the health of poor people is compromised because they do not have the options, choices, and discretion to deal with life challenges.

The Ypsilanti Preschool Program and the California Wellness Project are offered as two examples of programs that are designed to enhance skills in solving problems and accessing relevant services. Syme, of course, does not ignore, and nor should we, the very real material differences that exist between people in different social class positions, for example, differential access to goods and services, differential exposure to harmful environmental pollutants, and differential quality of the community infrastructure. Moreover, even if socioeconomic status cannot be readily altered, it may alter the effectiveness of a public health intervention. In other words, the success of a public health intervention may be modified by the socioeconomic status level of a neighborhood, either by enhancing or impeding the intervention.

As part of this discussion, we also should highlight the distinction between programs that, on the one hand, *inoculate* individuals and populations against risk factors and, on the other hand, programs that are designed to *eliminate* those risk factors. As noted earlier, Aaron Antonovsky (1979) argued that most research and practice in public health are based on *pathogenesis,* meaning a focus on the factors that cause people to become ill. Noting that most people remain healthy, in spite of exposures to noxious agents, he reasoned that perhaps a more fruitful approach would be based on *salutogenesis,* a consideration of the factors that cause people to remain or become healthy. The task, then, is to ask, "What is it about this person or this population that prevents them from becoming ill, even in the face of a noxious exposure or unhealthy behavior?" Moreover, Antonovsky argued that if that factor could be determined, then perhaps it could be introduced or provided to the individuals or populations—an inoculation.

Evidence-Based Community Interventions

There is a growing recognition of the importance of developing specific criteria to establish the utility of specific public health interventions. How do we distinguish between the programs that work and those that do not? In addition, what are the criteria for examining bodies to identify possible interventions? The Guide to Community Preventive Services has been developed in the United States to address these issues (Truman, Smith-Akin, Hinman, Gebbie, Brownson, Novick, et al., 2000). A nonfederal Task Force on Community Preventive Services has been established to make recommendations for the use of public health programs and policies based on scientific evidence about the practices that have worked to improve health (Briss, Brownson, Fielding, & Zaza, 2004). This includes a review of evidence on effectiveness, the applicability of effectiveness data, economic impact, and barriers to implementation of interventions. The specific procedures for conducting this research include the following (Briss, Zaza, Pappaioanou, Fielding, Wright-De Aguero, Truman, et al., 2000):

1. The establishment of multidisciplinary development teams
2. The development of a conceptual approach, which includes organizing, grouping, selecting, and evaluating the interventions in each area
3. The selection and summarization of evidence of effectiveness
4. The searching for and retrieving of evidence
5. Assessment of the quality of and summarization of the body of evidence of effectiveness
6. Translation of the body of evidence of effectiveness into recommendations
7. Consideration of information on evidence other than effectiveness
8. Identification and summarization of research gaps

Community guides have been developed to address the following areas: Tobacco-use prevention, physical activity, the social environment for child development, cancer prevention, diabetes, vaccine practice, oral health, motor vehicle safety, and violence prevention. To date, there has been no information about age-related differences in the effectiveness of different interventions nor have there been evaluations of interventions that have been designed specifically for older populations (P. A. Briss, personal communication, February 10, 2004).

Included in this discussion is a consideration of the specificity of the intervention. Clearly, there are some factors that are designed to address a particular factor, for example, programs to screen for high blood pressure or breast cancer. Other programs are designed to address a variety of outcomes. For example, one of the compelling aspects for exercise interventions is that they are associated with a variety of important health outcomes. In addition to a reduction in the risks for heart disease, stroke, and depression, exercise interventions are associated with improvement in physical and cognitive functioning.

The RE-AIM Framework

The RE-AIM framework, an acronym for Reach, Efficacy, Adoption, Implementation, and Maintenance, was developed as a comprehensive strategy to design and evaluate public health interventions (Glasgow,

Vogt, & Boles, 1999; Dzewaltowski, Glasgow, Klesges, Estabrooks, & Brock, 2004). Most important for our purposes, the framework was specifically developed to incorporate the key components of an ecological model to facilitate the translation of research into practice. Commentators have argued that the impact of an intervention is due to both its *reach*, i.e., the percentage of the population exposed to the intervention, as well as its *efficacy*, i.e., the extent to which the intervention achieves its intended purpose (Abrams, Orleans, Niaura, Goldstein, Prochaska, & Velier, 1996). Although reach and efficacy represent important, individual-level variables, other variables that operate more at the organizational level are also necessary to provide a more detailed assessment of interventions, especially in everyday settings. While *reach* refers to the percentage of individuals in a population exposed to an intervention, *adoption* refers to an organizational variable that better reflects the representativeness of the setting (Glasgow et al., 1999). *Implementation* refers to the extent to which a program is introduced as originally designed, also at the organizational or collective level. In fact, the *efficiency* of a program in combination with its actual *implementation* reflects the program's *effectiveness*. As reported by Glasgow and colleagues (Glasgow, McKay, Piette, & Reynolds, 2001, p. 120), "A major feature of the RE-AIM is that it shifts the focus from short-term efficacy among restricted samples of participants in randomized efficacy trials to longer-term effectiveness in real-world settings." Finally, *maintenance* refers to the timing of the intervention as well as the extent to which the outcomes of the intervention are sustained. The impact of the intervention can be maintained at both the level of the individual and at the level of the organization. Often the sustenance of the program at the organizational level is referred to as the institutionalization of that program.

Criteria have been developed to provide an overall assessment of a program intervention by the assignment of scores to each of the components of the RE-AIM framework (Dzewaltowski et al., 2004). Although the RE-AIM framework is a relatively new scheme for evaluating public health interventions, it holds great promise for providing a more comprehensive strategy than is provided by more conventional approaches. The evaluation of the Mediterranean Lifestyle Trial is an example of the use of the RE-AIM framework to evaluate a program intervention for older women (Toobert, Strycker, Glasgow, Barrera, & Bagdade, 2002). In particular, RE-AIM was used to assess strategies to improve the long-term maintenance of this lifestyle program.

Health Impact Assessment

One of the messages of the ecological model is that patterns of health in the population are due to a complex set of factors, as we have noted repeatedly in this book—a complex interplay of biologic, behavioral, social, and environmental factors that interact over the life course. It follows, then, that programs and policies that affect health are *not* limited to those that are explicitly designed to enhance health. Following from the field of environmental impact assessment, health impact assessment (HIA) is a new area of research and evaluation. The purpose of work in this area is to identify the health effects of programs and policies that were designed, administered, and evaluated for reasons other than health. In a paper on the principles of HIA, Margaret Douglas and colleagues (2001, p. 148) characterize this approach in the following way:

> An evidence-based approach to these tasks requires an assessment of: the ways that each policy might have an impact on health, how to improve this impact, and how to ensure that the combined effects of diverse policies avoid contradictory effects and create synergistic benefits. Health impact assessment (HIA) is a method of doing this and has been defined as "a combination of procedures, methods, and tools by which a policy, programme, or project may be judged as to its potential effects on the health of a population, and the distribution of those effects within the population." In this context, health impacts have been defined as the "overall effects, direct and indirect, of a policy, strategy, programme or project on the health of a population" and include impacts on health determinants.

It is reported that there are at least three ways in which HIA might influence decision makers (Kemm, Parry, & Palmer, 2004):

1. By raising awareness among decision makers of the relationship between health and the physical, social, and economic environments, thereby ensuring that they always include a consideration of health consequences in their deliberations
2. By helping decision makers identify and assess possible health consequences and optimize overall outcomes of the decision
3. By helping those affected by policies to participate in policy formation and contribute to decision making

Nancy Krieger and colleagues (2003) agree with the last point, noting in particular that the criteria for conducting HIA should be clear and should reflect the interests of diverse groups in the population.

There are a number of examples of programs and policies that have health effects in older populations. For example, a zoning policy may be introduced that affects the location and types of stores and services in particular neighborhoods. Since we know that the frequency and routes for walking, especially in older populations, are determined by the type and location of destinations, the location of stores could affect the level of physical activity among seniors in a particular area. That level of activity, in turn, affects their level of health and functioning. In addition, the width of streets and the location of automated pedestrian crossings could affect the decision of seniors to walk in specific areas. The types of grocery stores and location of convenience stores could affect the type of food available to older people. Again, this could affect their level of activity. Street lighting and the surface construction of sidewalks could affect the risk of falls and injuries in older populations. The location and type of mass transportation, such as subways and buses, could affect the extent to which older people access goods and services, as well as the opportunity to visit friends and relatives. We noted earlier that involvement in social networks is associated with positive health outcomes.

Health Perceptions and Self-Care in Later Life

There are many interventions that are initiated and conducted either jointly or exclusively by older people themselves. The World Health Organization has defined self-care as follows (Hatch & Kichbush, p. 4, 1983):

> Self-care in health refers to the activities individuals, families, and communities undertake with the intention of enhancing health, preventing disease, limiting illness, and restoring health. These activities are derived from knowledge and skills from the pool of both professional and lay experience. They are undertaken by lay people on their own behalf, either separately or in particular collaboration with professionals.

Self-care behavior attempts to maintain control of life and "to do so with competence, autonomy, and self-reliance" (Konrad, 1998). An important issue is the motivation to care for oneself. A person's attribution of the reasons for illness and the identification of possible venues to reduce pain and suffering are central to the provision of care. It is reported that older people frequently attribute symptoms to the aging process (Stoller, 1998). In one study of the content of health diaries maintained by older people, over half of the respondents attributed at least one of their symptoms to normal aging, and 5% attributed all of their symptoms to normal aging, i.e., "something that happens to most people as they get older." In general, symptoms that are severe and have a rapid onset and course are interpreted as being due to some health condition rather than being symptomatic of the aging process. It is reported that older people who attributed symptoms to aging were more likely to say they would deal with the symptoms by: (a) waiting and watching; (b) accepting the symptoms; (c) denying or minimizing the threat; or (d) postponing or avoiding medical attention.

There is evidence that older people are likely to consult with a variety of sources, both lay and professional, to interpret symptoms and develop a plan to address those symptoms. It is reported, for example, that many people who experience an illness episode consult with family members and friends (Stoller, 1998). This consultation may take place at different times and may occur prior, concurrent, and/or subsequent to a consultation with a health professional. Indeed, a person may consult with family members and friends instead of contacting a physician or health professional. Married people, especially married men, are likely to consult with their spouse about their health. In contrast, married women are more likely to consult with a female friend. Moreover, women are also more likely than men to assume responsibility for the health of their spouse and other family members. Females, in general, serve as caregivers to the health care system.

Research on self-care has important implications for public health practice. Self-care is related to a variety of outcomes, including prevention, screening, treatment, and rehabilitation. It is important to identify the range of self-care behaviors of older people, their purpose, and their relative effectiveness. It is also important to determine the extent to which older people use self-care in combination with professional services. For example, understanding lay meanings of illness, treatment, and rehabilitation is important for ensuring compliance with recommended formal services (Stoller, 1998).

Prohaska (1998) argues that successful health education and health promotion programs include the following components: (a) provision of information on issues associated with the self-care practice; (b) methods to motivate the older individuals to adopt and maintain the self-care behaviors; (c) collection of meaningful and timely feedback; and (d) methods to maintain the self-care practice. Other recommendations include the following (Rakowski, 1998):

- Peer support may be a useful avenue to manipulate in future intervention research.
- The use of persons as the unit of analysis in most self-care interventions may change, as projects become larger to include more aggregated units of assignment (e.g., family, neighborhoods, organizations, and communities) and statistical methodologies become more sophisticated.
- Tailored or personalized interventions are likely to become more prominent.

In general, research on self-care underscores the important point that all public health interventions should take into account the informal strategies older people use to maintain their health and functioning.

Establishment of Partnerships

A final issue is the establishment of partnerships between public health professionals and members of the community (Best, Stokols, Green, Leischow, Holmes, & Buchholz, 2003; Israel, Schulz, Parker, & Becker, 1998; Leung, Yen, & Minkler, 2004). Many funding agencies now require that public health interventions include community advisory committees in the conduct of the administration and evaluation of a public health intervention. For example, the Centers for Disease Control and Prevention requires that its own university-based Prevention Research Centers include a community-based advisory board, as well as, in particular instances, community advisory committees for individual projects, such as the Centers for Disease Control and Prevention, Prevention Research Center, Healthy Aging Research Network (http://depts.washington.edu/harn/).

The specific role of the community partners is an issue of considerable debate and discussion. Perhaps one of the most controversial questions is the extent to which members of the community should participate in the identification of a public health problem to be addressed. For example, public health practitioners may decide that it is important to conduct an intervention among older residents of a community to reduce falls and injuries. This would seem to be a reasonable goal, especially in light of the research that we reviewed in Chapter 7. However, it may be that members of the community, perhaps as expressed through focus groups or representatives of community-based organizations, believe that a more useful program would be one that would address problems of support for caregivers or a program to improve access to stores that provide inexpensive and nutritious food. There are a number of possible outcomes. First, the researchers could simply ignore the wishes of community representatives and proceed. Of course, to the extent that community representatives accurately captured the will of the community, simply ignoring the recommendations will probably just doom the project to failure. Second, the researchers could negotiate with community representatives to conduct conjoint interventions or to develop a broader intervention that combined both objectives (fall prevention and caregiving support) into a more comprehensive program. Some commentators have recommended an alternative strategy that ideally would avoid this type of controversy and establish collaborative ties *prior* to the identification of a specific project. This was the objective of the Kellogg Foundation's Community-Based Public Health Program (Bruce & McKane, 2000). A number of sites around the country were funded to develop innovative organizational structures to accommodate partnerships among community-based organizations, health departments, and university-based researchers. Often the partnerships were based in specific communities or neighborhoods. The purpose was to develop an organizational structure and administration that would sustain a partnership and avoid what was perceived as a more traditional style in which the development and administration of public health interventions were developed primarily by public health researchers and practitioners at either universities or health departments.

This type of arrangement should not be thought of simply as a necessary strategy to gain access to particular community residents (i.e., a means to an end), but rather as a strategy to do better research. As Margaret Leung and colleagues (2004, p. 503) write:

> With community buy-in and participation, participants are more motivated to ensure that data gathered are meaningful for the local community. Epidemiologists' concerns with poor response rates may be countered, as community leaders and trusted lay people assist in recruiting, retaining, collecting, and recording data from harder-to-reach

members of a community. With the community invested in the research process and outcomes, attrition in longitudinal studies may decrease.

In addition, this type of partnership may lead to the emergence of new research questions as well as the more effective translation of that research into locally relevant policy and community action (Leung et al., 2004). It is also reported that this type of partnership may lead to community members learning basic research skills. In addition to being better able to identify problems through the collection of basic survey data, with these skills, community members may be more active and more effective partners in epidemiologic research and practice.

It is only fair to identify some of the limitations that have been noted about the establishment of such partnerships. First, it takes time to establish true partnerships. Unfortunately, the time required to establish such partnerships may exceed the time line of a grant. Funds to establish and sustain the partnerships may have to come from other sources. Second, it may not be possible to respond to particular requests for proposals, when those requests are not in keeping with the priorities of the partnership. Third, it is necessary to develop clear terms for the publication or presentation of research from the research or intervention. This can be a rather contentious issue. Publication and presentation of results are important to academic-based researchers and practitioners. Any interference in that process may be viewed as an infringement on academic freedom. On the other hand, members of the community may view study results as politically charged or embarrassing. It is a difficult question, but it is often resolved by establishing clear terms between the parties prior to it becoming an issue. Although the study results should be presented or published, it is important to present the results to the community before communicating the findings in other forums. Moreover, if it is a viable arrangement, the partners will work together to minimize or manage controversies in the community.

REPRESENTATIVE PUBLIC HEALTH INTERVENTIONS

While it is not possible to present a comprehensive listing of interventions, our objective here is to consider some representative programs that may serve as exemplars for some of the issues and principles that we have considered. The programs range from physical activity programs to programs such as the Experience Corps that places senior mentors in K–12 institutions and are designed to provide benefits for children as well as the seniors themselves. Finally, we will consider the significance of recommendations to enhance housing and transportation in the general population.

Physical Activity Programs

Physical activity programs are very promising (Burbank, Reibe, Padula, & Nigg, 2002; Conn, Minor, Burks, Rantz, & Pomeroy, 2003; van der Bij, Laurant, & Wensing, 2002). Research on healthy aging points to the significance of physical activity in the promotion of health and physical and cognitive functioning in the general elderly population as well as among older people who have been diagnosed and treated for a variety of chronic conditions. Exercise programs also have improved strength and balance and reduced the likelihood of falls and injuries. Finally, there are now programs that focus both on the individual and the characteristics of the physical environment. It is not enough to encourage older people to exercise; it is also necessary to provide settings that are safe and inviting. In addition to epidemiologic studies of the effects of physical activity, there are evaluations of intervention studies that provide evidence of the significance of this factor (Hoehner, Brennan, Brownson, Handy, & Killingsworth, 2002; Sallis, Bauman, & Pratt, 1998; Satariano, 1997; Stokols et al., 2002). In this way, physical activity programs represent an exemplar for public health interventions for older people that are based on the tenets of an ecological model (Satariano & McAuley, 2003).

There are very exciting results that indicate that it is possible to encourage older adults, even those with preexisting chronic disease, to participate in programs designed to promote physical activity (Jette, Lachman, Giorgetti, Assmann, Harris, Levenson, et al., 1999; King, Pruitt, Phillips, Oka, Rodenbrug, & Haskell, 2000; Stewart, Mills, Sepsis, King, McLellan, Roitz, et al., 1997). Stewart and colleagues (1997), for example, were able to show increased levels of physical activity in older adults through a program based on referrals to existing community classes and programs.

The Robert Wood Johnson (RWJ) Foundation has introduced a program, Active for Life, to assess the effectiveness of two well-established exercise programs to enhance physical activity among adults aged 55 years and older (Robert Wood Johnson, 2004). One program, Active Choices, was developed at Stanford University (Stanford University, 2004) and is an individualized program that includes regular telephone-based reinforcement. The second program, Active Living Everyday, developed at the Cooper Clinic in Dallas, Texas, is based on a group-based model (Cooper Clinic, 2004). The purpose of the RWJ Active for Life program is to introduce and evaluate these well-established programs in different community-based settings. Nine sites across the United States were selected to participate in the program. The sites include a health maintenance organization, a YMCA, community-based organizations, and church-based facilities. Each site selected one of the two programs as part of its proposal to the RWJ. The overall purpose of the Active for Life program is to determine what ways the intervention programs need to be adapted to be acceptable and feasible within diverse populations.

Physical activity programs also have been designed to meet the needs of older people who are recuperating from health problems and injuries (Ettinger & Afable, 1994). For example, a randomized trial examined the effects of exercise therapy on knee pain, functional limitations, and disability in older adults who had knee osteoarthritis (Rejeski, Brawley, Ettinger, Morgan, & Thompson, 1997). A total of 439 patients were randomly assigned to one of three arms of the study: health education control, aerobic exercise, or resistance exercise. The exercise therapy involved encouraging the participants to achieve a 3-month goal of 40 minutes of exercise performed 3 times each week. The exercise sessions were conducted in a structured center-based program for 3 months and then patients went to home-based training for another 15 months. Trained physical activity therapists used phone counseling to manage the home-based component. This counseling was tailored to each patient's needs and employed strategies such as problem solving, goal setting, self-monitoring, support, and reinforcement. Although both exercise conditions were successful when compared to the health education control group, participants in the aerobic exercise condition experienced the greatest reductions in knee pain and the most improvement on tests of physical performance and self-reported disability. Other studies of this population revealed that the effect of exercise therapy on change in physical performance scores was due to a reduction in pain and the enhancement of self-efficacy beliefs (Rejeski, Ettinger, Martin, & Morgan, 1998).

There is also evidence that a home-based exercise program can be quite effective in reaching older sedentary adults with some degree of physical disability (Jette et al., 1999). The program included cognitive and behavioral strategies designed to maximize participation and adherence. A randomized, controlled trial compared the effects of assigning 215 older persons to either a home-based resistance exercise training group or a waiting list control group. Assessments were conducted at baseline and at three and six months following randomization. The Strong-for-Life program consisted of a videotaped program of 11 exercise routines: an individualized exercise and strength plan; and subsequent home visits from a physical therapist. The results indicated that members of the experimental group improved significantly in measures of strength and function at three and six months. Improvements, although not statistically significant, were found for balance and mobility.

Physical exercise also has been included in a multifactorial intervention to reduce the risk of falling among older people living in the community (Tinetti, Baker, McAvay, Claus, Garrett, Cottschalk, et al., 1994). Subjects for this project included 301 male and female community residents aged 70 and older. These subjects had at least one of the following risk factors for falls and injuries: postural hypotension; use of sedatives; use of at least four prescription medications; and impairment in arm or leg strength or range of motion, balance, ability to move safely from bed to chair or to the bathtub or toilet (transfer skills), or gait. The subjects were randomly assigned to two treatment arms. Subjects in the experimental group were given a combination of adjustment in their medications, behavioral instructions, and exercise programs. Members of the control group, on the one hand, were given regular health care in addition to social visits. Over the course of a year, 35% of the intervention group fell, compared to 47% of the controls. It is reported that the multiple-risk factor intervention strategy resulted in a significant reduction in the risk of falling among elderly persons in the community. In addition, the proportion of persons who had targeted risk factors for falling was reduced in the intervention group, as compared with the control group.

Other studies have examined the effects of specific types of exercise programs. For example, the Frailty and Injuries: Cooperative Studies of Intervention Techniques (FICSIT) was designed to develop innovative strategies to improve frailty and reduce the risk of falls in older populations (Wolf, Barnhart, Kutner, NcNeely, Coogler, Xu, et al., 1996). Based on data from the Atlanta FICSIT, a study was conducted of the effects of two exercise approaches, tai chi and computerized balance training, on specified primary outcomes (biomedical, functional, and psychosocial indicators of frailty) and second outcomes (occurrence of falls). The results indicated that participation in a moderate tai chi program can improve a variety of health indicators, including blood pressure, fear of falling, and the risk of falling itself.

Social Involvement

Social engagement and involvement are important indicators of healthy aging. Those older people who have extensive friendship networks and participate in social and voluntary activities are in better health than those who are socially isolated (Seeman, 2000). There are a growing number of programs that are designed to increase the social involvement of older people. One of the most interesting is the Experience Corps (Glass, Freedman, Carlson, Hill, Frick, Ialongo, et al., 2004), a program sponsored by the Corporation for National Service, Johns Hopkins University and Public/Private Ventures, with funding from the Retirement Research Foundation. This program recruits older adults to serve on teams as volunteers in elementary schools. In addition to providing a more positive educational experience for children, it is hypothesized that volunteerism, or, as Glass and colleagues (2004) write, "generativity," may lead to positive health outcomes for the older volunteers through physical activity, social engagement, and cognitive stimulation. These mechanisms or pathways, in turn, could lead to positive health outcomes, such as enhanced global, physical, and cognitive functioning, quality of life, and reduced health care costs. Finally, it is argued that this program could enhance the general level of social capital in the community. Along these lines, Glass and colleagues (2004, p. 99) write:

> Experience Corps roles were designed to augment the effectiveness of paid staff and not to replace teachers or librarians. Otherwise, the presence of the program would place downward pressure on teacher salaries and would generate opposition from school professionals. In a policy climate in which volunteerism can justify retrenchment of school funding, Experience Corps has been crafted to ensure that volunteers play only adjuvant roles.

Although a full-scale evaluation of the program has not been conducted, Fried and colleagues (2004) have recently presented the results of a pilot study in Baltimore, Maryland. In this pilot study, 128 volunteers aged 60–86 years, 95% of whom were African-American, were assigned to ele-

mentary schools in the city. Pretest and posttest health indicators were compared between the experimental group of volunteers with an age-matched
control group. Over a 4- to 8-month period, the experimental group
demonstrated significantly higher health indicators than the control group.
These indictors included level of physical activity strength, cognitive activity, identification of a confidant, and walking speed. Fried and colleagues
concluded that the pilot study results suggest that the Experience Corps has
the potential "to improve health for an aging population and simultane-
ously improve the education outcomes for children" (Fried et al., 2004,
p. 64). The Experience Corps program holds great promise. In addition to
the potential health and educational benefits across generations, it may contribute to a redefinition of aging. Rather than viewing the aging population
as a social problem and a threat to the solvency of the Medicare and Social
Security programs, the Experience Corps is based on the proposition that
the aging population is a resource for society at large—perhaps, as some
have noted, our "only renewable national resource."

Land Use and the Associated Health Dividends

As we have seen, there are a number of programs that promote health, activity, and social engagement—factors that characterize healthy aging. There
are also programs, however, that may seem at first glance as not designed
specifically to promote health and functioning, but may clearly provide
"health dividends" (Cannuscio, Block, & Kawachi, 2003). Programs designed to promote better housing and transportation systems are based on a
reconsideration of the use of land—the physical and built environments.

Housing

Most older people in the United States live in adequate housing. Nearly
80% of people aged 55 and older own their own homes. Home equity
accounts for approximately 44% of the assets of older households.
Despite these positive reports, there are potential problems facing older
people. It is reported, for example, that large numbers of older people are
"burdened with high housing costs and are in urgent need of affordable
housing" (Pynoos, Matsuoka, & Liebig, 2001). In addition to the financial issues associated with affordability, there are also concerns about the
adequacy, accessibility, and appropriateness of housing for older adults. It
is reported, for example, that older adults tend to live in older homes that
were typically built before 1960. In addition to being in need of repair,
the accessibility and supportiveness of the housing become a significant

issue. Assistance is needed to help older people, especially low-income elderly, make basic improvements to ensure that their homes are safe and livable. Improvements are also required to ensure that basic activities of daily living can be achieved, in spite of the occupants' decline in physical and cognitive capacity. This may include modifications of lighting, expansion of doorways, installation of alternative appliances, fixtures, and grab bars. It is also recommended that "universal design" principles be incorporated in all new housing. Universal design is based on the proposition that all products and environments be functionally designed so that people with different levels of capacity can use them.

Cohousing or clustered housing represent an alternative to standard, single independent dwellings. Although the organization, design, and, in some cases, governance of these facilities differ, each includes some shared space. In some cases, the space may be a sitting room, a kitchen, or dining room. In other more elaborate village designs, the shared space may be a common house placed amid a cluster of separate homes. These facilities provide the opportunity for social interaction and engagement. Some facilities, in particular, are designed to facilitate intergenerational contact (McCamant, Durrett, & Hertzman, 1994). To our knowledge, there have been no systematic assessments of the extent to which this type of housing arrangement would facilitate social interaction among older residents of this type of area.

Assisted-living facilities represent another type of housing especially designed for older people who have special needs. These new facilities have been defined as a "residential long-term care alternative that involves the managed delivery of uniquely prescribed health and personal care services within a residential setting" (Regnier, Hamilton, & Yatable, 1995). Facilities may provide an important balance between independence and a supportive setting, which may, in turn, enhance health and functioning in older populations.

Together, these examples illustrate how recommendations for housing design may be incorporated into a broader public health agenda to promote health and well-being in older populations.

Transportation

Transportation and mobility are essential for everyday life, including access to goods and services and contacts with friends and relatives. The most common form of transportation in the United States, including among older people, is the automobile. With increasing age and associated declines in vision, physical, and cognitive functioning, the use of the private automobile becomes more difficult. As noted previously, the incidence of crashes, especially those involving lane changes and failure to yield the right of way, increases with chronological age. Crashes represent one of the leading causes of accidental death among older people. It is not surprising, therefore, that the use of automobiles declines with age. Although this may reduce the risk of the older person being involved in a crash, it may expose the older person to increased risk as a pedestrian. Other models of transportation, such as buses and vans, are underutilized and generally not considered to be as desirable. The overall result is a loss of mobility, less access to goods and services, and reduced contact with friends and relatives. This problem is especially pronounced in areas of low-density housing—the suburbs. Low-density residences are located some distance from stores and services, and wide streets, ending in cul-de-sacs, do not have sidewalks. As one commentator has written, contemporary suburban design isolates the very young and the very old (Calthorpe, 1993).

Proposals to reform the use of land space, with regard to both housing and transportation, may have important implications for promoting successful aging. City planners and environmentalists are calling for "smart growth" and "neotraditional" community designs for tomorrow's aging residents. These designs feature increased population densities, mixed land uses that place services and shopping in closer proximity to residences, grid street patterns and sidewalks, and more pedestrian-oriented design and activities (Wachs, 2001). This type of design also calls for the integration of "public space," such as parks, city halls, and governmental services, within private housing and commercial services.

Although there is a growing body of evidence that residents of high-density, multiuse areas are more likely to engage in physical activity, most notably, walking, there are still relatively few studies that have provided opportunities to examine age differences in activity across wide age spectrums. Nevertheless, the evidence to date suggests that this type of development is ideally suited for an aging population.

CONCLUSION

The translation of research into practice is one of the important tasks in aging and public health. It is not enough to conduct research and then assume that the findings can be simply applied to solve a public health problem or to enhance the health and well-being of a population. In this chapter, we outlined the utility of an ecological model for health promotion and disease prevention in the older population.

REFERENCES

Abrams, D. B., Orleans, C. T., Niaura, R. S., Goldstein, M. G., Prochaska, J. O., & Velier, W. (1996). Integrating individual and public health perspectives for treatment of tobacco dependence under managed health care: A combined stepped care and matching model. *Annals of Behavioral Medicine, 18,* 290–304.

Anetzberger, G. J. (2002). Community resources to promote successful aging. *Clinics in Geriatric Medicine, 18*(3), 611–625.

Antonovsky, A. (1979). *Health, stress, and coping.* San Francisco, CA: Jossey-Bass.

Best, A., Stokols, D., Green, L. W., Leischow, S., Holmes, B., & Buchholz, K. (2003). An integrative framework for community partnering to translate theory into effective health promotion strategy. *American Journal of Health Promotion, 18*(2), 168–176.

Briss, P. A., Brownson, R. C., Fielding, J. E., & Zaza, S. (2004). Developing and using the *Guide to Community Preventive Services:* Lessons learned about evidence-based public health. *Annual Review of Public Health, 25,* 281–302.

Briss, P. A., Zaza, S., Pappaioanou, M., Fielding, J., Wright-De Aguero, L., Truman, B. I., et al. (2001). Developing an evidence-based guide to community preventive services—methods. The Task Force on Community Preventive Services, *American Journal of Preventive Medicine, 18*(1 Suppl), 35–43.

Bruce, T. A., & McKane, S. U. (Eds.). (2000). *Community-based public health: A partnership model.* Washington, DC: American Public Health Association.

Burbank, P. M., Reibe, D., Padula, C. A., & Nigg, C. (2002). Exercise and older adults: Changing behavior with the transtheoretical model. *Orthopedic Nursing, 21*(4), 51–61.

Calthorpe, P. (1993). *The next american metropolis: Ecology, community, and the American dream.* New York: Princeton Architectural Press.

Cannuscio, C., Block, J., & Kawachi, I. (2003). Social capital and successful aging: The role of senior housing. *Annals of Internal Medicine, 139,* 395–399.

Committee on Health and Behavior. (2001). *Health and behavior: The interplay of biological, behavioral, and societal influences.* Washington, DC: National Academy Press.

Conn, V. S., Minor, M. A., Burks, K. J., Rantz, M. M., & Pomeroy, S. H. (2003). Integrative review of physical activity intervention research with aging adults. *Journal of the American Geriatrics Society, 51,* 1159–1168.

Cooper Clinic, Active Living Every Day Program, www.cooperinst.org., accessed December 12, 2004.

Douglas, M., Conway, L., Gorman, D., Gavin, S., & Hanolon, P. (2001). Developing principles for health impact assessment. *Journal of Public Health Medicine, 23*(2), 148–154.

Dzewaltowski, D. A., Glasgow, R. E., Klesges, L. M., Estabrooks, P. A., & Brock, E. (2004). RE-AIM: Evidence-based standards and a Web resource to improve translation of research into practice. *Annals of Behavioral Medicine, 28*(2), 75–80.

Emmons, K. M. (2000). Health behaviors in a social context. In L. F. Berkman & I. Kawachi (Eds.), *Social epidemiology.* New York: Oxford University Press, 242–266.

Ettinger, W. H. Jr., & Afable, R. F. (1994). Physical disability from knee osteoarthritis: The role of exercise as an intervention. *Medical Science Sports Exercise, 26(12),* 1435–1440.

Fried, L. P., Carlson, M. C., Freedman, M., Frick, K. D., Glass, T. A., Hill, J., et al. (2004). A social model for health promotion for an aging population: Initial evidence on the Experience Corps model. *Journal of Urban Health, 81*(1), 64–78.

Glasgow, R. E., McKay, H. G., Piette, J. D., & Reynolds, K. D. (2001). The RE-Aim framework for evaluating interventions: What can it tell us about approaches to chronic illness management? *Patient Education and Counseling, 44,* 119–127.

Glasgow, R. E., Vogt, T. M., & Boles, S. M. (1999). Evaluating the public health impact of health promotion interventions: The RE-AIM framework. *American Journal of Public Health, 89*(9), 1322–1327.

Glass, T. A., Freedman, M., Carlson, M. C., Hill, J., Frick, K. D., Ialongo, N., et al. (2004). Experience Corps: Design of an intergenerational program to boost social capital and promote the health of an aging society. *Journal of Urban Health, 81*(1), 94–105.

Hatch, S., & Kichbush, I. (Eds.). (1983). *Self-care and health in Europe: New approaches in health care.* Copenhagen, Denmark: World Health Organization.

Hazzard, W. R. (1997). Ways to make usual and successful aging synonymous. Preventive gerontology. *Western Journal of Medicine, 167*(4), 206–215.

Hoehner, C. M., Brennan, L. K., Brownson, R. C., Handy, S. L., & Killingsworth, R. (2002). Opportunities for integrating public health and urban planning approaches to promote active community environments. *American Journal of Health Promotion, 18*(1), 14–20.

Israel, B. A., Schulz, A. J., Parker, E. A., & Becker, A. B. (1998). Review of community-based research assessing partnership approaches to improve public health. *Annual Review of Public Health, 19,* 173–202.

Jette, A. M., Lachman, M., Giorgetti, M. M., Assmann, S. F., Harris, B. A., Levenson, C., et al. (1999). Exercise—It's never too late: The Strong-for-Life Program. *American Journal of Public Health, 89*(1), 66–72.

Kemm, J., Parry, J. & Palmer, S. (Eds.). (2004). *Health impact assessment: Concepts, theory, techniques, and applications.* New York: Oxford University Press.

King, A. C., Pruitt, L. A., Phillips, W., Oka, R., Rodenbrug, A., & Haskell, W. L. (2000). Comparative effects of two physical activity programs on measured and perceived physical functioning and other health-related quality of life outcomes on older adults. *Journals of Gerontology: Medical Sciences, 55*(2), M74–M83.

Konrad, T. D. (1998). The pattern of self-care among older adults in western industrialized societies. In M. G. Ory & G. H. DeFriese (Eds.), *Self-care in later life.* New York: Springer Publishers, 1–23.

Krieger, N., Northridge, M., Gruskin, S., Quinn, M., Kriebel, D., Smith, G. D., et al. (2003). Assessing health impact assessment: Multidisciplinary and international perspectives. *Journal of Epidemiology and Community Health, 57,* 659–662.

Kuh, D., & Ben-Shlomo, Y. (Eds.). (2004). *A life course approach to chronic disease epidemiology,* 2nd ed. New York: Oxford University Press.

Leung, M. W., Yen, I. H., & Minkler, M. (2004). Community-based participatory research: A promising approach for increasing epidemiology's relevance in the 21st century. *International Journal of Epidemiology, 33,* 499–506.

McCamant, K., Durrett C., & Hertzman E. (1994). *Cohousing: A contemporary approach to housing ourselves.* Berkeley, CA: Ten Speed Press.

McKinlay, J. (1995). The new public health approach to improving physical activity and autonomy in older populations. In E. Heikkinen, J. Kuusinen, & I. Ruoppola (Eds.), *Preparing for aging.* New York: Plenum Press.

Omenn, G. S., Beresford, S. A. A., Buchner, D. M., LaCroix, A., Martin, M., Patrick, D. L., et al. (1997). In T. Hickey, M. A. Speers, & T. R. Prohaska (Eds.), *Public health and aging.* Baltimore, MD: Johns Hopkins University Press, 107–127.

Prochaska, J. O., & DiClemente, C. C. (1983). Stages and processes of self-change of smoking: Toward an integrative model. *Journal of Consulting and Clinical Psychology, 51*(3), 390–395.

Prohaska, T. (1998). The research basis for the design and implementation of self-care programs. In M. G. Ory & G. H. DeFriese (Eds.), *Self-care in later life.* New York: Springer Publishers, 62–84.

Pynoos, J., Matsuoka, C., & Liebig, P. (2001). *Housing for older Californians.* California Policy Research Center Brief, University of California, Strategic Planning on Aging, No. 5, May 2001.

Rakowski, W. (1998). Evaluating psychosocial interventions for promoting self-care behaviors among older adults. In M. G. Ory & G. H. DeFriese (Eds.), *Self-care in later life.* New York: Springer Publishers, 85–117.

Regnier, V., Hamilton, J., & Yatable, S. (1995). *Assisted living for the aged and frail.* New York: Columbia University Press.

Rejeski, W. J., Brawley, L. R., Ettinger, W., Morgan, T., & Thompson, C. (1997). Compliance to exercise therapy in older participants with knee osteoarthritis: Implications for treating disability. *Medical Science Sports Exercise, 29*(8), 977–985.

Rejeski, W. J., Ettinger, W. H. Jr., Martin, K., & Morgan, T. (1998). Treating disability in knee osteoarthritis with exercise therapy: A central role for self-efficacy and pain. *Arthritis Care Research, 11*(2), 94–101.

Robert Wood Johnson Foundation Active for Life Program, www.activeforlife. org, accessed December 12, 2004.

Rose, G. (1985). Sick individuals and sick populations. *International Journal of Epidemiology, 14,* 32–38.

Sallis, J. F., Bauman, A., & Pratt, M. (1998). Environmental and policy interventions to promote physical activity. *American Journal of Preventive Medicine, 15*(4), 379–397.

Satariano, W. A. (1997). The disabilities of aging—looking to the physical environment. [Editorial]. *American Journal of Public Health, 87*(3), 331–332.

Satariano, W. A., & McAuley, E. (2003). Promoting physical activity among older adults: From ecology to the individual. *American Journal of Preventive Medicine, 25*(3sii), 184–192.

Seeman, T. E. (2000). Health promoting effects of friends and family on health outcomes in older adults. *American Journal of Health Promotion, 14*(6), 362–370.

Smedley, B. D., & Syme, S. L. (Eds.). (2000). *Promoting health: Intervention strategies from social and behavioral research.* Washington, DC: National Academy Press.

Stanford University, Prevention Sciences, Active Choices. Retrieved December 12, 2004 from www.prevention,stanford.edu.

Stewart, A. L., Mills, K. M., Sepsis, P. G., King, A. C., McLellan, B. Y., Roitz, K., et al. (1997). Evaluation of CHAMPS, a physical activity promotion program for older adults. *Annals of Behavioral Medicine, 19*(4), 353–361.

Stokols, D., Grzywacz, J. G., McMahan, S., & Phillips, K. (2002). Increasing the health promotive capacity of human environments. *American Journal of Health Promotion, 18*(1), 4–13.

Stoller, E. P. (1998). Dynamics and processes of self care in old age. In M. G. Ory & G. H. DeFriese (Eds.), *Self-care in later life.* New York: Springer Publishers, 24–61.

Syme, S. L. (1998). Social and economic disparities in health: Thoughts about intervention. *The Milbank Quarterly, 76,* 493–505.

Syme, S. L. (2003). Psychosocial interventions to improve successful aging. *Annals of Internal Medicine, 139,* 400–402.

Timiras, P. S. (Ed.). (2003). *Physiological basis of aging and geriatrics,* 3rd ed. Boca Raton, FL: CRC Publishers.

Tinetti, M. E., Baker, D. I., McAvay, G., Claus, E. B., Garrett, P., Cottschalk, M., et al. (1994). A multifactorial intervention to reduce the risk of falling among elderly people living in the community. *The New England Journal of Medicine, 331*(13), 821–827.

Toobert, D. J., Strycker, L. A., Glasgow, R. E., Barrera, M., & Bagdade, J. D. (2002). Enhancing support for health behavior change among women at risk for heart disease: The Mediterranean Lifestyle Trial. *Health Education Research, 17*(5), 574–585.

Truman, B. I., Smith-Akin, C. K., Hinman, A. R., Gebbie, K. M., Brownson, R., Novick, L. F., et al. (2000). Developing the *Guide to Community Preventive*

Services—Overview and rationale. *American Journal of Preventive Medicine,* *18*(1S), 18–26.

Van der Bij, A. K., Laurant, M. G. H., & Wensing, M. (2002). Effectiveness of physical activity interventions for older adults: A review. *American Journal of Preventive Medicine, 22*(2), 120–133.

Wachs, M. (2001). *Mobility, travel, and aging in California.* (California Policy Research Center Brief, Strategic Planning on Aging, No. 6), University of California Policy Research Center.

Wolf, S. L., Barnhart, H. X., Kutner, N. G., NcNeely, E., Coogler, C., Xu, T., et al. (1996). Reducing fraility and falls in older persons: An investigation of Tai chi and computerized balance training. *Journal of the American Geriatrics Society, 44,* 489–497.

CHAPTER 12

New Directions for Research and Policy

The aging of human populations, as we noted in Chapter 1, represents one of the most significant scientific and public policy issues facing society (Koplan & Fleming, 2000). It is not only the increase in the sheer number of older people that has focused scientific and public attention; it is their current and future levels of health and vitality. The main question is whether this increase in the proportion of older people will necessarily result in an increase in the prevalence of disease and disability. Research in the epidemiology of aging has contributed significantly to addressing this question—both in terms of how the question should be posed and how it should be answered. In this chapter, we will summarize from our previous discussion the important findings from the epidemiology of aging. What do we know and how do we know it? This, in turn, will set the stage for the next set of questions: Where do we go from here? What are the promising areas of research; and, what approaches and methods are being developed to investigate these areas and, it is hoped, answer the new questions (Morley, 2004; National Institute on Aging, 2001)?

Earlier, I argued that an ecological model is well suited for the study of the epidemiology of aging. In addition to providing a lens for viewing the current scope of research in this field, it also identifies the spatial and temporal points of intersection among biologic, behavioral, social, and environmental factors. The most exciting and challenging areas of research, practice, and policy are found at those points of intersection.

THE EPIDEMIOLOGY OF AGING: A REVIEW

It is well known that the incidence and prevalence of disease and disability increase with advancing age. What is less well known is that the incidence and prevalence of disease and disability vary among people of the same age. Epidemiologic research has contributed significantly to our understanding of this heterogeneity. In many ways, this has been one of the most notable contributions to the field—our understanding of aging, health, and longevity. It has refined our consideration of the expansion and compression of morbidity hypotheses, described in Chapter 1. As we noted earlier, those hypotheses have served to join the debate about what the future may hold. Will the aging of the population result in a dramatic increase in the incidence and prevalence rates of disease and disability, will the rates remain generally the same, or will there be a general improvement in those indicators of health and disability? Although there is a growing body of research that suggests the prevalence rates of functional limitations (defined in different ways) are lower among current cohorts of older people than in past cohorts, epidemiologic research has demonstrated significant differences in health and functioning among people of the same age. These differences, in turn, are associated with other factors, such as gender, race, ethnicity, and socioeconomics status; living arrangements and psychosocial factors; the number and types of health conditions; and specific behaviors, such as tobacco exposure, diet and nutrition, and physical activity.

As noted in Chapter 1, the following questions serve as the basis for epidemiologic research in this area:

1. What is the overall distribution of the health outcome in the population, such as number and types of disease, levels of functioning, disability, and survival?
2. To what extent do differences between and within age groups vary by gender, race and ethnicity, and socioeconomic status? One example of the difference between groups is the age of the onset of a particular condition.
3. To what extent do differences between and within age groups vary by other factors associated with health, functioning, behavior, social factors, and the physical environment? Although these factors are important in their own right, they also serve to explain the associa-

tions between health outcomes and age, gender, race and ethnicity, and socioeconomic status.

4. To what extent are differences between and within age groups associated with age differences in: (a) the prevalence of the same risk factors; (b) the salience or strength of the same risk factors; (c) the frequency and timing of exposure in the life course to the same risk factors; and (d) exposure to a different set of risk factors?

5. What are the biologic, behavioral, social, and environmental factors associated with maintenance of health and functioning among older people, or so-called healthy aging? Special attention should be given to those older people who maintain health and functioning, in spite of a risk-factor profile that would elevate their risk for disease, disability, and death.

An ecological model is being used increasingly in epidemiology and public health to promote a multidisciplinary, integrated research and practice agenda (Stokols, 1996). Following *Healthy People 2010* and other governmental and foundation reports (Committee on Health and Behavior: Research, Practice, and Policy, 2001; Smedley & Syme, 2000; United States Department of Health and Human Services, 2000), the ecological model is based on the premise that differences in health, vitality, and longevity are associated with the interplay of biologic, behavioral, social, and environmental factors. This multilevel interaction, in turn, unfolds over the life course of individuals, families, neighborhoods, and communities. In addition to serving as a model for research, the ecological model also identifies multiple points of possible intervention in public health, from the microbiologic to the environmental levels, to postpone the risk of disease, disability, and death; and enhance the chances for health, mobility, and longevity. The ecological model is particularly well suited to examine the epidemiology of aging. It incorporates the importance of human development over the life course, the association between physiological capacity and adaptation to the environment, and is consistent with other models that are used in epidemiologic and gerontological studies, such as Lawton's Environment and Aging Model (1980) and Verbrugge and Jette's Disablement Model (1994).

The association between aging and longevity, meaning duration of life, varies by geographic area, gender, race and ethnicity, and socioeconomic status. Although there are more older people alive today than any other time in history, the percentage of people aged 65 years and older varies around the world. The greatest percentage is found in so-called developed countries, but the greatest recent, percentage increase in the elderly population is found in the developing countries. Women live longer than men, but gender differences in life expectancy become less pronounced with increasing age. Similar findings are also found between African-American and non-Hispanic white populations, especially among men. The age-specific differences in survival, in the general population and among those diagnosed with specific conditions, are most pronounced among those in their middle years. One hypothesis is that the middle years represent an important watershed, a time in which there is an intersection between reduced physiological resistance and the accumulation of social and environmental insults. African-Americans and those of lower socioeconomic status who survive beyond their middle years may have a subsequent life expectancy that is comparable to that found for non-Hispanic whites and those of higher socioeconomic status. Although there is a fairly consistent finding, there is very little information about the extent to which these racial, ethnic, and socioeconomic differences are due to age, period, or cohort effects.

The number and types of health conditions (comorbidity) are associated with reduced longevity. Leading conditions associated with an elevated risk of death in the elderly include coronary heart disease, stroke, cancer, chronic obstructive pulmonary disease, and diabetes. The risk of death increases significantly among older people who have multiple, comorbid conditions. Presently, there is relatively little specific information that explains the effects of multiple, comorbid conditions. There is also an absence of information on the factors that cause comorbid conditions to occur.

The risk of premature death is increased with a history of particular types of behavior, such as history of tobacco exposure, poor nutrition, and physical inactivity. Again, however, the strength of this association between behavior and vital status tends to decline with increasing age. This suggests that there is an "age-associated window" associated with the salience of particular types of health behaviors. There is some evidence to suggest that particular types of behavior tend to cluster, meaning people who engage in one form of behavior are likely to engage in other types of behavior. Despite evidence of these behavioral clusters, there is very little research on how they vary by age.

Living arrangements and psychosocial factors are associated with an elevated risk of death. Social isolation, measured in terms of living arrangements with others, is associated with a risk of death for men and women. An absence of self-efficacy is also associated with ill health.

Functional limitations, both physical and cognitive, are independently associated with reduced longevity. Functioning is defined as the relative ease in the performance of tasks that are necessary for independence and mobility in everyday life. Functional measures may vary from basic, generic tasks such as reported difficulty in lifting items, to complicated, integrated activities, such as occupational and voluntary activities or driving a car.

Although aging is associated with reports of functional limitations, there is considerable variation by gender, race and ethnicity, and socioeconomic status. Unlike the findings for longevity, women are more likely than men to report functional limitations. This finding is most evident in studies of active life expectancy. Women live longer, but a greater proportion of their later years are spent in states of functional limitation and disability. Studies of racial, ethnic, and socioeconomic differences, however, are similar to that found in studies of longevity and survival. For example, African-American and Latino elders are more likely than non-Hispanic white elders to report functional limitations and disabilities. There is relatively little information about other racial and ethnic groups, most notably the various Asian ethnic groups, such as Chinese, Vietnamese, and Japanese elders.

The risks of functional limitations and disabilities are associated with the number and types of chronic health conditions. In most cases, the chronic conditions that elevate the risk of death also increase the likelihood for functional limitations and disabilities. These conditions include coronary heart disease, cerebrovascular disease, cancer, and chronic obstructive lung disease. In addition, there are conditions that are not necessarily lethal that can cause functional difficulties and disabilities. These disabling conditions include osteoarthritis, osteoporosis, cataracts, and macular degeneration. Like the results for studies of longevity, the presence of multiple conditions can elevate the risk of limitations and disabilities. Moreover, research indicates that specific combinations of conditions can have a multiplicative effect on the risk of limitations and disabilities.

Limitations in areas of physical performance, such as reduced lower-body strength, often precede reports of functional limitations and are indicative of "preclinical disability." Preclinical disability refers to a stage in which a person's functional limitations, as measured typically by tests of physical performance, do not interfere with his or her everyday responsibilities. Over time, however, people with pre-clinical disability are at elevated risk for developing frank disability. There are different explanations. The limitations may simply not be apparent, or the person may compensate for limitations by modifying the manner or timing in which he or she performs specific tasks or jobs.

The transition from functional limitations to disabilities is due to a variety of behavioral, social, and physical environmental factors. Research in this area is increasingly based on a "disablement model." The model assumes that the likelihood and timing of the transitions from one state to another are not only affected by characteristics of the index diseases (e.g., the type and severity of the condition), but also by characteristics of the person (e.g., age, gender, race, ethnicity); history of other health conditions (i.e., comorbidities); past and current health behaviors (e.g., tobacco exposure and level of physical exercise); social factors (e.g., living arrangements, social networks, and social support); and the characteristics of the physical environment (e.g., characteristics of the built environment). It should be noted that commentators have argued that the disablement model should not be restricted to processes that are initiated by a pathological condition. Age-related, physiological processes, such as reduced lung function, also can initiate the disablement process independently or in conjunction with pathological factors. In general, the model specifies a broad array of physiological, clinical, social, and environmental variables that interact over time to affect the process of disablement. In many ways, the disablement model represents a specific application of the more integrated ecological model. Moreover, there is clear evidence that aging is not associated with an inevitable and constant decline in functional vitality. Instead, there are patterns of functioning, decline, and recuperation.

Depression and anxiety are common in older populations, especially among women. There is also evidence that psychiatric disorders are more likely to be found in African-American and Latino elders than non-Hispanic elders. The prevalence of these conditions is also likely to co-occur with other physical and cognitive difficulties. Indeed, in some cases, it is difficult to distinguish between depression and cognitive dysfunction.

Aging is associated with the risk of falls, injuries, and automobile crashes. The etiology of falls is found to vary in older populations. Frailty, a geriatric syndrome, characterized by reduced walking speed and upper- and lower strength, fatigue, and weight loss, elevates the risk of falls in the home. In contrast, physically active older people are more likely to fall outside the home. The nature of the built environment, such as clutter and poor lighting, has been associated with the risk of falls. In fact, more attention has been given to the built environment in the study of falls than in any other. There is a bimodal association between aging and the risk of traffic injury. Along with drivers in their teens and twenties, people 65 years and older are at elevated risk of automobile crashes. Although older people tend to monitor their driving by restricting it to particular times and places, they are still at elevated risk of accidents, especially accidents in which they are the cause. In most cases, older drivers are involved in multiple car accidents that are often due to improper lane changes. Aging is also associated with the risk of pedestrian injury. Not surprisingly, when the force of the trauma is held constant, whether the trauma refers to a fall, injury, or crash, older people are more likely than younger people to suffer ill effects. In general, older people, because of reduced physiological resistance, are more vulnerable to trauma than younger people.

Most of the research on the epidemiology of chronic conditions has been based on middle-aged populations. There is a growing appreciation, however, that the etiology of specific diseases may differ depending on age at onset. The risk factors for conditions that occur in the early and middle years may be different from the factors associated with late-onset conditions. For example, the risk factors for early (premenopausal) and late (postmenopausal) breast cancer are different. Obesity, for example, is more likely to be associated with the risk of postmenopausal breast cancer than with the risk of premenopausal breast cancer. There is also evidence that the risk factors for early- and late-onset diabetes (type 1 and type 2) are different. Although there are differences across conditions, tobacco exposure and physical inactivity are associated with conditions, regardless of the timing of the onset of those conditions.

Although the epidemiology of aging typically focuses on the senior years, there is a growing appreciation that patterns of health and functioning in the later years are affected by conditions, behaviors, and events that took place much earlier in life. The study of aging is increasingly being placed into a broader context of human development. For example, there is a growing interest in the role of genetic factors in the risk of disease in older populations. Interestingly, in the past, genetic factors were likely to be implicated almost exclusively in the risk of conditions that occur early in life. Presently, APOE-4 allele has been implicated in the etiologies of both cardiovascular disease and Alzheimer's disease in older populations.

Geriatric syndromes, such as frailty and urinary incontinence, are associated with, but distinct from, comorbidity and disability. It is hypothesized that there may be different forms of frailty. Some forms of frailty may result from the occurrence of specific conditions, while others may occur independently of distinct chronic conditions and be associated with a constellation of physiologic factors associated with aging.

Older people who are physically active, socially connected, and maintain a reasonable body weight, are more likely than others to avoid chronic conditions and disability. Research on healthy aging is providing a foundation for clinical and public health programs to postpone disease and disability and enhance the likelihood of functional independence and mobility.

NEW DIRECTIONS FOR RESEARCH AND POLICY

Although there is a growing body of research in the epidemiology of aging, there are a number of unanswered questions. In this section, we will review some new directions for research. These recommendations are based, in part, on recent reports issued by the National Institutes of Health, the Institutes of Medicine, and other organizations, such as the Robert Wood Johnson Foundation (Bulatao & Anderson, 2004; Committee on Health & Behavior, 2001; Morley, 2004; National Institute on Aging, 2001; Smedley & Syme, 2000).

Given that many governmental and private organizations and committees have highlighted the utility of the ecological model, it is reasonable to believe that it will continue to serve as a useful framework for future research in the epidemiology of aging and for the translation of that research into aging practice and policy.

Research Objectives

1. The epidemiology of aging should be viewed from a global perspective. The aging of the human population, as noted previously, is not restricted to the so-called developed nations. In fact, although the percentage of people over the age of 65 years is

greater in the developed nations, the increase in the percentage of people over the age of 65 years is increasing more rapidly today in the developing world than previously occurred in the developed nations. Not only do these trends have important implications for understanding the mechanisms of population aging, but also for all aspects of contemporary life. It will be impossible to understand fully the global economic and political issues without an appreciation of the aging of the world population. This is a critical area of research.

2. The causes and consequences of health disparities in aging populations must be a priority in epidemiologic and public health research. Indeed, the identification and elimination of health disparities have been identified as guiding principles of *Healthy People 2010*. Because health disparities in the United States and elsewhere are associated with race, ethnicity, and socioeconomic status, it is important to undertake systematic research in this area. In 2004, the National Academy of Sciences published an excellent report, *Understanding Racial and Ethnic Differences in Health in Late Life: A Research Agenda* (Bulatao & Anderson, 2004). The report includes 18 research recommendations. These recommendations include the need to clarify and explain racial and ethnic differences in mortality and morbidity across the life course, and will involve an examination of the interaction of biologic, behavioral, social, and environmental factors. Special attention will be given to the role of socioeconomic status.

3. The epidemiology of aging should incorporate a life-course approach to understand patterns of aging, health, functioning, disability, and mortality (Dannefer, 2003; Kuh & Ben-Shlomo, 2004; Longino, 2003). This approach will include research to understand the interplay between (a) age, period, and cohort effects at the level of the population with (b) the process of human development at the level of the individual. This should help to clarify the factors associated with the timing of both onset, course, and transitions of health conditions, impairments, limitations, disabilities, and mortality of aging populations. It is necessary to have a clearer idea of the extent to which behaviors and exposures in childhood and adolescence affect the risk of subsequent health conditions, limitations, and disabilities. There is a current epi-

demic of childhood obesity. It is critical to understand the implications of this current epidemic for future levels of health and well-being as this cohort of children ages. Can we expect, for example, that the high prevalence of childhood obesity will elevate the risk of subsequent health problems and functional limitations? Although we might expect that childhood obesity will contribute to premature mortality, it is also important to consider to what extent childhood obesity will contribute to the prevalence of ill health and disabilities as members of that cohort enter their senior years.

4. The genetic epidemiology of aging also needs to be developed. It will be necessary to examine in particular to what extent specific forms of behavior, social, and environmental factors give expression to those genetic factors. Along these lines, the APOE-4 allele has been receiving attention. As noted previously, it is shown to be associated with late-onset Alzheimer's disease and cardiovascular disease. Research in this area should continue.

5. More attention needs to be given to the biologic mechanism associated with patterns of aging, health, and functioning. One of the most promising areas of research has focused on "allostasis" and "allostatic load" (McEwen & Seeman, 1999). It is necessary to refine this concept and ensure that the data that are necessary to assess allostasis are obtained. As a summary measure of physiologic adaptation, allostasis may represent a key biologic component in the ecological model (Satariano & McAuley, 2003).

6. The prognostic significance of patterns of health behaviors needs to be examined. Presently, research concentrates on such specific forms of behavior as physical activity, diet and nutrition, or alcohol consumption. Research is needed to determine the mechanisms for the health effects of physical activity. To what extent does physical activity enhance pulmonary function, lean body mass, and metabolic function? It is also necessary to determine the metabolic changes and nutrient needs of older populations (Wakimoto & Block, 2001). More research is needed to examine the health effects of specific patterns of health behavior. For example, Berrigan and colleagues (2003) examined the patterns of health behavior in a national sample of adults. It may be that a clearer picture of the behavioral etiology of health conditions will

be obtained by examining current and past combinations of health behaviors than would be the case by examining the independent effects of a specific health behavior, such as diet and nutrition, while holding the other factors constant.

7. Research on the nature and effects of the physical environment on health and well-being in older populations should be expanded. As noted previously, the physical environment is a general term that includes the natural environment, such as weather patterns and land topography; the built environment, such as land use patterns, housing, and transportation systems; and the level of chemical and toxic exposures. There are a growing number of studies that have underscored the significance of place. For example, such measures of the built environment as land use patterns should be expanded and refined to better capture the extent to which the environment affects patterns of walking, physical activity, and functioning in older populations. It will be worthwhile to consider multiple methods of assessment that will include geographic information systems, environmental audits, and self-reports (Rushton, Elmes, & McMaster, 2000). Self-reports will provide an opportunity for older people to evaluate the "walkability" of neighborhoods as well as evaluations of whether their interactions with others in the neighborhood are characterized by trust and reciprocity, both of which are elements of social capital that may affect whether older people feel comfortable walking in particular areas. It also will be necessary for future researchers to take stock of the volume of environmental data that are being collected. Although great strides have been made in the collection of environmental data, it is fair to say that less attention has been given to criteria for summarizing the data into meaningful descriptive and analytical categories, especially with an eye toward understanding the mechanisms associated with characteristics of the built environment and the type and frequency of physical activity. Attention also should be directed to research on the etiological effects of chemical and toxic exposures over the life course on health, functioning, and longevity in older populations. As noted previously, much of the work in this area has focused on infants, children, and workers. Less attention, however, has been given to the elderly. In addition to increased physiologic vulnerability to chemicals, older

people, in many cases, may have experienced a more sustained exposure to those chemicals. Understanding the long-term effects of these exposures on patterns of health and functioning should be a public health objective. The US Environmental Protection Agency has introduced a new initiative in this area. This initiative should be sustained by governmental research funding and coupled with a broader agenda that includes elements of the natural and built environments noted previously. This work, in turn, will help to expand research on "healthy communities."

8. Research on living arrangements, social networks, and social support should be continued (Committee on Health and Behavior, 2001). Rather than focusing exclusively on individuals' reports of social networks and social supports, research should examine the networks themselves. This will involve the collection of information from members of specific networks rather than focusing only on random samples of unrelated individuals. Work in this area should include an examination of the interaction among spouses and partners. For example, it will be useful to determine whether a decline in the health and functioning of one partner or spouse has a negative effect on the health and functioning of the other partner or spouse. There is evidence to suggest that the prevalence of depression tends to cluster among spouses. It would be useful to pursue this work in more detail and identify the possible mechanisms that account for this concordance among pairs of spouses. Work in this area will contribute significantly to research, practice, and policies involving caregiving.

9. There is a need to continue to conduct research on the epidemiology of aging and leading infectious and chronic conditions. Given the global burden of disease associated with cardiovascular disease and diabetes, research should focus on those conditions, with a special focus on age-related factors associated with their onset and course. Other conditions that have been identified for future research studies include Alzheimer's disease, human immunodeficiency virus/acquired immune deficiency syndrome, and severe acute respiratory syndrome, as well as the leading cancers, such as female breast, colon, and prostate. Research on the age-related natural histories of those cancers will contribute to the development of more effective strategies for cancer screening.

10. Research on multiple morbidities and comorbid conditions should continue (Gijsen, Hoeymans, Schellevis, Ruwaard, Satariano, & van den Bos, 2001). As noted previously, older people are not only at elevated risk for single conditions, but for multiple conditions as well. The term multiple morbidities refers to the causes and consequences of combinations of health conditions. Comorbidity, a subset of multiple morbidities, refers to the presence of one or more health conditions occurring among people diagnosed with a single, index condition (Satariano & Silliman, 2003). Most of the research in this area has focused on specific diagnosed conditions. With an increase in information on preclinical conditions, it has been recommended that measures of multiple morbidity and comorbidity be expanded to include them as subjects of investigation as well. Moreover, it is argued that the joint effects of specific combinations of impairments and functional limitations be included as well. What these approaches seem to have in common is an appreciation of the value of examining multiple conditions rather than focusing exclusively on single, categorical conditions, while holding other conditions and factors constant. As noted previously, because most research has focused on the effects of comorbidity and multiple morbidities, more attention should be devoted to the causes of multiple morbidities and comorbidities (Gijsen et al., 2001). Summary measures are often used in research in this area. It is recommended, therefore, that more attention be given to the study of specific combinations of conditions and the manner in which those combinations change over time. Finally, as noted previously, there are two bodies of research on comorbidity. One area of research comes from psychiatry and focuses exclusively on conditions in that area, for example, the co-occurrence of depression and general anxiety disorder. The other area of research is based in medicine and public health and focuses almost exclusively on physical conditions. It has been recommended that these research traditions be merged with an examination of the multiple and concurrent psychiatric and physical conditions.

11. Research on geriatric conditions should be expanded. Geriatric syndromes refer to complex health and behavioral profiles. Typical geriatric syndromes include urinary incontinence, sarcopenia, and

falls and injuries. New research in this area should include an examination of the causes, timing, and course of specific syndromes, as well as specific combinations of syndromes.

12. There should be an expansion of research on the extent to which technology affects functioning in older populations and, in particular, the extent to which technology affects the relationship between functional capacities on the one hand and environmental demands on the other. One specific area of attention has been and should continue to be the use of different modes of transportation and, in particular, the private automobile. Although the automobile enables elderly residents to have contact with friends and relatives and access to goods and services, automobile crashes involving older drivers is a topic of public concern. There is a need to combine human factors research with epidemiologic research to better understand to what extent specific features of different automobile models and street and roadway design serve to ether enhance or impede driving performance and functioning (Rizzo, McGehee, Dawson, & Anderson, 2001). Comparable research should be introduced to examine other forms of everyday technologies as well. Research of this kind, for example, studying technologies that affect the completion of everyday tasks, communication, and personal computing, may lead to a new generation of products. Research focusing on "elder tech" should be encouraged.

13. Following research on healthy aging and salutogenesis, there is a need to expand research to examine the independent and joint effects on biologic, behavioral, social, and environmental factors that contribute to resiliency, disease resistance, and wellness. Research of this kind will be quite valuable for understanding better those older people who age well, including centenarians, as well as the development of new preventive strategies for older populations.

Research Infrastructure

1. One of the most challenging tasks in the epidemiology of aging is to identify and recruit older people to participate in research studies. As noted previously, there are many barriers associated with the participation of older people in studies of this kind. A comparison of the strengths and limitations of alternative strategies for participant identification, recruitment, and retention of older subjects in longi-

tudinal studies needs to be conducted. In addition, national and international organizations, both private and governmental, need to support the development of coordinated systems of longitudinal studies to serve as resources for the study of health, vitality, and longevity in aging populations. There is also a need to investigate such outcomes across the life course. There is a growing appreciation, as noted previously, that studies of aging need to be expanded to be studies of human development across the life course. This approach will require new methods and strategies to assess time. Presently, the timing of interviews and assessments of subjects are somewhat arbitrary, for example, every six months to a year. These time periods are almost exclusively established by investigators. In the future, it will be worthwhile to consider strategies to enable subjects to determine the timing of assessments. For example, subjects may be instructed to record significant events, e.g., behavioral changes or the timing of particular exposures, when they occur. The records may be maintained by a health diary, a handheld tape machine, or calling a toll-free telephone number. Researchers also have developed procedures to measure change between the established time periods for assessments. For example, researchers affiliated with the Women's Health and Aging Study selected a sample of subjects from the larger study cohort (Mendes de Leon, Guralnik, & Bandeen-Roche, 2002). Members of the smaller sample were interviewed on a more regular basis than members of the larger cohort. This "nested" longitudinal study provided some important information about changes in function that may have occurred for the larger sample during the periods between the regular assessments.

As noted previously, one of the important recruitment issues is compensation for participation in studies of this kind. There is some controversy about the form of that compensation. Although money is often considered the most appropriate and readily quantifiable form of compensation, others disagree. This is a very important and very difficult issue. It is recommended that expert panels, consisting of both researchers and members of the general public, be convened to address this issue in more detail. Likewise, the related and more general issue of protecting human subjects needs to be revisited. There is no question that the rights of older participants must be protected. Participants should never feel coerced into participating in a study. Medical care or other regular services should never depend on the willingness of people to participate or continue to participate in a research study. There is growing debate, however, about the criteria for assessing whether older people should be approached to participate and whether the older person should be the final arbitrator of whether he or she should participate. In addition to a consideration of safeguards to protect people from harm resulting from participation in a study, it is also necessary that we focus attention on the ethical implications of not conducting research.

2. Efforts should be made to establish a common protocol of core items for epidemiologic studies of aging, health, and functioning. In the United States, the National Institute on Aging-supported Established Populations for Epidemiologic Studies of the Elderly were instrumental in the development of a protocol that included both self-reported and direct measures of physical functioning and physical performance. This should serve as a model for the development of a protocol that reflects current research in this area. For example, increasingly, home interviews and field assessments are being supplemented with laboratory assessments that include more detailed assessments for cognitive and physical functioning, such as those obtained through detailed assessments of pulmonary function and fitness. In some cases, biologic specimens, such as obtained through a blood draw, are being obtained to establish DNA banks. With growing attention being given to cognitive functioning, it may be possible in the future to incorporate neuroimaging assessment, especially of the prefrontal cortex, to obtain more complete information on anatomical and functional measurements of brain aging. In addition, technological devices, such as accelerometers to capture distance traveled on foot and global positioning system devices to assess locations traveled, will provide a more complete picture of how people use the physical environment. This will be valuable for studies of behavior, health, and functioning in older populations. Special studies are needed to assess the most feasible ways to incorporate these data into a standard protocol for epidemiologic studies in older populations.

It is also necessary to develop better methods of simulation of behavior in particular environmental settings. Presently, automobile driving simulators represent the most sophisticated methods of simulating activity (Rizzo et al., 2001). It will be useful to determine whether other simulators can be developed so that behavioral patterns can be examined in more controlled settings. In addition to these devices, it is necessary to determine how the ethnographic methods that are used in anthropology to obtain qualitative data of human interaction can be incorporated into the design of large population studies, perhaps in the form of more detailed studies nested within larger population cohorts.

3. Research on clinical trial design and methods should be conducted. The clinical trial remains the most definitive method to evaluate the effects of different interventions on health and functional outcomes. There is concern, however, that efforts to improve the internal validity of the study, for example, the recruitment of a sample of a healthy population of seniors to avoid possible health bias, may erode the external validity of the study, for example, the extent to which the results of a clinical trial based on a senior sample without competing health conditions can be generalized to the larger older population that often suffers from multiple health conditions. Along these lines, the Interventions on Frailty Working Group (Ferrucci, Guralnik, Studenski, Fried, Cultler, Waltson, 2004, p. 625) developed the following recommendations to screen, recruit, evaluate, and retain frail older persons in clinical trials:

a. Eligibility screening should include a multistage process to quickly exclude those who are doing too well and those who are too sick.

b. Inclusion criteria should target those most likely to benefit, be meaningful to clinicians, and reflect advancements in the frailty research area.

c. Disability outcome measures should include self-reported, objective, and proxy measures. Strategies to improve retention and compliance and to monitor their effectiveness should be an integral part of the study design.

d. Estimation of cost and sample size should contemplate high dropout rates and interference by competing outcomes.

In addition to these points, it has also been recommended that traditional clinical designs be modified to accommodate people with different levels of comorbidity and functional capacity (Satariano &

Silliman, 2003). For example, it may be possible to develop a stratified clinical trial. This would involve grouping participants in terms of their background levels of comorbidity (e.g., high, medium, and low). Within each of the three categories, respondents could be randomly assigned to different treatments. With this type of design, it is possible to generalize to populations with different levels of background comorbidity.

It also may be possible to develop multiple-level clinical trials, for example, an exercise intervention that takes into account neighborhood resources (Satariano & McAuley, 2003). As in the previous example, it may be possible to group participants in terms of some background characteristics, in this case, the presence of parks and recreation facilities and the general walkability of their neighborhoods. As in the previous example, within each category of neighborhood characteristics, participants could be randomly assigned to different exercise treatments. Not only would this design afford an opportunity to compare the effectiveness of different exercise interventions, but it also would determine to what extent the effectiveness of those interventions may vary across different neighborhood characteristics. This type of multi-level design is more in keeping with the principles of the ecological model.

4. Special efforts should be made to foster further development of statistical techniques that may be especially appropriate for studies in the epidemiology of aging. These techniques include, but are not limited to, multilevel analysis, grade-of-membership analysis, and marginal structural models. Each of these techniques contributes special information.

Research Training Programs

1. Develop and evaluate educational programs to train a new generation of scholars to conduct research and practice in the epidemiology of aging. These programs should be designed as part of existing MPH, DrPH, and PhD programs in epidemiology and other areas of public health. Based on the current and future research, practice, and policy needs in this area, the programs should be based on work from the biologic, behavioral, social, and environmental health sciences. Postdoctoral training programs also should be considered.

The Robert Wood Johnson Foundation Health and Society Program may serve as one model for this type of training program (see the Robert Wood Johnson Foundation Web site at www.rwjf. org/programs/hss/HealthSocietyScholars.jhtml).

2. Establish training programs that include public health professionals who are currently working in health departments and community-based organizations. Training programs of this kind should foster and sustain academic-practice collaborations in the field of aging.

3. Establish centers of excellence for clinical and public health research and practice in aging. For example, the California State Plan on Aging includes a recommendation for university-affiliated centers of this kind to be based in different regions of the state (Scharlach, Torres-Gil, & Kaskie, 2001). The placement of these centers would represent academic-practice collaborations and would be designed to reflect the geographic, racial, and ethnic diversity of the state. This plan may serve as a model for state-based centers in other regions of the country.

4. Continue to support research and practice support in the epidemiology of aging. Given that aging is a global issue, the World Health Organization and other international organizations should identify aging as a priority for future funding.

CONCLUSION

The epidemiology of aging represents an exciting area of study. The ecological model should continue to play an important role in guiding the multidisciplinary work that is needed to fulfill the promise of this field. In his letter to Thomas Jefferson, James Madison wrote, as we noted earlier, that the "web of mutual obligation" that binds generations serves as well in binding us as a civilized society. In the end, I believe that we will discover that the aging of the human population, perhaps our greatest natural, renewable resource, will serve to bind us globally as well.

REFERENCES

Berrigan, D., Dodd, K., Troiano, R. P., Krebs-Smith, S. M., & Barbash, R. B. (2003). Patterns of health behavior in U.S. adults. *Preventive Medicine, 36*(5), 615–623.

Bulatao, R. A., & Anderson, N. B. (2004). *Understanding racial and ethnic differences in health in late life: A research agenda.* Washington, DC: National Academy Press.

Committee on Health and Behavior: Research, Practice, and Policy (2001). *Health and behavior: The interplay of biological, behavioral, and social influences.* Washington DC: National Academy Press.

Dannefer, D. (2003). Cumulative advantage/disadvantage and the life course: Cross-fertilizing age and social science theory. *Journals of Gerontology: Social Sciences, 58B*(6), S327–S337.

Ferrucci, L., Guralnik, J. M., Studenski, S., Fried, L. P., Cultler, G. B., & Waltson, J. D., for the Interventions on Frailty Working Group. (2004). Designing randomized, controlled trials aimed at preventing or delaying functional decline and disability in frail, older persons: A consensus report. *Journal of the American Geriatrics Society, 52*, 625–634.

Gijsen, R., Hoeymans, N., Schellevis, F. G., Ruwaard, D., Satariano, W. A., & van den Bos, G. A. (2001). Causes and consequences of comorbidity: A review. *Journal of Clinical Epidemiology, 54*(7), 661–674.

Koplan, J. P., & Fleming, D. W. (2000). Current and future public health challenges. *Journal of the American Medical Association, 284*, 1696–1698.

Kuh, D., & Ben-Shlomo, Y. (Eds.). (2004). *A life course approach to chronic disease epidemiology,* 2nd ed. New York: Oxford University Press.

Lawton, M. P. (1980). *Environment and aging.* Belmont, CA: Brooks-Cole.

Longino, C. F. Jr. (2003). Editorial: Why we are suddenly interested in the life course. *Journals of Gerontology: Social Sciences, 58B*(6), S326.

McEwen, B. S., & Seeman, T. (1999). Protective and damaging effects of mediators of stress: Elaborating and testing the concepts of allostasis and allostatic load. *Annals of the New York Academy of Sciences, 896*, 30–47.

Mendes de Leon, C., Guralnik, J. M., Bandeen-Roche, K. (2002). Short term change in physical function and disability: The Women's Health and Aging Study. *Journals of Gerontology: Social Sciences, 57*(6), S355–S365.

Morley, J. E. (2004). Editorial: The top 10 hot topics in aging. *Journals of Gerontology: Medical Sciences, 59A*(1), 24–33.

National Institute on Aging. (2001). *Action Plan for Aging Research: Strategic Plan for Fiscal Years 2001–2005.* Washington, DC: National Institutes of Health (NIH Publication No. 01-4951). www2.nia.nih.gov/strat-plan/2001–2005/ Accessed December 4, 2004.

Rizzo, M., McGehee, D. V., Dawson, J. D., & Anderson, S. N. (2001). Simulated car crashes at intersections in drivers with Alzheimer's disease. *Alzheimer's Disease and Associated Disorders, 15*(1), 10–20.

Rushton, G., Elmes, G., & McMaster, R. (2000). Considerations for improving geographic information system research in public health. *URISA Journal, 12*(2), 31–49.

Satariano, W. A., & McAuley, E. (2003). Promoting physical activity among older adults: From ecology to the individual. *American Journal of Preventive Medicine, 25*(3Sii), 184–192.

Satariano, W. A., & Silliman, R. A. (2003). Comorbidity: Implications for research and practice in geriatric oncology. *Critical Reviews in Oncology/Hematology, 48,* 239–248.

Scharlach, A., Torres-Gil, F., & Kaskie, B. (2001). *Strategic planning framework for an aging population.* Berkeley, CA: Regents of the University of California, California Policy Research Center.

Smedley, B. D., & Syme, S. L. (Eds.). (2000). *Promoting health: Intervention strategies from social and behavioral research.* Washington, DC: National Academy Press.

Stokols, D. (1996). Translating social ecological theory into guidelines for community health promotion. *American Journal of Health Promotion, 10*(4), 282–298.

U.S. Department of Health and Human Services. (2000). *Healthy People 2010: Understanding and improving health.* Washington, DC: U.S. Department of Health and Human Services, 2000.

Verbrugge, L. M., & Jette, A. M. (1994). The disablement process. *Social Science and Medicine, 38,* 1–14.

Wakimoto, P., & Block, G. (2001). Dietary intake, dietary patterns, and changes with age: An epidemiological perspective. *Journals of Gerontology: Medical Sciences, 56* (Spec No. 2), 65–80.

INDEX

depression, 115. *See also* depression
disease and comorbidities, 112. *See also*
    disease and comorbidities
falls and injuries, 113. *See also* falls and
    injuries
fixed life span, 13–14
health behavior, 109–111. *See also* health
    behavior
improvement vs. decline, 20
physical and cognitive functioning, 114.
    See also functioning and disability
physical environment, 104–106. *See also*
    physical environment
psychological mechanisms, 115–116
psychosocial factors, 111. *See also*
    psychosocial factors
social capital, 107–109. *See also* social
    capital
socioeconomic status, 101–104. *See also*
    socioeconomic status
survival studies, 90–92
motor skills. *See* physical functioning
motor vehicle records, 331
MPTP (1-methyl-4-
    phenyltetrahydropyridine), 289
multimorbidity research, 293–295. *See also*
    disease and comorbidities
multiple-level clinical trials, 348–349, 398
multistate models of active life expectancy,
    127
musculoskeletal disease, 157
myopia, cataracts and, 285–286

N

National Health Interview Survey, 345
National Long-Term Care Survey, 345
nationality. *See* race and ethnicity
nations, relationships between, 23
natural resources, availability of, 22
need for assistance, 134, 136
neighborhoods. *See* built environment;
    geography and regional
    differences; social relations
networks, social. *See* social relations

neurodegenerative diseases, 184–185
    Alzheimer's disease, 173, 286–288
    cognitive functioning, effects on,
        187
    depression with, 219–220
    falls and injuries, 254
    Parkinson's disease, 184, 288–289
    depression with, 220
NHAP (nursing home–acquired
    pneumonia), 289–290
nicotine, 184. *See also* tobacco exposure
NIH conferences (1970s), 25–27
norms of reciprocity. *See* social capital
NRB measures, 147–148
nuclear cataracts, 285
nursing home–acquired pneumonia
    (NHAP), 289–290
nursing homes, 332, 374
nurturance, 50–51
nutrition. *See* diet and nutrition

O

obesity. *See* diet and nutrition
occupational exposures. *See* physical
    environment
occupational status. *See* socioeconomic
    status
older populations
    identifying, 328–334, 394–398
    recruiting, 334–338, 394–398
onset of disease, age at, 270–272, 387
osteoarthritis. *See* arthritis
outcome measures, 397
outdoor vs. indoor falls, 233, 236
overall health, 303–307
    measures and predictors, 306–307
oxidative damage. *See* free-radical theories

P

pandemics, age of, 10
parental death, 205
Parkinson's disease (PD), 184, 288–289
    depression with, 220